GRAPH CLASSIFICATION
AND CLUSTERING
BASED ON VECTOR
SPACE EMBEDDING

SERIES IN MACHINE PERCEPTION AND ARTIFICIAL INTELLIGENCE*

Editors: **H. Bunke** (Univ. Bern, Switzerland)
P. S. P. Wang (Northeastern Univ., USA)

*For the complete list of titles in this series, please write to the Publisher.

Series in Machine Perception and Artificial Intelligence – Vol. 77

GRAPH CLASSIFICATION AND CLUSTERING BASED ON VECTOR SPACE EMBEDDING

Kaspar Riesen & Horst Bunke

University of Bern, Switzerland

World Scientific

NEW JERSEY · LONDON · SINGAPORE · BEIJING · SHANGHAI · HONG KONG · TAIPEI · CHENNAI

Published by

World Scientific Publishing Co. Pte. Ltd.

5 Toh Tuck Link, Singapore 596224

USA office: 27 Warren Street, Suite 401-402, Hackensack, NJ 07601

UK office: 57 Shelton Street, Covent Garden, London WC2H 9HE

British Library Cataloguing-in-Publication Data
A catalogue record for this book is available from the British Library.

**GRAPH CLASSIFICATION AND CLUSTERING BASED ON
VECTOR SPACE EMBEDDING**
Series in Machine Perception and Artificial Intelligence — Vol. 77

Copyright © 2010 by World Scientific Publishing Co. Pte. Ltd.

ISBN-13 978-981-4304-71-9
ISBN-10 981-4304-71-9

Printed in Singapore.

Kaspar Riesen dedicates this book to Madeleine and Emilie
Horst Bunke dedicates this book to Helga

Preface

Due to the ability of graphs to represent properties of entities and binary relations at the same time, a growing interest in graph based object representation can be observed in science and engineering. Yet, graphs are still not the common data structure in pattern recognition and related fields. The reason for this is twofold. First, working with graphs is unequally more challenging than working with feature vectors, as even basic mathematic operations cannot be defined in a standard way for graphs. Second, we observe a significant increase of the complexity of many algorithms when graphs rather than feature vectors are employed. In conclusion, almost none of the standard methods for pattern recognition can be applied to graphs without significant modifications and thus we observe a severe lack of graph based pattern recognition tools.

This thesis is concerned with a fundamentally novel approach to graph based pattern recognition based on vector space embeddings of graphs. We aim at condensing the high representational power of graphs into a computationally efficient and mathematically convenient feature vector. Based on the explicit embedding of graphs, the considered pattern recognition task is eventually carried out. Hence, the whole arsenal of algorithmic tools readily available for vectorial data can be applied to graphs. The key idea of our embedding framework is to regard dissimilarities of an input graph to some prototypical graphs as vectorial description of the graph. Obviously, by means of such an embedding we obtain a vector space where each axis is associated with a prototype graph and the coordinate values of an embedded graph are the distances of this graph to the individual prototypes.

Our graph embedding framework crucially relies on the computation of graph dissimilarities. Despite adverse mathematical and computational conditions in the graph domain, various procedures for evaluating the dissimilarity of graphs have been proposed in the literature. In the present thesis the concept of graph edit distance is actually used for this task. Basically, the edit distance of graphs aims at deriving a dissimilarity measure from the number as well as the strength of distortions one has to apply to one graph in order to transform it into another graph. As it turns out, graph edit distance meets the requirements of applicability to a wide range of graphs as well as the adaptiveness to various problem domains. Due to this flexibility, the proposed embedding procedure can be applied to virtually any kind of graphs.

In our embedding framework, the selection of the prototypes is a critical issue since not only the prototypes themselves but also their number affect the resulting graph mapping, and thus the performance of the corresponding pattern recognition algorithm. In the present thesis an adequate selection of prototypes is addressed by various procedures, such as prototype selection methods, feature selection algorithms, ensemble methods, and several other approaches.

In an experimental evaluation the power and applicability of the proposed graph embedding framework is empirically verified on ten graph data sets with quite different characteristics. There are graphs that represent line drawings, gray scale images, molecular compounds, proteins, and HTML webpages. The main finding of the experimental evaluation is that the embedding procedure using dissimilarities with subsequent classification or clustering has great potential to outperform traditional approaches in graph based pattern recognition. In fact, regardless of the subsystems actually used for embedding, on most of the data sets the reference systems directly working on graph dissimilarity information are outperformed, and in the majority of the cases these improvements are statistically significant.

Kaspar Riesen and Horst Bunke

Acknowledgments

I am grateful to Prof. Dr. Horst Bunke for directing me through this work. On countless occasions, his excellent advise and open attitude towards new ideas have been a tremendous support. I would also like to thank Prof. Dr. Xiaoyi Jiang for acting as co-referee of this work and Prof. Dr. Matthias Zwicker for supervising the examination. Furthermore, I am very grateful to Susanne Thüler for her support in all administrative concerns. I would like to acknowledge the funding by the Swiss National Science Foundation (Project 200021-113198/1).

Many colleagues have contributed invaluable parts to this work. Dr. Michel Neuhaus, Dr. Andreas Schlapbach, Dr. Marcus Liwicki, Dr. Roman Bertolami, Dr. Miquel Ferrer, Dr. Karsten Borgwardt, Dr. Adam Schenker, David Emms, Vivian Kilchherr, Barbara Spillmann, Volkmar Frinken, Andreas Fischer, Emanuel Indermühle, Stefan Fankhauser, Claudia Asti, Anna Schmassmann, Raffael Krebs, Stefan Schumacher, and David Baumgartner — thank you very much.

A very special thank goes out to my very good friends David Baumgartner, Peter Bigler, Andreas Gertsch, Lorenzo Mercolli, Christian Schaad, Roman Schmidt, Stefan Schumacher, Pascal Sigg, Sandra Rohrbach, Annie Ryser, Godi Ryser, Julia Ryser, and Römi Ryser.

I am very grateful to my family for their support and encouragement during the time as a PhD student. Very special thanks to my parents Max and Christine Riesen, to my brothers and their wives Niklaus and Daniela as well as Christian and Anita, to my parents-in-law Markus and Marlis Steiner, and my sister-in-law Cathrine.

Finally, I would like to thank my wife Madeleine Steiner. You believed in me long before I did. It is impossible to put into words what your faith in me has done for me. This thesis is dedicated to you.

Contents

Introduction and Basic Concepts

1

> The real power of human thinking is based on recognizing patterns.

Ray Kurzweil

1.1 Pattern Recognition

Pattern recognition describes the act of determining to which category, referred to as *class*, a given pattern belongs and taking an action according to the class of the recognized pattern. The notion of a *pattern* thereby describes an observation in the real world. Due to the fact that pattern recognition has been essential for our survival, evolution has led to highly sophisticated neural and cognitive systems in humans for solving pattern recognition tasks over tens of millions of years [1]. Summarizing, recognizing patterns is one of the most crucial capabilities of human beings.

Each individual is faced with a huge amount of various pattern recognition problems in every day life [2]. Examples of such tasks include the recognition of letters in a book, the face of a friend in a crowd, a spoken word embedded in noise, the chart of a presentation, the proper key to the locked door, the smell of coffee in the cafeteria, the importance of a certain message in the mail folder, and many more. These simple examples illustrate the essence of pattern recognition. In the world there exist classes of patterns we distinguish according to certain knowledge that we have learned before [3].

Most pattern recognition tasks encountered by humans can be solved intuitively without explicitly defining a certain method or specifying an exact algorithm. Yet, formulating a pattern recognition problem in an algorithmic way provides us with the possibility to delegate the task to a machine. This can be particularly interesting for very complex as well as for cumbersome tasks in both science and industry. Examples are the prediction of the properties of a certain molecule based on its structure, which is known to be very difficult, or the reading of handwritten payment orders, which might become quite tedious when their quantity reaches several hundreds.

Such examples have evoked a growing interest in adequate modeling of the human pattern recognition ability, which in turn led to the establishment of the research area of pattern recognition and related fields, such as machine learning, data mining, and artificial intelligence [4]. The ultimate goal of pattern recognition as a scientific discipline is to develop methods that mimic the human capacity of perception and intelligence. More precisely, pattern recognition as computer science discipline aims at defining mathematical foundations, models and methods that automate the process of recognizing patterns of diverse nature.

However, it soon turned out that many of the most interesting problems in pattern recognition and related fields are extremely complex, often making it difficult, or even impossible, to specify an explicit programmed solution. For instance, we are not able to write an analytical program to recognize, say, a face in a photo [5]. In order to overcome this problem, pattern recognition commonly employs the so called *learning methodology*. In contrast to the *theory driven* approach, where precise specifications of the algorithm are required in order to solve the task analytically, in this approach the machine is meant to learn itself the concept of a class, identify objects, and discriminate between them.

Typically, a machine is fed with training data, coming from a certain problem domain, whereon it tries to detect significant rules in order to solve the given pattern recognition task [5]. Based on this training set of samples and particularly the inferred rules, the machine becomes able to make predictions about new, i.e. unseen, data. In other words, the machine acquires generalization power by learning. This approach is highly inspired by the human ability to recognize, for instance, what a dog is, given just a few examples of dogs. Thus, the basic idea of the learning methodology is that a few examples are sufficient to extract important knowledge about their respective class [4]. Consequently, employing this approach requires computer scientists to provide mathematical foundations to a machine allowing it to learn from examples.

Pattern recognition and related fields have become an immensely important discipline in computer science. After decades of research, reliable and accurate pattern recognition by machines is now possible in many formerly very difficult problem domains. Prominent examples are mail sorting [6, 7], e-mail filtering [8, 9], text categorization [10–12], handwritten text recognition [13–15], web retrieval [16, 17], writer verification [18, 19], person identification by fingerprints [20–23], gene detection [24, 25], activity predictions for molecular compounds [26, 27], and others. However, the indispensable necessity of further research in automated pattern recognition systems becomes obvious when we face new applications, challenges, and problems, as for instance the search for important information in the huge amount of data which is nowadays available, or the complete understanding of highly complex data which has been made accessible just recently. Therefore, the major role of pattern recognition will definitely be strengthened in the next decades in science, engineering, and industry.

1.2 Learning Methodology

The key task in pattern recognition is the analysis and the classification of patterns [28]. As discussed above, the learning paradigm is usually employed in pattern recognition. The learning paradigm states that a machine tries to infer classification and analysis rules from a sample set of training data. In pattern recognition several learning approaches are distinguished. This section goes into the taxonomy of *supervised, unsupervised,* and the recently emerged *semi-supervised* learning. All of these learning methodologies have in common that they incorporate important information captured in training samples into a mathematical model.

Supervised Learning   In the supervised learning approach each training sample has an associated class label, i.e. each training sample belongs to one and only one class from a finite set of classes. A class contains similar objects, whereas objects from different classes are dissimilar. The key task in supervised learning is *classification.* Classification refers to the process of assigning an unknown input object to one out of a given set of classes. Hence, supervised learning aims at capturing the relevant criteria from the training samples for the discrimination of different classes. Typical classification problems can be found in biometric person identification [29], optical character recognition [30], medical diagnosis [31], and many other domains.

Formally, in the supervised learning approach, we are dealing with a pattern space $\mathcal{X}$, and a space of class labels Ω. All patterns $x \in \mathcal{X}$ are potential candidates to be recognized, and $\mathcal{X}$ can be any kind of space (e.g. the real vector space $\mathbb{R}^n$, or a finite or infinite set of symbolic data structures[1]). For *binary classification* problems the space of class labels is usually defined as $\Omega = \{-1, +1\}$. If the training data is labeled as belonging to one of k classes, the space of class labels $\Omega = \{\omega_1, \ldots, \omega_k\}$ consists of a finite set of discrete symbols, representing the k classes under consideration. This task is then referred to as *multiclass classification*. Given a set of N labeled training samples $\{(x_i, \omega_i)\}_{i=1,\ldots,N} \subset \mathcal{X} \times \Omega$ the aim is to derive a prediction function $f : \mathcal{X} \to \Omega$, assigning patterns $x \in \mathcal{X}$ to classes $\omega_i \in \Omega$, i.e. *classifying* the patterns from $\mathcal{X}$. The prediction function f is commonly referred to as *classifier*. Hence, supervised learning employs some algorithmic procedures in order to define a powerful and accurate prediction function[2].

Obviously, an overly complex classifier system $f : \mathcal{X} \to \Omega$ may allow perfect classification of all training samples $\{x_i\}_{i=1,\ldots,N}$. Such a system, however, might perform poorly on unseen data $x \in \mathcal{X} \setminus \{x_i\}_{i=1,\ldots,N}$. In this particular case, which is referred to as *overfitting*, the classifier is too strongly adapted to the training set. Conversely, *underfitting* occurs when the classifier is unable to model the class boundaries with a sufficient degree of precision. In the best case, a classifier integrates the trade-off between underfitting and overfitting in its training algorithm. Consequently, the overall aim is to derive a classifier from the training samples $\{x_i\}_{i=1,\ldots,N}$ that is able to correctly classify a majority of the unseen patterns x coming from the same pattern space $\mathcal{X}$. This ability of a classifier is generally referred to as *generalization power*. The underlying assumption for generalization is that the training samples $\{x_i\}_{i=1,\ldots,N}$ are sufficiently representative for the whole pattern space $\mathcal{X}$.

Unsupervised Learning   In unsupervised learning, as opposed to supervised learning, there is no labeled training set whereon the class concept is learned. In this case the important information needs to be extracted from the patterns without the information provided by the class

---

[1]We will revisit the problem of adequate pattern spaces in the next section.

[2]The supervised learning approach can be formulated in a more general way to include other recognition tasks than classification, such as *regression*. Regression refers to the case of supervised pattern recognition in which rather than a class $\omega_i \in \Omega$, an unknown real-valued feature $y \in \mathbb{R}$ has to be predicted. In this case, the training sample consists of pairs $\{(x_i, y_i)\}_{i=1,\ldots,N} \subset \mathcal{X} \times \mathbb{R}$. However, in this book considerations in supervised learning are restricted to pattern classification problems.

label [5]. Metaphorically speaking, in this learning approach no teacher is available defining which class a certain pattern belongs to, but only the patterns themselves. More concretely, in the case of unsupervised learning, the overall problem is to partition a given collection of unlabeled patterns $\{x_i\}_{i=1,...,N}$ into k meaningful groups $C_1, \ldots, C_k$. These groups are commonly referred to as *clusters*, and the process of finding a natural division of the data into homogeneous groups is referred to as *clustering*. The *clustering algorithm*, or *clusterer*, is a function mapping each pattern $\{x_i\}_{i=1,...,N}$ to a cluster C_j. Note that there are also *Fuzzy clustering* algorithms available, allowing a pattern to be assigned to several clusters at a time. Yet, in the present book only *hard clusterings*, i.e. clusterings where patterns are assigned to exactly one cluster, are considered.

Clustering is particularly suitable for the exploration of interrelationships among individual patterns [32, 33]. That is, clustering algorithms are mainly used as data exploratory and data analysis tool. The risk in using clustering methods is that rather than finding a natural structure in the underlying data, we are imposing an arbitrary and artificial structure [3]. For instance, for many of the clustering algorithms the number of clusters k to be found in the data set has to be set by the user in advance. Moreover, given a particular set of patterns, different clustering algorithms, or even the same algorithm randomly initialized, might lead to completely different clusters. An open question is in which scenarios to employ a clustering approach at all [34].

An answer can be found in the concept of a cluster. Although both concepts, class and cluster, seem to be quite similar, their subtle difference is crucial. In contrast to the concept of a class label, the assignment of a pattern to a certain cluster is not intrinsic. Changing a single feature of a pattern, or changing the distance measurement between individual patterns, might change the partitioning of the data, and therefore the patterns' cluster membership. Conversely, in a supervised learning task the class membership of the patterns of the labeled training set never changes. Hence, the objective of clustering is not primarily the classification of the data, but an evaluation and exploration of the underlying distance measurement, the representation formalism, and the distribution of the patterns.

Semi-supervised Learning Semi-supervised learning is halfway between supervised and unsupervised learning [35]. As the name of this approach indicates, both labeled and unlabeled data are provided to the learning algorithm. An important requirement for semi-supervised learning approaches to work properly is that the distribution of the underlying patterns, which the unlabeled data will help to learn, is relevant for the given classification problem. Given this assumption, there is evidence that a classifier can lead to more accurate predictions by also taking into account the unlabeled patterns. In the present book, however, this learning approach is not explicitly considered, but only purely supervised and unsupervised learning methods, i.e. classification and clustering algorithms.

1.3   Statistical and Structural Pattern Recognition

The question how to represent patterns in a formal way such that a machine can learn to discriminate between different classes of objects, or find clusters in the data, is very important. Consider, for instance, a pattern classification task where images of dogs have to be distinguished from images of birds. Obviously, a person might come up with the classification rule that birds have two legs, two wings, plumes, and a pecker. Dogs, on the other hand, have four legs, no wings, a fur, and no pecker. Based on this knowledge every human will be able to assign images showing dogs and birds to one of the two categories.

Yet, for a machine the concepts of *leg*, *fur*, or *wing* have no predefined meaning. That is, the knowledge about the difference between dogs and birds established above, has no relevance for machines. Consequently, the first and very important step in any pattern recognition system is the task of defining adequate data structures to represent the patterns under consideration. That is, the patterns have to be encoded in a machine readable way. There are two major ways to tackle this crucial step: the *statistical* and the *structural* approach[3]. In this section we examine both approaches and discuss drawbacks and advantages of them.

Statistical Pattern Recognition   In statistical pattern recognition objects or patterns are represented by feature vectors. That is, a pattern is formally represented as vector of n measurements, i.e. n numerical features. Hence, an object can be understood as a point in the n-dimensional real space, i.e. $\mathbf{x} = (x_1, \ldots, x_n) \in \mathbb{R}^n$. As pointed out in [4], in a rigorous mathematical sense, *points* and *vectors* are not the same. That is, points

---

[3]Note that there exists also the *syntactical* approach where the patterns of a certain class are encoded as strings of a formal language [36]. Language analysis can then be used in order to discriminate between different classes of objects. The present book, however, is restricted to statistical and structural pattern recognition.

are defined by a fixed set of coordinates in $\mathbb{R}^n$, while vectors are defined by differences between points. Hoewever, in statistical pattern recognition both terminologies are used interchangeably. Patterns are represented as points in $\mathbb{R}^n$, but for the sake of convenience, they are treated as vectors so that all vector space operations are well defined.

Representing objects or patterns by feature vectors $\mathbf{x} \in \mathbb{R}^n$ offers a number of useful properties, in particular, the mathematical wealth of operations available in a vector space. That is, computing the sum, the product, the mean, or the distance of two entities is well defined in vector spaces, and moreover, can be efficiently computed. The convenience and low computational complexity of algorithms that use feature vectors as their input have eventually resulted in a rich repository of algorithmic tools for statistical pattern recognition and related fields [1, 5, 37].

However, the use of feature vectors implicates two limitations. First, as vectors always represent a predefined set of features, all vectors in a given application have to preserve the same length regardless of the size or complexity of the corresponding objects. Second, there is no direct possibility to describe binary relationships that might exist among different parts of a pattern. These two drawbacks are severe, particularly when the patterns under consideration are characterized by complex structural relationships rather than the statistical distribution of a fixed set of pattern features [38].

Structural Pattern Recognition Structural pattern recognition is based on symbolic data structures, such as *strings*, *trees*, or *graphs*. Graphs, which consist of a finite set of nodes connected by edges, are the most general data structure in computer science, and the other common data types are special cases of graphs. That is, from an algorithmic perspective both strings and trees are simple instances of graphs[4]. A string is a graph in which each node represents one character, and consecutive characters are connected by an edge [39]. A tree is a graph in which any two nodes are connected by exactly one path. In Fig. 1.1 an example of a string, a tree, and a graph are illustrated. In the present book graphs are used as representation formalism for structural pattern recognition. Although focusing on graphs, the reader should keep in mind that strings and trees are always included as special cases.

---

[4]Obviously, also a feature vector $\mathbf{x} \in \mathbb{R}^n$ can be represented as a graph, whereas the contrary, i.e. finding a vectorial description for graphs, is highly non-trivial and one of the main objectives of this book.

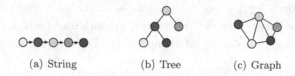

(a) String   (b) Tree   (c) Graph

Fig. 1.1   Symbolic data structures.

The above mentioned drawbacks of feature vectors, namely the size constraint and the lacking ability of representing relationships, can be overcome by graph based representations [40]. In fact, graphs are not only able to describe properties of an object, but also binary relationships among different parts of the underlying object by means of edges. Note that these relationships can be of various nature, viz. spatial, temporal, or conceptual. Moreover, graphs are not constrained to a fixed size, i.e. the number of nodes and edges is not limited a priori and can be adapted to the size or the complexity of each individual object under consideration.

Due to the ability of graphs to represent properties of entities and binary relations at the same time, a growing interest in graph-based object representation can be observed [40]. That is, graphs have found widespread applications in science and engineering [41–43]. In the fields of bioinformatics and chemoinformatics, for instance, graph based representations have been intensively used [27, 39, 44–46]. Another field of research where graphs have been studied with emerging interest is that of web content mining [47, 48]. Image classification from various fields is a further area of research where graph based representations draw the attention [49–55]. In the fields of graphical symbol and character recognition, graph based structures have also been used [56–59]. Finally, it is worth to mention computer network analysis, where graphs have been used to detect network anomalies and predict abnormal events [60–62].

One drawback of graphs, when compared to feature vectors, is the significant increase of the complexity of many algorithms. For example, the comparison of two feature vectors for identity can be accomplished in linear time with respect to the length of the two vectors. For the analogous operation on general graphs, i.e. testing two graphs for isomorphism, only exponential algorithms are known today. Another serious limitation in the use of graphs for pattern recognition tasks arises from the fact that there is little mathematical structure in the domain of graphs. For example, computing the (weighted) sum or the product of a pair of entities (which are elementary operations required in many classification and clustering algorithms) is not possible in the domain of graphs, or is at least not defined in a standardized way. Due to these general problems in the graph domain, we observe a lack of algorithmic tools for graph based pattern recognition.

Bridging the Gap A promising approach to overcome the lack of algorithmic tools for both graph classification and graph clustering is graph embedding in the real vector space. Basically, an embedding of graphs into vector spaces establishes access to the rich repository of algorithmic tools for pattern recognition. However, the problem of finding adequate vectorial representations for graphs is absolutely non-trivial. As a matter of fact, the representational power of graphs is clearly higher than that of feature vectors, i.e. while feature vectors can be regarded as unary attributed relations, graphs can be interpreted as a set of attributed unary and binary relations of arbitrary size. The overall objective of all graph embedding techniques is to condense the high representational power of graphs into a computationally efficient and mathematically convenient feature vector.

The goal of the present book is to define a new class of graph embedding procedures which can be applied to both directed and undirected graphs, as well as to graphs without and with arbitrary labels on their nodes and edges. Furthermore, the novel graph embedding framework is distinguished by its ability to handle structural errors. The presented approach for graph embedding is primarily based on the idea proposed in [4, 63–66] where the *dissimilarity representation* for pattern recognition in conjunction with feature vectors was first introduced. The key idea is to use the dissimilarities of an input graph g to a number of training graphs, termed *prototypes*, as a vectorial description of g. In other words, the dissimilarity representation rather than the original graph representation is used for pattern recognition.

1.4 Dissimilarity Representation for Pattern Recognition

Human perception has reached a mature level and we are able to recognize common characteristics of certain patterns immediately. Recognizing a face, for instance, means that we evaluate several characteristics at a time and make a decision within a fraction of a second whether or not we know the person standing vis-a-vis[5]. These discriminative characteristics of a pattern are known as *features*. As we have seen in the previous sections,

---

[5]There exists a disorder of face recognition, known as *prosopagnosia* or face blindness, where the ability to recognize faces is impaired, while the ability to recognize other objects may be relatively intact.

there are two major concepts in pattern recognition, differing in the way the features of a pattern are represented. However, whether we use real vectors or some symbolic data structure, the key question remains the same: How do we find good descriptors for the given patterns to solve the corresponding pattern recognition task.

The traditional goal of the *feature extraction* task is to characterize patterns to be recognized by measurements whose values are very similar for objects of the same class, and very dissimilar for objects of different classes [1]. Based on the descriptions of the patterns a similarity measure is usually defined, which in turn is employed to group together similar objects to form a class. Hence, the similarity or dissimilarity measure, which is drawn on the extracted features, is fundamental for the constitution of a class. Obviously, the concept of a class, the similarity measure, and the features of the pattern are closely related, and moreover, crucially depend on each other.

Due to this close relationship, the dissimilarity representation has emerged as a novel approach in pattern recognition [4, 63–68]. The basic idea is to represent objects by vectors of dissimilarities. The dissimilarity representation of objects is based on pairwise comparisons, and is therefore also referred to as *relative representation*. The intuition of this approach is that the notion of proximity, i.e. similarity or dissimilarity, is more fundamental than that of a feature or a class. Similarity groups objects together and, therefore, it should play a crucial role in the constitution of a class [69–71]. Using the notion of similarity, rather than features, renews the area of pattern recognition in one of its foundations, i.e. the representation of objects [72–74].

Given these general thoughts about pattern representation by means of dissimilarities, we revisit the key problem of structural pattern recognition, namely the lack of algorithmic tools, which is due to the sparse space of graphs containing almost no mathematical structure. Although for graphs basic mathematical operations cannot be defined in a standardized way, and the application-specific definition of graph operations often involves a tedious and time-consuming development process [28], a substantial number of graph matching paradigms have been proposed in the literature (for an extensive review of graph matching methods see [40]). Graph matching refers to the process of evaluating the structural similarity or dissimilarity of two graphs. That is, for the discrimination of structural patterns various proximity measures are available. Consequently, the dissimilarity representation for pattern recognition can be applied to graphs, which builds a natural bridge for unifying structural and statistical pattern recognition.

In Fig. 1.2 an illustration of the procedure which is explored in the present book is given. The intuition behind this approach is that, if $p_1, \ldots, p_n$ are arbitrary prototype graphs from the underlying pattern space, important information about a given graph g can be obtained by means of the dissimilarities of g to $p_1, \ldots, p_n$, i.e. $d(g, p_1), \ldots, d(g, p_n)$. Moreover, while the flattening of the depth of information captured in a graph to a numerical vector in a standardized way is impossible, pairwise dissimilarities can be computed in a straightforward way. Through the arrangement of the dissimilarities in a tupel, we obtain a vectorial description of the graph under consideration. Moreover, by means of the integration of graph dissimilarities in the vector, a high discrimination power of the resulting representation formalism can be expected. Finally, and maybe most importantly, through the use of dissimilarity representations the lack of algorithmic tools for graph based pattern recognition is instantly eliminated.

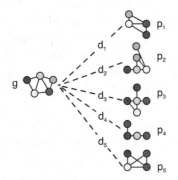

Fig. 1.2 The dissimilarity representation for graph based data structures. A graph g is formally represented as a vector of its dissimilarities $(d_1, \ldots d_n)$ to n predefined graphs $p_1, \ldots, p_n$ (here $n = 5$).

The concept of dissimilarity representation applied to graphs appeals very elegant and straightforward in order to overcome the major drawback of graphs. However, the proposed approach stands and falls with the answer to the overall question, whether or not we are able to outperform traditional pattern recognition systems that are directly applied in the graph domain. That is, the essential and sole quality criterion to be applied to the novel approach is the degree of improvement in the recognition accuracy. More pessimistically one might ask, is there any improvement at all? As one might guess from the size of the present book, in principle the answer is "yes". However, a number of open issues have to be investigated to reach that answer. For instance, how do we select the prototype graphs, which serve us as reference points for the transformation of a given graph into a real vector? Obviously, the prototype graphs, and also their numbering, have a pivotal impact on the resulting vectors. Hence, a well defined set of prototype graphs seems to be crucial to succeed with the proposed graph embedding framework. The present book approaches this question and comes up with solutions to this and other problems arising with the dissimilarity approach for graph embedding.

1.5   Summary and Outline

In the present introduction, the importance of pattern recognition in our everyday life, industry, engineering, and in science is emphasized. Pattern recognition covers the automated process of analyzing and classifying patterns occurring in the real world. In order to cope with the immense complexity of most of the common pattern recognition problems (e.g. recognizing the properties of a molecular compound based on its structure), the learning approach is usually employed. The general idea of this approach is to endow a machine with mathematical methods such that it becomes able to infer general rules from a set of training samples.

Depending on whether the samples are labeled or not, supervised or unsupervised learning is applied. Supervised learning refers to the process where the class structure is learned on the training set such that the system becomes able to make predictions on unseen data coming from the same source. That is, a mathematical decision function is learned according to the class structure on the training set. In the case of unsupervised learning, the patterns under consideration are typically unlabeled. In this learning scheme, the structure of the patterns and especially the interrelationships between different patterns are analyzed and explored. This is done by means of clustering algorithms that partition the data set into meaningful groups, i.e. clusters. Based on the partitioning found, the distribution of the data can be conveniently analyzed. Note the essential difference between classification and clustering: The former aims at predicting a class label for unseen data, the latter performs an analysis on the data at hand.

There are two main directions in pattern recognition, viz. the statistical and the structural approach. Depending on how the patterns in a specific problem domain are described, i.e. with feature vectors or with symbolic data structures, the former or the latter approach is employed. In the present book, structural pattern recognition is restricted to graph based representation. However, all other symbolic data structures, such as strings or trees, can be interpreted as simple instances of graphs.

Particularly, if structure plays an important role, graph based pattern representations offer a versatile alternative to feature vectors. A severe drawback of graphs, however, is the lack of algorithmic tools applicable in the sparse space of graphs. Feature vectors, on the other hand, benefit from the mathematically rich concept of a vector space, which in turn led to a huge amount of pattern recognition algorithms. The overall objective of the present book is to bridge the gap between structural pattern recognition (with its versatility in pattern description) and statistical pattern recognition (with its numerous pattern recognition algorithms at hand). To this end, the dissimilarity representation is established for graph structures.

The dissimilarity representation aims at defining a vectorial description of a pattern based on its dissimilarities to prototypical patterns. Originally, the motivation for this approach is based on the argument that the notion of proximity (similarity or dissimilarity) is more fundamental than that of a feature or a class [4]. However, the major motivation for using the dissimilarity representation for graphs stems from to the fact that though there is little mathematical foundation in the graph domain, numerous procedures for computing pairwise similarities or dissimilarities for graphs can be found in the literature [40]. The present book aims at defining a stringent foundation for graph based pattern recognition based on dissimilarity representations and ultimately pursues the question whether or not this approach is beneficial.

The remainder of this book is organized as follows (see also Fig. 1.3 for an overview). Next, in Chapter 2 the process of graph matching is introduced. Obviously, as the graph embedding framework employed in this book is based on dissimilarities of graphs, the concept of graph matching is essential. The graph matching paradigm actually used for measuring the dissimilarity of graphs is that of graph edit distance. This particular graph matching model, which is known to be very flexible, is discussed in Chapter 3. A repository of graph data sets, compiled and developed within this book and suitable for a wide spectrum of tasks in pattern recognition and machine learning is described in Chapter 4. The graph repository consists of ten graph sets with quite different characteristics. These graph sets are used throughout the book for various experimental evaluations. Kernel

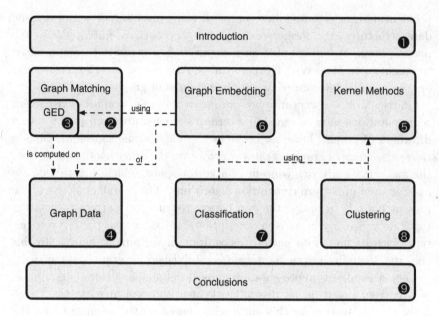

Fig. 1.3   Overview of the present book.

methods, a relatively novel approach in pattern recognition, are discussed in Chapter 5. Particularly, the support vector machine, kernel principal component analysis, and kernel k-means algorithm, are reviewed. These three kernel machines are employed in the present book for classification, transformation, and clustering of vector space embedded graphs, respectively. Moreover, the concept of graph kernel methods, which is closely related to the proposed approach of graph embedding, is discussed in detail in Chapter 5. The general procedure of our graph embedding framework is described in Chapter 6. In fact, the embedding procedure for graphs can be seen as a foundation for a novel class of graph kernels. However, as we will see in Chapter 6, the embedding procedure is even more powerful than most graph kernel methods. Furthermore, more specific problems, such as prototype selection and the close relationship of the presented embedding framework to *Lipschitz embeddings*, are discussed in this chapter. An experimental evaluation of classification and clustering of vector space embedded graphs is described in Chapters 7 and 8, respectively. For both scenarios exhaustive comparisons between the novel embedding framework and standard approaches are performed. Finally, the book is summarized and concluded in Chapter 9.

Graph Matching

2

The study of algorithms is at
the very heart of computer
science.

Alfred Aho, John Hopcroft and
Jeffrey Ullman

Finding adequate representation formalisms, which are able to capture
the main characteristics of an object, is a crucial task in pattern recognition.
If the underlying patterns are not appropriately modeled, even the most
sophisticated pattern recognition algorithm will fail. In problem domains
where the patterns to be explored are characterized by complex structural
relationships, graph structures offer a versatile alternative to feature vectors. In fact, graphs are universal data structures able to model networks of
relationships between substructures of a given pattern. Thereby, the size as
well as the complexity of a graph can be adopted to the size and complexity
of a particular pattern[1].

However, after the initial enthusiasm induced by the "smartness" and
flexibility of graph representations in the late seventies, graphs have been
practically left unused for a long period of time [40]. The reason for this
is twofold. First, working with graphs is unequally more challenging than
working with feature vectors, as even basic mathematic operations cannot
be defined in a standard way, but must be provided depending on the specific application. Hence, almost none of the standard methods for pattern
recognition can be applied to graphs without significant modifications [28].

Second, graphs suffer from their own flexibility [39]. For instance, consider the homogeneous nature of feature vectors, where each vector has

---

[1]For a thorough discussion on different representation formalisms in pattern recognition,
i.e. the statistical and structural approach in pattern recognition, see Section 1.3.

equal dimensions, and each vector's entry at position i describes the same property. Obviously, with such a rigid pattern description, the comparison of two objects is straightforward and can be accomplished very efficiently. That is, computing the distances of a pair of objects is linear in the number of data items in the case where vectors are employed [75]. The same task for graphs, however, is much more complex, since one cannot simply compare the sets of nodes and edges since they are generally unordered and of arbitrary size. More formally, when computing graph dissimilarity or similarity one has to identify common parts of the graphs by considering all of their subgraphs. Regarding that there are $O(2^n)$ subgraphs of a graph with n nodes, the inherent difficulty of graph comparisons becomes obvious.

Despite adverse mathematical and computational conditions in the graph domain, various procedures for evaluating the similarity or dissimilarity[2] of graphs have been proposed in the literature [40]. In fact, the concept of similarity is an important issue in many domains of pattern recognition [76]. In the context of the present work, computing graph (dis)similarities is even one of the core processes. The process of evaluating the dissimilarity of two graphs is commonly referred to as *graph matching*. The overall aim of graph matching is to find a correspondence between the nodes and edges of two graphs that satisfies some, more or less, stringent constraints [40]. By means of a graph matching process similar substructures in one graph are mapped to similar substructures in the other graph. Based on this matching, a dissimilarity or similarity score can eventually be computed indicating the proximity of two graphs.

Graph matching has been the topic of numerous studies in computer science over the last decades [77]. Roughly speaking, there are two categories of tasks in graph matching: *exact graph matching* and *inexact graph matching*. In the former case, for a matching to be successful, it is required that a strict correspondence is found between the two graphs being matched, or at least among their subparts. In the latter approach this requirement is substantially relaxed, since also matchings between completely non-identical graphs are possible. That is, inexact matching algorithms are endowed with a certain tolerance to errors and noise, enabling them to detect similarities in a more general way than the exact matching approach. Therefore, inexact graph matching is also referred to as *error-tolerant graph*

---

[2]Clearly, similarity and dissimilarity are closely related, as both a small dissimilarity value and a large similarity value for two patterns at hand indicate a close proximity. There exist several methods for transforming similarities into dissimilarities, and vice versa.

matching.

For an extensive review of graph matching methods and applications, the reader is referred to [40]. In this chapter, basic notations and definitions are introduced and an overview of standard techniques for exact as well as for error-tolerant graph matching is given.

2.1 Graph and Subgraph

Depending on the considered application, various definitions for graphs can be found in the literature. The following well-established definition is sufficiently flexible for a large variety of tasks.

Definition 2.1 (Graph). *Let L_V and L_E be a finite or infinite label sets for nodes and edges, respectively. A graph g is a four-tuple $g = (V, E, \mu, \nu)$, where*

- *V is the finite set of nodes,*
- *$E \subseteq V \times V$ is the set of edges,*
- *$\mu : V \to L_V$ is the node labeling function, and*
- *$\nu : E \to L_E$ is the edge labeling function.*

The number of nodes of a graph g is denoted by $|g|$, while $\mathcal{G}$ represents the set of all graphs over the label alphabets L_V and L_E.

Definition 2.1 allows us to handle arbitrarily structured graphs with unconstrained labeling functions. For example, the labels for both nodes and edges can be given by the set of integers $L = \{1, 2, 3, \ldots\}$, the vector space $L = \mathbb{R}^n$, or a set of symbolic labels $L = \{\alpha, \beta, \gamma, \ldots\}$. Given that the nodes and/or the edges are labeled, the graphs are referred to as *labeled graphs*[3]. *Unlabeled graphs* are obtained as a special case by assigning the same label ε to all nodes and edges, i.e. $L_V = L_E = \{\varepsilon\}$.

Edges are given by pairs of nodes (u, v), where $u \in V$ denotes the source node and $v \in V$ the target node of a directed edge. Commonly, two nodes u and v connected by an edge (u, v) are referred to as *adjacent*. A graph is termed *complete* if all pairs of nodes are adjacent. The *degree* of a node $u \in V$, referred to as *deg(u)*, is the number of adjacent nodes to u, i.e. the number of *incident* edges of u. More precisely, the *indegree* of a node $u \in V$ denoted by *in(u)* and the *outdegree* of a node $u \in V$ denoted by *out(u)* refers to the number of incoming and outgoing edges of

---

[3] *Attributes* and *attributed graphs* are sometimes synonymously used for *labels* and *labeled graphs*, respectively.

node u, respectively. *Directed graphs* directly correspond to Definition 2.1. However, the class of *undirected graphs* can be modeled as well, inserting a reverse edge $(v, u) \in E$ for each edge $(u, v) \in E$ with an identical label, i.e. $\nu(u, v) = \nu(v, u)$. In this case, the direction of an edge can be ignored, since there are always edges in both directions. In Fig. 2.1 some example graphs (directed/undirected, labeled/unlabeled) are shown.

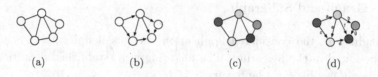

(a)   (b)   (c)   (d)

Fig. 2.1   Different kinds of graphs: (a) undirected and unlabeled, (b) directed and unlabeled, (c) undirected with labeled nodes (different shades of grey refer to different labels), (d) directed with labeled nodes and edges.

The class of *weighted graphs* is obtained by defining the node and edge label alphabet as $L_N = \{\varepsilon\}$ and $L_E = \{x \in \mathbb{R} \mid 0 \leq x \leq 1\}$. In *bounded-valence graphs* or *fixed-valence graphs* every node's degree is bounded by, or fixed to, a given value termed *valence*. Clearly, valence graphs satisfy the definition given above [78, 79]. Moreover, Definition 2.1 also includes *planar graphs*, i.e. graphs which can be drawn on the plane in such a way that its edges intersect only at their endpoints [52, 80], *trees*, i.e. acyclic connected graphs where each node has a set of zero or more children nodes, and at most one parent node [81–85], or graphs with unique node labels [60–62], to name just a few.

In analogy to the subset relation in set theory, we define parts of a graph as follows.

Definition 2.2 (Subgraph). *Let* $g_1 = (V_1, E_1, \mu_1, \nu_1)$ *and* $g_2 = (V_2, E_2, \mu_2, \nu_2)$ *be graphs. Graph* g_1 *is a subgraph of* g_2, *denoted by* $g_1 \subseteq g_2$, *if*

(1) $V_1 \subseteq V_2$,
(2) $E_1 \subseteq E_2$,
(3) $\mu_1(u) = \mu_2(u)$ for all $u \in V_1$, and
(4) $\nu_1(e) = \nu_2(e)$ for all $e \in E_1$.

By replacing condition *(2)* by the more stringent condition

(2') $E_1 = E_2 \cap V_1 \times V_1$,

g_1 becomes an *induced subgraph* of g_2. A complete subgraph is referred to as a *clique*. Obviously, a subgraph g_1 is obtained from a graph g_2 by removing some nodes and their incident, as well as possibly some additional edges from g_2. For g_1 to be an induced subgraph of g_2, some nodes and only their incident edges are removed from g_2, i.e. no additional edge removal is allowed. Fig. 2.2 (b) and 2.2 (c) show an induced and a non-induced subgraph of the graph in Fig. 2.2 (a), respectively.

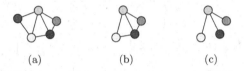

(a)   (b)   (c)

Fig. 2.2   Graph (b) is an induced subgraph of (a), and graph (c) is a non-induced subgraph of (a).

2.2   Exact Graph Matching

The process of graph matching primarily aims at identifying corresponding substructures in the two graphs under consideration. Through the graph matching procedure, an associated similarity or dissimilarity score can be easily defined. We refer to the key problem of computing graph proximity as *graph comparison problem* [39].

Definition 2.3 (Graph Comparison Problem [39]). *Given two graphs g_1 and g_2 from a graph domain $\mathcal{G}$, the graph comparison problem is to find a function*

$$d : \mathcal{G} \times \mathcal{G} \to \mathbb{R}$$

such that $d(g_1, g_2)$ quantifies the dissimilarity (or alternatively the similarity) of g_1 and g_2.

In a rigorous sense, graph matching and graph comparison do not refer to the same task as they feature a subtle difference. The former aims at a mapping between graph substructures and the latter at an overall (dis)similarity score between the graphs. However, in the present book graph matching is exclusively used for the quantification of graph proximity. Consequently, in the context of the present work, both terms 'graph matching' and 'graph comparison' describe the same task and are therefore used interchangeable.

The aim in exact graph matching is to determine whether two graphs, or at least part of them, are identical in terms of structure and labels. A common approach to describe the structure of a graph g is to define the *degree matrix*, the *adjacency matrix*, or the *Laplacian matrix* of g.

Definition 2.4 (Degree Matrix). *Let $g = (V, E, \mu, \nu)$ be a graph with $|g| = n$. The degree matrix $\mathbf{D} = (d_{ij})_{n \times n}$ of graph g is defined by*

$$d_{ij} = \begin{cases} deg(v_i) & \text{if } i = j \\ 0 & \text{otherwise} \end{cases}$$

where v_i is a node from g, i.e. $v_i \in V$.

Clearly, the i-th entry in the main diagonal of the degree matrix $\mathbf{D}$ indicates the number of incident edges of node $v_i \in V$.

Definition 2.5 (Adjacency Matrix). *Let $g = (V, E, \mu, \nu)$ be a graph with $|g| = n$. The adjacency matrix $\mathbf{A} = (a_{ij})_{n \times n}$ of graph g is defined by*

$$a_{ij} = \begin{cases} 1 & \text{if } (v_i, v_j) \in E \\ 0 & \text{otherwise} \end{cases}$$

where v_i and v_j are nodes from g, i.e. $v_i, v_j \in V$.

The entry a_{ij} of the adjacency matrix $\mathbf{A}$ is equal to 1 if there is an edge (v_i, v_j) connecting the i-th node with the j-th node in g, and 0 otherwise.

Definition 2.6 (Laplacian Matrix). *Let $g = (V, E, \mu, \nu)$ be a graph with $|g| = n$. The Laplacian matrix $\mathbf{L} = (l_{ij})_{n \times n}$ of graph g is defined by*

$$l_{ij} = \begin{cases} deg(v_i) & \text{if } i = j \\ -1 & \text{if } i \neq j \text{ and } (v_i, v_j) \in E \\ 0 & \text{otherwise} \end{cases}$$

where v_i and v_j are nodes from g, i.e. $v_i, v_j \in V$.

The Laplacian matrix $\mathbf{L}$ is obtained by subtracting the adjacency matrix from the degree matrix[4], i.e. $\mathbf{L} = \mathbf{D} - \mathbf{A}$. Hence, the main diagonal of $\mathbf{L}$ indicates the number of incident edges for each node $v_i \in V$, and the remaining entries l_{ij} in $\mathbf{L}$ are equal to -1 if there is an edge (v_i, v_j) connecting the i-th node with the j-th node in g, and 0 otherwise.

---

[4]This holds if, and only if, $u \neq v$ for all edges $(u, v) \in E$ in a given graph $g = (V, E, \mu, \nu)$. That is, there is no edge in g connecting a node with itself.

Generally, for the nodes (and also the edges) of a graph there is no unique canonical order. Thus, for a single graph with n nodes, $n!$ different degree, adjacency, and Laplacian matrices exist, since there are $n!$ possibilities to arrange the nodes of g. Consequently, for checking two graphs for structural identity, we cannot simply compare their structure matrices. The identity of two graphs g_1 and g_2 is commonly established by defining a function, termed graph isomorphism, mapping g_1 to g_2.

Definition 2.7 (Graph Isomorphism). *Assume that two graphs* $g_1 = (V_1, E_1, \mu_1, \nu_1)$ *and* $g_2 = (V_2, E_2, \mu_2, \nu_2)$ *are given. A graph isomorphism is a bijective function* $f : V_1 \to V_2$ *satisfying*

(1) $\mu_1(u) = \mu_2(f(u))$ *for all nodes* $u \in V_1$
(2) for each edge $e_1 = (u, v) \in E_1$, *there exists an edge* $e_2 = (f(u), f(v)) \in E_2$ *such that* $\nu_1(e_1) = \nu_2(e_2)$
(3) for each edge $e_2 = (u, v) \in E_2$, *there exists an edge* $e_1 = (f^{-1}(u), f^{-1}(v)) \in E_1$ *such that* $\nu_1(e_1) = \nu_2(e_2)$

Two graphs are called isomorphic if there exists an isomorphism between them.

Obviously, isomorphic graphs are identical in both structure and labels. Therefore, in order to verify whether a graph isomorphism exists a one-to-one correspondence between each node of the first graph and each node of the second graph has to be found such that the edge structure is preserved and node and edge labels are consistent. Formally, a particular node u of graph g_1 can be mapped to a node $f(u)$ of g_2, if, and only if, their corresponding labels are identical, i.e. $\mu_1(u) = \mu_2(f(u))$ (Condition *(1)*). The same holds for the edges, i.e. their labels have to be identical after the mapping as well. If two nodes (u, v) are adjacent in g_1, their maps $f(u)$ and $f(v)$ in g_2 have to be adjacent, too (Condition *(2)*). The same holds in the opposite direction (Condition *(3)*). The relation of graph isomorphism satisfies the conditions of reflexivity, symmetry, and transitivity and can therefore be regarded as an equivalence relation on graphs [28].

Unfortunately, no polynomial runtime algorithm is known for the problem of graph isomorphism [86][5]. In the worst case, the computational

---

[5]Note that in the year 1979 in [86] three decision problems were listed for which it was not yet known whether they are P or NP-complete, and it was assumed that they belong to NP-incomplete. These three well known problems are *linear programming* (LP), *prime number testing* (PRIMES), and the problem of *graph isomorphism* (GI). In the meantime, however, it has been proved that both LP and PRIMES belong to P

complexity of any of the available algorithms for graph isomorphism is exponential in the number of nodes of the two graphs. However, since the scenarios encountered in practice are usually different from the worst cases, and furthermore, the labels of both nodes and edges very often help to substantially reduce the search time, the actual computation time can still be manageable. Polynomial algorithms for graph isomorphism have been developed for special kinds of graphs, such as trees [90], ordered graphs [91], planar graphs [80], bounded-valence graphs [78], and graphs with unique node labels [61].

Standard procedures for testing graphs for isomorphism are based on tree search techniques with backtracking. The basic idea is that a partial node matching, which assigns nodes from the two graphs to each other, is iteratively expanded by adding new node-to-node correspondences. This expansion is repeated until either the edge structure constraint is violated or node or edge labels are inconsistent. In either case a backtracking procedure is initiated, i.e. the last node mappings are undone until a partial node matching is found for which an alternative expansion is possible. Obviously, if there is no further possibility for expanding the partial node mapping without violating the constraints, the algorithm terminates indicating that there is no isomorphism between the two considered graphs. Conversely, finding a complete node-to-node correspondence without violating any of the structure or label constraints proves that the investigated graphs are isomorphic. In Fig. 2.3 (a) and (b) two isomorphic graphs are shown.

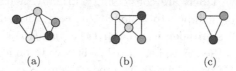

(a)   (b)   (c)

Fig. 2.3   Graph (b) is isomorphic to (a), and graph (c) is isomorphic to a subgraph of (a). Node attributes are indicated by different shades of grey.

(proofs can be found in [87] and [88] for LP $\in$ P and PRIMES $\in$ P, respectively). Yet, for the graph isomorphism problem there are no indications that this particular problem belongs to P. Moreover, there are strong assumptions that indicate that GI is neither NP-complete [89]. Hence, GI is currently the most prominent decision problem for which it is not yet proved whether it belongs to P or NP-complete. Futhermore, it is even assumed that it is NP-incomplete, which would be a proof for the P$\neq$NP assumption (considered as the most important unsolved question in theoretical computer science for which the Clay Mathematics Institute (http://www.claymath.org) has offered a \$1 million prize for the first correct proof).

A well known, and despite its age still very popular algorithm implementing the idea of a tree search with backtracking for graph isomorphism is described in [92]. A more recent algorithm for graph isomorphism, also based on the idea of tree search, is the VF algorithm and its successor VF2 [57, 93, 94]. Here the basic tree search algorithm is endowed with an efficiently computable heuristic which substantially reduces the search time. In [95] the tree search method for isomorphism is sped up by means of another heuristic derived from *Constraint Satisfaction*. Other algorithms for exact graph matching, not based on tree search techniques, are *Nauty* [96], and decision tree based techniques [97, 98], to name just two examples. The reader is referred to [40] for an exhaustive list of exact graph matching algorithms developed since 1973.

Closely related to graph isomorphism is subgraph isomorphism, which can be seen as a concept describing subgraph equality. A subgraph isomorphism is a weaker form of matching in terms of only requiring that an isomorphism holds between a graph g_1 and a subgraph of g_2. Intuitively, subgraph isomorphism is the problem of detecting whether a smaller graph is identically present in a larger graph. In Fig. 2.3 (a) and (c), an example of subgraph isomorphism is given.

Definition 2.8 (Subgraph Isomorphism). *Let* $g_1 = (V_1, E_1, \mu_1, \nu_1)$ *and* $g_2 = (V_2, E_2, \mu_2, \nu_2)$ *be graphs. An injective function* $f : V_1 \to V_2$ *from* g_1 *to* g_2 *is a subgraph isomorphism if there exists a subgraph* $g \subseteq g_2$ *such that* f *is a graph isomorphism between* g_1 *and* g.

The tree search based algorithms for graph isomorphism [92–95], as well as the decision tree based techniques [97, 98], can also be applied to the subgraph isomorphism problem. In contrast with the problem of graph isomorphism, subgraph isomorphism is known to be NP-complete [86]. As a matter of fact, subgraph isomorphism is a harder problem than graph isomorphism as one has not only to check whether a permutation of g_1 is identical to g_2, but we have to decide whether g_1 is isomorphic to any of the subgraphs of g_2 with size $|g_1|$.

Graph isomorphism as well as subgraph isomorphism provide us with a binary similarity measure, which is 1 (maximum similarity) for (sub)graph isomorphic, and 0 (minimum similarity) for non-isomorphic graphs. Hence, two graphs must be completely identical, or the smaller graph must be identically contained in the other graph, to be deemed similar. Consequently, the applicability of this graph similarity measure is rather limited. Consider a case where most, but not all, nodes and edges in two graphs are identical. The rigid concept of (sub)graph isomorphism fails in such a situation in the sense of considering the two graphs to be totally dissimilar. Regard, for instance, the two graphs in Fig. 2.4 (a) and (b). Clearly, from an objective point of view, the two graphs are similar as they have three nodes including their adjacent edges in common. Yet, neither the graph matching paradigm based on graph isomorphism nor the weaker form of subgraph isomorphism hold in this toy example; both concepts return 0 as the similarity value for these graphs. Due to this observation, the formal concept of the largest common part of two graphs is established.

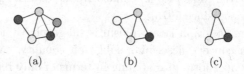

(a)   (b)   (c)

Fig. 2.4   Graph (c) is a maximum common subgraph of graph (a) and (b).

Definition 2.9 (Maximum Common Subgraph, mcs). *Let g_1 and g_2 be graphs. A graph g is called a common subgraph of g_1 and g_2 if there exist subgraph isomorphisms from g to g_1 and from g to g_2. The largest common subgraph with respect to the cardinality of nodes $|g|$ is referred to as a maximum common subgraph (mcs) of g_1 and g_2.*

The maximum common subgraph of two graphs g_1 and g_2 can be seen as the intersection of g_1 and g_2. In other words, the maximum common subgraph refers to the largest part of two graphs that is identical in terms of structure and labels. Note that in general the maximum common subgraphs needs not to be unique, i.e. there might be more than one maximum common subgraph of identical size for two given graphs g_1 and g_2. In Fig. 2.4 (c) the maximum common subgraph is shown for the two graphs in Fig. 2.4 (a) and (b).

A standard approach for computing the maximum common subgraph of two graphs is related to the *maximum clique problem* [99]. The basic idea of this approach is to build an *association graph* representing all node-to-node correspondences between the two graphs that violate neither the structure nor the label consistency of both graphs. A maximum clique in the association graph is equivalent to a maximum common subgraph of the two underlying graphs. Also for the detection of the maximum clique, tree search algorithms using some heuristics can be employed [100, 101]. In [102] other approaches to the maximum common subgraph problem are reviewed and compared against one another (e.g. the approach presented in [103] where an algorithm for the maximum common subgraph problem is introduced without converting it into the maximum clique problem).

Various graph dissimilarity measures can be derived from the maximum common subgraph of two graphs. Intuitively speaking, the larger a maximum common subgraph of two graphs is, the more similar the two graphs are. For instance, in [104] such a distance measure is introduced, defined by

$$d_{MCS}(g_1, g_2) = 1 - \frac{|mcs(g_1, g_2)|}{\max\{|g_1|, |g_2|\}} \ .$$

Note that, whereas the maximum common subgraph of two graphs is not uniquely defined, the d_{MCS} distance is. If two graphs are isomorphic, their d_{MCS} distance is 0; on the other hand, if two graphs have no part in common, their d_{MCS} distance is 1. It has been shown that d_{MCS} is a metric and produces a value in $[0, 1]$.

A second distance measure which has been proposed in [105], based on the idea of *graph union*, is

$$d_{WGU}(g_1, g_2) = 1 - \frac{|mcs(g_1, g_2)|}{|g_1| + |g_2| - |mcs(g_1, g_2)|} \ .$$

By graph union it is meant that the denominator represents the size of the union of the two graphs in the set-theoretic sense. This distance measure behaves similarly to d_{MCS}. The motivation of using graph union in the denominator is to allow for changes in the smaller graph to exert some influence on the distance measure, which does not happen with d_{MCS}. This measure was also demonstrated to be a metric and creates distance values in $[0, 1]$.

A similar distance measure [106] which is not normalized to the interval $[0, 1]$ is

$$d_{UGU}(g_1, g_2) = |g_1| + |g_2| - 2 \cdot |mcs(g_1, g_2)| \ .$$

In [107] it has been proposed to use a distance measure based on both the maximum common subgraph and the *minimum common supergraph*, which is the complimentary concept of maximum common subgraph.

Definition 2.10 (Minimum Common Supergraph, MCS). *Let $g_1 = (V_1, E_1, \mu_1, \nu_1)$ and $g_2 = (V_2, E_2, \mu_2, \nu_2)$ be graphs. A common supergraph* *of g_1 and g_2, $CS(g_1, g_2)$, is a graph $g = (V, E, \mu, \nu)$ such that there exist subgraph isomorphisms from g_1 to g and from g_2 to g. We call g a minimum common supergraph of g_1 and g_2, $MCS(g_1, g_2)$, if there exists no other common supergraph of g_1 and g_2 that has less nodes than g.*

In Fig. 2.5 (a) the minimum common supergraph of the graphs in Fig. 2.5 (b) and (c) is given. The computation of the minimum common supergraph can be reduced to the problem of computing a maximum common subgraph [108].

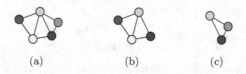

(a)   (b)   (c)

Fig. 2.5   Graph (a) is a minimum common supergraph of graph (b) and (c).

The distance measure proposed in [107] is now defined by

$$d_{MMCS}(g_1, g_2) = |MCS(g_1, g_2)| - |mcs(g_1, g_2)| \ .$$

The concept that drives this particular distance measure is that the maximum common subgraph provides a "lower bound" on the similarity of two graphs, while the minimum supergraph is an "upper bound". If two graphs are identical, i.e. isomorphic, then both their maximum common subgraph and minimum common supergraph are the same as the original graphs and $|g_1| = |g_2| = |MCS(g_1, g_2)| = |mcs(g_1, g_2)|$, which leads to $d_{MMCS}(g_1, g_2) = 0$. As the graphs become more dissimilar, the size of the maximum common subgraph decreases, while the size of the minimum supergraph increases. This in turn leads to increasing values of $d_{MMCS}(g_1, g_2)$. For two graphs with an empty maximum common subgraph, the distance becomes $|MCS(g_1, g_2)| = |g_1| + |g_2|$. The distance $d_{MMCS}(g_1, g_2)$ has also been shown to be a metric, but it does not produce values normalized to the interval $[0, 1]$, unlike d_{MCS} or d_{WGU}. We can also create a version of this distance measure which is normalized to $[0, 1]$ by defining

$$d_{MMCSN}(g_1, g_2) = 1 - \frac{|mcs(g_1, g_2)|}{|MCS(g_1, g_2)|} \ .$$

Note that, because of $|MCS(g_1, g_2)| = |g_1| + |g_2| - |mcs(g_1, g_2)|$, d_{UGU} and d_{MMCS} are identical. The same is true for d_{WGU} and d_{MMCSN}.

The main advantage of exact graph matching methods is their stringent definition and solid mathematical foundation [28]. This main advantage may turn into a disadvantage, however. In exact graph matching for finding two graphs g_1 and g_2 to be similar, it is required that a significant part of the topology together with the corresponding node and edge labels in g_1 and g_2 is identical. To achieve a high similarity score in case of graph isomorphism, the graphs must be completely identical in structure and labels. In case of subgraph isomorphism, the smaller graph must be identically contained in the larger graph. Finally, in cases of maximum common subgraph and minimum common supergraph large part of the graphs need to be isomorphic so that a high similarity or low dissimilarity is obtained. These stringent constraints imposed by exact graph matching are too rigid in some applications.

For this reason, a large number of error-tolerant, or inexact, graph matching methods have been proposed, dealing with a more general graph matching problem than the one formulated in terms of (sub)graph isomorphism. These inexact matching algorithms measure the discrepancy of two graphs in a broader sense that better reflects the intuitive understanding of graph similarity or dissimilarity.

2.3 Error-tolerant Graph Matching

Due to the intrinsic variability of the patterns under consideration, and the noise resulting from the graph extraction process, it cannot be expected that two graphs representing the same class of objects are completely, or at least in a large part, identical in their structure. Moreover, if the node or edge label alphabet L is used to describe non-discrete properties of the underlying patterns, and the label alphabet therefore consists of continuous labels, $L \subseteq \mathbb{R}^n$, it is most probable that the actual graphs differ somewhat from their ideal model. Obviously, such noise crucially affects the applicability of exact graph matching techniques, and consequently exact graph matching is rarely used in real-world applications.

In order to overcome this drawback, it is advisable to endow the graph matching framework with a certain tolerance to errors. That is, the matching process must be able to accommodate the differences of the graphs by relaxing – to some extent – the constraints of the matching process [40]. For instance, rather than simply evaluating whether or not two node labels are equal, an error-tolerant graph matching process should measure how similar the respective labels are. Hence, by means of such an approach mappings of nodes from one graph to nodes of another graph with different labels become possible. The same holds for the edges, of course. By assigning a high cost to mappings where the labels are dissimilar, and vice versa, a low cost to mappings where the labels are similar, the matching process still ensures that similar substructures of both graphs are matched with each other. Furthermore, whereas in the exact approach, the matching between two nodes must preserve the edge structure in any case, in error-tolerant graph matching node mappings violating the structure are not forbidden, but only penalized. Hence, the overall aim of error-tolerant graph matching is to find a mapping from one graph to another such that the overall cost of the matching is minimized.

Various approaches to error-tolerant graph matching have been proposed in the literature. In the next paragraphs some important categories are briefly described.

Graph Edit Distance and Related Approaches   The idea of a tree search employed for the (sub)graph isomorphism problem can also be applied to inexact graph matching. The idea first emerged in [109] where error-correcting graph isomorphism is computed by means of a tree search algorithm. Yet, the proposed framework allows neither deletions nor insertions of both nodes and edges, i.e. the graphs to be matched must be structurally isomorphic. In [110] this drawback is resolved by allowing both insertions and deletions of nodes as well as edges. In [111] an improved heuristic for speeding up the search for an optimal mapping is presented. The idea of *graph edit distance*, that is the approach where the dissimilarity between graphs is captured in terms of a cost function measuring the strength of the transformation of one graph into another, emerged in [112, 113]. In order to compute graph edit distance and related measures often A* based search techniques using some heuristics are employed [114–117]. A* is a best-first search algorithm [118] which is *complete* and *admissable*, i.e. it always finds a solution if there is one and it never overestimates the cost of reaching the goal.

The problem of optimizing the cost of an error-tolerant graph matching is known to be NP-hard. That is, the computational complexity of related algorithms, whether or not a heuristic function is used to govern the tree traversal process, is exponential in the number of nodes of the involved graphs. This means that the running time and space complexity may be huge even for rather small graphs.

In order to cope better with the problem of graph edit distance, *approximate*, or *suboptimal*, matching algorithms can be used instead of exact, or optimal, ones. In contrast to *optimal* error-tolerant graph matching, approximate algorithms do not guarantee to find the global minimum of the matching cost, but only a local one. Usually this approximation is not very far from the global one, but there are no guarantees, of course [40]. The approximate nature of such suboptimal algorithms is usually repaid by polynomial matching times. Local optimization criteria [28, 119, 120], for instance, are used to solve the error-tolerant graph matching problem in a more efficient way. Another idea for efficient graph edit distance is to prune the underlying search tree and consequently reduce both the search space and the matching time [121]. Linear programming for computing the edit distance of graphs with unlabeled edges is proposed in [122]. Finding an optimal match between the sets of subgraphs by means of dynamic programming [123, 124] or a bipartite matching procedure [125, 126] is another possibility for speeding up the computation of graph edit distance.

Genetic Algorithms Optimization procedures for error-tolerant graph matching based on *genetic algorithms* have also been proposed [127–130]. The basic idea of this approach is to formalize matchings as states (chromosomes) with a corresponding performance (fitness). An initial pool of these chromosomes, i.e. matchings, evolves iteratively into other generations of matchings. To this end, different genetic operations, such as *reproduction, crossover,* and *mutation,* are applied to the current matchings. That is, the pool of node-to-node correspondences is iteratively modified by some randomized operations. Though the search space is explored in a random fashion, genetic algorithms tend to favor promising chromosomes, i.e. well fitting matchings, and further improve them by specific genetic operations. The main advantage of genetic algorithms is that they offer an efficient way to cope with huge search spaces. However, the final result crucially depends on the initial states which are commonly randomly generated. Moreover, due to its random procedure, genetic algorithm based graph matching is obviously non-deterministic.

Relaxation Labeling Another class of error-tolerant graph matching methods employs *relaxation labeling technique.* The basic idea of this particular approach is to formulate the graph matching problem as a labeling problem. Each node of one graph is to be assigned to one label out of a discrete set of possible labels, specifying a matching node of the other graph. During the matching process, Gaussian probability distributions are used to model compatibility coefficients measuring how suitable each candidate label is. The initial labeling, which is based on the node attributes, node connectivity, or other information available, is then refined in an iterative procedure until a sufficiently accurate labeling, i.e. a matching of two graphs, is found. Based on the pioneering work presented in [131], the idea of relaxation labeling has been refined in several contributions. In [132, 133] the probabilistic framework for relaxation labeling is endowed with theoretical foundation. The main drawback of the initial formulation of this technique, namely the fact that node and edge labels are used only in the initialization of the matching process, is overcome in [134]. A significant extension of the framework is introduced in [135] where a Bayesian consistency measure is adapted to derive a graph distance. In [136] this method is further improved by also taking edge labels into account in the evaluation of the consistency measure. The concept of Bayesian graph edit distance, which in fact builds up on the idea of probabilistic relaxation, is presented in [137]. The concept has been also successfully applied to special kinds of graphs, such as trees [84].

Graph Kernel   Kernel methods were originally developed for vectorial representations, but the kernel framework can be extended to graphs in a very natural way. A number of *graph kernels* have been designed for graph matching [5, 138–140]. A seminal contribution is the work on convolution kernels, which provides a general framework for dealing with complex objects that consist of simpler parts [141, 142]. Convolution kernels infer the similarity of complex objects from the similarity of their parts. The ANOVA kernel [143] or the graphlet kernel [144], for instance, are convolution kernels.

A second class of graph kernels is based on the analysis of random walks in graphs. These kernels measure the similarity of two graphs by the number of random walks in both graphs that have all or some labels in common [44, 45, 140, 145–147]. In [140] it is shown that the number of matching walks in two graphs can be computed by means of the product graph of two graphs, without the need to explicitly enumerate the walks. In order to handle continuous labels the random walk kernel has been extended in [44]. This extension allows one to also take non-identically labeled walks into account. In [45] two kernels, the so-called all-path and the shortest-path kernel, are introduced. These kernels consider paths between two pairs of nodes in a graph and use the similarity of two pairs of paths in order to derive the final similarity value. Another kernel that considers paths and label sequences encountered along the paths in two graphs is described in [46].

A third class of graph kernels is given by diffusion kernels. The kernels of this class are defined with respect to a base similarity measure which is used to construct a valid kernel matrix [148–153]. This base similarity measure only needs to satisfy the condition of symmetry and can be defined for any kind of objects.

A number of additional kernels are discussed in [154, 155]. These kernels are based on finding identical substructures in two graphs, such as common subgraphs, subtrees, and cycles. In a recent book [28], graph kernels that are derived from graph edit distance are introduced. These kernels can cope with any type of graph and are applicable to a wide spectrum of different applications.

For a more thorough introduction to kernel methods, and particularly to graph kernels, the reader is referred to Chapter 5.

Spectral Methods *Spectral methods* constitute a further class of graph matching procedures [156–162]. The general idea of this approach is based on the following observation. The eigenvalues and the eigenvectors of the adjacency or Laplacian matrix of a graph are invariant with respect to node permutations. Hence, if two graphs are isomorphic, their structural matrices will have the same eigendecomposition. The converse, i.e. deducing from the equality of eigendecompositions to graph isomorphism, is not true in general. However, by representing the underlying graphs by means of the eigendecomposition of their structural matrix, the matching process of the graphs can be conducted on some features derived from their eigendecomposition. The main problem of spectral methods is, however, that they are rather sensitive towards structural errors, such as missing or spurious nodes [28]. Moreover, most of these methods are purely structural, in the sense that they are only applicable to unlabeled graphs, or they allow only severely constrained label alphabets.

Artificial Neural Networks One class of error-tolerant graph matching methods employs *artificial neural networks*. In two seminal papers [163, 164] it is shown that neural networks can be used to classify directed acyclic graphs. The algorithms are based on an energy minimization framework, and use some kind of Hopfield network [165]. Hopfield networks consist of a set of neurons connected by synapses such that, upon activation of the network, the neuron output is fed back into the network. By means of an iterative learning procedure the given energy criterion is minimized.

Similar to the approach of relaxation labeling, compatibility coefficients are used to evaluate whether two nodes or edges constitute a successful match.

In [166] the optimization procedure is stabilized by means of a Potts MFT network. In [167] a self-organizing Hopfield network is introduced that learns most of the network parameters and eliminates the need for specifying them a priori. In [168, 169] the graph neural network is extended such that also undirected and acyclic graphs can be processed. The general idea is to represent the nodes of a graph in an encoding network. In this encoding network local transition functions and local output functions are employed, expressing the dependency of a node on its neighborhood and describing how the output is produced, respectively. As both functions are implemented by feedforward neural networks, the encoding network can be interpreted as a recurrent neural network.

Further examples of graph matching based on artificial neural networks can be found in [170–175].

Miscelanous Methods   Several other error-tolerant graph matching methods have been proposed in the literature. For instance, graph matching based on the Expectation Maximization algorithm [176, 177], on replicator equations [178], and on graduated assignment [179]. Moreover, random walks in graphs [180, 181], approximate least-squares and interpolation theory algorithms [182, 183], and random graphs [184, 185] are also employed for error-tolerant graph matching.

2.4   Summary and Broader Perspective

This chapter reviews the most important graph matching paradigms developed in the last decades. Graph matching methods are used for the crucial task of computing graph similarity. We distinguish between exact graph matching and error-tolerant graph matching. The former approach is based on the idea of determining graph equality by means of the general concept of graph isomorphism. Two isomorphic graphs are identical in terms of structure and labels. The idea of subgraph isomorphism provides us with the possibility to find out whether a smaller graph is contained in a larger one. Finally, by means of maximum common subgraph and minimum common supergraph, it can be determined whether two graphs share identical parts, and if so, use the size of the common parts as a foundation for various graph metrics. A major issue in exact graph matching approaches is the restriction that large part of the two graphs have to be completely identical in terms of structure and labels to be deemed similar. In fact, this scenario is often too restrictive, as subtle differences in the graphs are not considered in this approach.

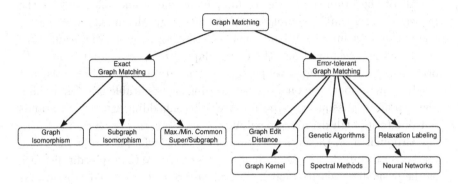

Fig. 2.6   A taxonomy of graph matching approaches.

Error-tolerant graph matching overcomes this general problem by not enforcing strict matchings. That is, in error-tolerant graph matching the labels of the substructures to be matched do not need necessarily to be equal. Moreover, while in exact graph matching the edge-structure has to be always preserved by the matching, in error-tolerant graph matching the edge-structure can be violated. Through the introduction of a cost for non-consistent labels and violated edge-structures, the matching process becomes a problem of cost minimization. A huge amount of error-tolerant graph matching procedures have been proposed, among them methods using tree search algorithms, relaxation labeling techniques, genetic algorithms, kernel methods, spectral approaches, artificial neural networks, and many others. In Fig. 2.6 an overview of exact as well as error-tolerant graph matching methods is given.

Graph matching is a core process in the graph based pattern recognition framework to be established in the present book. The general idea of the proposed framework is that rather than directly operating on the graphs, one first explicitly maps them to a vector space. Hence, from a conceptional point of view, this approach is somewhat similar to spectral methods, where vectorial descriptions of graphs are derived from the eigendecomposition of their structural matrices. However, the framework established in the present book uses a novel idea for graph embedding, viz. the dissimilarity representation. Roughly speaking, this approach transforms any data structure, in our case graphs, into a vector of n dissimilarities $(d_1, \ldots, d_n)$. Hence, graph (dis)similarity computation, i.e. graph matching, is particularly crucial for the proposed book.

All of the graph matching techniques available and discussed in the present chapter could be employed for the task of graph embedding. That is, one of the most important components of the graph embedding framework can be easily exchanged and therefore adapted to specific applications. In other words, from a high-level perspective the graph embedding procedure can be seen as operating on a black-box using some suitable graph matching algorithms. Consequently, the novel graph embedding framework stands out due to its high degree of flexibility.

Although it is theoretically possible to use different graph matching methods for embedding, the present book is restricted to graph edit distance as the basic dissimilarity model. As a matter of fact, graph edit distance is recognized as one of the most flexible and universal error-tolerant matching paradigms. Particularly, graph edit distance is not restricted to a special class of graphs, but can cope with arbitrary graphs with unconstrained label alphabets for nodes and edges. The next chapter is devoted to a detailed description of graph edit distance and its computation.

Graph Edit Distance 3

When in doubt, use brute force.

Kenneth Thompson

In the previous chapter, several approaches to the problem of graph matching were discussed. The approaches based on the paradigm of exact graph matching ((sub)graph isomorphism, maximum common subgraph, and minimum common supergraph) are clearly too constrained to provide us with a general purpose graph matching tool. The requirement that a significant part of the topology together with the node and edge labels have to be identical to achieve a high similarity value, makes the general applicability of such rigid methods impossible in most real-world applications.

Error-tolerant graph matching methods, on the other hand, offer a framework for structural matching that reflects the intuitive understanding of graph similarity in a much broader sense. In general, the error-tolerant nature of such algorithms allows the mapping between substructures of two graphs even if the corresponding structures and labelings are not completely identical. In other words, differences on the labels of two nodes or edges to be matched are accepted and rather penalized than merely forbidden. The penalty, or cost, is dependent on the strength of the difference between the actual label information. The same applies for the edge structure of two graphs to be matched. That is, the structures of the considered graphs do not have to be preserved in any case, and structure violations are also imposed with a cost (usually depending on the magnitude of the structure violation). The overall aim that all error-tolerant graph matching methods have in common is the minimization of the cost of a complete matching. Clearly, for a matching of similar graphs (in terms of structure and labels), an overall low cost is to be expected, and vice versa, for a matching of dissimilar graphs, an overall high cost will be the result of the matching.

Thus, the sum of cost inferred from the resulting matching provides us with a flexible dissimilarity measure on graphs.

Regarding the huge variety of error-tolerant graph matching methods available (see the previous chapter and [40] for a survey), a potential developer of a graph matching framework has a number of options. The right choice of an error-tolerant graph matching model suitable for a particular recognition problem is inherently difficult. If the area of application is confined to a certain class of graphs, it is often possible to come up with specialized methods exploiting specific properties of the underlying graphs [28]. As an example consider the case where purely structural graphs are powerful enough to model the objects of a certain problem domain. In other words, neither node nor edge labels are necessary for capturing the important information in the graphs. In such a particular case, employing a graph matching method based on spectral methods, which are perfectly suited for unlabeled graphs, could be a promising way to be explored.

Though it might be beneficial in some applications to use a graph matching approach explicitly tailored to a special class of graphs, the present book addresses the issue of processing arbitrarily structured and arbitrarily labeled graphs. Hence, the graph matching method actually employed has to be able to cope with directed and undirected, as well as with labeled and unlabeled graphs. If there are labels on nodes, edges, or both, no constraints on the label alphabet should compromise the representational power of the employed graphs. Anyhow, the matching framework should in any case be flexible enough to be adopted and tailored to certain problem specifications. As it turns out, graph edit distance [109, 112, 113, 123] meets both requirements, due to its applicability to a wide range of graphs and its adaptiveness to various problem domains. Therefore the concept of edit distance is used throughout this book as the basic graph matching approach.

Originally, the concept of edit distance has been proposed in the context of string matching [186, 187]. Generally, procedures for edit distance computation aim at deriving a dissimilarity measure from the number as well as the strength of distortions one has to apply to one pattern in order to transform it into another pattern. The concept of edit distance has been extended from strings to more general data structures such as trees [188] and graphs [109, 112, 113, 123]. The overall idea of graph edit distance is to define the dissimilarity of two graphs by the minimum amount of distortion that is needed to transform one graph into another.

There are various applications where the edit distance has proved to be suitable for error-tolerant graph matching [21, 53, 189]. In [21], for instance, graph edit distance is employed for the difficult task of fingerprint classification. In [53], graph edit distance is used for the task of diatom identification[1]. Finally, clustering of color images based on the edit distance of graphs is treated in [189].

3.1 Basic Definition and Properties

Compared to other graph matching methods, graph edit distance stands out due to its ability to cope with arbitrary structured graphs with unconstrained label alphabets for both nodes and edges. Besides the fact that graph edit distance is very flexible, the concept of edit distance can be tailored to specific applications by defining a cost for edit operations. Hence, in the very first step of edit distance based graph matching, the underlying distortion model needs to be defined. A standard set of distortion operations is given by *insertions, deletions,* and *substitutions* of both nodes and edges. We denote the substitution of two nodes u and v by $(u \to v)$, the deletion of node u by $(u \to \varepsilon)$, and the insertion of node v by $(\varepsilon \to v)$. For edges we use a similar notation. Other operations, such as *merging* and *splitting* of nodes [53, 191, 192], can be useful in certain applications, but are not considered in the present book.

Given two graphs, the source graph g_1 and the target graph g_2, the idea of graph edit distance is to delete some nodes and edges from g_1, relabel (substitute) some of the remaining nodes and edges, and insert some nodes and edges in g_2, such that g_1 is eventually transformed into g_2. A sequence of edit operations $e_1, \ldots, e_k$ that transform g_1 completely into g_2 is called an *edit path* between g_1 and g_2. In Fig. 3.1 an example of an edit path between two graphs g_1 and g_2 is given. This edit path consists of three edge deletions, one node deletion, one node insertion, two edge insertions, and two node substitutions.

Fig. 3.1 A possible edit path between graph g_1 and graph g_2 (node labels are represented by different shades of grey).

---

[1] Diatoms are unicellular algae found in humid places where light provides the basis for photosynthesis. The identification of diatoms is useful for various applications such as environmental monitoring and forensic medicine [190].

Obviously, for every pair of graphs (g_1, g_2), there exist an infinite number of different edit paths transforming g_1 into g_2. For instance, deleting all nodes and edges from the first graph g_1 and inserting all nodes and edges in the second graph g_2 is always an admissible way of editing the first graph into the second one. However, such a trivial edit path would be definitely inappropriate for deriving some information of the considered graphs' proximity. From the general point of view, substitutions of both nodes and edges can be regarded as positive matches as their labels are similar enough to find a low cost edit operation on them, namely a substitution. Deletions and insertions, on the other hand, represent nodes or edges where no positive match can be found. More precisely, whenever a node or edge substitution is insufficiently accurate, i.e. the cost of the actual substitution would be too high, the considered nodes or edges have to be deleted and inserted in g_1 and g_2, respectively. Clearly, every edit path between two graphs g_1 and g_2 is a model describing the correspondences found between the graphs' substructures. That is, the nodes of g_1 are either deleted or uniquely substituted with a node in g_2, and analogously, the nodes in g_2 are either inserted or matched with a unique node in g_1. The same applies for the edges.

In [193] the idea of fuzzy edit paths is reported where both nodes and edges can be simultaneously mapped to several nodes and edges. The optimal fuzzy edit path is then determined by means of quadratic programming. However, for the sake of clarity the present book is restricted to the traditional approach of graph edit distance where only one-to-one correspondences between nodes and edges are allowed.

Let $\Upsilon(g_1, g_2)$ denote the set of all possible edit paths between two graphs g_1 and g_2. To find the most suitable edit path out of $\Upsilon(g_1, g_2)$, one introduces a cost for each edit operation, measuring the strength of the corresponding operation. The idea of such a cost is to define whether or not an edit operation represents a strong modification of the graph. Obviously, the cost is defined with respect to the underlying node or edge labels, i.e. the cost $c(e)$ is a function depending on the edit operation e. Consider, for instance, three nodes u, v, and w labeled with integer values; $\nu(u) = 1$, $\nu(v) = 2$, and $\nu(w) = 5$. The cost of substituting u with v should intuitively be lower than the cost of substituting u with w, as the former edit operation is clearly more moderate than the latter one. Formally, $c(u \to v) < c(u \to w)$. Similarly, the cost of a substitution, where the respective labels differ only marginally, should be lower than the cost of a deletion or an insertion. Hence, the overall aim of the cost function is to favor weak distortions over strong modifications of the graph.

Clearly, between two similar graphs, there should exist an inexpensive edit path, representing low cost operations, while for dissimilar graphs an edit path with high cost is needed. Consequently, the *edit distance* of two graphs is defined by the minimum cost edit path between two graphs.

Definition 3.1 (Graph Edit Distance). *Let $g_1 = (V_1, E_1, \mu_1, \nu_1)$ be the source and $g_2 = (V_2, E_2, \mu_2, \nu_2)$ the target graph. The graph edit distance between g_1 and g_2 is defined by*

$$d(g_1, g_2) = \min_{(e_1,\ldots,e_k) \in \Upsilon(g_1,g_2)} \sum_{i=1}^{k} c(e_i),$$

where $\Upsilon(g_1, g_2)$ denotes the set of edit paths transforming g_1 into g_2, and c denotes the cost function measuring the strength $c(e)$ of edit operation e.

3.1.1 Conditions on Edit Cost Functions

The cost $c(e)$ of a particular edit operation e reflects the strength of the distortion applied by operation e to the underlying graph. The definition of adequate and application-specific cost functions is a key task in edit distance based graph matching. As the definition of the cost is usually depending on the underlying label alphabet, i.e. the meaning of the graphs, prior knowledge of the graphs' labels is often inevitable for graph edit distance to be a suitable proximity measure. This fact is often considered as one of the major drawbacks of graph edit distance. Contrariwise, the possibility to parametrize graph edit distance by means of a cost function crucially amounts for the versatility of this particular dissimilarity model. That is, by means of graph edit distance it is possible to integrate domain specific knowledge about object similarity, if available, when defining the cost of the elementary edit operations. Furthermore, if in a particular case prior knowledge about the labels and their meaning is not available, automatic procedures for learning the edit cost from a set of sample graphs are available as well [194–197].

Note that the set of edit paths $\Upsilon(g_1, g_2)$ between two graphs g_1 and g_2 is infinite as it is always possible to extend a valid edit path $(e_1, \ldots, e_k) \in \Upsilon(g_1, g_2)$ with an arbitrary number of additional insertions $(\varepsilon \rightarrow v_1), \ldots, (\varepsilon \rightarrow v_n)$ followed by their corresponding deletions $(v_1 \rightarrow \varepsilon), \ldots, (v_n \rightarrow \varepsilon)$, where $\{v_i\}_{i=1,\ldots,n}$ are arbitrary nodes. In practice, however, a few weak conditions on the cost function c are sufficient so that only a finite number of edit paths have to be evaluated to find the minimum cost edit path among all valid paths between two given graphs. First, we define the cost function to be non-negative, i.e.

$$c(e) \geq 0 \quad , \text{ for all node and edge edit operations } e. \qquad (3.1)$$

We refer to this condition as *non-negativity*. Since the cost function assigns a penalty cost to a certain edit operation, this condition is certainly reasonable. However, it does not prevent an edit path to contain insertions of a particular node or edge followed by the corresponding deletion. Such an unnecessary sequence of edit operations is eliminated by means of the following condition on the cost of both deletions and insertions of nodes as well as edges.

$$c(e) > 0 \quad , \text{ for all node and edge deletions and insertions } e. \qquad (3.2)$$

In other words, only substitutions of both nodes and edges are allowed to possibly add a zero cost to the sum of total cost of an actual edit path. Therefore, during the process of finding the minimum cost edit operations, edit paths containing an insertion of a node or edge followed by its subsequent deletion can be safely omitted.

Next, we want to prevent adding unnecessary substitutions to an actual edit path. This is achieved by asserting that the elimination of such unnecessary substitutions from edit paths will not increase the corresponding sum of edit operation cost [28]. Formally,

$$c(u \rightarrow w) \leq c(u \rightarrow v) + c(v \rightarrow w) \qquad (3.3)$$
$$c(u \rightarrow \varepsilon) \leq c(u \rightarrow v) + c(v \rightarrow \varepsilon)$$
$$c(\varepsilon \rightarrow v) \leq c(\varepsilon \rightarrow u) + c(u \rightarrow v)$$

for all nodes u, v, w and corresponding node substitutions, deletions, and insertions. We refer to this condition as *triangle-inequality*. For instance, instead of substituting u with v and then substituting v with w (line 1), one can safely replace the two right-hand side operations by the edit operation $(u \rightarrow w)$ on the left and will never miss out a minimum cost edit path. The same accounts for unnecessary substitutions of edges, of course. Therefore, each edit path $(e_1, \ldots, e_k) \in \Upsilon(g_1, g_2)$ containing superfluous substitutions of both nodes and edges, can be replaced by a shorter edit path with a total cost that is equal to, or lower than, the sum of cost of the former edit path.

Given the above stated conditions 3.1, 3.2, and 3.3 on the edit cost function, it is guaranteed that for evaluating the minimum cost edit path between two graphs $g_1 = (V_1, E_1, \mu_1, \nu_1)$ and $g_2 = (V_2, E_2, \mu_2, \nu_2)$ only the nodes and edges of the graphs g_1 and g_2 have to be considered. That is, adding edit operations to an edit path $(e_1, \ldots, e_k) \in \Upsilon(g_1, g_2)$ containing operations on nodes or edges not involved in the graphs at hand will possibly increase, and definitely not decrease, the overall edit cost of the edit path. Consequently, in order to find the minimum cost edit path among all possible edit paths $\Upsilon(g_1, g_2)$ between the source graph g_1 and the target graph g_2, we only consider the $|V_1|$ node deletions, the $|V_2|$ node insertions, and the $|V_1| \times |V_2|$ possible node substitutions[2]. Similarly, only the $|E_1| + |E_2| + |E_1| \times |E_2|$ edge edit operations have to be considered for finding the minimum cost edit path. Consequently, the size of the set of possible edit paths $\Upsilon(g_1, g_2)$ between two graphs to be matched is bounded by a finite number of edit paths containing edit operations of this kind only.

Note that graph distance measures based on the edit distance are not necessarily metric. That is, the four axioms *non-negativity*, *identity of indiscernibles*, *symmetry*, and *triangle inequality* on a distance measure to be metric need not to be fulfilled in any case using graph edit distance. For instance, it is theoretically possible that the graph edit distance is defined to be non-symmetric, i.e. $d(g_1, g_2) \neq d(g_2, g_1)$ may hold true for some specific definitions of the cost function. However, adding the following two conditions on the cost function c to the above stated conditions of *non-negativity* and *triangle inequality* (Conditions 3.1 and 3.3) ensures the graph edit distance measure to be metric [113]. First, we define identical substitutions to have zero cost, i.e.

$$c(e) = 0 \ , \tag{3.4}$$

if, and only if, edit operation e is an identical node or edge substitution (*identity of indiscernibles*). Second, we define the cost function c to be symmetric, i.e.

$$c(e) = c(e^{-1}) \ , \tag{3.5}$$

for any edit operation e on nodes and edges, where e^{-1} denotes the inverse edit operation to e (*Symmetry*).

3.1.2 Examples of Edit Cost Functions

Typically, the similarity of two nodes or edges to be substituted is measured by means of some distance function defined on the label alphabet L_N or L_E.

---

[2] Remember that the source graph g_1 is edited such that it is transformed into the target graph g_2. Hence, the edit direction is essential and only nodes in g_1 can be deleted and only nodes in g_2 can be inserted.

For instance, for numerical node and edge labels the Euclidean distance can be used to model the cost of a substitution operation on the graphs[3]. For deletions and insertions of both nodes and edges a constant cost is assigned. We refer to this cost function as *Euclidean Cost Function*.

Definition 3.2 (Euclidean Cost Function). *For two graphs $g_1 = (V_1, E_1, \mu_1, \nu_1)$ and $g_2 = (V_2, E_2, \mu_2, \nu_2)$, where $L_N, L_E \subseteq \mathbb{R}^n$, the Euclidean cost function is defined for all nodes $u \in V_1$, $v \in V_2$ and edges $p \in E_1$ and $q \in E_2$ by*

$$c(u \to \varepsilon) = \alpha \cdot \tau_{node}$$
$$c(\varepsilon \to v) = \alpha \cdot \tau_{node}$$
$$c(u \to v) = \alpha \cdot \|\mu_1(u) - \mu_2(v)\|$$
$$c(p \to \varepsilon) = (1 - \alpha) \cdot \tau_{edge}$$
$$c(\varepsilon \to q) = (1 - \alpha) \cdot \tau_{edge}$$
$$c(p \to q) = (1 - \alpha) \cdot \|\nu_1(p) - \nu_2(q)\|$$

where $\tau_{node}, \tau_{edge} \in \mathbb{R}^+$ are non-negative parameters representing the cost of a node and edge deletion/insertion, respectively. The weighting parameter $\alpha \in [0, 1]$ controls whether the edit operation cost on the nodes or on the edges is more important.

The Euclidean cost function defines the substitution cost proportional to the Euclidean distance of two respective labels. The basic intuition behind this approach is that the further away two labels are, the stronger is the distortion associated with the corresponding substitution. For the sake of symmetry, an identical cost τ_{node} for node deletions and node insertions, and an identical cost τ_{edge} for edge deletions and insertions is defined. Note that any node substitution having a higher cost than $2 \cdot \tau_{node}$ will be replaced by a composition of a deletion and an insertion of the involved nodes (the same accounts for the edges). This behavior reflects the basic intuition that substitutions should be favored over deletions and insertions to a certain degree. Given that $0 < \alpha < 1$, the Euclidean cost function satisfies the condition of non-negativity, identity of indiscernibles, symmetry, and triangle inequality and therefore graph edit distance using this cost function is a metric.

In fact, the Euclidean cost function is flexible enough for many problems. However, in some applications the node and/or edge labels are not

---

[3]Obviously, other dissimilarity measures such as Minkowski or Mahalanobis distance could be used as well.

numerical and other distance functions are employed to measure the cost of a particular substitution operation. For instance, the label alphabet can be given by the set of all strings of arbitrary size over a finite set of symbols. In such a case a distance model on strings such as the string edit distance [186, 187] can be used for measuring the cost of a substitution. In another problem domain, the label alphabet might be given by a finite set of symbolic labels $L_{N/E} = \{\alpha, \beta, \gamma, \ldots\}$. In such a case a substitution cost model using a Dirac function, which returns zero when the involved labels are identical and a non-negative constant otherwise, could be the best choice.

A special case of graph edit distance is obtained by defining the cost function as follows.

Definition 3.3 (Subgraph Isomorphism Cost Function). *For two graphs $g_1 = (V_1, E_1, \mu_1, \nu_1)$ and $g_2 = (V_2, E_2, \mu_2, \nu_2)$, where $|g_2| \leq |g_1|$, the subgraph isomorphism cost function is defined for all nodes $u \in V_1$, $v \in V_2$ and edges $p \in E_1$ and $q \in E_2$ by*

$$c(u \to \varepsilon) = 0$$

$$c(\varepsilon \to v) = \infty$$

$$c(u \to v) = \begin{cases} 0 & \text{if } \mu(u) = \mu(v). \\ \infty & \text{otherwise.} \end{cases}$$

$$c(p \to \varepsilon) = \begin{cases} 0 & \text{if } p \to \varepsilon \text{ is implied by a node deletion.} \\ \infty & \text{otherwise.} \end{cases}$$

$$c(\varepsilon \to q) = \infty$$

$$c(p \to q) = \begin{cases} 0 & \text{if } \nu(p) = \nu(q). \\ \infty & \text{otherwise.} \end{cases}$$

Using this cost model, g_2 is a subgraph of g_1 if, and only if, $d(g_1, g_2) = 0$. Hence, subgraph isomorphism can be regarded as a special case of determining the graph edit distance [198][4].

---

[4]Therefore, it cannot be expected to find a polynomial algorithm for the graph edit distance problem.

3.2 Exact Computation of GED

The computation of the edit distance is usually carried out by means of a tree search algorithm which explores the space of all possible mappings of the nodes and edges of the first graph to the nodes and edges of the second graph. A widely used method is based on the A* algorithm [118] which is a best-first search algorithm. The basic idea is to organize the underlying search space as an ordered tree. The root node of the search tree represents the starting point of our search procedure, inner nodes of the search tree correspond to partial solutions, and leaf nodes represent complete – not necessarily optimal – solutions. Such a search tree is constructed dynamically at runtime by iteratively creating successor nodes linked by edges to the currently considered node in the search tree. In order to determine the most promising node in the current search tree, i.e. the node which will be used for further expansion of the desired mapping in the next iteration, a heuristic function is usually used. Formally, for a node p in the search tree, we use $g(p)$ to denote the cost of the optimal path from the root node to the current node p, and we use $h(p)$ for denoting the estimated cost from p to a leaf node. The sum $g(p) + h(p)$ gives the total cost assigned to an open node in the search tree. One can show that, given that the estimation of the future cost $h(p)$ is lower than, or equal to, the real cost, the algorithm is admissible. Hence, an optimal path from the root node to a leaf node is guaranteed to be found [118].

In Algorithm 3.1 the A*-based method for optimal graph edit distance computation is given. The nodes of the source graph are processed in the order $u_1, u_2, \ldots, u_{|V_1|}$. The deletion (line 12) and the substitution of a node (line 11) are considered simultaneously, which produces a number of successor nodes in the search tree. If all nodes of the first graph have been processed, the remaining nodes of the second graph are inserted in a single step (line 14). The set $OPEN$ of partial edit paths contains the search tree nodes to be processed in the next steps. The most promising partial edit path $p \in OPEN$, i.e. the one that minimizes $g(p) + h(p)$, is always chosen first (line 5). This procedure guarantees that the complete edit path found by the algorithm first is always optimal in the sense of providing minimal cost among all possible competing paths (line 7).

Note that edit operations on edges are implied by edit operations on their adjacent nodes. Whether an edge is substituted, deleted, or inserted, depends on the edit operations performed on its adjacent nodes. Formally, let $u, u' \in V_1 \cup \{\varepsilon\}$ and $v, v' \in V_2 \cup \{\varepsilon\}$, and assume that the two node

---

Algorithm 3.1 Graph edit distance algorithm.

Input: Non-empty graphs $g_1 = (V_1, E_1, \mu_1, \nu_1)$ and
$g_2 = (V_2, E_2, \mu_2 \nu_2)$, where $V_1 = \{u_1, \ldots, u_{|V_1|}\}$ and
$V_2 = \{v_1, \ldots, v_{|V_2|}\}$

Output: A minimum cost edit path from g_1 to g_2
e.g. $p_{min} = \{u_1 \to v_3, u_2 \to \varepsilon, \ldots, \varepsilon \to v_2\}$

1: initialize $OPEN$ to the empty set $\{\}$
2: For each node $w \in V_2$, insert the substitution $\{u_1 \to w\}$ into $OPEN$
3: Insert the deletion $\{u_1 \to \varepsilon\}$ into $OPEN$
4: **loop**
5:    Remove $p_{min} = argmin_{p \in OPEN}\{g(p) + h(p)\}$ from $OPEN$
6:    **if** p_{min} is a complete edit path **then**
7:        Return p_{min} as the solution
8:    **else**
9:        Let $p_{min} = \{u_1 \to v_{i1}, \cdots, u_k \to v_{ik}\}$
10:       **if** $k < |V_1|$ **then**
11:           For each $w \in V_2 \setminus \{v_{i1}, \cdots, v_{ik}\}$, insert $p_{min} \cup \{u_{k+1} \to w\}$ into $OPEN$
12:           Insert $p_{min} \cup \{u_{k+1} \to \varepsilon\}$ into $OPEN$
13:       **else**
14:           Insert $p_{min} \cup \bigcup_{w \in V_2 \setminus \{v_{i1}, \cdots, v_{ik}\}} \{\varepsilon \to w\}$ into $OPEN$
15:       **end if**
16:   **end if**
17: **end loop**

---

operations $(u \to v)$ and $(u' \to v')$ have been executed. We distinguish three cases.

(1) Assume there are edges $e_1 = (u, u') \in E_1$ and $e_2 = (v, v') \in E_2$ in the corresponding graphs g_1 and g_2. Then the edge substitution $(e_1 \to e_2)$ is implied by the node operations given above.

(2) Assume there is an edge $e_1 = (u, u') \in E_1$ but there is no edge $e_2 = (v, v') \in E_2$. Then the edge deletion $(e_1 \to \varepsilon)$ is implied by the node operations given above. Obviously, if $v = \varepsilon$ or $v' = \varepsilon$ there cannot be any edge $(v, v') \in E_2$ and thus an edge deletion $(e_1 \to \varepsilon)$ has to be performed.

(3) Assume there is no edge $e_1 = (u, u') \in E_1$ but an edge $e_2 = (v, v') \in E_2$. Then the edge insertion $(\varepsilon \to e_2)$ is implied by the node operations given above. Obviously, if $u = \varepsilon$ or $u' = \varepsilon$ there cannot be any edge $(u, u') \in E_1$. Consequently, an edge insertion $(\varepsilon \to e_2)$ has to be performed.

Obviously, the implied edge operations can be derived from every partial or complete edit path during the search procedure given in Algorithm 3.1. The cost of these implied edge operations are dynamically added to the corresponding paths in $OPEN$.

In order to integrate more knowledge about partial solutions in the search tree, it has been proposed to use heuristics [118]. Basically, such heuristics for a tree search algorithm aim at the estimation of a lower bound $h(p)$ of the future cost. In the simplest scenario this lower bound estimation $h(p)$ for the current node p is set to zero for all p, which is equivalent to using no heuristic information about the present situation at all. The other extreme would be to compute for a partial edit path the actual optimal path to a leaf node, i.e. perform a complete edit distance computation for each node of the search tree. In this case, the function $h(p)$ is not a lower bound, but the exact value of the optimal cost. Of course, the computation of such a perfect heuristic is unreasonable. Somewhere in between the two extremes, one can define a function $h(p)$ evaluating how many edit operations have to be applied in a complete edit path at least [113]. One possible function of this type is described in the next paragraph.

Let us assume that a partial edit path at a position in the search tree is given, and let the number of unprocessed nodes of the first graph g_1 and second graph g_2 be n_1 and n_2, respectively. For an efficient estimation of the remaining optimal edit operations, we first attempt to perform as many node substitutions as possible. To this end, we potentially substitute each of the n_1 nodes from g_1 with any of the n_2 nodes from g_2. To obtain a lower bound of the exact edit cost, we accumulate the cost of the $\min\{n_1, n_2\}$ least expensive of these node substitutions, and the cost of $\max\{0, n_1 - n_2\}$ node deletions and $\max\{0, n_2 - n_1\}$ node insertions. Any of the selected substitutions that is more expensive than a deletion followed by an insertion operation is replaced by the latter. The unprocessed edges of both graphs are handled analogously. Obviously, this procedure allows multiple substitutions involving the same node or edge and, therefore, it possibly represents an invalid way to edit the remaining part of g_1 into the remaining part of g_2. However, the estimated cost certainly constitutes a lower bound of the exact cost and thus an optimal edit path is guaranteed to be found [118]. Moreover, the complexity for $h(p)$ is clearly lower than for computing the exact cost. In the following, we refer to this method as *Heuristic-A**.

3.3   Efficient Approximation Algorithms

The method described in the previous section finds an optimal edit path between two graphs. Due to the fact that the error-tolerant nature of edit distance potentially allows every node of a graph g_1 to be mapped to every node of another graph g_2, the computational complexity of the edit distance algorithm, whether or not a heuristic function $h(p)$ is used to govern the tree traversal process, is exponential in the number of nodes of the involved graphs. Consequently, the edit distance can be computed for graphs of a rather small size only.

In recent years, a number of methods addressing the high computational complexity of graph edit distance computation have been proposed. In some approaches, the basic idea is to perform a local search to solve the graph matching problem, that is, to optimize local criteria instead of global, or optimal ones [119, 120]. In [122], a linear programming method for computing the edit distance of graphs with unlabeled edges is proposed. The method can be used to derive lower and upper edit distance bounds in polynomial time. Two fast but suboptimal algorithms for graph edit distance computation are proposed in [121]. The authors propose simple variants of an optimal edit distance algorithm that make the computation substantially faster. Another approach to efficient graph edit distance has been proposed in [123, 124]. The basic idea is to decompose graphs into sets of subgraphs. These subgraphs consist of a node and its adjacent structure, i.e. edges including their nodes. The graph matching problem is then reduced to the problem of finding an optimal match between the sets of subgraphs by means of dynamic programming. A common way to make graph matching more efficient is to restrict considerations to special classes of graphs. Examples include the classes of ordered graphs [91], planar graphs [80], bounded-valence graphs [78], trees [85], and graphs with unique node labels [60]. Recently, a suboptimal edit distance algorithm has been proposed [52] that requires the nodes of graphs to be planarly embeddable, which is satisfied in many, but not all computer vision applications of graph matching.

3.3.1   *Bipartite Graph Matching*

In the present section another efficient algorithm for solving the problem of graph edit distance computation is introduced. This approach is some-what similar to the method described in [123, 124] in that the graph edit distance is approximated by finding an optimal match between nodes and their local structure of two graphs. However, in order to find the optimal match between local structures a bipartite matching procedure rather than dynamic programming is used. Because of its local nature, this method does not generally return the optimal edit path, but only an approximate one.

The novel approach for graph edit distance computation is based on the *assignment problem*. The assignment problem considers the task of finding an optimal assignment of the elements of a set A to the elements of a set B, where A and B have the same cardinality. Assuming that a numerical cost is given for each assignment pair, an optimal assignment is one which minimizes the sum of the assignment cost. Formally, the assignment problem can be defined as follows.

Definition 3.4 (The Assignment Problem). *Let us assume there are two sets A and B together with an $n \times n$ cost matrix $\mathbf{C} = (c_{ij})_{n \times n}$ of real numbers given, where $|A| = |B| = n$. The matrix elements c_{ij} correspond to the cost of assigning the i-th element of A to the j-th element of B. The assignment problem can be stated as finding a permutation $p = p_1, \ldots, p_n$ of the integers $1, 2, \ldots, n$ that minimizes the overall cost $\sum_{i=1}^{n} c_{ip_i}$.*

The assignment problem can be reformulated by means of a *bipartite graph*, and is therefore also referred to as the bipartite graph matching problem. A bipartite graph $b = (V, E, \mu, \nu)$ is a graph whose nodes V can be divided into two disjoint sets V' and V'' such that every edge $(u, v) \in E$ connects a node $u \in V'$ to a node $v \in V''$ (or vice versa). That is, there are no edges connecting two nodes coming from the same node set V' or V''.

Definition 3.5 (Bipartite Graph). *A bipartite graph b is a four-tuple $b = (V, E, \mu, \nu)$ according to Definition 2.1, where $V = V' \cup V''$, $V' \cap V'' = \emptyset$, and $E \subseteq V' \times V'' \cup V'' \times V'$.*

The assignment problem of Definition 3.4 can be represented as a bipartite graph $b = (V, E, \mu, \nu)$ where the elements of set A and set B are represented by the nodes in V' and V'', respectively. Hence, the bipartite graph b is used to represent the matching of the underlying graphs' nodes. In graph b, the node labeling function μ assigns a label to the nodes in V such that the elements of both sets A and B are uniquely identified. An edge $(u, v) \in E$ is present in b, if, and only if, the assignment of the two elements represented by node $u \in V'$ and $v \in V''$ is possible. The edge labeling function ν assigns the cost of matching node $u \in V'$ with node $v \in V''$ to the corresponding edge $(u, v) \in E$. Commonly an assignment has no direction, and therefore bipartite graphs are usually undirected, i.e for each edge $(u, v) \in E$ a reverse edge $(v, u) \in E$ is inserted in b. In the formalization of the assignment problem all elements of A can be assigned to all elements in B. Hence, every node of the first node set V' is connected to every node of the second node set V'' (and vice versa). Such a bipartite graph b is termed complete.

A *matching* in a bipartite graph $b = (V, E, \mu, \nu)$ is a set of edges $E' \subseteq E$ without common nodes, which means that no two edges $p, q \in E'$ of the matching share a common node $u \in V$. A matching is termed *maximum matching* if it contains the largest possible number of edges. If a matching covers all nodes $V = V' \cup V''$ it is termed a *complete matching*. An *optimal matching* minimizes the sum of matching cost of a complete matching in b. Obviously, such an optimal matching is equivalent to the optimal solution of the assignment problem.

Solving the assignment problem in a brute force manner by enumerating all permutations and selecting the one that minimizes the objective function leads to an exponential complexity which is unreasonable, of course. However, there exists an algorithm which is known as Munkres' algorithm [199][5] that solves the bipartite matching problem in polynomial time. (In the worst case the maximum number of operations needed by Munkres' algorithm is $O(n^3)$, where n is the dimension of the cost matrix $\mathbf{C}$.)

In Algorithm 3.2, Munkres method is described in detail. The assignment cost matrix $\mathbf{C}$ given in Definition 3.4 is the algorithm's input, and the output corresponds to the optimal permutation, i.e. the assignment pairs resulting in the minimum cost. In the description of Munkres' method in Algorithm 3.2 some lines (rows or columns) of the cost matrix $\mathbf{C}$ and some zero elements are distinguished. They are termed *covered* or *uncovered* lines and *starred* or *primed* zeros, respectively.

Intuitively, Munkres' algorithm transforms the original cost matrix $\mathbf{C} = (c_{ij})_{n \times n}$ into an equivalent matrix $\mathbf{C}' = (c'_{ij})_{n \times n}$.

Theorem 3.1 (Equivalent Matrices). *Given a cost matrix $\mathbf{C} = (c_{ij})_{n \times n}$ as defined in Definition 3.4, a column vector $\mathbf{c} = (c_1, \ldots, c_n)$, and a row vector $\mathbf{r} = (r_1, \ldots, r_n)$, the square matrix $\mathbf{C}' = (c'_{ij})_{n \times n}$ with elements $c'_{ij} = c_{ij} - c_i - r_j$ has the same optimal assignment solution as the original cost matrix $\mathbf{C}$. $\mathbf{C}$ and $\mathbf{C}'$ are said to be equivalent.*

Proof. [201] Let p be a permutation of the integers $1, 2, \ldots, n$ minimizing

---

[5]Munkres' algorithm is a refinement of an earlier version by Kuhn [200] and is also referred to as Kuhn-Munkres, or Hungarian algorithm.

Algorithm 3.2 Munkres' algorithm for the assignment problem.

Input: A cost matrix $C = (c_{ij})_{n \times n}$ with dimensionality n
Output: The minimum-cost assignment pairs

1: For each row r in C, subtract its smallest element from every element in r
2: For each column c in C, subtract its smallest element from every element in c
3: For all zeros z_i in C, mark z_i with a star if there is no starred zero in its row or column
4: **STEP 1**:
5: **for** Each column containing a starred zero **do**
6:     cover this column
7: **end for**
8: **if** n columns are covered **then GOTO** DONE **else GOTO** STEP 2 **end if**
9: **STEP 2**:
10: **if** C contains an uncovered zero **then**
11:     Find an arbitrary uncovered zero Z_0 and prime it
12:     **if** There is no starred zero in the row of Z_0 **then**
13:         **GOTO** STEP 3
14:     **else**
15:         Cover this row, and uncover the column containing the starred zero **GOTO** STEP 2.
16:     **end if**
17: **else**
18:     Save the smallest uncovered element e_{min} **GOTO** STEP 4
19: **end if**
20: **STEP 3**: Construct a series S of alternating primed and starred zeros as follows:
21: Insert Z_0 into S
22: **while** In the column of Z_0 exists a starred zero Z_1 **do**
23:     Insert Z_1 into S
24:     Replace Z_0 with the primed zero in the row of Z_1. Insert Z_0 into S
25: **end while**
26: Unstar each starred zero in S and replace all primes with stars. Erase all other primes and uncover every line in C **GOTO** STEP 1
27: **STEP 4**: Add e_{min} to every element in covered rows and subtract it from every element in uncovered columns. **GOTO** STEP 2
28: **DONE**: Assignment pairs are indicated by the positions of starred zeros in the cost-matrix.

$\sum_{i=1}^{n} c_{ip_i}$, then

$$\sum_{i=1}^{n} c'_{ip_i} = \sum_{i=1}^{n} c_{ip_i} - \sum_{i=1}^{n} c_i - \sum_{j=1}^{n} r_j$$

The values of the last two terms are independent of permutation p so that if p minimizes $\sum_{i=1}^{n} c_{ip_i}$, it also minimizes $\sum_{i=1}^{n} c'_{ip_i}$.   □

The equivalent matrix $\mathbf{C}' = (c'_{ij})_{n \times n}$ established through Munkres' algorithm has n independent zero elements, i.e. each row and each column of $\mathbf{C}'$ contains exactly one of these zero elements. This independent set of zero elements exactly corresponds to the optimal solution to the assignment problem. Consequently, if we find a new matrix $\mathbf{C}' = (c'_{ij})_{n \times n}$ equivalent to the initial cost matrix $\mathbf{C} = (c_{ij})_{n \times n}$, and a permutation $p = p_1, \ldots, p_n$ with $c'_{ip_i} = 0$ for $i = 1, \ldots, n$, then p also minimizes $\sum_{i=1}^{n} c_{ip_i}$.

The operations executed in lines 1 and 2, and STEP 4 of Algorithm 3.2 find a matrix equivalent to the initial cost matrix (Theorem 3.1). In lines 1 and 2 the column vector $\mathbf{c} = (c_1, \ldots, c_n)$ is constructed by $c_i = \min\{c_{ij}\}_{j=1,\ldots,n}$, and the row vector $\mathbf{r} = (r_1, \ldots, r_n)'$ by $r_j = \min\{c_{ij}\}_{i=1,\ldots,n}$. In STEP 4 the vectors $\mathbf{c}$ and $\mathbf{r}$ are defined by the rules

$$c_i = \begin{cases} e_{min} & \text{if row } i \text{ is covered} \\ 0 & \text{otherwise} \end{cases} \tag{3.6}$$

$$r_j = \begin{cases} 0 & \text{if column } j \text{ is covered} \\ e_{min} & \text{otherwise} \end{cases} \tag{3.7}$$

where e_{min} is the smallest uncovered element in the cost matrix $\mathbf{C}$.

STEP 1, 2, and 3 of Algorithm 3.2 are constructive procedures to find a maximum set of n' independent zeros and a minimum set of n' lines which contain all zero elements of $\mathbf{C}$. Note that the independent zeros in $\mathbf{C}$ are covered by columns due to König's Theorem.

Theorem 3.2 (König's Theorem). *Given a matrix $\mathbf{C} = (c_{ij})_{n \times n}$, if n' is the maximum number of independent zero elements in $\mathbf{C}$, then there are n' lines (rows or columns) which contain all the zero elements of $\mathbf{C}$.*

We now revisit the formalism of a bipartite graph representing the assignment problem. Assume that the i-th element of set A can be matched with the j-th element of set B, if, and only if, the corresponding cost c_{ij} is equal to zero. The corresponding situation can be represented by means of a bipartite graph $b = (V' \cup V'', E, \mu, \nu)$ where node $u \in V'$ is connected to node $v \in V''$ if, and only if, the matching cost of the corresponding assignment is zero. The maximum number n' of independent zero elements in $\mathbf{C}$ corresponds to the maximum matching which is currently possible in b. Remember that the rows and columns of $\mathbf{C}$ represent the nodes of V' and V'', respectively. The n' rows or columns (stated in Theorem 3.2) which contain all zero elements of $\mathbf{C}$ can be regarded as node cover for the corresponding bipartite graph b. A node cover for a bipartite graph $b = (V, E, \mu, \nu)$ is a subset $V^\circ \subseteq V$ such that for each edge $(u, v) \in E$ at least one of the involved nodes, u or v, is in V°. That is, the n' rows or columns correspond to covered nodes in V' and V'', respectively. König's theorem states that in any bipartite graph b, the number of edges in a maximum matching in b equals the number of nodes in a minimum node cover for b[6].

---

[6]While the maximum matching problem can be solved in polynomial time for gen-

3.3.2   Graph Edit Distance Computation by Means of Munkres' Algorithm

Munkres' algorithm as introduced in the last section provides us with an optimal solution to the assignment problem in cubic time. The same algorithm can be used to derive an approximate solution to the graph edit distance problem as described below.

Let us assume a source graph $g_1 = (V_1, E_1, \mu_1, \nu_1)$ and a target graph $g_2 = (V_2, E_2, \mu_2, \nu_2)$ of equal size, i.e. $|V_1| = |V_2|$, are given. One can use Munkres' algorithm in order to map the nodes of V_1 to the nodes of V_2 such that the resulting node substitution cost is minimal, i.e. we solve the assignment problem of Definition 3.4 with $A = V_1$ and $B = V_2$. In our solution we define the cost matrix $\mathbf{C} = (c_{ij})_{n \times n}$ such that entry c_{ij} corresponds to the cost of substituting the i-th node of V_1 with the j-th node of V_2. Formally, $c_{ij} = c(u_i \to v_j)$, where $u_i \in V_1$ and $v_j \in V_2$, for $i, j = 1, \ldots, |V_1|$.

The constraint that both graphs to be matched are of equal size is too restrictive since it cannot be expected that all graphs in a specific problem domain always have the same number of nodes. However, Munkres' algorithm can be applied to non-quadratic matrices, i.e. to sets with unequal size, as well [201]. In an early version of the present approach to suboptimal graph edit distance, Munkres' algorithm has been applied to rectangular cost matrices [125]. In this approach Munkres' algorithm first finds the $\min\{|V_1|, |V_2|\}$ node substitutions which minimize the total cost. Then the cost of $\max\{0, |V_1| - |V_2|\}$ node deletions and $\max\{0, |V_2| - |V_1|\}$ node insertions are added to the minimum-cost node assignment such that all nodes of both graphs are processed. Using this approach, all nodes of the smaller graph are substituted and the nodes remaining in the larger graph are either deleted (if they belong to g_1) or inserted (if they belong to g_2).

Later the idea proposed in [125] was extended by defining a new cost matrix $\mathbf{C}$ which is more general in the sense that it allows insertions or deletions to occur not only in the larger, but also in the smaller of the two graphs under consideration [126]. In contrast with the scenario of [125], this new setting now perfectly reflects the graph edit distance model of Definition 3.1. Moreover, matrix $\mathbf{C}$ is by definition quadratic. Consequently, the original method as described in Algorithm 3.2 can be used to find the

---

eral graphs, the minimum node cover problem is NP-complete. Yet, the equivalence of matching and covering in bipartite graphs articulated in König's Theorem allows minimum node covers to be computed in polynomial time for bipartite graphs.

minimum cost assignment.

Definition 3.6 (Cost Matrix). *Let* $g_1 = (V_1, E_1, \mu_1, \nu_1)$ *be the source and* $g_2 = (V_2, E_2, \mu_2, \nu_2)$ *be the target graph with* $V_1 = \{u_1, \ldots, u_n\}$ *and* $V_2 = \{v_1, \ldots, v_m\}$, *respectively. The cost matrix* $\mathbf{C} = (c_{ij})_{(n+m) \times (n+m)}$ *is defined as*

$$
\mathbf{C} =
\left[
\begin{array}{cccc|cccc}
c_{11} & c_{12} & \cdots & c_{1m} & c_{1\varepsilon} & \infty & \cdots & \infty \\
c_{21} & c_{22} & \cdots & c_{2m} & \infty & c_{2\varepsilon} & \ddots & \vdots \\
\vdots & \vdots & \ddots & \vdots & \vdots & \ddots & \ddots & \infty \\
c_{n1} & c_{n2} & \cdots & c_{nm} & \infty & \cdots & \infty & c_{n\varepsilon} \\
\hline
c_{\varepsilon 1} & \infty & \cdots & \infty & 0 & 0 & \cdots & 0 \\
\infty & c_{\varepsilon,2} & \ddots & \vdots & 0 & 0 & \ddots & \vdots \\
\vdots & \ddots & \ddots & \infty & \vdots & \ddots & \ddots & 0 \\
\infty & \cdots & \infty & c_{\varepsilon m} & 0 & \cdots & 0 & 0
\end{array}
\right]
$$

where c_{ij} *denotes the cost of a node substitution* $c(u_i \to v_j)$, $c_{i\varepsilon}$ *denotes the cost of a node deletion* $c(u_i \to \varepsilon)$, *and* $c_{\varepsilon j}$ *denotes the cost of a node insertion* $c(\varepsilon \to v_j)$ *(*$u_i \in V_1$ *and* $v_j \in V_2$*).*

Obviously, the left upper corner of the cost matrix represents the cost of all possible node substitutions, the diagonal of the right upper corner the cost of all possible node deletions, and the diagonal of the bottom left corner the cost of all possible node insertions. Note that each node can be deleted or inserted at most once. Therefore, any non-diagonal element of the right-upper and left-lower part is set to ∞. The bottom right corner of the cost matrix is set to zero since substitutions of the form $(\varepsilon \to \varepsilon)$ should not cause any cost.

On the basis of the new cost matrix $\mathbf{C}$ defined above, Munkres' algorithm [199] can be executed (Algorithm 3.2). This algorithm finds the minimum cost permutation $p = p_1, \ldots, p_{n+m}$ of the integers $1, 2, \ldots, n+m$ that minimizes $\sum_{i=1}^{n+m} c_{ip_i}$. Obviously, this is equivalent to the minimum cost assignment of the nodes of g_1 represented by the rows to the nodes of g_2 represented by the columns of matrix $\mathbf{C}$. That is, Munkres' algorithm indicates the minimum cost assignment pairs with starred zeros in the transformed cost matrix $\mathbf{C}'$. These starred zeros are independent, i.e. each row and each column of $\mathbf{C}'$ contains exactly one starred zero. Consequently, each node of graph g_1 is either uniquely assigned to a node of g_2 (left upper corner of $\mathbf{C}'$), or to the deletion node ε (right upper corner of $\mathbf{C}'$). Vice versa, each node of graph g_2 is either uniquely assigned to a node of g_1 (left upper corner of $\mathbf{C}'$), or to the insertion node ε (bottom left corner of $\mathbf{C}'$). The ε-nodes in g_1 and g_2 corresponding to rows $n + 1, \ldots, n + m$ and columns $m + 1, \ldots, m + n$ in $\mathbf{C}'$ that are not used cancel each other out without any cost (bottom right corner of $\mathbf{C}'$).

So far the proposed algorithm considers the nodes only and takes no information about the edges into account. In order to achieve a better approximation of the true edit distance, it would be highly desirable to involve edge operations and their cost in the node assignment process as well. In order to achieve this goal, an extension of the cost matrix is needed. To each entry c_{ij}, i.e. to each cost of a node substitution $c(u_i \rightarrow v_j)$, the minimum sum of edge edit operation cost, implied by node substitution $u_i \rightarrow v_j$, is added. Formally, assume that node u_i has incident edges E_{ui} and node v_j has incident edges E_{vj}. With these two sets of edges, E_{ui} and E_{vj}, an individual cost matrix similarly to Definition 3.6 can be established and an optimal assignment of the elements E_{ui} to the elements E_{vj} according to Algorithm 3.2 can be performed. Clearly, this procedure leads to the minimum sum of edge edit cost implied by the given node substitution $u_i \rightarrow v_j$. This edge edit cost is added to the entry c_{ij}. Clearly, to the entry $c_{i\varepsilon}$, which denotes the cost of a node deletion, the cost of the deletion of all incident edges of u_i is added, and to the entry $c_{\varepsilon j}$, which denotes the cost of a node insertion, the cost of all insertions of the incident edges of v_j is added.

Note that Munkres' algorithm used in its original form is optimal for solving the assignment problem, but it provides us with a suboptimal solution for the graph edit distance problem only. This is due to the fact that each node edit operation is considered individually (considering the local structure only), such that no globally implied operations on the edges can be inferred dynamically. The result returned by Munkres' algorithm corresponds to the minimum cost mapping, according to matrix $\mathbf{C}$, of the nodes of g_1 to the nodes of g_2. Given this node mapping, the implied edit operations of the edges are inferred, and the accumulated cost of the individual edit operations on both nodes and edges can be computed. This cost serves us as an approximate graph edit distance. The approximate edit distance values obtained by this procedure are equal to, or larger than, the exact distance values, since our suboptimal approach finds an optimal solution in a subspace of the complete search space. In other words, it might be that the minimum cost assignment of the local structures eventually leads to additional edge operations which in turn potentially increase the true graph edit distance. In the following we refer to this suboptimal graph edit distance algorithm as *Bipartite*, or *BP* for short.

3.4 Exact vs. Approximate Graph Edit Distance – An Experimental Evaluation

The purpose of the experiments presented in this section is to empirically verify the feasibility of the proposed suboptimal graph edit distance algorithm Bipartite. First of all, we compare the runtime of Bipartite with the runtime of an optimal graph edit distance algorithm. For comparison we use the optimal tree search algorithm (Heuristic-A*) described in Section 3.2. Second, we aim at answering the question whether the resulting suboptimal graph edit distances remain sufficiently accurate for pattern recognition applications. To this end we consider a classification task. There are various approaches to graph classification that make use of graph edit distance in some form, including, for instance, graph kernels [28, 202, 203]. In the present section we make use of a nearest-neighbor classifier to assess the quality of the resulting edit distances because it directly uses these distances without any additional classifier training. Obviously, if a suboptimal algorithm leads to edit distances with poor quality, the classification accuracy of this classifier is expected to decrease.

3.4.1 *Nearest-Neighbor Classification*

The traditional approach to graph matching using edit distance is based on k-nearest-neighbor classification (k-NN). In contrast with for other classifiers such as artificial neural networks, Bayes classifiers, or decision trees [1], the underlying pattern space need not to be rich in mathematical operations for nearest-neighbor classifiers to be applicable. In order to use the nearest-neighbor paradigm, only a pattern dissimilarity measure must be available. Therefore, the k-NN classifier is perfectly suited for the graph domain, where several graph dissimilarity models, but only little mathematical structure is available.

The k-NN classifer in the graph domain proceeds as follows. Given a labeled set of training graphs, an unknown graph is assigned to the class that occurs most frequently among the k graphs from the training set having the smallest edit distances to the unknown graph. The decision boundary of this classifier is a piecewise linear function which makes it very flexible compared to the Bayes classifier and other classification algorithms. On the other hand, if $k = 1$ the k-NN classifier's decision is based on just one element from the training set, no matter if this element is an outlier or a true class representative. That is, the decision boundaries are largely based on empirical arguments. A choice of parameter $k > 1$ reduces the influence of outliers by evaluating which class occurs most frequently in a neighborhood around the test pattern to be classified.

For a formal description of nearest-neighbor classifiers, let us assume that a pattern space $\mathcal{X}$, a pattern dissimilarity measure $d : \mathcal{X} \times \mathcal{X} \to \mathbb{R}$, a set of labels Ω, and a labeled set of training samples $\{(x_i, \omega_i)\}_{1 \leq i \leq n} \subseteq \mathcal{X} \times \Omega$ is given. The 1-nearest-neighbor classifier (1-NN) is defined by assigning a test pattern $x \in \mathcal{X}$ to the class of its most similar training pattern. Accordingly, the 1-NN classifier $f : \mathcal{X} \to \Omega$ is defined by

$$f(x) = \omega_j \quad , \text{ where } j = \operatorname*{argmin}_{1 \leq i \leq n} d(x, x_i) \quad .$$

To render nearest-neighbor classification less prone to outlier patterns from the training set, it is common to consider not only the single most similar pattern from the training set, but evaluate several of the most similar patterns. Formally, if $\{(x_{(1)}, \omega_{(1)}), \dots, (x_{(k)}, \omega_{(k)})\} \subseteq \{(x_i, \omega_i)\}_{1 \leq i \leq n}$ are those k patterns in the training set that have the smallest distance $d(x, x_{(i)})$ to a test pattern x, the k-NN classifier $f : \mathcal{X} \to \Omega$ is defined by

$$f(x) = \operatorname*{argmax}_{\omega \in \Omega} |\{(x_{(i)}, \omega_{(i)}) : \omega_{(i)} = \omega\}| \quad .$$

Clearly, nearest-neighbor classifiers provide us with a natural way to classify graphs based on graph edit distance. However, the major restriction of nearest-neighbor classifiers is that a sufficiently large number of training samples covering a substantial part of the pattern space must be available. In case of graph edit distance, this requirement is particularly cumbersome since the larger the training set, the more graph edit distance computations have to be carried out. Regarding the exponential time complexity of exact computation, the need of efficient graph edit distance becomes obvious.

3.4.2   Graph Data Set

The classification task considered in this section includes the recognition of distorted letter line drawings. We consider the 15 capital letters of the Roman alphabet that consist of straight lines only (*A, E, F, H, I, K, L, M, N, T, V, W, X, Y, Z*). For each class, a prototype line drawing is manually constructed. These prototype drawings are then converted into prototype graphs by representing lines by undirected edges and ending points of lines by nodes. Each node is labeled with a two-dimensional attribute giving its position relative to a reference coordinate system. Edges are unlabeled. The graph database consists of a training set, a validation set, and a test set of size 750 each. The graphs are uniformly distributed over the 15 classes. In order to test classifiers under different conditions, distortions are applied on the prototype graphs with three different levels of strength, viz. *low, medium* and *high*. Hence, our experimental data set comprises 6,750 graphs altogether. In Fig. 3.2 the prototype graph and a graph instance for each distortion level representing the letter *A* are illustrated. Note that in Chapter 4 the Letter data set and several other graph sets are discussed in greater detail.

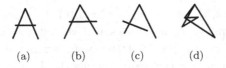

(a)   (b)   (c)   (d)

Fig. 3.2   Instances of letter *A*: Original and distortion levels *low, medium* and *high* (from left to right).

3.4.3   *Experimental Setup and Validation of the Meta Parameters*

As for the letter graphs the node labels are vectors of real numbers andthe substitution cost of a pair of labels is given by the Euclidean distance. Hence, the Euclidean cost function (see Definition 3.2) is employed. The elements of the training set are used as the prototypes in the k-NN classifier. The validation set is used to determine the values of the meta parameters τ_{node}, which corresponds to the cost of a node deletion or insertion, τ_{edge}, which corresponds to the cost of an edge deletion or insertion, $\alpha \in [0,1]$ which corresponds to the weighting parameter that controls whether the edit operation cost on the nodes or on the edges is more important, and the parameter k which determines the number of neighbors considered by the k-NN classifier.

The validation procedure on the Letter data set with lowest distortion is illustrated in Fig. 3.3 and Fig. 3.4 for exact and approximate graph edit distance, respectively. Here the classification results on the validation set are plotted as a function of the two edit cost parameters τ_{node} and

Table 3.1 Best performing meta parameters $(\tau_{node}, \tau_{edge}, \alpha, k)$ and corresponding classification accuracy on the validation set achieved with exact graph edit distance (e) and approximate graph edit distance (a).

Data Set	τ_{node}	τ_{edge}	α	k	Accuracy	
Letter low	0.3	0.5	0.75	3	99.7	(e)
	0.3	0.1	0.25	5	99.7	(a)
Letter medium	0.7	0.7	0.5	5	95.3	(e)
	0.7	1.9	0.75	5	95.2	(a)
Letter high	0.9	2.3	0.75	5	90.9	(e)
	0.9	1.7	0.75	5	90.9	(a)

τ_{edge} for $k = \{1, 3, 5\}$ and $\alpha = \{0.25, 0.5, 0.75\}$. Note the very subtle differences of the validation accuracies achieved by exact and approximate graph edit distance. In Table 3.1 the best performing meta parameter values are shown including the corresponding classification accuracy on the validation set. Note that on Letter low and Letter high both exact and approximate graph edit distance perform equally. On the data set with medium distortion level a slight deterioration (from 95.3% to 95.2%) is observed when using approximate distances rather than exact ones. This deterioration, however, is not statistically significant (using a Z-test with $\alpha = 0.05$).

Finally for both scenarios, the exact and the approximate graph edit distance, the parameter quadruple $(\tau_{node}, \tau_{edge}, \alpha, k)$ that leads to the highest classification accuracy on the validation set is used on the independent test set to perform graph edit distance computation and nearest-neighbor classification. These test results are presented in the next section.

3.4.4 *Results and Discussion*

As the bipartite graph edit distance procedure offers polynomial time complexity, a significant speed-up of Bipartite compared to the exact procedure can be expected. However, the question remains whether the approximate edit distances found by BP are accurate enough for pattern recognition tasks. As mentioned before, the distances found by BP are equal to, or larger than, the exact graph edit distance. In fact, this can be seen in the correlation scatter plots in Fig. 3.5, 3.6, and 3.7. These scatter plots give us a visual representation of the accuracy of the suboptimal method BP on

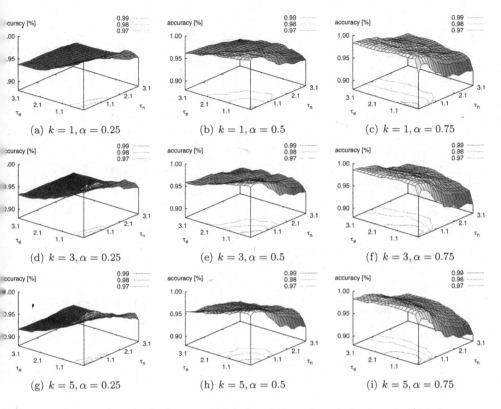

Fig. 3.3 Exact graph edit distance. Validation of the node and edge insertion/deletion penalty τ_n and τ_e, number of nearest neighbors k, and weighting parameter α on the Letter low data set.

the Letter data at all distortion levels. We plot for each pair consisting of one test and one training graph its exact (horizontal axis) and approximate (vertical axis) distance value. We distinguish intra-class and inter-class distances. The former refer to distances computed between graphs from the same class and the latter to distances between graphs from different classes. Note that for this kind of visualization for both exact and approximate graph edit distance the same deletion/insertion cost for nodes and edges has to be applied, of course (the best performing parameter values for τ_{node}, τ_{edge}, and α evaluated for the approximate graph edit distance Bipartite are used).

Based on the scatter plots given in Fig. 3.5, 3.6, and 3.7 we find that BP approximates small distance values accurately in general, i.e. small approximate distances are often equal to the exact distances. On the other hand,

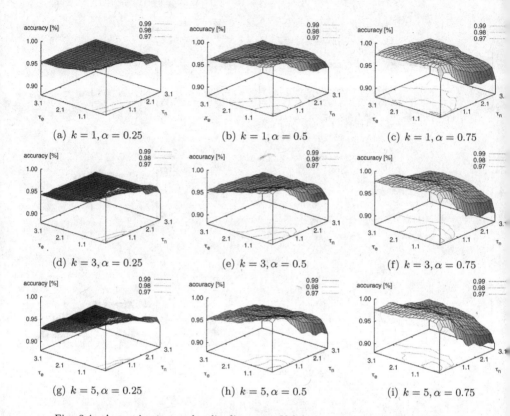

Fig. 3.4   Approximate graph edit distance. Validation of the node and edge insertion/deletion penalty τ_n and τ_e, number of nearest neighbors k, and weighting parameter α on the Letter low data set.

relatively large distance values tend to be overestimated. Based on the fact that graphs within the same class usually have a smaller distance than graphs belonging to two different classes this means that the suboptimality of BP mainly increases inter-class distances, while most of the intra-class distances are not, or only marginally, affected.

BP considers the local edge structure of the graphs only. Hence, in comparison with Heuristic-A*, our novel algorithm BP might find an optimal node mapping which eventually causes additional edge operations. These additional edge edit operations are often deletions or insertions. This leads to an additional cost of a multiple of the edit cost parameter τ_{edge}. This might explain the accumulation of points in the line-like areas parallel to the diagonal in the distance scatter plot in Fig. 3.5 (a), Fig. 3.6 (a), and Fig. 3.7 (a). Compared to the low distortion level, the parameter value τ_{edge}

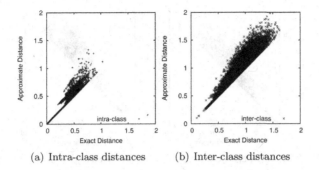

(a) Intra-class distances   (b) Inter-class distances

Fig. 3.5   Scatter plots of the exact edit distances (x-axis) and the approximate edit distances (y-axis) on Letter low.

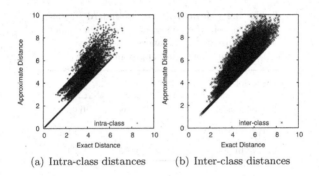

(a) Intra-class distances   (b) Inter-class distances

Fig. 3.6   Scatter plots of the exact edit distances (x-axis) and the approximate edit distances (y-axis) on Letter medium.

is increased for both medium and high distortion level. Hence, the difference between exact and approximate graph edit distance is also increased. In Table 3.2 the mean and the standard deviation of the differences between exact and approximate edit distances are given for all distortion levels. Additionally, the correlation coefficient ρ between exact and approximate graph edit distance is given.

The effect on the classification accuracy of a k-NN classifier, when we substitute the exact edit distances by approximate ones, can be observed in Table 3.3. On Letter low the classification accuracy is deteriorated, while on Letter med the accuracy is improved. However, both changes are not statistically significant (using a Z-test with $\alpha = 0.05$). The deterioration of the accuracy on Letter high is statistically significant. From the results reported in Table 3.3, we can conclude that in general the classification

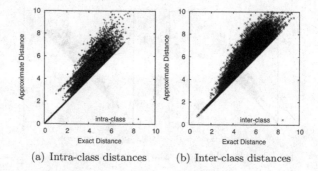

(a) Intra-class distances   (b) Inter-class distances

Fig. 3.7   Scatter plots of the exact edit distances (x-axis) and the approximate edit distances (y-axis) on Letter high.

Table 3.2   Mean (μ) and standard deviation (σ) of the difference between exact and approximate distances and correlation (ρ) between exact and approximate distance.

Data Set	μ	σ	ρ
Letter low	0.05	0.08	0.96
Letter medium	0.52	0.64	0.91
Letter high	0.41	0.55	0.94

accuracy of the k-NN classifier is not negatively affected by using the approximate rather than the exact edit distances. This is due to the fact that most of the overestimated distances belong to inter-class pairs of graphs, while intra-class distances are not strongly affected. Obviously, intra-class distances are of much higher importance for a distance based classifier than inter-class distances. Graphs which belong to the same class (according to the ground truth) often remain near, while graphs from different classes are pulled apart from each other. Note that for a k-NN classifier not to be negatively affected it is sufficient that only few intra-class distances remain lower than the smallest inter-class distances. For a 1-NN classifier, for instance, only one small intra-class distance is needed per graph to achieve a high classification accuracy. Moreover, assuming that critically small inter-class distances are increased due to the suboptimality of Bipartite, even a moderate overestimation of the intra-class distances can be compensated. Obviously, if the approximation is too inaccurate, the similarity measure and the underlying classifier may be unfavorably distorted.

Table 3.3 Classification accuracy and running time in seconds of exact (Heuristic-A*) and approximate (Bipartite) algorithm for graph edit distance.

Data Set	Classification accuracy		Running time	
	Heuristic-A*	Bipartite	Heuristic-A*	Bipartite
Letter low	99.6	99.3	10,225	178
Letter medium	94.0	94.4	31,839	186
Letter high	90.4	89.1	31,920	210

The computation time in Table 3.3 corresponds to the time elapsed while performing all graph edit distance computations on a given data set, which amounts to $750 \cdot 750 = 562,500$ matchings in total. Comparing the runtime of our suboptimal method, Bipartite, with the reference system we observe a massive speed-up[7]. On the Letter data at the lowest distortion level, for instance, the bipartite edit distance algorithm is about 58 times faster than the exact algorithm Heuristic-A*. On the Letter graphs at medium and high distortion level the corresponding speed-ups of the novel algorithm are even higher (171 and 152 times faster, respectively). In other words, the optimal computation of graph edit distance needs some tens of seconds per matching in average, while Bipartite needs less than one millisecond per matching in average for all distortion levels,

We conclude that a trade-off between accuracy of graph edit distance and computation time can be made by using either the exact or the approximate algorithm. In applications where an overestimation of certain distances is acceptable, the approximate algorithm with its superior running time is the method of choice. If exact pairwise distances are needed in any case, the optimal algorithm has to be carried out at the cost of time consuming distance computation.

3.5 Summary

In the present chapter, the problem of graph edit distance computation is considered. The edit distance of graphs is a powerful and flexible concept that has found various applications in pattern recognition and related areas. A serious drawback is, however, the exponential complexity of graph edit

---

[7]Both systems are implemented in JAVA and the experiments have been carried out on a 2 × 2.66 GHz Dual-Core Intel Xeon with 4GB memory.

distance computation. Hence using optimal, or exact, algorithms restricts the applicability of the edit distance to graphs of rather small size.

In the current chapter, we propose a suboptimal approach to graph edit distance computation, which is based on Munkres' algorithm for solving the assignment problem. The assignment problem consists in finding an assignment of the elements of two sets with each other such that a cost function is minimized. In the current chapter it is shown how the graph edit distance problem can be transformed into the assignment problem. The proposed solution allows for the insertion, deletion, and substitution of both nodes and edges, but considers these edit operations in a rather independent fashion from each other. Therefore, while Munkres' algorithm returns the optimal solution to the assignment problem, the proposed solution yields only a suboptimal, or approximate, solution to the graph edit distance problem. However, the time complexity is only cubic in the number of nodes of the two underlying graphs.

In the experimental section of this chapter we compute edit distance on letter graphs. Two main findings can be reported. First, the suboptimal procedure Bipartite achieves remarkable speed-ups compared to the exact method Heuristic-A*. Second, suboptimal graph edit distance does not necessarily lead to a deterioration of the classification accuracy of a distance based classifier. This can be explained by the fact that all distances computed by the suboptimal method are equal to, or larger than, the true distances. An experimental analysis shows that the larger the true distances are the larger the observed overestimation is. In other words, smaller distances are computed more accurately than larger distances by our suboptimal algorithm. This means that inter-class distances are more affected than intra-class distances by the suboptimal algorithm. In turn, for a nearest neighbor classifier, small distances have more influence on the decision than large distances. Therefore, no serious deterioration of the classification accuracy occurs when our novel suboptimal algorithm is used instead of an exact method.

Due to the satisfactory results achieved by the novel bipartite graph edit distance procedure, we use this particular approximation scheme in all remaining chapters of this book. Crucial for choosing the bipartite matching algorithm is its superior run time with (almost) invariant classification accuracies compared to the exact computation.

Graph Data

4

In statistical pattern recognition and machine learning, the UCI Machine Learning Repository [204] is well established and widely used for benchmarking different algorithms. In addition to this repository, there exist various other data sets that are frequently used in statistical pattern recognition and machine learning (e.g. [205]). Yet, a lack of standardized data sets for benchmarks in graph based pattern recognition and machine learning can be observed. For an early discussion of benchmarking graph matching algorithms see [206]. As of today, however, there is only one standard set of graphs adequate for graph matching tasks publicly available to the knowledge of the author, namely the TC-15 graph database [79]. However, this data set consists of synthetically generated graphs only. Furthermore the graphs are particularly generated for exact graph matching algorithms rather than general matching tasks. In [207] benchmarks for graph problems are described. These benchmarks, however, are defined for special problems in graph theory, such as the maximum clique or vertex coloring problem. In particular, they are not related to pattern recognition and machine learning. The present chapter describes a first step towards creating a graph repository that is suitable for a wide spectrum of tasks in pattern recognition and machine learning. The graph data sets emerged in the context of recent work on graph kernels [28, 44] and graph embedding [208]. The introduced data sets are employed for empirical evaluation of various algorithms throughout this book. All graph data sets discussed in the present chapter have been made publicly available by the author under www.iam.unibe.ch/fki/databases/iam-graph-database.

Table 4.1   Summary of graph data set characteristics.

Letter low/medium/high	
Patterns	Letter line drawings
Classes	15 (A, E, F, H, I, K, L, M, N, T, V, W, X, Y, Z)
Size of *tr*, *va*, *te*	750, 750, 750 / 750, 750, 750 / 750, 750, 750
Node labels	(x, y) coordinates
Edge labels	none
Average per graph	4.7/4.7/4.7 nodes, 3.1/3.2/4.5 edges
Maximum per graph	8/9/9 nodes, 6/7/9 edges
Balanced	yes

4.1   Graph Data Sets

Each of the data sets presented in the next subsections is divided into three disjoint subsets, which can be used for training, validation, and testing structural pattern recognition algorithms. If appropriate, all three or two out of the three subsets can be merged.

4.1.1   *Letter Graphs*

Typically, when one is asked to visualize graphs, circles and lines are used to represent nodes and edges, respectively. Hence, it seems to be natural to interpret points in the plane as nodes (implicitly associated with their coordinates) and lines connecting these points by edges. The first graph data set presented in this section involves graphs that represent such line drawings in the plane.

In order to arrive at an intuitive and simple pattern recognition scenario, we consider drawings of the 15 capital letters of the Roman alphabet that consist of straight lines only (*A, E, F, H, I, K, L, M, N, T, V, W, X, Y, Z*). For each class, a prototype line drawing is manually constructed. An illustration of these prototype drawings is provided in Fig. 4.1. These prototype drawings are then converted into prototype graphs by representing lines by undirected edges and ending points of lines by nodes. Each node is labeled with a two-dimensional label giving its position relative to a reference coordinate system. Edges are unlabeled.

Next, distortions are applied on the prototype graphs with three different levels of strength, viz. *low*, *medium* and *high*. These distortions consist of randomly removing, inserting, and displacing edges including their corresponding nodes. For each class and for each distortion level, 150

Fig. 4.1   Prototypes of letters *A* to *Z*.

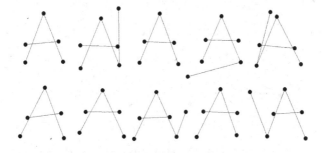

Fig. 4.2   Instances of letter *A* at distortion level *low*.

noisy patterns are generated from each clean prototype. Hence, the graphs are uniformly distributed over the 15 classes (referred to as *balanced*). In Fig. 4.2, 4.3, and 4.4 ten graph instances for each distortion level representing the letter *A* are illustrated. Note that letters that undergo distortions of medium and high strength are difficult to recognize even for a human observer.

Each of the three letter data set consists of a training set, a validation set, and a test set of size 750 each. Hence, our experimental data set comprises 6,750 graphs altogether. Note that this graph data set is particularly useful for investigations of how certain pattern recognition methods behave under increasingly noisy conditions. In Table 4.1 a summary of the Letter

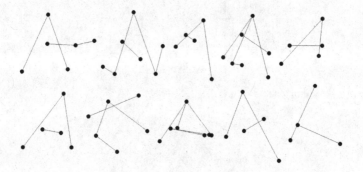

Fig. 4.3   Instances of letter A at distortion level *medium*.

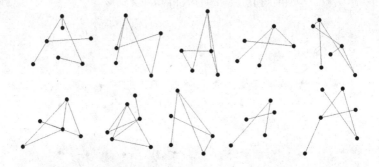

Fig. 4.4   Instances of letter A at distortion level *high*.

data set together with some basic characteristic properties is given.

4.1.2 *Digit Graphs*

The automatic recognition of handwritten digits is an important task in many applications (e.g. automatic bank check readers). The digit data set consists of graphs representing handwritten digits [209]. The original version of this database includes 10,992 handwritten digits from ten classes (*0, 1, 2, . . . , 9*). The data was created by 44 different writers which have been asked to write 250 digits each in random order. For data acquisition a pressure sensitive tablet PC and a cordless pen have been used. During the recording of the digits, the position of the pen was sampled with a constant frequency (100 milliseconds) resulting in sequences of (x, y) coordinates. In

Table 4.2   Summary of graph data set characteristics.

Digit	
Patterns	Digit line drawings
Classes	10 (0, 1, 2, 3, 4, 5, 6, 7, 8, 9)
Size of *tr, va, te*	1,000, 500, 2,000
Node labels	two (x, y) coordinates (starting- and ending point of a line)
Edge labels	none
Average per graph	8.9 nodes, 7.9 edges
Maximum per graph	17 nodes, 16 edges
Balanced	yes

Fig. 4.5   Five instances of the digit classes *0, 1, 2, 3, 4*.

Fig. 4.5 and 4.6 five instances for each digit class are illustrated.

The digit data set is quite similar to the letter data set in the sense that line drawings are considered as basic patterns. However, rather than using artificial distortions to simulate the variety of different writers, the underlying data represents real world data allocated by humans. Moreover, the conversion of the line drawings into graphs is fundamentally different to the approach described above. In contrast to the letter data set where ending

Fig. 4.6   Five instances of the digit classes *5, 6, 7, 8, 9*.

points of lines are represented by nodes, in the present data set nodes represent line segments of a handwritten digit. More formally, the sequences of (x, y) coordinates are converted into graphs by grouping coordinate points together forming subpaths of similar length. Starting with the first coordinate point in the underlying sequence, the handwritten line is traced until the length of the covered path exceeds a certain threshold θ. This procedure is iteratively repeated until the whole digit drawing is covered by subpaths which are in turn encoded by nodes. Subpaths are therefore represented by nodes labeled with their starting and ending position relative to a reference coordinate system (i.e. the first and last (x, y) coordinates from the respective subpath). Successive subpaths are connected by undirected and unlabeled edges. Finally, the derived graphs are normalized such that each graph has equal width and height.

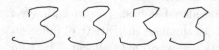

Fig. 4.7   Representing a digit with subpaths of various length ($\theta = 0, 10, 20, 30$ from left to right).

Table 4.3 Summary of graph data set characteristics.

GREC	
Patterns	Line drawings of electronic and architectural symbols
Classes	22 (antenna, capacitor, washbasin, etc.)
Size of *tr, va, te*	836, 836, 1,628
Node labels	Type (end, corner, intersection, circle) and (x, y) coordinates
Edge labels	Type (line, arc)
Average per graph	11.5 nodes, 12.2 edges
Maximum per graph	25 nodes, 30 edges
Balanced	yes

Clearly, by varying the value of threshold θ, the resulting graph representation is crucially modified. The larger the threshold θ, the longer the subpaths, and, consequently, the less nodes are used to capture the whole digit. That is, by increasing θ the number of nodes is reduced. Simultaneously, the quality of the representation decreases. In Fig. 4.7 the impact of threshold θ is illustrated. Starting with $\theta = 0$, where each successive pair of (x, y)-coordinates in the sequence is converted into a node, θ is increased by steps of ten. Clearly, defining θ too large, the resulting subpaths will not be able to capture the characteristic contours of different digits, rendering the recognition task rather difficult. Contrariwise, using a threshold θ which is too small, we end up with graphs with too many nodes and edges making graph comparisons rather inefficient. In our experiments a threshold of 30 is used, leading to graphs with a reasonable number of nodes in average.

For our data set a randomly selected subset of totally 3,500 digits is used. This set is split into a training set of size 1,000, a validation set of size 500, and a test set of size 2,000. The digit graphs are uniformly distributed over the 10 classes. In Table 4.2 a summary of the Digit data set together with some basic characteristic properties is given.

4.1.3 *GREC Graphs*

Automatic conversion of line drawings from paper to electronic form requires the recognition of geometric primitives like lines, arcs, circles etc. in scanned documents [210]. The GREC data set consists of graphs representing symbols made of such geometric primitives from architectural and electronic drawings. From the original GREC database [211], 22 classes are considered. In Fig. 4.8 the prototype images of each class are provided.

The images occur with so-called *salt-and-pepper noise* at five different

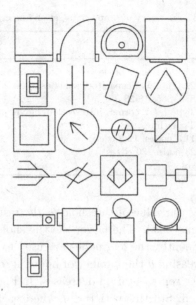

Fig. 4.8   The prototype images of the 22 GREC classes.

distortion levels. In Fig. 4.9 for each distortion level three examples of a drawing are given. Depending on the distortion level, either *erosion*, *dilation*, *opening* (erosion followed by dilation), or *closing* (dilation followed by erosion) operations are applied for noise removal. For all of these morphological operations a *structuring element* is needed. Structuring elements used for the conversion of images to graphs are defined as binary $n \times m$ pixel matrices where foreground and background pixel are represented by ones and zeros, respectively. In the present work a square $n \times n$ matrix, where the corner entries are set to zero and all other entires are set to one, is employed for noise removal.

In case of erosion, for each black pixel at position (i, j) in the image the structuring element is superimposed such that the center of the structuring element lies at position (i, j). If not all foreground pixels of the image are matched by a foreground pixel of the structuring element, the current pixel is flagged. Eventually, each flagged pixel is changed to be a background pixel. Clearly, erosion shrinks the foreground pixels of the image by changing black pixels from the margin of a drawing to white pixels. Dilation can be seen as a reverse operation to erosion. That is, for each white pixel in the image the structuring element is superimposed. If a foreground pixel of the structuring element matches at least one foreground pixel of the image,

Fig. 4.9   The five distortion levels (from bottom to top) applied to three sample images.

the current pixel is flagged. Eventually, each flagged pixel is changed to be a foreground pixel, i.e. changed from white to black. Hence, by means of dilation the margin of a drawing is expanded. Applying closing to an image changes spurious background pixels to foreground pixels, i.e. removes salt noise (small white regions). Opening, on the other hand, changes spurious foreground pixels to background pixels, i.e. removes pepper noise (small black regions).

The noise removed image is thinned to obtain lines of one pixel width. To this end, the thinning method described in [212] is applied. Finally, graphs are extracted from the resulting denoised images by tracing the one-pixel wide lines from end to end and detecting intersections as well as corners. Ending points, corners, intersections and circles are represented by nodes and labeled with a two-dimensional attribute giving their position. These nodes are possibly connected by undirected edges which are labeled as *line* or *arc* depending on whether a straight or curvy line connects the nodes under consideration.

For an adequately sized set, the five graphs per distortion level are individually distorted 30 times to obtain a data set containing 3,300 graphs uniformly distributed over the 22 classes. These distortions consists of translations and scalings of the graphs in a certain range, and random deletions and insertions of both nodes and edges. The resulting set is split into a training and a validation set of size 836 each, and a test set of size 1,628. In Table 4.3 a summary of the GREC data set together with some

Table 4.4   Summary of graph data set characteristics.

Fingerprint	
Patterns	Fingerprint images from the NIST-4 database
Classes	4 (arch, left loop, right loop, whorl)
Size of *tr, va, te*	500, 300, 2,000
Node labels	none
Edge labels	angle
Average per graph	5.4 nodes, 4.4 edges
Maximum per graph	26 nodes, 25 edges
Balanced	no

basic characteristic properties is given.

4.1.4 *Fingerprint Graphs*

The Fingerprint data set stems from the emerging field of *biometric person authentication*. Biometric person authentication refers to the task of automatically recognizing the identity of a person from his or her physiological or behavioral characteristics [28]. Typical examples of biometric person authentication are fingerprint identification, signature verification, voice recognition, face recognition, iris recognition, and many more. Fingerprint images are particularly interesting as a biometric measurement since each person possess this biometric, persons are believed to have unique fingerprints, and fingerprints do not change over time. Moreover, fingerprint images are rather easy to be captured by sensors.

Given the fingerprints captured by means of a sensor, two tasks of fingerprint recognition are distinguished: *fingerprint verification* and *fingerprint identification*. In the former case, the identity of the person is known and the captured fingerprint only needs to be compared to the relevant person's fingerprint template in some database. In cases where the captured and the stored fingerprint match (i.e. they can be viewed as similar), the authentication is verified, otherwise not. In the process of fingerprint identification, the identity of the person belonging to a given fingerprint is not known beforehand and must be established by searching databases of fingerprints. Commonly, these fingerprint databases are very large, containing millions of possible fingerprint candidates (e.g. the FBI database of fingerprints containing more than 200 million fingerprints).

Regarding such huge databases the need for efficient querying techniques is obvious. One possibility to render fingerprint identification more efficient

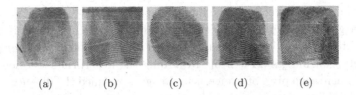

(a)   (b)   (c)   (d)   (e)

Fig. 4.10   Fingerprint examples from the Galton-Henry class *Arch*.

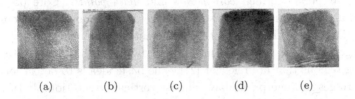

(a)   (b)   (c)   (d)   (e)

Fig. 4.11   Fingerprint examples from the Galton-Henry class *Left loop*.

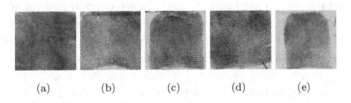

(a)   (b)   (c)   (d)   (e)

Fig. 4.12   Fingerprint examples from the Galton-Henry class *Right loop*.

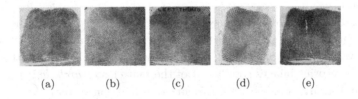

(a)   (b)   (c)   (d)   (e)

Fig. 4.13   Fingerprint examples from the Galton-Henry class *Whorl*.

is to reduce the number of stored fingerprints to be compared. An old but still widely used classification system for fingerprints is the so called *Galton-Henry classification system* developed more than 100 years ago [213]. This particular classification scheme stems from the fact that fingerprints can be grouped into classes of global ridge patterns, viz. *arch, left loop, right loop*, and *whorl*. For examples of these four fingerprint classes, see Fig. 4.10, 4.11, 4.12, and 4.13. Clearly, in order to identify an input fingerprint, one has to consider only those fingerprints from the database coming from the same Galton-Henry class as the input fingerprint.

The graph extraction approach pursued for the present data set is closely related to the traditional method based on the detection of *singular points* in fingerprint images [214, 215]. Regarding the fingerprints as orientation fields, where each pixel of a fingerprint image is assigned the direction of the local ridge line, singular points are those points for which it is impossible to determine a unique orientation. There exist two different categories of singular points termed *core points* and *delta points*. Core points are located at the center of a whorl or at the center of a loop. Delta points are at positions where ridges from three different directions meet.

Fingerprints are converted into graphs by filtering the images and extracting regions that are relevant [21]. The basic idea is to detect locations where ridges in fingerprints have almost vertical orientation. It turns out that each core point is connected to a delta point by a region consisting only of vertical orientation. In order to obtain graphs from fingerprint images, these relevant regions are binarized and a noise removal and thinning procedure is applied [212]. This results in a skeletonized representation of the extracted regions. Ending points and bifurcation points of the skeletonized regions are represented by nodes. Additional nodes are inserted in regular intervals between ending points and bifurcation points. Finally, undirected edges are inserted to link nodes that are directly connected through a ridge in the skeleton. Nodes are unlabeled, while edges are attributed with an angle denoting the orientation of the edge with respect to the horizontal direction.

The Fingerprint data set used in our experiments is based on the NIST-4 reference database of fingerprints [216]. It consists of a training set of size 500, a validation set of size 300, and a test set of size 2,000. Thus, there are 2,800 fingerprint images totally out of the four classes *arch*, *left loop*, *right loop*, and *whorl* from the Galton-Henry classification system. Note that in our benchmark test only the four-class problem of fingerprint classification is considered, i.e. the fifth class *tented arch*, sometimes used in the Galton-Henry scheme, is merged with the class *arch*. Therefore, the first class (arch) consists of about twice as many graphs as the other three classes (left loop, right loop, whorl). In Table 4.4 a summary of the Fingerprint data set together with some basic characteristic properties is given.

Table 4.5 Summary of graph data set characteristics.

AIDS	
Patterns	Chemical compounds
Classes	2 (confirmed active, confirmed inactive)
Size of *tr*, *va*, *te*	250, 250, 1,500
Node labels	Chemical symbol
Edge labels	none
Average per graph	15.7 nodes, 16.2 edges
Maximum per graph	95 nodes, 103 edges
Balanced	no

4.1.5 *AIDS Graphs*

Chemical compounds constitute a good example of patterns for which a structural pattern description is obviously better suited than a statistical one. Clearly, a molecular structure consisting of atoms and covalent bonds can be represented by a graph in a very natural and straightforward manner by representing atoms as nodes and the covalent bonds as edges. Nodes may be labeled with their corresponding chemical symbol and edges by the valence of the linkage. Since it is well-known that there is a close relationship between the structure of a certain molecular compound and its activity, graph based representation seems to be a suitable data description technique.

The AIDS data set consists of graphs representing molecular compounds from the AIDS Antiviral Screen Database of Active Compounds [217] provided by the US National Cancer Instititute (NCI). Since 1999, the NCI carries out AIDS antiviral screen tests to discover chemical compounds that might be capable of inhibiting the HIV virus. The aim of these screen tests is to measure how strongly the compounds under consideration are able to protect human cells from infection by the HIV virus. The experiment is carried out in two stages. In a first experiment, those chemical compounds that are able to provide a protection from an HIV infection in at least half of the cases are selected for a second experiment. Chemical compounds that reproducibly provide a perfect protection from HIV in this second experiment are labeled *confirmed active (CA)*, while compounds that are only able to protect cells from infection in at least 50% of the cases are labeled *moderately active (MA)*. All of the remaining molecules are labeled *confirmed inactive (CI)*. In total, 42,438 chemical compounds were screened, whereof 406 were found to belong to the CA category, 1,056 to the MA

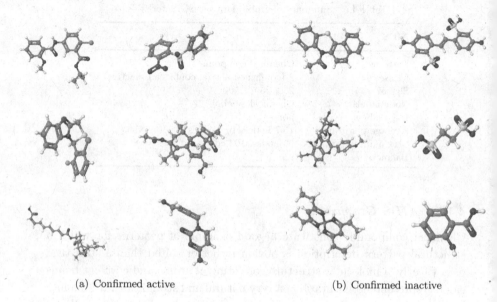

(a) Confirmed active   (b) Confirmed inactive

Fig. 4.14   Example compounds of both classes.

category, and the vast majority (40,976) to the CI category.

The data set actually employed in the present book consists of 2,000 graphs representing molecular compounds from two classes *CA* and *CI*, which represent molecules with and without activity against HIV (400 active elements and 1,600 inactive elements). In Fig. 4.14 some molecular compounds of both classes are illustrated. Different shades of gray represent different chemical symbols, i.e. different node labels. We use a training set and a validation set of size 250 each, and a test set of size 1,500. In Table 4.5 a summary of the AIDS data set together with some basic characteristic properties is given.

4.1.6   *Mutagenicity Graphs*

The Mutagenicity data set is similar to the AIDS data set since also molecular compounds are considered. *Mutagenicity* is the ability of a chemical compound to cause mutations in DNA and is therefore one of the numerous adverse properties of a compound that hampers its potential to become a marketable drug [218]. A mutagenic compound's reactivity toward DNA can result in the creation of DNA adducts or base deletions, which crucially

Table 4.6   Summary of graph data set characteristics.

Mutagenicity	
Patterns	Chemical compounds
Classes	2 (confirmed mutagen, confirmed non-mutagen)
Size of *tr, va, te*	500, 500, 1,500
Node labels	Chemical symbol
Edge labels	none
Average per graph	30.3 nodes, 30.8 edges
Maximum per graph	417 nodes, 112 edges
Balanced	yes

distort the DNA structure. Hence, mutagenic compounds pose a toxic risk to humans and screening of drug candidates for mutagenicity is a regulatory requirement for drug approval [218].

The Chemical Carcinogenicity Research Information System (CCRIS) database [219] contains scientifically evaluated test data for approximately 7,000 compounds. The data set used in the present book was originally prepared by the authors of [218]. From this data set we use a training and validation set of size 500 each, and a test set of size 1,500. Thus, there are 2,500 chemical compounds totally. In order to convert molecular compounds of the mutagenicity data set into attributed graphs the same procedure as for the AIDS data set is applied. The mutagenicity data set is divided into two classes *mutagen* and *nonmutagen* of equal size (1,250 mutagenic elements and 1,250 nonmutagenic elements). In Table 4.6 a summary of the Mutagenicity data set together with some basic characteristic properties is given.

4.1.7   *Protein Graphs*

Proteins are organic compounds made of amino acids sequences joined together by peptide bonds. In fact, a huge amount of proteins have been sequenced over recent years, and the structures of thousands of proteins have been resolved so far. The best known role of proteins in the cell is as enzymes which catalyze chemical reactions. There are about 4,000 such reactions known. Yet, the experimental determination of the function of a protein with known sequence and structure is still a difficult, time and cost intensive task [44]. Being able to predict protein function from its structure could save both time and money.

The protein data set employed in the present book consists of graphs

Table 4.7 Summary of graph data set characteristics.

Protein	
Patterns	Proteins
Classes	6 (EC1, EC2, EC3, EC4, EC5, EC6)
Size of *tr, va, te*	200, 200, 200
Node labels	Type (helix, sheet, loop) and amino acid sequence
Edge labels	Type (sequential, structural) and length
Average per graph	32.6 nodes, 62.1 edges
Maximum per graph	126 nodes, 149 edges
Balanced	yes

representing proteins originally used in [39]. The graphs are constructed from the Protein Data Bank [220] and labeled with their corresponding enzyme class labels from the BRENDA enzyme database [221]. The proteins database consists of six classes (*EC1, EC2, EC3, EC4, EC5, EC6*), which represent proteins out of the six enzyme commission top level hierarchy (EC classes). The EC numbering of proteins is a numerical classification scheme based on the chemical reactions they catalyze. That is, two proteins having the same EC number catalyze the same reaction. For instance, proteins from the EC3 class are hydrolases meaning they use water to break up some other molecule.

The proteins are converted into graphs by representing the structure, the sequence, and chemical properties of a protein by nodes and edges. Nodes represent secondary structure elements (SSE) within the protein structure, labeled with their type (helix, sheet, or loop) and their amino acid sequence. Every pair of nodes is connected by an edge if they are neighbors along the amino acid sequence (sequential edges) or if they are neighbors in space within the protein structure (structural edges). Every node is connected to its three nearest spatial neighbors. In case of sequential relationships, the edges are labeled with their length in amino acids, while in case of structural edges a distance measure in Ångstroms is used as a label. In Fig. 4.15 to 4.20 three images of proteins for all six EC classes are given.

There are 600 proteins totally, 100 per class. We use a training, validation, and test set of equal size (200). The classification task on this data set consists in predicting the enzyme class membership. In Table 4.7 a summary of the Protein data set together with some basic characteristic properties is given.

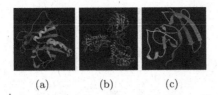

Fig. 4.15   Protein examples of top level class EC1.

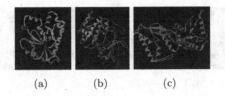

Fig. 4.16   Protein examples of top level class EC2.

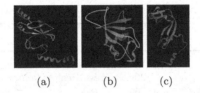

Fig. 4.17   Protein examples of top level class EC3.

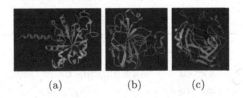

Fig. 4.18   Protein examples of top level class EC4.

4.1.8   *Webpage Graphs*

In [47] several methods for creating graphs from webpage documents are introduced. For the graphs included in the present data set, the following method was applied. First, all words occurring in the webpage document – except for approximately 600 stop words such as "the" or "and", which contain only little information – are converted into nodes in the resulting webpage graph. We attribute each node with the corresponding word and

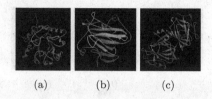

(a)   (b)   (c)

Fig. 4.19   Protein examples of top level class EC5.

(a)   (b)   (c)

Fig. 4.20   Protein examples of top level class EC6.

Table 4.8   Summary of graph data set characteristics.

Webpage	
Patterns	Webpages hosted at Yahoo as news pages
Classes	20 (Business, Health, Politics, etc.)
Size of *tr, va, te*	780, 780, 780
Node labels	Word and its frequency
Edge labels	Section type(s) (title, link, text)
Average per graph	186.1 nodes, 104.6 edges
Maximum per graph	834 nodes, 596 edges
Balanced	no

its frequency. That is even if a word appears more than once in the same webpage document we create only one unique node for it and store its total frequency as an additional node attribute. Hence, this data set is special in the sense of providing graphs with unique node labels. Next, different sections of the webpage document are investigated individually. These sections are *title*, which contains the text related to the document's title, *link*, which is text in a clickable hyperlink, and *text*, which comprises any of the readable text in the web document. If a word w_i immediately precedes word w_{i+1} in any of the sections *title*, *link*, or *text*, a directed edge from the node corresponding to word w_i to the node corresponding to the word w_{i+1} is inserted in our webpage graph. The resulting edge is attributed with the corresponding section label. Although word w_i might immediately precede word w_{i+1} in more than just one section, only one edge is inserted. Therefore, an edge is possibly labeled with more than one section label. Finally, only the most frequently used words (nodes) are kept in the graph and the terms are conflated to the most frequently occurring forms.

In our experiments we make use of a data set that consists of 2,340 documents from 20 categories (*Business, Health, Politics, Sports, Technology, Entertainment, Art, Cable, Culture, Film, Industry, Media, Multimedia, Music, Online, People, Review, Stage, Television,* and *Variety*). The last 14 categories are sub-categories related to entertainment. The number of documents of each category varies from only 24 (Art) up to about 500 (Health). These webpage documents were originally hosted at Yahoo as news pages (http://www.yahoo.com). The database is split into a training, a validation, and a test set of equal size (780). In Table 4.8 a summary of the Webpage data set together with some basic characteristic properties is given.

4.2 Evaluation of Graph Edit Distance

This section provides an experimental evaluation of traditional edit distance based nearest-neighbor classification. Basically, the nearest-neighbor classifier assigns a test pattern to the most frequent class of its most similar training patterns. For a thorough introduction to nearest-neighbor classification see Section 3.4.1. The basic dissimilarity model used throughout the present book is that of graph edit distance. The very first step in graph edit distance applications is an appropriate choice of the underlying cost function (for a more detailed introduction into graph edit distance and cost functions we refer to Chapter 3). For graph edit distance computation the approximate algorithm Bipartite (see Section 3.3.1) is employed. Note that the aim of the present section is twofold. First, we establish a traditional reference classification system in the graph domain. Second, the optimized graph edit distances obtained through this reference system are used for dissimlarity based graph embedding in real vector spaces (to be described in the upcoming chapters of the present book).

In our experiments each data set is divided into three disjoint subsets, viz. the training, the validation, and the test set. The training set is used to construct and train the classifier. In case of nearest-neighbor classifiers, the graphs from the training set are used as labeled prototypes to find the nearest neighbors. The validation set is used to determine those meta parameters that cannot directly be obtained from the training procedure.

For all of our graph sets, the substitution cost of nodes and edges is defined with respect to the underlying label information using an appropriate dissimilarity measure. Hence, the parameters to be validated are the node insertion/deletion cost τ_{node}, the edge insertion/deletion cost τ_{edge}, and the weighting parameter $\alpha \in [0, 1]$ which controls what is more important, the edit operation cost on the nodes or on the edges. For k-nearest-neighbor classification (k-NN) the only meta parameter to be tuned is the number of neighbors k considered for classification.

For validation of the quadruple $(\tau_{node}, \tau_{edge}, \alpha, k)$, edit distances of graphs from the validation set to graphs from the training set are computed. Based on the obtained distances the graphs from the validation set are classified using a k-NN classifier. Obviously, changing the edit cost parameters will strongly affect the edit distance measure and therefore the accuracy of the resulting classifier as well. We first run the classifier with different meta parameters $(\tau_{node}, \tau_{edge}, \alpha, k)$ and report the accuracies achieved on the validation set. To obtain a parameter configuration that is as well performing on the validation set as possible, a grid search in the four dimensional parameter space with respect to the classification accuracy on the validation set is employed. Note that in our experiments no cross-validation is carried out, but three disjoint subsets are used for training, validation, and testing the underlying algorithm.

For a summary of the best performing parameters on the validation set and the corresponding classification accuracy achieved on both the validation and test set, see Table 4.9. Note that for the Webpage data set another dissimilarity model than graph edit distance is employed for which the parameters $(\tau_{node}, \tau_{edge}, \alpha)$ have not to be defined (for details see below). In the next subsections the validation of the cost function is described in detail for each data set.

Letter Graphs   For the letter graphs, the Euclidean cost function is employed (see Definition 3.2 in Section 3.1.2). That is, the cost of a node substitution is set proportional to the Euclidean distance of the two considered node labels. Since the edges of the letter graphs are unlabeled, edge substitutions can be carried out for free in this cost model.

In Fig. 4.21 the validation procedure is illustrated on the Letter high data set (the same Figures for Letter low and Letter medium data set are given in Appendix A). In this illustration, the classification accuracy on

Table 4.9 Best performing meta parameters $(\tau_{node}, \tau_{edge}, \alpha, k)$ and corresponding classification accuracy on the validation set (va) and on the test set (te).

Data Set	τ_{node}	τ_{edge}	α	k	va	te
Letter low	0.3	0.1	0.25	5	99.7	99.3
Letter medium	0.7	1.9	0.75	5	95.2	94.4
Letter high	0.9	1.7	0.75	5	90.9	89.1
Digit	65.0	1.9	0.25	3	98.4	97.4
Fingerprint	0.7	0.5	0.75	3	81.7	79.1
GREC	90.0	15.0	0.50	5	96.5	82.2
AIDS	1.1	0.1	0.25	1	95.6	94.9
Mutagenicity	11.0	1.1	0.25	5	70.8	66.9
Protein	11.0	1.0	0.75	1	68.5	68.5
Webpage	-	-	-	5	78.7	80.6

the validation set is plotted as a function of τ_{node} and τ_{edge} for $k = \{1, 2, 3\}$ and $\alpha = \{0.25, 0.5, 0.75\}$. On the Letter low data set, the empirically optimal parameters $\tau_{node} = 0.3$, $\tau_{edge} = 0.1$, $\alpha = 0.25$, and $k = 5$ (see Fig. 4.22 (a)) result in a classification accuracy of 99.7% and 99.3% on the validation and test set, respectively. On Letter medium, the optimal parameters are determined to be $\tau_{node} = 0.7$, $\tau_{edge} = 1.9$, $\alpha = 0.75$, and $k = 5$ (see Fig. 4.22 (b)), resulting in a classification accuracy of 95.2% on the validation set and 94.4% on the independent test set. Finally, on Letter high the best performing parameters on the validation set are $\tau_{node} = 0.9$, $\tau_{edge} = 1.7$, $\alpha = 0.75$, and $k = 5$ (see Fig. 4.22 (c)), which result in a classification accuracy of 90.9% and 89.1% on the validation and test set, respectively.

Digit Graphs For the Digit graph data set the same cost model as for the Letter graph is used. However, the Euclidean distance between nodes has to be adjusted since the nodes of these graphs bear two (x, y)-coordinates representing the starting- and ending point of a line segment. We use the sum of distances between starting- and ending points of the two nodes under consideration. Edge substitutions are free of costs since these graphs have no edge labels. Similarly to Fig. 4.21, in Appendix A the validation procedure for the quadruple $(\tau_{node}, \tau_{edge}, \alpha, k)$ is illustrated on the Digit data set. On the validation set, the steepest-ascent search procedure de-

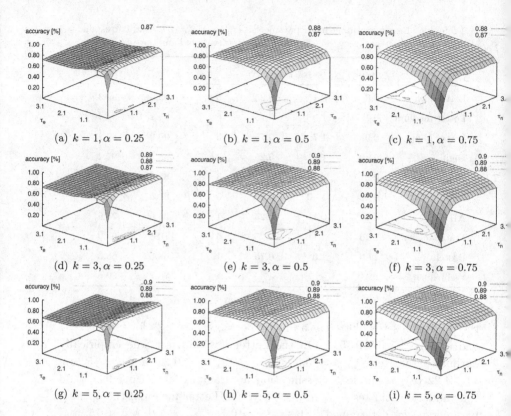

Fig. 4.21 Validation of the node and edge insertion/deletion penalty τ_n and τ_e, number of nearest neighbors k, and weighting parameter α on the Letter high data set.

termines optimal parameters $\tau_{node} = 65$, $\tau_{edge} = 1.9$, $\alpha = 0.25$, and $k = 3$ (see Fig. 4.23 (a)). The classification accuracy obtained on the validation set amounts to 98.4% and the one on the test set to 97.4%.

GREC Graphs Additionally to (x, y) coordinates, the nodes of graphs from the GREC data set are labeled with a type (ending point, corner, intersection, circle). The same accounts for the edges where two types (line, arc) are employed. The Euclidean cost model is adopted accordingly. That is, for node substitutions the type of the involved nodes is compared first. For identically typed nodes, the Euclidean distance is used as node substitution cost. In case of non-identical types on the nodes, the substitution cost is set to $2 \cdot \tau_{node}$, which reflects the intuition that nodes with different type label cannot be substituted but have to be deleted and inserted, respectively. For edge substitutions, we measure the dissimilarity of two types

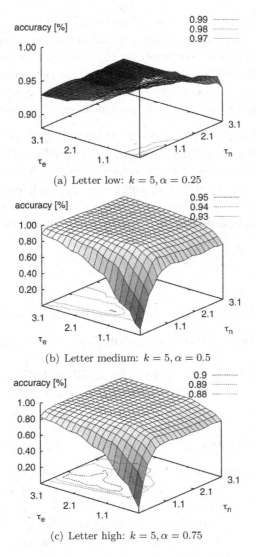

(a) Letter low: $k = 5, \alpha = 0.25$

(b) Letter medium: $k = 5, \alpha = 0.5$

(c) Letter high: $k = 5, \alpha = 0.75$

Fig. 4.22 Validation of the node and edge insertion/deletion penalty τ_n and τ_e for optimal k and α on the Letter low, medium, and high data set.

with a Dirac function returning 0 if the two types are equal, and $2 \cdot \tau_{edge}$ otherwise. The validation of the quadruple $(\tau_{node}, \tau_{edge}, \alpha, k)$ is illustrated on the GREC data set in Appendix A. The highest classification accuracy on the validation set returned by a steepest-ascent search procedure is achieved with $\tau_{node} = 90$, $\tau_{edge} = 15$, $\alpha = 0.5$, and $k = 5$ (see Fig. 4.23 (b)).

The classification accuracy is 96.5% on the validation set and only 82.2% on the test set. Note that the significantly higher recognition rate on the validation set compared to the test set indicates that the nearest-neighbor classifier strongly overfits the validation set. That is, the optimized parameter quadruple is too strongly adopted to the classification scenario on the validation set and therefore poorly generalizes on the unseen test set.

Fingerprint Graphs The angle attributes attached to edges in fingerprint graphs specify an undirected orientation of a line. That is, the angle value $\nu(e)$ of each edge e is in the interval $\nu(e) \in (-\pi/2, +\pi/2]$. Because of the cyclic nature of angular measurements, the Euclidean distance is not appropriate for measuring the dissimilarity of edges. Therefore, for fingerprint graphs a modified dissimilarity measure for undirected orientations is used, defined by

$$d : (-\pi/2, +\pi/2] \times (-\pi/2, +\pi/2] \to [0, \pi/2] \quad ,$$

where

$$d(\nu(e), \nu(e')) = \min(\pi - |\nu(e) - \nu(e')|, |\nu(e) - \nu(e')|) \quad .$$

Node substitutions have no cost since the characteristic information of the fingerprints is captured in the labels attached to the edges. The validation of the quadruple $(\tau_{node}, \tau_{edge}, \alpha, k)$ is illustrated on the Fingerprint data set in Appendix A. On the validation set, the steepest-ascent search procedure determines optimal parameters $\tau_{node} = 0.7$, $\tau_{edge} = 0.5$, $\alpha = 0.75$, and $k = 3$ (see Fig. 4.23 (c)). The classification accuracy achieved on the validation set amounts to 81.7% and the one on the test set to 79.1%.

AIDS and Mutagenicity Graphs In some preliminary experiments it turned out that the information attached to the edges of graphs representing molecular compounds is of marginal significance for graph edit distance computations. Hence, edge substitutions are free of cost. For node substitutions, we measure the dissimilarity of two chemical symbols with a Dirac function returning 0 if the two symbols are equal, and $2 \cdot \tau_{node}$ otherwise. The validation of the quadruple $(\tau_{node}, \tau_{edge}, \alpha, k)$ is illustrated on both the AIDS and Mutagenicity data set in Appendix A. The highest classification accuracy on the validation set of the AIDS data set returned by a steepest-ascent search procedure is achieved with $\tau_{node} = 1.1$, $\tau_{edge} = 0.1$, $\alpha = 0.25$, and $k = 1$ (see Fig. 4.24 (a)). The classification accuracy amounts to 95.6% on the validation set and 94.9% on the test set. On the Mutagenicity data set the optimal parameters are determined by $\tau_{node} = 11$, $\tau_{edge} = 1.1$,

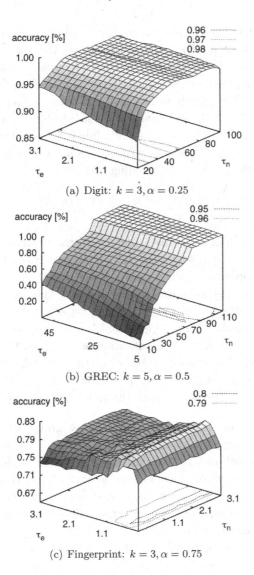

(a) Digit: $k = 3, \alpha = 0.25$

(b) GREC: $k = 5, \alpha = 0.5$

(c) Fingerprint: $k = 3, \alpha = 0.75$

Fig. 4.23 Validation of the node and edge insertion/deletion penalty τ_n and τ_e for optimal k and α on the Digit, GREC, and Fingerprint data set.

$\alpha = 0.25$, and $k = 5$ (see Fig. 4.24 (b)). With these parameters a classification accuracy of 70.8% on the validation set and 66.9% on the test set is achieved.

Protein Graphs For the protein graphs, a cost model based on the amino acid sequences is used. For node substitutions, the type of the involved nodes is compared first. If two types are identical, the amino acid sequences of the nodes to be substituted are compared by means of string edit distance [187]. Similarly to graph edit distance, string edit distance is defined as the cost of the minimal edit path between a source string and a target string. More formally, given an alphabet L and two strings s_1, s_2 defined on L ($s_1, s_2 \in L^*$), we allow substitutions, insertions, and deletions of symbols and define the corresponding cost as

$$c(u \to v) = c(u \to \varepsilon) = c(\varepsilon \to u) = 1, \quad c(u \to u) = 0$$

for $u, v \in L, u \neq v$.

Hence, node substitution cost is defined as the minimum cost sequence of edit operations that has to be applied to the amino acid sequence of the source node in order to transform it into the amino acid sequence of the target node. For edge substitutions, we measure the dissimilarity with a Dirac function returning 0 if the two edge types are equal, and $2 \cdot \tau_{edge}$ otherwise. The validation of the quadruple $(\tau_{node}, \tau_{edge}, \alpha, k)$ is illustrated in Appendix A. The highest classification accuracy on the validation set returned by a steepest-ascent search procedure is achieved with $\tau_{node} = 11.0$, $\tau_{edge} = 1.0$, $\alpha = 0.75$, and $k = 1$ (see Fig. 4.24 (c)). The classification accuracy amounts to 68.5% on both the validation and test set.

Webpage Graphs In contrast to the other graph sets, the webpage graphs offer the property of unique node labels. That is, it is guaranteed that each label on a node occurs at most once in a given graph. The impact of this property on the matching process is huge. In our cost model, identical node substitutions are free of cost while non-identical node substitutions are not admissible. For all other edit operations the cost is set to an arbitrary constant greater than zero (in our experiments we set this constant to 1). In order to edit a graph g_1 into a graph g_2 one only needs to perform the following three steps [47]:

(1) Delete all nodes from g_1 that do not appear in g_2.
(2) Substitute all identically labeled nodes
(3) Insert all nodes in g_2 that do not appear in g_1

Given this unique mapping between nodes from g_1 and nodes from g_2, the corresponding edge operations can be inferred. That is, all edges incident to a deleted node of g_1 are also deleted. Conversely, incident edges of an

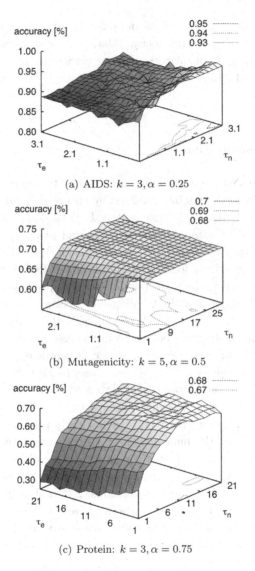

(a) AIDS: $k = 3, \alpha = 0.25$

(b) Mutagenicity: $k = 5, \alpha = 0.5$

(c) Protein: $k = 3, \alpha = 0.75$

Fig. 4.24 Validation of the node and edge insertion/deletion penalty τ_n and τ_e for optimal k and α on the AIDS, Mutagenicity, and Protein data set.

inserted node in g_2 are also inserted. Finally, edges between two nodes which have been successfully substituted are also substituted if their corresponding section type is identical (otherwise they have to be deleted and inserted, respectively). The distance between two graphs g_1 and g_2 is then defined as the sum of all insertions and deletions applied to both nodes and edges. Consequently, no edit cost validation is needed for this data set. With the optimized k for nearest-neighbor classification ($k = 5$) a classification accuracy of 78.7% on the validation set and 80.6% on the test set is achieved.

4.3   Data Visualization

Given the optimized distance function according to nearest-neighbor classification, the data sets can be visualized by means of *distance plots*. These plots visualize the square distance matrix $\mathbf{D} = (d_{ij})_{n \times n}$, where d_{ij} represents the graph edit distance between the i-th and j-th graph of the training set. The resulting grey scale pixel matrix uses dark pixels for low dissimilarities and bright pixels for high dissimilarities. Hence, the smaller the distance d_{ij}, the darker the corresponding pixel at position (i, j) in the distance plot. If the graphs of the training set are ordered according to their class membership Ω_i ($i = 1, \ldots, k$), pixels inside the k square areas of size $|\Omega_i|$ along the main diagonal belong to intra-class distances, i.e. distances between graphs from the same class. Hence, it can be expected that pixels in these squares are generally darker than other pixels in the distance plots.

In Fig. 4.25 (a) the distance plot obtained on Letter low data set is shown. Due to the marginal differences between graphs from the same class, a 15×15 checker-board pattern is clearly observable. Moreover, the 15 squares along the main diagonal, corresponding to the intra-class distances, are the darkest squares compared to the other squares for each column in the checker-board. Although representing inter-class distances, the squares in the checker-board at positions $(2, 3)$ and $(3, 2)$ are quite dark. Note that these pixels belong to distances between letters from class E and F which are quite similar in their respective structure. The distance plot in Fig. 4.25 (a) reflects the high recognition rate achieved by the k-NN classifier on this data set.

Given the square dissimilarity matrix $\mathbf{D} = (d_{ij})_{n \times n}$ representing pairwise dissimilarities between training graphs, multidimensional scaling (MDS) [222–224] can be also applied for data visualization. MDS aims at a low-dimensional vectorial representation of the underlying data preserving the pairwise dissimilarities between data objects as well as possible. That is, MDS projects the original data points in a low-dimensional space (in our case a two-dimensional plane) such that the overall difference between the

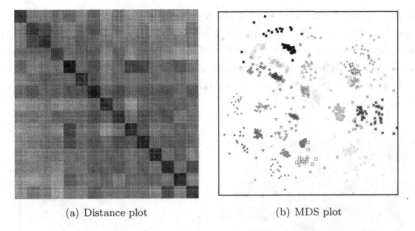

(a) Distance plot　　　　　　　　(b) MDS plot

Fig. 4.25　Distance and MDS plots of Letter low data set.

pairwise original distances d_{ij} and the corresponding distances δ_{ij} in the low-dimensional space is minimized. MDS is realized by the minimization of a certain loss function commonly referred to as *stress*. Various definitions of stress can be found in the literature such as *raw stress* [222] and *least squares scaling loss* [224] (see [4] for an exhaustive review on stress functions in MDS). In the present book the *Sammon stress* [225] is used as loss function. This particular stress function can be defined in a number of ways [226]. The objective function actually minimized in our case is defined as

$$E = \frac{1}{\sum_{i=1}^{n-1} \sum_{j=i+1}^{n} d_{ij}^2} \sum_{i=1}^{n-1} \sum_{j=i+1}^{n} (d_{ij} - \delta_{ij})^2 \quad ,$$

where d_{ij} refers to the original distance between the i-th and j-th pattern and δ_{ij} to the distance between the projections of the considered patterns. Most of the minimization algorithms employed in MDS are based on gradient methods [223].

In Fig. 4.25 (b) MDS is applied to the dissimilarity matrix obtained on the training set of the Letter low data set. The elements for each of the 15 classes are shown in diversely colored and shaped points in the plane (the elements from the structurally similar classes E and F are displayed in green and red color, respectively.). This visualization clearly indicates the good separability of the classes already observed on both the distance plots and the classification accuracy. Increasing the distortion level from low to medium and high, the good class separability is more and more lost. The distance plots for medium and high distortion in Fig. 4.26 (a) and 4.27 (a) show how the checker-board pattern is blurred when the distortion level is increased. Also the MDS plots (Fig. 4.26 (b) and 4.27 (b)) indicate that the increased distortion levels render the classification task more difficult. In Appendix B, both distance and MDS plots for the remaining data sets are provided.

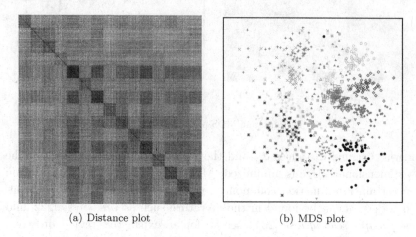

    (a) Distance plot   (b) MDS plot

Fig. 4.26   Distance and MDS plots of Letter medium data set.

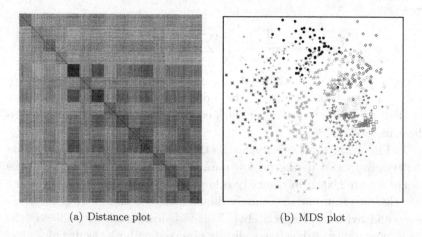

    (a) Distance plot   (b) MDS plot

Fig. 4.27   Distance and MDS plots of Letter high data set.

4.4   Summary

The present chapter introduces ten graph data sets with quite different characteristics. For instance, there are graphs with and without labels on the nodes or edges. If there are labels on the nodes or edges or both, the label alphabets are diverse, ranging from numerical to symbolic attributes. The average number of nodes varies from below ten up to more than 180 per graph (similar variations can be observed for the edges). Moreover, the ten classification scenarios involve both two-class as well as multi-class problems. Finally, there are graph sets where the graphs are uniformly distributed over the classes and others where the individual classes are not balanced.

The meaning of the graphs is also quite diverse. There are graphs that represent line drawings, gray scale images, molecular compounds, proteins, and HTML webpages. In Table 4.10 a summary of all graph datasets and their corresponding characteristics is provided. In addition to a description of the data sets, classification results achieved with a reference system based on a k-nearest-neighbor classifier are given as well. In fact, for such classifiers to work properly, the underlying pattern space only needs to be endowed with a dissimilarity model (e.g. graph edit distance). Hence, the nearest-neighbor paradigm for classification is particularly well suited for graph based pattern recognition. This traditional approach for graph classification is used as a reference system throughout the rest of this book.

Table 4.10   Summary of graph data set characteristics, viz. the size of the training (tr), the validation (va) and the test set (te), the number of classes ($|\Omega|$), the label alphabet of both nodes and edges, the average and maximum number of nodes and edges ($\varnothing$/max $|V|/|E|$), whether the graphs are uniformly distributed over the classes or not (balanced), and the classification accuracy of a k-NN classifier.

Database	size (tr, va, te)	$|\Omega|$	node labels	edge labels	$\varnothing$ $|V|/|E|$	max $|V|/|E|$	balanced	k-NN
Letter (*low*)	750, 750, 750	15	(x, y) coord.	none	4.7/3.1	8/6	yes	99.3%
Letter (*medium*)	750, 750, 750	15	(x, y) coord.	none	4.7/3.2	9/7	yes	94.4%
Letter (*high*)	750, 750, 750	15	(x, y) coord.	none	4.7/4.5	9/9	yes	89.1%
Digit	1,000, 500, 2,000	10	(x, y) coord.	none	8.9/7.9	17/16	yes	97.4%
GREC	836, 836, 1,628	22	Type/(x, y) coord.	Type	11.5/12.2	25/30	yes	82.2%
Fingerprint	500, 300, 2,000	4	none	Angle	5.4/4.4	26/25	no	79.1%
AIDS	250, 250, 1,500	2	Chem. symbol	none	15.7/16.2	95/103	no	94.9%
Mutagenicity	500, 500, 1,500	2	Chem. symbol	none	30.3/30.8	417/112	yes	66.9%
Protein	200, 200, 200	6	Type/AA-seq.	Type/Length	32.6/62.1	126/149	yes	68.5%
Webpage	780, 780, 780	20	Word/Frequency	Type(s)	186.1/104.6	834/596	no	80.6%

Kernel Methods

5

> Young man, in mathematics
> you don't understand things.
> You just get used to them.
>
> John von Neumann

5.1 Overview and Primer on Kernel Theory

Kernel machines constitute a very powerful class of algorithms. As a matter of fact, kernel methods are increasingly used to solve typical problems in pattern recognition and machine learning, such as image classification [50, 227], protein prediction [44, 228, 229], molecule classification [27, 46], text classification [230], handwriting recognition [231], feature selection problems [232–234], or face and fingerprint authentification [23, 235]. The idea of using kernels functions for function approximation can be traced back at least to 1950 [236]. Also the principle of using kernels as dot products is rather old and was introduced in the midsixties of the last century in the work on *potential function classifiers* in conjunction with radial basis function kernels [237]. In the first edition of a popular textbook on pattern recognition published in the early seventies [238], this particular work on potential function classifiers is mentioned in an inconspicuous footnote[1]. It took again over 30 years until the idea of kernel machines was revisited to construct support vector machines as a generalization of large margin classifiers [239]. This seminal work ulti-

---

[1]In the same book it is noted that the suggestions for constructing potential functions via symmetric kernels is more appealing for their mathematical beauty than their practical usefulness. A clear evidence that – once again – the practical importance of mathematical results was initially heavily underestimated [138].

mately led to a reanimation of the notion of kernels in both the machine learning and pattern recognition community. Summarizing, although some of the mathematical foundation of kernel theory has been known for a long time, the practical usefulness in pattern recognition and related areas has been recognized only recently.

During the past ten years kernel methods have become one of the most rapidly emerging sub-fields in intelligent information processing. The reason for this is twofold. First, kernel theory makes standard algorithms for classification or clustering (originally developed for vectorial data) applicable to more complex data structures such as strings, trees, or graphs. That is, the issue of data representation is overcome and kernel methods can therefore be seen as a fundamental theory bridging the gap between statistical and structural pattern recognition. Second, kernel methods allow one to extend basic linear algorithms to complex non-linear ones in a unified and elegant manner. Hence, by means of kernel methods the issue of non-linear regularities in the data is inherently coped with. There is theoretical evidence that under some conditions kernel methods are more appropriate for difficult pattern recognition tasks than traditional methods [28]. In various areas, the advantage of kernel methods over other methods has empirically been confirmed [5, 138, 240–243].

This chapter gives a brief introduction to kernel methods. (For a more thorough introduction to kernel methods the reader is referred to [5, 138].) First, in Section 5.2, kernel functions and some basic properties for patterns given in terms of vectors are introduced. Later in this chapter, the extension of kernel functions to structural data and in particular to graph based representations is described. In Section 5.3, the fundamental relation between feature and pattern space and the so-called kernel trick are described in detail. Kernel machines are described in Section 5.4. Such machines are algorithms that operate on pairwise kernel values derived from some kernel function rather than on individual patterns. Finally, an experimental evaluation of a specific kernel machine, the support vector machine, in conjunction with an edit distance based graph kernel is given.

5.2   Kernel Functions

Traditionally, in statistical pattern recognition the input patterns are given by real valued vectors, while in structural pattern recognition graphs can be employed for representing the data at hand. Given this explicit representation of patterns, the algorithms for analysis or recognition are usually designed in such way that they directly operate on the actual data structures in the specific pattern space.

The key idea of kernel methods is based on an essentially different way how the underlying data is represented [240]. In the kernel approach, an explicit data representation is of secondary interest. That is, rather than defining individual representations for each pattern or object, the data at hand is represented by pairwise comparisons only. More formally, let us assume that a pattern space $\mathcal{X}$ with N patterns or objects $\{x_1, \ldots, x_N\} \subseteq \mathcal{X}$ to be processed by a certain algorithm, and a real valued similarity function $\kappa : \mathcal{X} \times \mathcal{X} \to \mathbb{R}$, referred to as *kernel function*, are given. This function defines a kernel which represents the whole pattern space $\mathcal{X}$ in an implicit fashion by pairwise kernel values $\kappa_{ij} = \kappa(x_i, x_j)$.

Given this implicit representation, algorithms are designed in such way that they operate on pairwise kernel values rather than on individual data entities. Simply put, the only requirement for a kernel based algorithm to be applicable to patterns from some pattern space $\mathcal{X}$ is the existence of a kernel function $\kappa : \mathcal{X} \times \mathcal{X} \to \mathbb{R}$. Hence, by means of kernel methods pattern recognition tasks can be accomplished in a unified manner regardless of the pattern representation formalism actually used. Hence, kernel methods are distinguished in that they can be applied to any pattern space whereon a kernel can be defined[2].

Although kernel methods do not depend upon individual pattern representations, kernel functions still do. That is, the kernel function to be employed in $\mathcal{X}$ is defined with respect to the patterns in $\mathcal{X}$. For instance, there are kernels exclusively applicable to vectors or kernels particularly designed for graphs. In this section the patterns $x \in \mathcal{X}$ are vectors from some possibly infinite dimensional vector space $\mathcal{H}$, whereas later in this chapter the pattern space $\mathcal{X}$ will be given by a certain graph domain $\mathcal{G}$.

Kernel functions are used to extract information from patterns that is relevant for classification, clustering, or other tasks. Most kernel methods can only process kernel values which are established by symmetric and *positive definite* kernel functions [138, 244].

Definition 5.1 (Positive Definite Kernel). *A kernel function* $\kappa : \mathcal{X} \times \mathcal{X} \to \mathbb{R}$ *is a symmetric function, i.e.* $\kappa(x_i, x_j) = \kappa(x_j, x_i)$, *mapping pairs of patterns* $x_i, x_j \in \mathcal{X}$ *to real numbers. A kernel function* κ *is called positive*

---

[2]Note that it is not even intrinsically necessary for $\mathcal{X}$ to have more mathematical structure beyond the existence of a kernel function κ.

definite[3], *if, and only if, for all* $N \in \mathbb{N}$,

$$\sum_{i,j=1}^{N} c_i c_j \kappa(x_i, x_j) \geq 0$$

for all $\{c_1, \ldots, c_N\} \subseteq \mathbb{R}$, *and any choice of* N *objects* $\{x_1, \ldots, x_N\} \subseteq \mathcal{X}$.

Kernel functions that are positive definite are often called *valid kernels, admissible kernels*, or *Mercer kernels*. Clearly, imposing a kernel to be positive definite restricts the class of valid kernel functions substantially. However, the property of positive definiteness is crucial for the definition of kernel machines and turns out to be sufficiently strong to implicate a considerable number of theoretical properties associated with kernel functions [28].

Next, we define the *kernel matrix*, sometimes referred to as *Gram matrix*, based on a given kernel κ.

Definition 5.2 (Kernel Matrix, Gram Matrix). *Given a kernel* κ *and a training set of* N *patterns* $\{x_1, \ldots, x_N\} \subseteq \mathcal{X}$, *we are able to form a* $N \times N$ *square matrix*

$$\mathbf{K} = \begin{bmatrix} \kappa_{11} & \kappa_{12} & \cdots & \kappa_{1N} \\ \kappa_{21} & \kappa_{22} & \cdots & \kappa_{2N} \\ \vdots & \vdots & \ddots & \vdots \\ \kappa_{N1} & \kappa_{n2} & \cdots & \kappa_{NN} \end{bmatrix}$$

of real numbers $(k_{ij})_{1 \leq i,j \leq N}$ *commonly referred to as kernel or Gram matrix. The kernel matrix* $\mathbf{K} = (\kappa_{ij})_{N \times N}$ *contains the kernel function evaluated on all pairs of patterns in* $\{x_1, \ldots, x_N\}$.

To verify whether a kernel function is positive definite, one can check if the condition in Def. 5.1 is satisfied. This is equivalent for the kernel matrix $\mathbf{K} = (\kappa_{ij})_{N \times N}$ to be positive definite. Therefore it is sufficient to check any of the following three conditions (for proofs we refer to [5]). The kernel function κ is positive definite if, and only if,

(1) all N eigenvalues $\{\lambda_i(\mathbf{K})\}_{1 \leq i \leq N}$ of the kernel matrix $\mathbf{K}$ are non-negative, or
(2) $\mathbf{K} = \mathbf{B}^T \mathbf{B}$ for some real matrix $\mathbf{B}$, or

---

[3]Note that positive definite functions according to the definition given in this chapter are sometimes called positive semi-definite since $\sum_{i,j=1}^{n} c_i c_j \kappa(x_i, x_j)$ can be zero and need not be strictly positive.

(3) all of the *principal minors* of $\mathbf{K}$ are non-negative. The principal minors of a matrix are the determinants of its submatrices obtained by removing a certain number of columns and the corresponding rows.

As the reader might guess, the kernel matrix $\mathbf{K} = (\kappa_{ij})_{N \times N}$ plays a central role in the development of kernel methods. This matrix acts as an information bottleneck, as all the information available to a kernel algorithm is extracted from $\mathbf{K}$ [5]. In other words, the kernel matrix $\mathbf{K}$ acts as an interface between the pattern space $\mathcal{X}$ and the algorithm to be employed.

A first example of a kernel defined on pairs of vectors $x, x' \in \mathcal{H}$ is the dot product defined in a vector space $\mathcal{H}$.

Definition 5.3 (Dot Product). *A dot product in a vector space $\mathcal{H}$ is a function $\langle \cdot, \cdot \rangle : \mathcal{H} \times \mathcal{H} \to \mathbb{R}$ satisfying*

- $\langle x, x' \rangle = \langle x', x \rangle$ *(Symmetry)*
- $\langle \alpha x + \beta x', x'' \rangle = \alpha \langle x, x'' \rangle + \beta \langle x', x'' \rangle$ *(Bilinearity)*
- $\langle x, x \rangle = 0$ *for $x = 0$*
- $\langle x, x \rangle > 0$ *for $x \neq 0$*

for vectors $x, x', x'' \in \mathcal{H}$ and scalars $\alpha, \beta \in \mathbb{R}$. If $\mathcal{H} = \mathbb{R}^n$ the standard dot product of two real vectors $\mathbf{x} = (x_1, \ldots, x_n), \mathbf{x}' = (x_1', \ldots, x_n') \in \mathbb{R}^n$ is given by $\langle \mathbf{x}, \mathbf{x}' \rangle = \sum_{i=i}^{n} = x_i x_i'$.

It can be easily verified that any dot product $\langle \cdot, \cdot \rangle : \mathcal{H} \times \mathcal{H} \to \mathbb{R}$ is a valid kernel, i.e. symmetric and positive definite [240]. Usually the kernel $\kappa_{\langle \rangle} : \mathcal{H} \times \mathcal{H} \to \mathbb{R}$ employing the dot product is referred to as *linear kernel*

$$\kappa_{\langle \rangle}(x, x') = \langle x, x' \rangle \quad .$$

Kernels can be seen as pattern similarity measures satisfying the condition of symmetry and positive definiteness. In view of this, the standard dot product in $\mathbb{R}^n$ interpreted as kernel makes sense as it is maximal if two feature vectors $\mathbf{x}, \mathbf{x}' \in \mathbb{R}^n$ point in the same direction, and minimal if they point in opposite directions.

The real vector space $\mathbb{R}^n$ with the standard dot product is an example of a *Hilbert space*

Definition 5.4 (Hilbert space). *A vector space $\mathcal{H}$ endowed with a dot product $\langle \cdot, \cdot \rangle : \mathcal{H} \times \mathcal{H} \to \mathbb{R}$ for which the induced norm gives a complete metric space, is termed Hilbert space.*

Provided that a vector space $\mathcal{H}$ is in fact a Hilbert space, some functions measuring how patterns are related to each other in geometrical terms can be derived from dot products. These geometrical relations comprise the *norm* of a vector $x \in \mathcal{H}$

$$\|x\| = \sqrt{\langle x, x \rangle} \quad ,$$

the *distance* of two vectors $x, x' \in \mathcal{H}$

$$\|x - x'\| = \sqrt{\langle x, x \rangle + \langle x', x' \rangle - 2\langle x, x' \rangle} \quad ,$$

and the *angle* between two vectors $x, x' \in \mathcal{H}$

$$\angle(x, x') = \arccos \frac{\langle x, x' \rangle}{\|x\| \cdot \|x'\|} \quad .$$

As a matter of fact, many pattern recognition and analysis algorithms are defined in geometrical terms and can therefore be entirely reformulated in terms of dot products. This observation will be crucial for further development of kernel theory and builds one of the major building blocks of kernel methods' great success.

As it is the kernel function (or the kernel matrix) which represents the underlying data, it might be worth to design intermediate processing steps in order to improve the data representation through more sophisticated kernels than the linear one. In fact, from given kernels one can easily construct derived kernels as kernel functions satisfy a number of closure properties. (For proofs we refer to [5, 138].)

Lemma 5.1 (Closure properties). *Let κ_1 and κ_2 be valid kernels over $\mathcal{X} \times \mathcal{X}$, κ_3 a valid kernel over $\mathcal{H} \times \mathcal{H}$, $\varphi : \mathcal{X} \to \mathcal{H}$, $f : \mathcal{X} \to \mathbb{R}$, and $a \in \mathbb{R}^+$. Then the kernel functions defined by*

(1) $\kappa(x, x') = \kappa_1(x, x') + \kappa_2(x, x')$
(2) $\kappa(x, x') = \kappa_1(x, x')\kappa_2(x, x')$
(3) $\kappa(x, x') = a\kappa_1(x, x')$
(4) $\kappa(x, x') = f(x)f(x')$
(5) $\kappa(x, x') = \kappa_3(\varphi(x), \varphi(x'))$

are also valid kernels.

We will now derive some standard kernels from the linear kernel $\kappa_{\langle\rangle}$ and extend them to non-vectorial data with a workaround under the closure properties.

Taking into account the first three kernel constructions *(1)*, *(2)*, and *(3)* in conjunction with the kernel in *(4)* with $f(x) = c$, where $c \geq 0$, it becomes clear that any polynomial $p(\kappa(x, x'))$ with positive coefficients applied to a valid kernel $\kappa(x, x')$ is also valid. Hence, the well known *polynomial kernel* for vectors $x, x' \in \mathcal{H}$

$$\kappa_{poly}(x, x') = (\langle x, x' \rangle + c)^d$$

with $d \in \mathbb{N}$ and $c \geq 0$ can be derived from the linear kernel $\kappa_{\langle\rangle}$ under the closure properties.

The kernel matrix corresponding to the kernel constructed in *(2)*, that is $\kappa_1 \kappa_2$, is known as the *Schur product* $\mathbf{H}$ of $\mathbf{K}_1$ and $\mathbf{K}_2$. Taking the Schur product of a basic kernel $\kappa(x, x')$ and the kernel in *(4)* with $f(x) = \left(\sqrt{\kappa(x, x)}\right)^{-1}$ leads to the so called *normalized kernel*

$$\hat{\kappa}(x, x') = \frac{\kappa(x, x')}{\sqrt{\kappa(x, x)\kappa(x', x')}} \quad .$$

The exponential function can be arbitrarily closely approximated by polynomials with positive coefficients and the positive definiteness property is closed under pointwise convergence [244]. Hence, the exponentiation $\exp(\kappa(x, x'))$ of a valid kernel $\kappa(x, x')$ is also valid. By normalizing this particular kernel we obtain the so called *radial basis function kernel*, or *RBF kernel* for short[4]

$$\kappa_{rbf}(x, x') = \exp\left(-\gamma||x - x'||^2\right)$$

with $\gamma > 0$. In fact, RBF kernels are the most widely used kernels for vectorial data and have been extensively studied in neighboring fields [5].

The kernels defined so far are applicable to patterns from some pattern space $\mathcal{X}$ endowed with a dot product only and are therefore quite limited in their application. However, consider the kernel constructed in *(5)* where κ_3 is one of the derived vector kernels ($\kappa_{\langle\rangle}, \kappa_{poly}, \kappa_{rbf}$). By means of a mapping $\varphi : \mathcal{X} \to \mathcal{H}$ general data structures $x \in \mathcal{X}$ can be mapped from the original space $\mathcal{X}$ into a vector space $\mathcal{H}$ endowed with a dot product. Any vector kernel κ can thus be applied to general data structures $x \in \mathcal{X}$, viz.

$$\kappa(x, x') = \kappa(\varphi(x), \varphi(x')) \quad ,$$

resulting in a valid kernel on any kind of data $x \in \mathcal{X}$, regardless of the mapping $\varphi : \mathcal{X} \to \mathcal{H}$.

In Table 5.1 some prominent kernel functions defined for vectors $x, x' \in \mathcal{H}$ are summarized. Note that the first three kernels in Table 5.1 are actually

---

[4]The RBF kernel is also referred to as *Gaussian kernel*.

Table 5.1   Sample kernel functions defined on vectors $x, x' \in \mathcal{H}$.

Kernel	Definition	Parameter
Linear kernel	$\kappa_{\langle\rangle}(x, x') = \langle x, x' \rangle$	–
RBF kernel	$\kappa_{rbf}(x, x') = \exp\left(-\gamma\|x - x'\|^2\right)$	$\gamma > 0$
Polynomial kernel	$\kappa_{poly}(x, x') = (\langle x, x' \rangle + c)^d$	$d \in \mathbb{N}$ and $c \geq 0$
Sigmoid kernel	$\kappa_{sig}(x, x') = \tanh(\alpha\langle x, x' \rangle + \beta)$	$\alpha > 0$ and $\beta < 0$

positive definite, while the Sigmoid kernel is not always valid. However, this particular kernel has been successfully used in practice and moreover, it has been shown that if the kernel parameter β is small enough and α is close to zero, the Sigmoid kernel behaves similar to the RBF kernel [245].

5.3   Feature Map vs. Kernel Trick

Linear methods in pattern recognition have a long tradition. Various efficient algorithms have been developed addressing basic problems such as the linear separation of classes or the detection of dominant linear relations in the underlying data set. Principal component analysis [246, 247], for instance, is an efficient algorithm able to detect dominant linear directions in a data set. Yet, linear methods are quite limited as in real world data very often non-linear regularities appear. In such cases linear methods will fail as they are apparently limited to understanding and processing linear data. Hence, quite an effort was made in order to develop algorithms capable of handling non-linear data with the same level of efficiency and the same statistical guarantees that linear methods provide.

In the mid 1980s the field of pattern recognition underwent a non-linear revolution with the introduction of approaches able of detecting non-linear patterns as well (e.g. decision tree learning algorithms [248]). However, these non-linear algorithms suffered from some severe problems. For instance, as many of the proposed methods are based on gradient descent or greedy heuristics and, moreover, their actual statistical behavior was not well understood, they suffered from both local optima and overfitting [5].

With the rise of kernel methods a more universal solution to the problem of non-linear data has found its way into pattern recognition. The basic idea of the kernel approach is to modify the problem domain such that non-linear regularities are turned into linear ones. That is, rather than defining an algorithm able to detect non-linear relations in the original problem domain, the underlying pattern space $\mathcal{X}$ is mapped into a new feature space $\mathcal{F}$ via a non-linear function $\phi : \mathcal{X} \to \mathcal{F}$. As a first toy example consider the two class problem given in Fig. 5.1 (a). Obviously, the gray dots can be separated from the black dots by means of a second-order function f with respect to the two features x_1, x_2 only. For instance, the function

$$f(\mathbf{x}) = -(x_1 - m_1)^2 - (x_2 - m_2)^2 + r^2$$

of the circle with appropriate radius r and center (m_1, m_2) almost perfectly separates the two classes. Obviously, any algorithm designed for linear separation will always be insufficient for this particular problem. Yet, by mapping the two dimensional pattern space $\mathcal{X} = \mathbb{R}^2$ to a higher dimensional feature space $\mathcal{F} = \mathbb{R}^3$ by means of $\phi : \mathcal{X} \to \mathcal{F}$ with $\phi(\mathbf{x}) = (x_1^2, x_2^2, \sqrt{2}x_1x_2)$ the problem of non-linearity can easily be solved. In Fig. 5.1 (b–c) the mapping $\phi : \mathcal{X} \to \mathcal{F}$ is illustrated. Clearly, for the data in the transformed space $\mathcal{F}$ a linear function, namely a plane, is now sufficient for separation while previously in $\mathcal{X}$ a second-order function was necessary.

In order to justify the procedure of mapping the pattern space $\mathcal{X}$ into a high-dimensional feature space $\mathcal{F}$ using a feature map $\phi : \mathcal{X} \to \mathcal{F}$ often Cover's Theorem [249] is consulted [138].

Theorem 5.1 (Cover's Theorem). *Given is an n-dimensional pattern space $\mathcal{X}$ and N points $\{x_1, \ldots, x_N\} \subseteq \mathcal{X}$ in general position. If $N \le n + 1$, all 2^N separations are possible in $\mathcal{X}$. If $N > n + 1$, the number of linear separations amounts to*

$$2 \sum_{i=0}^{n} \binom{N-1}{i} .$$

Cover's theorem formalizes the intuition that the number of linear separations increases with the dimensionality [138]. Note, however, that the theorem does not strictly make a statement about the separability of a given data set in a certain feature space $\mathcal{X}$ [240]. That is, the difficult problem to be solved in the context of mapping data into a higher dimensional feature space is the definition of the mapping function ϕ and its corresponding feature space $\mathcal{F}$. Nevertheless, mapping the original data from $\mathcal{X}$ to a higher dimensional feature space $\mathcal{F}$ increases at least the probability that the data at hand is eventually separable by linear functions. In other words, even if it is unknown whether the properties of a high dimensional feature space will render the recognition problem easier, the mere construction of such a

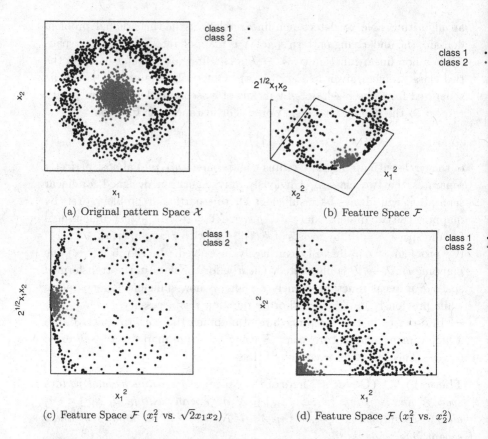

(a) Original pattern Space $\mathcal{X}$

(b) Feature Space $\mathcal{F}$

(c) Feature Space $\mathcal{F}$ (x_1^2 vs. $\sqrt{2}x_1x_2$)

(d) Feature Space $\mathcal{F}$ (x_1^2 vs. x_2^2)

Fig. 5.1   In the original pattern space $\mathcal{X}$ the two classes can be separated by a non-linear decision boundary only. Yet, mapping the patterns from $\mathcal{X}$ to $\mathcal{F}$ via $\phi : \mathcal{X} \to \mathcal{F}$ where $\phi(\mathbf{x}) = (x_1^2, x_2^2, \sqrt{2}x_1x_2)$, the patterns can be separated by a linear function, namely a plane.

feature space in conjunction with a non-linear mapping $\phi : \mathcal{X} \to \mathcal{F}$ is on the average advantageous [28].

Yet, applying a non-linear mapping $\phi : \mathcal{X} \to \mathcal{F}$ to the original pattern space $\mathcal{X}$ is often costly. In particular, when the dimensionality of the resulting feature space $\mathcal{F}$ is high, such mappings turn out to be computationally demanding and are often not feasible. Kernel theory offers an elegant solution to this severe problem. Continuing with the example presented above, the standard dot product of two patterns mapped from $\mathcal{X} = \mathbb{R}^2$ to $\mathcal{F} = \mathbb{R}^3$ according to

$$\phi(\mathbf{x}) = (x_1^2, x_2^2, \sqrt{2}x_1x_2)$$

amounts to

$$\langle \phi(\mathbf{x}), \phi(\mathbf{x}') \rangle = \langle \phi(x_1, x_2), \phi(x_1', x_2') \rangle$$
$$= x_1^2 x_1'^2 + x_2^2 x_2'^2 + 2x_1 x_2 x_1' x_2'$$
$$= (x_1 x_1' + x_2 x_2')^2$$
$$= \langle \mathbf{x}, \mathbf{x}' \rangle^2$$

Obviously, the dot product in the higher dimensional space $\mathcal{F}$ can be inferred by the squared dot product in the original space $\mathcal{X}$. According to Lemma 5.1, $\kappa(\mathbf{x}, \mathbf{x}') = \langle \mathbf{x}, \mathbf{x}' \rangle^2$ is a valid kernel. Hence, for computing spatial relationships in the feature space $\mathcal{F}$, for instance the distance $\|\phi(\mathbf{x}) - \phi(\mathbf{x}')\|$ between two feature maps $\phi(\mathbf{x}), \phi(\mathbf{x}') \in \mathcal{F}$, the mapping $\phi : \mathcal{X} \to \mathcal{F}$ has not to be explicitly computed, as the necessary information is available in the original pattern space $\mathcal{X}$ via the kernel function κ. More formally,

$$\|\phi(\mathbf{x}) - \phi(\mathbf{x}')\| = \sqrt{\langle \phi(\mathbf{x}), \phi(\mathbf{x}) \rangle + \langle \phi(\mathbf{x}'), \phi(\mathbf{x}') \rangle - 2\langle \phi(\mathbf{x}), \phi(\mathbf{x}') \rangle}$$
$$= \sqrt{\langle \mathbf{x}, \mathbf{x} \rangle^2 + \langle \mathbf{x}', \mathbf{x}' \rangle^2 - 2\langle \mathbf{x}, \mathbf{x}' \rangle^2}$$
$$= \sqrt{\kappa(\mathbf{x}, \mathbf{x}) + \kappa(\mathbf{x}', \mathbf{x}') - 2\kappa(\mathbf{x}, \mathbf{x}')}$$

In this toy example, the kernel function κ constitutes a shortcut for computing the dot product in $\mathcal{F} = \mathbb{R}^3$. The following theorem generalizes this crucial observation for other valid kernel functions and for high-, or even infinite-dimensional, Hilbert spaces (for proofs see [5, 138]).

Theorem 5.2. [5, 138] *Let $\kappa : \mathcal{X} \times \mathcal{X} \to \mathbb{R}$ be a valid kernel on a pattern space $\mathcal{X}$. There exists a possibly infinite-dimensional Hilbert space $\mathcal{F}$ and a mapping $\phi : \mathcal{X} \to \mathcal{F}$ such that*

$$\kappa(x, x') = \langle \phi(x), \phi(x') \rangle \quad ,$$

for all $x, x' \in \mathcal{X}$ where $\langle \cdot, \cdot \rangle$ denotes the dot product in a Hilbert space $\mathcal{F}$.

This theorem gives a good intuition what kernel functions really are. Every kernel κ can be thought of as a dot product $\langle \cdot, \cdot \rangle$ in some (implicitly existing) feature space $\mathcal{F}$. In other words, instead of mapping patterns from $\mathcal{X}$ to the feature space $\mathcal{F}$ and computing their dot product there, one can simply evaluate the value of the kernel function in $\mathcal{X}$ [28].

Consider now an algorithm formulated entirely in terms of dot products. Such algorithms are commonly referred to as *kernel machines*. Clearly, any kernel machine can be turned into an alternative algorithm by merely replacing the dot product $\langle \cdot, \cdot \rangle$ by a valid kernel $\kappa(\cdot, \cdot)$. This procedure is commonly referred to as *kernel trick* [5, 138]. Note that any valid kernel function can be interpreted as a dot product in a feature space $\mathcal{F}$ and therefore the kernel trick is admissible.

From a higher level perspective, the kernel trick allows one to run algorithms in implicitly existing feature spaces $\mathcal{F}$ without computing the mapping $\phi : \mathcal{X} \to \mathcal{F}$. Hence, kernel machines can be interpreted to some extent as algorithms operating on black-boxes where the dot product builds the interface to the underlying data. By changing the dot product to a kernel function, the kernel machine is applied to vectors $\phi(x) \in \mathcal{F}$ rather than to original patterns $x \in \mathcal{X}$. In Fig. 5.2 the general principle of the kernel trick is illustrated.

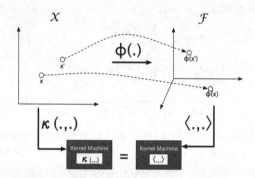

Fig. 5.2   Kernel machines can be seen as operating on black boxes. Changing the dot product to a kernel function enables us to run a kernel algorithm in a higher dimensional feature space $\mathcal{F}$ without explicitly performing the mapping $\phi : \mathcal{X} \to \mathcal{F}$.

Given that the kernel function κ satisfies the conditions of symmetry and positive-definiteness, it is guaranteed that the kernel implicitly represents vectors in the feature space $\mathcal{F}$ where the geometry of $\mathcal{F}$ is based on κ. The kernel trick has a huge impact in practice and offers two crucial properties which are highly beneficial. First, kernel theory allows us to compute geometrical properties of patterns $x, x' \in \mathcal{X}$ though $\mathcal{X}$ possibly contains no, or only little, mathematical structure. That is, by means of the kernel trick and kernel machines, a possible lack of mathematical tools can easily be bypassed. For instance, consider a pattern space $\mathcal{X}$ without any mathematical operations available beyond the existence of a kernel ($\mathcal{X}$ can be thought of as the domain of graphs $\mathcal{G}$ which usually provides no mathematical structure). Clearly, in such a space the angle between two patterns $x, x' \in \mathcal{X}$ is not defined in general. However, by means of a kernel function $\kappa : \mathcal{X} \times \mathcal{X} \to \mathbb{R}$ the patterns x and x' can be implicitly mapped to a feature space $\mathcal{F}$ where the desired computation is eventually carried out. More formally, given a mapping $\phi : \mathcal{X} \to \mathcal{F}$. The computation of the angle $\angle(x, x')$ between two given patterns $x, x' \in \mathcal{X}$ is now carried out in $\mathcal{F}$ by

$$\angle(x, x') = \arccos \frac{\langle \phi(x), \phi(x') \rangle}{||\phi(x)|| \cdot ||\phi(x')||}$$

which amounts to

$$\angle(x, x') = \arccos \frac{\kappa(x, x')}{\sqrt{\kappa(x, x)\kappa(x', x')}} \quad .$$

Hence, the computation of the angle between two patterns x, x', which is not defined in the original pattern space, can be computed in $\mathcal{F}$ using the kernel trick. Similarly any other geometrical relation (which can be expressed through dot products) can be computed in the feature space $\mathcal{F}$.

Second, even if there is mathematical structure in $\mathcal{X}$ (e.g. $\mathcal{X} = \mathbb{R}^n$) kernel methods exhibit beneficial properties. Consider a problem where non-linear regularities in the data points in $\mathcal{X}$ have to be detected (similar to the toy example discussed above). Rather than defining a non-linear algorithm in $\mathcal{X}$, the kernel trick allows one to carry out a linear algorithm in $\mathcal{F}$ without explicitly computing the mapping $\phi : \mathcal{X} \to \mathcal{F}$ for each pattern. The tremendous benefit of this procedure is that the solution of a linear algorithm in the implicit feature space has a non-linear counterpart in the original pattern space. In other words, due to the non-linearity of $\phi(\cdot)$ and the special relation between pattern and feature space established through the kernel, the kernel trick allows one to find non-linear relations in $\mathcal{X}$ with an efficient and statistically well understood linear algorithm.

It is the conceptual simplicity of kernel methods that makes them extremely powerful. In order to modify a linear algorithm to have non-linear behavior, one has to change the algorithm's input from a matrix of dot products to a matrix of kernel values only. Moreover, by changing the kernel function's parameter, or the kernel function itself, a new variant of the considered algorithm is obtained with minimal effort. That is, by means of the kernel trick any kernel machine can be adopted to a specific problem allowing us to learn virtually any complex regularities in the data set at hand.

5.4   Kernel Machines

In recent years, a huge amount of important algorithms have been *kernelized*, i.e. reformulated in terms of dot products. These algorithms include, support vector machine, nearest-neighbor classifier, perceptron algorithm, principal component analysis, Fisher discriminant analysis, canonical correlation analysis, k-means clustering, self organizing map, partial least squares regression, and many more [5, 138]. In the present thesis three kernel machines are actually used: the support vector machine for classification, the principal component analysis for feature extraction, and the k-means algorithm for clustering. These three kernel machines are discussed in greater detail in the next sections.

5.4.1   *Support Vector Machine (SVM)*

Support vector machines (SVMs) are the most popular kernel machines for pattern classification. Originally, SVMs are linear classifiers able to derive a linear function for classification only. Yet, since the SVM training procedure can be entirely formulated in terms of dot products, the kernel trick can be applied to the basic SVM. That is, the training procedure is carried out in an implicitly existing feature space $\mathcal{F}$. Through the non-linearity of the mapping $\phi : \mathcal{X} \to \mathcal{F}$ the derived classification function, which is actually linear in $\mathcal{F}$, corresponds to a non-linear decision function in the original pattern space $\mathcal{X}$. Moreover, through the kernel trick not only the problem of non-linearity is resolved but also the issue of pattern representation. By means of kernels for structured data, the extremely powerful SVM can be applied to strings, trees, or graphs, hence making SVMs very flexible in its application.

Consider a pattern space $\mathcal{X}$, a space of class labels Ω, and a labeled training set of N objects $\{(x_i, \omega_i)\}_{1 \le i \le N} \subseteq \mathcal{X} \times \Omega$. SVMs are kernel machines able to derive a function $f : \mathcal{X} \to \Omega$ from the training set which can be used to predict the label of unseen data out of the underlying pattern space $\mathcal{X}$. The training procedure of SVMs for learning the prediction function f is based on results from statistical learning theory. That is, the SVM training explicitly aims at reducing the risk of overfitting, which means SVMs aim at learning the class boundaries of the hidden underlying population rather than the class boundaries of the training set. Therefore, the decision function learned by an SVM can be expected to generalize well on unseen data. Moreover, SVMs are not only interesting because

of their well founded statistical theory, but also because they show superior performance in comparison with traditional classifiers on various data
sets [5, 138, 240–243].

The basic idea of SVMs is to separate different classes from the training
set by hyperplanes. Hyperplanes derived from SVM training are characterized by the property that they are placed in such way that their distance to
the closest element of either class is maximal. Such hyperplanes are commonly referred to as *maximum-margin hyperplanes*. In Fig. 5.3 a labeled
training set with two classes is shown. Obviously, the three hyperplanes
shown correctly separate the two classes, i.e. the white and black dots. Yet,
the hyperplane shown in a solid line is the maximum-margin hyperplane,
i.e. the hyperplane that maximizes the distances to the nearest element from
both classes. Intuitively, this specific hyperplane will perform the best on
unseen test data, i.e. the solid line hyperplane's generalization power is the
highest among all proposed prediction functions.

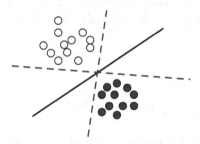

Fig. 5.3 A labeled training set with two classes (white vs. black dots). All three
hyperplanes discriminate the white circles from the black ones without a mistake. The
solid line hyperplane, however, is the maximum-margin hyperplane and would intuitively
be considered the most suitable hyperplane separating the two classes.

In the following, let us assume that the pattern space is the real vector
space ($\mathcal{X} = \mathbb{R}^n$) and consider a two class problem ($\Omega = \{-1, +1\}$). Later
in this section we will be able to generalize both the pattern space $\mathcal{X}$ and
the number of classes in Ω. A given decision function

$$f(\mathbf{x}) = \langle \mathbf{w}, \mathbf{x} \rangle + b \qquad (5.1)$$

with $\mathbf{w} \in \mathbb{R}^n$ and $b \in \mathbb{R}$ can be used to assign labels to the data entities
$\mathbf{x} \in \mathcal{X}$ according to the sign of $f(\mathbf{x})$. That is, this hyperplane-defining
function assigns a label $\omega = +1$ to patterns $\mathbf{x}$ with $f(\mathbf{x}) \geq 0$, and a label
$\omega = -1$ to patterns $\mathbf{x}$ with $f(\mathbf{x}) < 0$. In order to estimate the power
of a derived decision function f, a natural criterion might be the number

of misclassifications on the training set made by f. This general principle, which minimizes the number of training patterns $(\mathbf{x}_i, \omega_i)$ where $\omega_i f(\mathbf{x}_i) < 0$, is known as *empirical risk minimization*. However, as shown in Fig. 5.3 the minimization of training errors does not lead to a unique solution, even when it is possible to perfectly separate the training set's classes by a linear function.

The theory underlying SVMs stems from general results on learning theory developed in particular by Vapnik and Chervonenkis [250, 251]. SVMs are unique in that they are able to focus on the confidence of a hyperplane and not only on the number of misclassifications resulting from a specific decision boundary [240]. The SVM training can be interpreted as a *structural risk minimization* process. In contrast to empirical risk, which quantifies how well a classifier f performs on the current training set, the structural risk minimization quantifies the degree of underfitting and overfitting and therefore helps in determining which classifier f can be expected to achieve the best performance on unseen data. In order to see this let us first multiply the parameters $\mathbf{w}$ and b of a given hyperplane with a positive constant such that

$$\min_{1 \leq i \leq N} |\langle \mathbf{w}, \mathbf{x}_i \rangle + b| = 1$$

which is equivalent to

$$\omega_i(\langle \mathbf{w}, \mathbf{x}_i \rangle + b) \geq 1$$

for all $i = 1, \ldots, N$.

Such a hyperplane is commonly referred to as *canonical* with respect to the training data. Geometrically interpreted, $\mathbf{w}$ is a vector perpendicular to the hyperplane, and b is a scalar which corresponds to the distance of the hyperplane to the origin of the coordinate system. This distance amounts to $|b|/||\mathbf{w}||$. The distance of any pattern $\mathbf{x}' \in \mathcal{X}$ to the hyperplane $f(\mathbf{x}) = \langle \mathbf{w}, \mathbf{x} \rangle + b$ is given by $f(\mathbf{x}')/||w||$. Therefore, given that the hyperplane is in canonical form, the distance of any patterns from either class closest to the hyperplane $f(\mathbf{x}) = \langle \mathbf{w}, \mathbf{x} \rangle + b$ amounts to $1/||\mathbf{w}||$. The distance of the closest points from either class to the hyperplane is commonly termed *margin* of the hyperplane with respect to training set. Consequently, the smaller the length of the weight vector $||\mathbf{w}||$ of the canonical hyperplane, the larger the margin. Obviously, large margin hyperplanes are definitely to be favored over small-margin hyperplanes, since a larger margin corresponds to a better separability of the classes.

The objective of SVM training boils down to minimizing the training error (i.e. minimizing the empirical risk) by simultaneously maximizing the margin of the hyperplane (i.e. minimizing the structural risk). Formally, the term to be optimized is

$$\min_{\mathbf{w} \in \mathbb{R}^n} \frac{1}{2} ||\mathbf{w}||^2 \tag{5.2}$$

subject to

$$\omega_i(\langle \mathbf{w}, \mathbf{x} \rangle + b) \geq 1 \quad \text{for } 1 \leq i \leq N \quad . \tag{5.3}$$

The minimization of the squared length of the weight vector $\mathbf{w}$ in Eq. 5.2 corresponds to maximizing the margin of the hyperplane while simultaneously classifying the training set without error (Eq. 5.3).

The minimization problem to be solved by the SVM belongs to the class of linearly constrained convex optimization problems and can be solved by quadratic programming [252, 253]. The particular minimization task given in Eq. 5.2 is commonly termed *primal optimization problem*. The corresponding so-called *dual problem* [254], which has the same solution as Eq. 5.2, is derived through the following Lagrangian

$$L(\mathbf{w}, b, \boldsymbol{\alpha}) = \frac{1}{2} ||\mathbf{w}||^2 - \sum_{i=1}^{N} \alpha_i(\omega_i(\langle \mathbf{x}_i, \mathbf{w} \rangle + b) - 1) \tag{5.4}$$

where $\alpha_i \geq 0$ are Lagrange multipliers. The Lagrangian L has to be maximized with respect to $\boldsymbol{\alpha} = (\alpha_1, \ldots, \alpha_N)$ and minimized with respect to $\mathbf{w}$ and b. Hence, $\boldsymbol{\alpha} \in \mathbb{R}^N$ and $b \in \mathbb{R}$ are obtained from the SVM optimization. At the saddle point, the derivatives of L with respect to the primal variables must vanish [138]. Formally,

$$\frac{d}{db}L(\mathbf{w}, b, \boldsymbol{\alpha}) = 0 \quad \text{and} \quad \frac{d}{d\mathbf{w}}L(\mathbf{w}, b, \boldsymbol{\alpha}) = 0$$

which leads to

$$\sum_{i=1}^{N} \alpha_i \omega_i = 0 \quad ,$$

and

$$\mathbf{w} = \sum_{i=1}^{N} \alpha_i \omega_i \mathbf{x}_i \quad . \tag{5.5}$$

Thus, the weight vector $\mathbf{w}$ can be expressed as a linear combination of the training examples $\mathbf{x}_1, \ldots, \mathbf{x}_N$ with coefficients $\alpha_i \omega_i$. Using Eq. 5.5 in the SVM's decision function in Eq. 5.1, we obtain the following expression

$$f(\mathbf{x}) = \sum_{i=1}^{N} \alpha_i \omega_i \langle \mathbf{x}_i, \mathbf{x} \rangle + b \tag{5.6}$$

for SVM classification of an input pattern $\mathbf{x} \in \mathcal{X}$.

It turns out that only training patterns located closely to the hyperplane contribute to the sum in Eq. 5.6. Formally, for training patterns $\mathbf{x}_i$ correctly classified by the decision function with large confidence, the corresponding Lagrange multiplier α_i becomes zero. The training patterns $\mathbf{x}_i$ with $\alpha_i > 0$ are commonly referred to as *support vectors*. Hence, in order to learn the decision function f, the set of support vectors contains all the information necessary. That is, the solution found by the SVM does not change when non-support vectors are removed from, or added to, the training set.

The tremendous benefit of the expression in Eq. 5.6 is that for a given test pattern $\mathbf{x} \in \mathcal{X}$ the prediction of the class membership depends on dot products of $\mathbf{x}$ and training patterns $\{\mathbf{x}_i\}_{1 \le i \le N}$ only. This means that in order to determine in which subspace defined by the separating hyperplane a given test pattern lies, one merely needs to know the Lagrange multipliers $\alpha_1, \ldots, \alpha_N$, the constant b, and the dot products $\langle \mathbf{x}, \mathbf{x}_i \rangle$ between the test pattern and all training patterns. The kernel trick can therefore be applied to perform the SVM optimization in a feature space $\mathcal{F}$. Clearly, the constraint that $\mathcal{X}$ is a vector space can now be omitted. Instead we define a valid kernel function $\kappa : \mathcal{X} \times \mathcal{X} \to \mathbb{R}$ on the pattern space $\mathcal{X}$ of any kind. By replacing the dot product $\langle \cdot, \cdot \rangle$ with this kernel function, the SVM is trained in an implicit existing feature space $\mathcal{F}$. The resulting decision function is linear in $\mathcal{F}$, of course. However, the corresponding decision boundary in the original pattern space $\mathcal{X}$ can be more complex because of the non-linearity of the feature mapping $\phi : \mathcal{X} \to \mathcal{F}$.

Examples of non-linear separations are illustrated in Fig. 5.4, where an SVM endowed with an RBF kernel is applied to a two class problem. Note the influence of parameter γ in the RBF kernel function. The larger the values of γ, the more peaked the Gaussians around the vectors become, allowing a classifier to learn quite complex decision boundaries.

As it cannot be expected that the training set can be separated by a linear decision function in any case, the constraint that every training sample is classified correctly is too severe for real world applications (cf. Eq. 5.3). Moreover, by demanding every training pattern to be correctly classified by the decision function, outliers might crucially affect the generalization power of the SVM's decision boundary. Therefore, it might be beneficial to include some sort of error-tolerance in the SVM training procedure. In order to be able to cope with linearly non-seperable data as well as with outliers, so called slack variables ξ_i are used to allow for misclassification [255]. For each training pattern $\mathbf{x}_i$ being misclassified by the hyperplane, the cor-

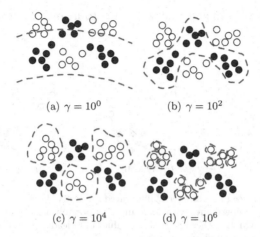

(a) $\gamma = 10^0$ (b) $\gamma = 10^2$

(c) $\gamma = 10^4$ (d) $\gamma = 10^6$

Fig. 5.4 The influence of parameter γ illustrated for an RBF SVM. For large values of γ the Gaussians around the vectors become more peaked allowing a classifier to learn complex decision boundaries but also risking overfitting.

responding slack variable ξ_i is greater than zero. Formally, we relax the separation constraint of Eq. 5.3 to

$$\omega_i(\langle \mathbf{w}, \mathbf{x}_i \rangle + b) \geq 1 - \xi_i \text{ (where } \xi_i \geq 0) \quad \text{for } 1 \leq i \leq N \quad . \tag{5.7}$$

Clearly, the relaxed constraint imposed in Eq. 5.7 can always be met by making the slack variables ξ_i large enough. However, in order not to obtain this trivial solution, we penalize the slack variables in the objective function [138]. Formally, the term to be optimized by SVM is now written as

$$\min_{\mathbf{w} \in \mathbb{R}^n} \frac{1}{2} ||\mathbf{w}||^2 + C \sum_{i=1}^{N} \xi_i \quad , \tag{5.8}$$

where $C \geq 0$ is a weighting parameter that controls the trade off between the requirements of large margin (i.e. small $||\mathbf{w}||$) and few misclassifications. In other words, C controls what is more important, the minimization of the structural risk or the minimization of the empirical risk. In Fig. 5.5 the influence of parameter C can be observed in an example. Clearly, small values of C lead to hyperplanes with large margins but possibly more errors on the training data. Conversely, large values of C correspond to hyperplanes with smaller margin but more training data correctly classified.

An alternative realization of the SVM uses the ν parameter instead of the C parameter [138]. In this case, the parameter $\nu \in [0, 1]$ is used to determine the lower- and upper bound of the number of training data that will be support vectors and that will come to lie on the wrong side of the hyperplane [240].

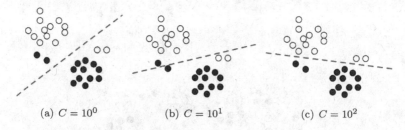

(a) $C = 10^0$ (b) $C = 10^1$ (c) $C = 10^2$

Fig. 5.5 The influence of parameter C illustrated for an SVM with linear kernel. Small values of C lead to hyperplanes with large margins possibly misclassifying some of the training elements. On the other hand, larger values of C lead to hyperplanes with fewer errors on the training set but smaller margins.

Until now, only binary classification scenarios are covered by the SVM. However, many real world applications deal with more than only two classes. A widely used method to overcome this limitation of SVMs is to reformulate the multiclass problem as a number of two-class problems and eventually combining the results of these binary SVMs. Two different approaches are well known in the literature, referred to as the *one-against-all* and the *one-against-one* scheme. In the former case, the problem of k classes is transformed into k binary problems. That is, for each of the k classes in Ω an individual SVM is trained. Thereby, the i-th SVM finds a decision boundary between the i-th class and all other classes. In this way k decision boundaries $f_1, \ldots, f_k$ are obtained. For classifying an unknown test object, a maximum rule is applied, which means that the test pattern is assigned to the class corresponding to the SVM that outputs the largest score. More formally, given a test element $x \in \mathcal{X}$ and the SVM decision values $f_1(x), \ldots, f_k(x)$. The pattern x is assigned to class ω_i if $f_i(x) = \max\{f_j(x) | 1 \leq j \leq k\}$. In the latter approach, for every pair of classes an individual binary SVM is trained resulting in $k(k-1)/2$ different SVMs. An unknown test element is assigned to the class that occurs most frequently among the $k(k-1)/2$ decisions.

The structural risk minimization principle, the maximum-margin hyperplane, and the SVM formulation in terms of dot products leading to a non-linear classifier applicable to any kind of data, all that accounts for the mathematical appeal of SVMs. Furthermore, SVM classification has been applied to a wide range of recognition problems and has frequently outperformed traditional classifiers [5, 138, 240–243]. These convincing results, obtained on various difficult real world data sets, made the SVM to the state-of-the art algorithm for classification problems.

5.4.2 *Principal Component Analysis (PCA)*

Principal Component Analysis (PCA) [246, 247] is a well-known technique for data analysis and dimensionality reduction. PCA is a linear transformation which basically seeks the projection that best represents the data with respect to the variance of the underlying features. More formally, PCA finds a new pattern space whose basis vectors correspond to the directions of the maximum variance of the data in the original space. Hence, the idea of PCA is to extract those features that best describe the dominant linear directions in a vectorial data set. In the resulting linearly decorrelated data set, the components are ordered according to their importance [28]. PCA is an unsupervised transformation method, i.e. PCA does not take any class label information into account. Let us assume that N objects are given in terms of n-dimensional vectors $\{\mathbf{x}_1, \ldots, \mathbf{x}_N\} \subset \mathbb{R}^n$ (later in this section we show that PCA is kernelizable thus relaxing this explicit data representation formalism). We first normalize the data by shifting the sample mean

$$\mathbf{m} = \frac{1}{N} \sum_{k=1}^{N} \mathbf{x}_k$$

to the origin of the coordinate system, i.e. we center the data. Next we compute the covariance matrix $\mathbf{C}$ of the centered data which is defined as

$$\mathbf{C} = \frac{1}{N} \sum_{k=1}^{N} \mathbf{x}_k \mathbf{x}_k' \quad .$$

The covariance matrix $\mathbf{C}$ is symmetric and, therefore, an orthogonal basis can be defined by finding the eigenvalues λ_i and the corresponding eigenvectors $\mathbf{e}_i$ of $\mathbf{C}$. To this end the following eigenstructure decomposition has to be solved:

$$\lambda_i \mathbf{e}_i = \mathbf{C} \mathbf{e}_i$$

The eigenvectors $\mathbf{W} = (\mathbf{e}_1, \ldots, \mathbf{e}_n)$ are also called *principal components*, and they build an orthogonal basis. Consequently, the matrix $\mathbf{W}$ represents a linear transformation that maps the original data points $\{\mathbf{x}_k\}_{k=1,\ldots,N} \subset \mathbb{R}^n$ to new data points $\{\mathbf{y}_k\}_{k=1,\ldots,N} \subset \mathbb{R}^n$ where

$$\mathbf{y}_k = \mathbf{W}^t \mathbf{x}_k, \; k = 1, \ldots, N$$

That is, the data is projected into the space spanned by the eigenvectors. The eigenvalues λ_i of the covariance matrix represent the variance of the data points in the direction of the corresponding eigenvector $\mathbf{e}_i$. Hence, the eigenvectors $\mathbf{e}_i$ can be ordered according to decreasing magnitude of their corresponding eigenvalues. Consequently, the first principal component points in the direction of the highest variance and, therefore, includes the most information about the data. The second principal component is perpendicular to the first principal component and points in the direction of the second highest variance, and so on. In order to project the n-dimensional data $\{\mathbf{x}_k\}_{k=1,\ldots,N} \subset \mathbb{R}^n$ into a subspace of lower dimensionality, we retain only the $n' < n$ eigenvectors $\mathbf{W}_{n'} = (\mathbf{e}_1, \ldots, \mathbf{e}_{n'})$ with the highest n' eigenvalues. Formally, the mapping of $\{\mathbf{x}_k\}_{k=1,\ldots,N} \subset \mathbb{R}^n$ to $\{\tilde{\mathbf{y}}_k\}_{k=1,\ldots,N} \subset \mathbb{R}^{n'}$ is defined by

$$\tilde{\mathbf{y}}_k = \mathbf{W}_{n'}^t \mathbf{x}_k, \ k = 1, \ldots, N$$

Note that the larger the resulting dimensionality n' is defined, the greater is the fraction of the captured variance. In Fig. 5.6 an example of a PCA decorrelation is given. In this toy example $\tilde{\mathbf{y}}_1$ points in the direction of the highest variance in the data, while $\tilde{\mathbf{y}}_2$ can be regarded as noise and can thus be omitted.

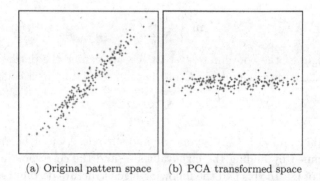

(a) Original pattern space   (b) PCA transformed space

Fig. 5.6   Decorrelated data set after applying PCA.

As a matter of fact, PCA can be reformulated in terms of dot products only, i.e. PCA is kernelizable [256]. In order to see this, let us first assume that we apply the mapping $\phi : \mathbb{R}^n \to \mathcal{F}$ explicitly to our data. For further processing we assume that the data is centered in the kernel feature space[5].

---

[5]We will come back to this point later in this section.

We compute the covariance matrix $\mathbf{C}$ in the feature space $\mathcal{F}$

$$\mathbf{C} = \frac{1}{N} \sum_{i=1}^{N} \phi(\mathbf{x}_i)\phi(\mathbf{x}_i)' \quad .$$

Similarly to PCA the principal components of this feature space are extracted by means of the eigenstructure decomposition

$$\lambda \mathbf{w} = \mathbf{C}\mathbf{w} \quad . \tag{5.9}$$

From the definition of $\mathbf{C}$ follows that $\mathbf{C}\mathbf{w}$ is a linear combination of the training samples $\phi(\mathbf{x}_i)$. Formally,

$$\mathbf{C}\mathbf{w} = \sum_{i=1}^{N} (\langle \phi(\mathbf{x}_i), \mathbf{w} \rangle) \phi(\mathbf{x}_i) \quad .$$

Thus, all solutions $\mathbf{w}$ must lie in the span of $\phi(\mathbf{x}_1), \ldots, \phi(\mathbf{x}_N)$. This observation is crucial since it allows us to rewrite $\mathbf{w}$ as a linear combination of the vectors $\phi(\mathbf{x}_i)$ with coefficients α_i $(i = 1, \ldots, N)$

$$\mathbf{w} = \sum_{i=1}^{N} \alpha_i \phi(\mathbf{x}_i) \quad . \tag{5.10}$$

Furthermore, Eq. 5.9 can now be rewritten as

$$\lambda \sum_{i=1}^{N} \alpha_i \phi(\mathbf{x}_i) = \frac{1}{N} \sum_{i,j=1}^{N} \alpha_i \phi(\mathbf{x}_j) \langle \phi(\mathbf{x}_j), \phi(\mathbf{x}_i) \rangle \quad .$$

This is equivalent to N equations $(k = 1, \ldots, N)$

$$\lambda \sum_{i=1}^{N} \alpha_i \langle \phi(\mathbf{x}_i), \phi(\mathbf{x}_k) \rangle = \frac{1}{N} \sum_{i,j=1}^{N} \alpha_i \langle \phi(\mathbf{x}_j), \phi(\mathbf{x}_k) \rangle \langle \phi(\mathbf{x}_j), \phi(\mathbf{x}_i) \rangle \quad . \tag{5.11}$$

The tremendous benefit of Eq. 5.11 is that it is entirely formulated in terms of dot products. Hence, we can define a kernel matrix $\mathbf{K} = (\kappa_{ij})_{N \times N}$ where $\kappa_{ij} = \langle \phi(\mathbf{x}_i), \phi(\mathbf{x}_j) \rangle$ and replace the dot products in Eq. 5.11 by the kernel function. Formally,

$$N\lambda \mathbf{K}\boldsymbol{\alpha} = \mathbf{K}^2 \boldsymbol{\alpha} \quad , \tag{5.12}$$

where $\boldsymbol{\alpha} = (\alpha_1, \ldots, \alpha_N)'$. $\mathbf{K}$ is by definition symmetric and has a set of eigenvectors that span the whole space. It can be shown [138] that Eq. 5.12 is equivalent to

$$N\lambda \boldsymbol{\alpha} = \mathbf{K}\boldsymbol{\alpha} \quad .$$

Consequently, all solutions $\boldsymbol{\alpha}$ for each principal component can be obtained by the eigendecomposition of the kernel matrix $\mathbf{K}$.

Let $\lambda_1 \leq \lambda_2 \leq \ldots \leq \lambda_N$ denote the eigenvalues and $\boldsymbol{\alpha}^1, \ldots, \boldsymbol{\alpha}^N$ the corresponding eigenvectors of $\mathbf{K}$. The principal components, i.e. eigenvectors $\mathbf{w}^k$ in the feature space $\mathcal{F}$, need to be normalized to have unit length, i.e. $||\mathbf{w}^k||^2 = 1$. This can also be achieved by means of the kernel matrix $\mathbf{K}$ only, leading to a normalization rule for $\boldsymbol{\alpha}^k$ ($k = 1, \ldots, N$).

$$
\begin{aligned}
1 &= ||\mathbf{w}^k||^2 \\
&= \sum_{i,j=1}^{N} \alpha_i^k \alpha_j^k \langle \phi(\mathbf{x}_i), \phi(\mathbf{x}_j) \rangle \\
&= \langle \boldsymbol{\alpha}^k, \mathbf{K}\boldsymbol{\alpha}^k \rangle \\
&= N\lambda_k \langle \boldsymbol{\alpha}^k, \boldsymbol{\alpha}^k \rangle
\end{aligned}
$$

In order to compute a projection of $\phi(\mathbf{x}) \in \mathcal{F}$ onto a subspace spanned by the first n' eigenvectors $(\mathbf{w}^1, \ldots, \mathbf{w}^{n'})$ the following equation is used

$$
\begin{aligned}
\tilde{\mathbf{y}} &= \left(\langle \mathbf{w}^k, \phi(\mathbf{x}) \rangle \right)_{k=1}^{n'} \\
&= \left(\sum_{i=1}^{N} \alpha_i^k \langle \phi(\mathbf{x}_i), \phi(\mathbf{x}) \rangle \right)_{k=1}^{n'} \\
&= \left(\sum_{i=1}^{N} \alpha_i^k \kappa(\mathbf{x}_i, \mathbf{x}) \right)_{k=1}^{n'}
\end{aligned}
$$

Note that for the purpose of kernel PCA the principal components in $\mathcal{F}$ are not explicitly extracted. Instead, the mapping of $\phi(\mathbf{x}) \in \mathcal{F}$ onto the principal components in $\mathcal{F}$ is computed by means of the kernel matrix $\mathbf{K}$ and the normalized coefficients $\boldsymbol{\alpha}^k$ only.

So far we assumed that the data is centered. Usually, this is not fulfilled, of course. In an explicit fashion one would center the data by

$$
\hat{\phi}(\mathbf{x}) = \phi(\mathbf{x}) - \frac{1}{N} \sum_{k=1}^{N} \phi(\mathbf{x}_k) \quad .
$$

However, it turns out that the centering of the data need not be done explicitly. That is, the kernel matrix $\mathbf{K} = (\kappa_{ij})_{N \times N}$ can be replaced by

$\hat{\mathbf{K}} = (\hat{\kappa}_{ij})_{N \times N}$ which is defined by

$$
\begin{aligned}
\hat{\kappa}_{ij} &= \langle \hat{\phi}(\mathbf{x}_i), \hat{\phi}(\mathbf{x}_j) \rangle \\
&= \left\langle \phi(\mathbf{x}_i) - \frac{1}{N} \sum_{k=1}^{N} \phi(\mathbf{x}_k), \phi(\mathbf{x}_j) - \frac{1}{N} \sum_{k=1}^{N} \phi(\mathbf{x}_k) \right\rangle \\
&= \langle \phi(\mathbf{x}_i), \phi(\mathbf{x}_j) \rangle - \frac{1}{N} \sum_{k=1}^{N} \langle \phi(\mathbf{x}_i), \phi(\mathbf{x}_k) \rangle - \frac{1}{N} \sum_{k=1}^{N} \langle \phi(\mathbf{x}_j), \phi(\mathbf{x}_k) \rangle + \\
&\quad \frac{1}{N^2} \sum_{k,l=1}^{N} \langle \phi(\mathbf{x}_k), \phi(\mathbf{x}_l) \rangle \\
&= \kappa_{ij} - \frac{1}{N} \sum_{k=1}^{N} \kappa_{ik} - \frac{1}{N} \sum_{k=1}^{N} \kappa_{jk} + \frac{1}{N^2} \sum_{k,l=1}^{N} \kappa_{kl} \quad .
\end{aligned}
$$

Provided that a suitable kernel function is employed, Kernel PCA differs from traditional PCA in that non-linear regularities in the data at hand can be detected as well. Note that PCA applied in $\mathcal{F}$ is still linear, but in the original space $\mathcal{X}$ the extracted features correspond to non-linear directions.

In Fig. 5.7 (a) a two-class data set with a clearly non-linear regularity is shown. Applying traditional PCA to this data set merely results in a rotation of the data points (Fig. 5.7 (b)). That is, PCA, which is able to detect linear regularities, fails in this particular example. However, using kernel PCA instead of linear PCA, various transformations of the original data set can be observed. Note that kernel PCA can be understood as visualization of the pattern distribution in an implicitly existing, but unknown feature space $\mathcal{F}$ [28]. In other words, kernel PCA extracts those principal components that best explain the variance of the data in $\mathcal{F}$. In Fig. 5.7 (c–f) kernel PCA using an RBF kernel varying the parameter value γ is illustrated ($\gamma \in \{2^{-5}, 2^{-4}, 2^{-3}, 2^{-2}\}$). Obviously, by varying the meta parameter, different feature extractions of the same data set can be obtained with minimal effort. Moreover, whereas in the original pattern space $\mathcal{X}$ a complex classifier is required to solve the two class problem, in the feature space $\mathcal{F}$ obtained by kernel PCA with RBF kernel and $\gamma = 2^{-3}$ a linear classifier defined with respect to the first principal component would be perfectly sufficient.

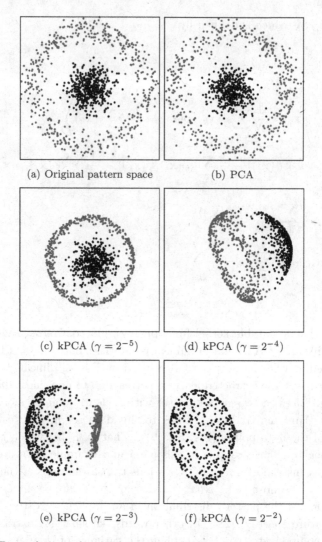

Fig. 5.7   Decorrelating a data set by means of PCA and kernel PCA with RBF kernel and various parameter values γ.

5.4.3   *k-Means Clustering*

Clustering, a common task in pattern recognition, data mining, machine learning, and related fields, refers to the process of dividing a set of given objects into homogeneous groups. In recent years a large amount of clustering algorithms have been proposed in the literature (see [32] for a survey).

The k-means algorithm [257] is one of the most popular clustering algorithms in pattern recognition and related areas. Let us assume that N objects $\{x_1, \ldots, x_N\} \subseteq \mathcal{X}$ are given. The initialization of k-means is commonly done with a random selection of k cluster centers, i.e. a set of $k < N$ objects $\mathcal{M}_k = \{m_1, \ldots, m_k\} \subset \{x_1, \ldots, x_N\}$. Next each of the N objects is assigned to its closest cluster center in $\mathcal{M}_k$. Based on this initial clustering, the cluster centers are recomputed. The two preceding steps, i.e. the assignment of objects to the nearest cluster center and the recomputation of the centers, are repeated until a predefined termination criterion is met (e.g. no reassignment of objects from one cluster to another has taken place during the last iteration). In Algorithm 5.1 the algorithmic procedure for k-means clustering is given.

Algorithm 5.1 k-means clustering algorithm.

Input:	N objects $\{x_1, \ldots, x_N\} \subseteq \mathcal{X}$, number of clusters k
Output:	A clustering of the objects into k disjoint clusters $C_1, \ldots, C_k$

1: Select k initial cluster centers $\{m_1, \ldots, m_k\} \subset \{x_1, \ldots, x_N\}$
2: **repeat**
3:     Assign each object x_i to the nearest cluster center
4:     Recompute cluster centers
5: **until** Termination criterion is met

K-means clustering makes use of the squared error criterion as an objective function. Formally, the k-means algorithm finds k clusters $C_1, \ldots, C_k$ such that the objective function

$$f\left(\{C_j\}_{j=1}^k\right) = \sum_{j=1}^{k} \sum_{x_i \in C_j} d(x_i, m_j)^2$$

is minimized. In this formula, the j-th cluster is denoted by C_j, a clustering by $\{C_j\}_{j=1}^k$, d is an appropriate distance function defined on the patterns $x \in \mathcal{X}$, and m_j refers to the mean of cluster C_j.

Note that the objects x_i are usually given in terms of vectors. In this case, the dissimilarity function d can be defined as the Euclidean distance, and m_j is the mean vector of C_j, i.e.

$$m_j = \frac{1}{|C_j|} \sum_{x_i \in C_j} x_i \quad .$$

However, k-means clustering can be slightly modified such that is becomes applicable to structured data and in particular to graphs. If the objects x_i are given in terms of graphs, the distance function d can be given by the graph edit distance and the mean m_j of the j-th cluster can be defined, for instance, as the set median graph [258][6]

$$m_j = \operatorname*{argmin}_{g_1 \in C_j} \sum_{g_2 \in C_j} d(g_1, g_2) \quad .$$

The median graph of cluster C_j is the graph $g \in C_j$ that minimizes the sum of distances to all other objects in this cluster. Commonly, k-means clustering applied to graphs using the concept of set median graph is referred to as k-medians clustering [259].

A well known drawback of k-means clustering is that the individual clusters C_j need to be spherical in order to achieve satisfactory results. (This drawback directly follows from the minimization of the squared error criterion.) In other words, k-means clustering forms spherical clusters whether or not the underlying data distribution meets this form.

Let us now assume that a function $\phi : \mathcal{X} \to \mathcal{F}$ is given, mapping the original patterns $x_i \in \mathcal{X}$ into a higher dimensional feature space $\mathcal{F}$. Applying k-means clustering in the resulting feature space $\mathcal{F}$, i.e. finding spherical clusters C_j in $\mathcal{F}$, corresponds to finding (possibly) non-spherical clusters in the original pattern space $\mathcal{X}$. Due to the non-linearity of function ϕ we are able to form virtually any kind of clusters in the original pattern space $\mathcal{X}$. Hence, this clustering procedure is much more powerful than the conventional k-means algorithm.

The objective function for k-means clustering in the higher dimensional feature space $\mathcal{F}$ can be written as the minimization of

$$f\left(\{C_j\}_{j=1}^{k}\right) = \sum_{j=1}^{k} \sum_{\mathbf{x}_i \in C_j} \|(\phi(x_i) - m_j\| \quad ,$$

where

$$m_j = \frac{1}{|C_j|} \sum_{x_i \in C_j} \phi(x_i) \quad .$$

In fact, it turns out that the k-means algorithm can be written as a kernel machine, i.e. can be reformulated in terms of pairwise dot products only.

---

[6]Note that there is no standard mean m defined in the domain of graphs $\mathcal{G}$. This is due to the fact that basic mathematical operations such as the computation of sums is not defined for graphs in general.

Formally, the squared Euclidean distance $||(\phi(x) - m||^2$ between vector x and the mean m of cluster C can be rewritten as

$$||\phi(x)-m||^2 = \langle \phi(x), \phi(x) \rangle + \frac{1}{|C|^2} \sum_{x_i \in C} \sum_{x_j \in C} \langle \phi(x_i), \phi(x_j) \rangle - \frac{2}{|C|} \sum_{x_i \in C} \langle \phi(x), \phi(x_i) \rangle \quad .$$

(5.13)

Obviously, now we can replace the dot products $\langle \cdot, \cdot \rangle$ in Eq. 5.13 with a valid kernel function $\kappa(\cdot, \cdot)$ to represent the dot product in an implicit feature space $\mathcal{F}$.

$$||\phi(x) - m||^2 = \kappa(x, x) + \frac{1}{|C|^2} \sum_{x_i \in C} \sum_{x_j \in C} \kappa(x_i, x_j) - \frac{2}{|C|} \sum_{x_i \in C} \kappa(x, x_i) \quad .$$

(5.14)

That is, one can apply k-means in an implicitly existing feature space $\mathcal{F}$. The resulting procedure is commonly referred to as kernel k-means clustering [260].

Note that the cluster mean $m \in \mathcal{F}$ cannot be explicitly computed. Yet, there is no need to do so as we merely need the distances between any object $\phi(x) \in \mathcal{F}$ and the cluster means. In view of this, line 4 in Algorithm 5.1 is dispensable as the cluster centers are implicitly given through the respective members.

5.5 Graph Kernels

So far only kernel functions for vectorial pattern descriptions have been discussed. A workaround for non-vectorial patterns $x \in \mathcal{X}$ is shown in Section 5.2. The basic idea is to define a mapping $\varphi : \mathcal{X} \to \mathcal{H}$ in order to embed the general patterns x in some vector space $\mathcal{H}$ endowed with a dot product. Based on the maps $\varphi(x) \in \mathcal{H}$ a kernel defined for vectors can be applied accordingly. In fact, we have not yet discussed how such a function $\varphi : \mathcal{X} \to \mathcal{H}$ could be defined in practice. The main objective of the present book is to provide a general framework for building such functions for structural data and in particular for graphs. This procedure will be discussed in detail in the next chapter. In this section another solution for non-vectorial data is reviewed, viz. kernels directly defined for graphs.

While it might be cumbersome to define mathematical operations in some graph domain $\mathcal{G}$, a kernel $\kappa : \mathcal{G} \times \mathcal{G} \to \mathbb{R}$ might be much easier to obtain[7]. By means of suitable kernel functions, graphs can be implicitly

---

[7]Remember that a kernel function is a measure of similarity satisfying the conditions of symmetry and positive definiteness.

mapped into dot product spaces $\mathcal{F}$. That is, rather than defining hand-crafted operations or quantities in $\mathcal{G}$, these operations are carried out in $\mathcal{F}$ by means of the kernel trick. Consequently, a large class of algorithms for pattern recognition (all kernel machines), most of them originally developed for vectors, become applicable to graphs.

Clearly, by means of graph kernels one can benefit from both the high representational power of graphs and the large repository of algorithmic tools available for feature vector representations. A number of graph kernels have been proposed in the literature. For an early survey see [139]. In the present section four classes of graph kernels are discussed whereof one graph kernel is used as second reference system for our further experimental evaluation.

Diffusion Kernels   A first class of graph kernels is given by diffusion kernels. The kernels of this class are defined with respect to a base similarity measure which is used to construct a kernel matrix [148–153]. This base similarity measure only needs to satisfy the condition of symmetry to guarantee that the resulting kernel matrix is positive definite. Obviously, the diffusion kernel can be defined for any kind of objects and particularly for graphs. Assume that a graph set $\{g_1, \ldots, g_N\} \subseteq \mathcal{G}$, a decay factor $0 < \lambda < 1$, and a similarity measure $s : \mathcal{G} \times \mathcal{G} \to \mathbb{R}$ defined on graphs are given. The $N \times N$ matrix $\mathbf{S} = (s_{ij})_{N \times N}$ of pairwise similarities s_{ij} can be turned into a positive definite kernel matrix $\mathbf{K} = (\kappa_{ij})_{N \times N}$ through the *exponential diffusion kernel* [148] defined by

$$\mathbf{K} = \sum_{k=0}^{\infty} \frac{1}{k!} \lambda^k \mathbf{S}^k = \exp(\lambda \mathbf{S})$$

or the *von Neumann diffusion kernel* [149] defined by

$$\mathbf{K} = \sum_{k=0}^{\infty} \lambda^k \mathbf{S}^k \quad .$$

The decay factor λ assures that the weighting factor λ^k will be negligibly small for sufficiently large k. Therefore, only the first t addends in the diffusion kernel sums have to be evaluated in practice. The key idea of diffusion kernels is to enhance the base similarity measure by considering not only the similarity of two patterns, but also the number of similar patterns they have in common. Of course, any graph (dis)similarity measure can be used to build a diffusion kernel for graphs. In [28], for instance, a diffusion kernel from graph edit distance $d : \mathcal{G} \times \mathcal{G} \to \mathbb{R}$ is derived. To this end, the authors turn the edit distance for graphs into a similarity measure by some simple transformations.

Convolution Kernel A seminal contribution in the field of graph kernel is the work on convolution kernels, which provides a general framework for dealing with complex objects that consist of simpler parts [141, 142]. Convolution kernels infer the similarity of composite objects from the similarity of their parts. The rationale behind this approach is that a similarity function might more easily be defined or more efficiently be computed for smaller parts rather than for the whole composite object. Given the similarities between the simpler parts of the underlying objects, a convolution operation is eventually applied in order to turn them into a kernel function.

Clearly, graphs g from some graph domain $\mathcal{G}$ are complex composite objects as they consist of nodes and edges. The concept of decomposing a graph g into its parts is mathematically denoted by a relation R, where $R(g_1, \ldots, g_d, g)$ represents the decomposition of g into parts $(g_1, \ldots, g_d)$. By $R^{-1}(g) = \{(g_1, \ldots, g_d) : R(g_1, \ldots, g_d, g)\}$ we denote the set of decompositions of any graph $g \in \mathcal{G}$. For a simple example, assume that the set of all decompositions of a graph $g = (V, E, \mu, \nu) \in \mathcal{G}$ is defined by $R^{-1}(g) = V$. Hence, all of g's nodes are a valid decomposition of g. For the definition of the convolution kernel, a kernel function κ_i is required for each part of a decomposition $\{g_i\}_{1 \le i \le d}$. For instance, if $R^{-1}(g) = V$, a kernel function measuring the similarity of the involved nodes could be employed for κ_i. The convolution kernel function for graphs $g, g' \in \mathcal{G}$ can then be written as

$$\kappa(g, g') = \sum_{\substack{(g_1, \ldots, g_d) \in R^{-1}(g) \\ (g'_1, \ldots, g'_d) \in R^{-1}(g')}} \prod_{i=1}^{d} \kappa_i(g_i, g'_i) \ .$$

Hence, this graph kernel derives the similarity between two graphs g and g' from the sum, over all decompositions, of the similarity product of the parts of g and g' [28]. The ANOVA kernel [143], for instance, is a particular convolution kernel, which uses a subset of the components of a composite object for comparison.

Walk Kernel A third class of graph kernels is based on the analysis of random walks in graphs. These kernels measure the similarity of two graphs by the number of random walks in both graphs that have all or some labels in common [44, 45, 140, 145–147]. In [140] an important result is reported. It is shown that the number of matching walks in two graphs can be computed by means of the *direct product graph* of two graphs, without the need to explicitly enumerate the walks. This allows us to consider random walks of arbitrary length.

Definition 5.5 (Direct Product Graph). *The direct product graph of two graphs* $g = (V, E, \mu, \nu)$ *and* $g' = (V', E', \mu', \nu')$ *is the graph* $(g \times g') = (V_\times, E_\times, \mu_\times, \nu_\times)$ *where*

- $V_\times = \{(u, u') \in V \times V' : \mu(u) = \mu'(u')\}$
- $E_\times = \{((u, u'), (v, v')) \in V_\times \times V_\times : (u, v) \in E \text{ and } (u', v') \in E' \text{ and } \nu(u, v) = \nu'(u', v')\}$.

The direct product graph, by definition, identifies the compatible nodes and edges in the two graphs. Given a weighting parameter $\lambda \geq 0$, one can derive a kernel function for graphs $g, g' \in \mathcal{G}$ from the adjacency matrix $\mathbf{A}_\times$ of their product graph $(g \times g')$ by defining

$$\kappa(g, g') = \sum_{i,j=1}^{|V_\times|} \left[\sum_{n=0}^{\infty} \lambda^n \mathbf{A}_\times^n \right]_{ij} .$$

With a weighting factor $\lambda < 1$ it is assured that the contribution of $\lambda^n \mathbf{A}_\times^n$ to the overall sum will be negligibly small for sufficiently large n. Therefore, only the first t terms in the random walk kernel sums have to be evaluated.

In order to handle continuous labels, the random walk kernel has been extended in [44]. This extension allows one to also take non-identically labeled walks into account. In [45] two kernels, the so-called all-path and the shortest-path kernel, are introduced. These kernels consider paths between two pairs of nodes in a graph and use the similarity of two pairs of paths in order to derive the final kernel value. Another kernel that considers paths and label sequences encountered along the paths in two graphs is described in [46]. The problem of tottering is addressed in [27]. Tottering is the phenomenon that, in a walk, a node may be revisited immediately after it has been left. In order to prevent tottering, the random walk transition probability model is appropriately modified in [27].

Similarity Kernel from Graph Graph Edit Distance In case of graphs, the edit distance already provides us with a flexible and widely used graph dissimilarity measure $d : \mathcal{G} \times \mathcal{G} \to \mathbb{R}$. Hence, it might be tempting to turn the existing dissimilarity d into a similarity measure s. The advantage of such an approach is that the cumbersome definition of novel kernel functions measuring the similarity of graphs is not required [28].

Instead, one simply uses the transformed distances as kernel values to be fed into a kernel machine.

The proposed approach basically turns the existing dissimilarity measure (graph edit distance) into a similarity measure by mapping low distance values to high similarity values and vice versa. To this end we use a monotonically decreasing transformation. Given the edit distance $d(g, g')$ of two graphs g and g', the similarity kernel is defined by

$$\kappa(g, g') = \exp(-\gamma d(g, g')^2) \quad ,$$

where $\gamma > 0$. In [261] this similarity kernel is explicitly suggested for classifying distance-based data. Note that this kernel function is not positive definite in general. However, there is theoretical evidence that using kernel machines in conjunction with indefinite kernels may be reasonable if some conditions are fulfilled [28, 261].

5.6 Experimental Evaluation

The present experimental evaluation considers the similarity kernel derived from graph edit distance in conjunction with an SVM for a classification task. The purpose of this experimental evaluation is to find out whether it is beneficial to feed the kernel values derived from the distance information into a kernel machine rather than directly using the same information with a distance based classifier. One of the few classifiers directly applicable to arbitrary graphs is the k-nearest-neighbor classifier (k-NN) in conjunction with graph edit distance. Hence, as reference system this classifier is employed (see Section 4.2). We use all available data sets previously described in Chapter 4. For the similarity kernel two meta parameters have to be tuned, viz. C (weighting parameter in the SVM) and λ (weighting parameter in the kernel function). Both parameters are optimized on the validation set, and the best performing parameter pair is eventually applied to the independent test set.

In Table 5.2 the classification accuracies on all data sets on the validation and test set are given. In the first column, the reference system's accuracy is indicated. On eight out of ten data sets, the SVM in conjunction with the similarity kernel outperforms the traditional k-NN directly applied in the graph domain. Note that five of these improvements are statistically significant. Hence, using the distance information given by the graph edit distance, transforming it in order to derive kernel values, and finally feeding them into the powerful support vector machine for classification, is clearly

Table 5.2 Classification accuracy of an optimized k-NN on the test set (first reference system described in Section 3.4.1 and 4.2) and classification accuracy of the similarity kernel $\kappa = \exp(-\gamma d(g_i, g_j))$ on the validation set (va) and on the test set (te).

| | k-NN | Similarity Kernel | |
Data Set	te	va	te
Letter low	99.3	99.7	99.6
Letter medium	94.4	96.4	94.9
Letter high	89.1	94.0	92.9 ①
Digit	97.4	97.8	98.1 ①
Fingerprint	79.1	82.3	82.0 ①
GREC	82.2	90.4	71.6 ❶
AIDS	94.9	98.0	97.0 ①
Mutagenicity	66.9	72.4	68.6
Protein	68.5	64.0	68.5
Webpage	80.6	81.8	83.0 ①

Z-test for testing statistical significance ($\alpha = 0.05$):

① Stat. significant improvement over the first reference system (k-NN).
❶ Stat. significant deterioration compared to the first reference system (k-NN).

beneficial. That is, the kernel approach generally leads to an improvement of the classification accuracy compared to distance based nearest-neighbor classifiers.

For the remainder of this book, this similarity kernel will serve as a second reference system for classification scenarios. Comparing the performance of our proposed graph embedding framework with this particular kernel might be the first step towards understanding whether the power of our framework is primarily due to sophisticated kernel machines or rather the strength of the novel embedding procedure developed within this book.

5.7 Summary

Kernel theory allows one to carry out the extension of basic linear algorithms to complex non-linear methods, preserving the efficiency previously reserved for linear methods [5]. Assume a possibly non-linear function $\phi : \mathcal{X} \to \mathcal{F}$ mapping patterns from the original space $\mathcal{X}$ to some feature space $\mathcal{F}$ of high or even infinite dimensionality is given. As shown in this chapter, a kernel function $\kappa(x, x')$ returns the dot product $\langle \phi(x), \phi(x') \rangle$ between two maps $\phi(x)$ and $\phi(x')$ in this (implicitly existing) feature space $\mathcal{F}$. Hence, kernel functions enable us to evaluate the dot product of two patterns in the feature space $\mathcal{F}$ without explicitly computing their coordinates in $\mathcal{F}$ via mapping $\phi(\cdot)$. This procedure, which can be seen as a shortcut for the efficient computation of dot products in high-dimensional spaces, is commonly termed kernel trick. In Fig. 5.8 the kernel trick is illustrated.

The kernel trick has a huge impact in practice and in particular in the design of algorithms. That is, any algorithm that can be reformulated in terms of dot products only, can be extended implicitly in the feature space $\mathcal{F}$ by replacing each dot product $\langle \cdot, \cdot \rangle$ by a kernel evaluation $\kappa(\cdot, \cdot)$. Such algorithms together with some kernel function are commonly referred to as kernel machines. For instance, support vector machines, principal component analysis, and k-means clustering are kernel machines and will actually be employed in the present book.

Applying a linear algorithm (e.g. an SVM which is a linear classifier) in an implicit feature space $\mathcal{F}$ rather than in the original pattern space $\mathcal{X}$ has enormous potential. In fact, given an appropriate non-linear mapping $\phi : \mathcal{X} \to \mathcal{F}$, a linear decision boundary in $\mathcal{F}$ corresponds to a non-linear decision boundary in $\mathcal{X}$. Consequently, by means of kernel machines, linear methods can be extended to detect non-linear regularities in $\mathcal{X}$ without loosing their efficiency and well-founded mathematical and statistical properties.

The main result of kernel theory is that it is perfectly sufficient to extract information about pairwise similarity of patterns from the problem domain by means of a kernel function in order to apply non-linear versions of well-known algorithms for pattern recognition. Consequently, this provides us with another crucial advantage over traditional methods. In fact, using a kernel function for graphs, the original patterns from some graph domain can be implicitly mapped to a dot product space. The tremendous benefit of applying such an embedding to graphs is that it instantly eliminates the lack of mathematical structure in the domain of graphs.

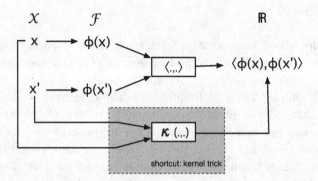

Fig. 5.8   Comparing the explicit mapping of patterns x and x' in a feature space $\mathcal{F}$ via ϕ and subsequent dot product computation with the shortcut *kernel-trick*. Note that the pattern space $\mathcal{X}$ can be any domain (e.g. the domain of graphs $\mathcal{G}$, or a vector space $\mathcal{H}$).

In a preliminary experiment a graph kernel directly derived from graph edit distances is tested on the graph data sets featured in this book. The results clearly suggests that using kernel machines in conjunction with such a kernel, rather than using the same distance information in a more direct fashion, is clearly beneficial. This particular similarity kernel will serve us as a further reference system in the remainder of this book.

Graph Embedding Using Dissimilarities

6

> It's very satisfying to take a
> problem we thought difficult
> and find a simple solution. The
> best solutions are always
> simple.
>
> Ivan Edward Sutherland

After decades of focusing on independent and identically-distributed representation formalisms, more and more effort is now rendered in various research fields on structured data (e.g. in chemoinformatics [46] or in document analysis [48]). That is, the intensive study of problems where the objects under consideration consist of interrelated entities has emerged rapidly in the last decade. Therefore, a continuously growing interest in graph-based object representations for pattern recognition and machine learning can be observed [40, 43, 75, 262]. As a matter of fact, object representations by means of graphs is advantageous compared to vectorial approaches because of two reasons. First, graphs are able to represent not only the values of object properties, i.e. features, but can be used to explicitly model relations that exist between different parts of an object. Second, graphs do not suffer from the constraint of fixed dimensionality. That is, the number of nodes and edges in a graph is not limited a priori and depends on the size and the complexity of the actual object to be modeled.

Yet, one drawback of graphs, when compared to feature vectors, is the significantly increased complexity of many algorithms. Nevertheless, new computer generations, which are now able to more efficiently handle complex data structures, as well as the development of fast approximate algorithms for graph comparisons definitively empowered researchers to use graphs in their respective problem domains [40]. Yet, another serious limitation in the use of graphs for object classification or clustering arises from the fact that there is little mathematical structure in the domain of graphs. For example, computing the (weighted) sum or the product of a pair of entities is not possible in the domain of graphs, or is at least not defined in general for graph structures.

In order to overcome the resulting lack of algorithmic tools applicable to graphs, the traditional approach is to give up the universality of graphs in favor of efficient feature vectors, even in problem domains where graphs would be the method of choice [39]. Yet, with the extension of kernel methods to structured data [262] and in particular to graphs [39, 139, 262, 263], the sacrifice of losing representational power and flexibility in the data structure to be used has no longer to be made. As seen in the previous chapter, graph kernels aim at an implicit embedding of graphs from some graph domain $\mathcal{G}$ in a feature space $\mathcal{F}$. The term "implicit" stems from the fact that the feature space $\mathcal{F}$ remains unknown. The only fact we know is that $\mathcal{F}$ exists and that the dot product in $\mathcal{F}$ is equal to the evaluated kernel function in the original graph domain $\mathcal{G}$. Pattern recognition tasks which can be accomplished with kernel machines, i.e. with algorithms that use pairwise dot products rather than individual patterns, can therefore be implicitly carried out in $\mathcal{F}$ by means of graph kernels.

The present book's objective is similar to that of graph kernels, i.e. we want to benefit from both the universality of graphs for pattern representation and the computational convenience of vectors for pattern recognition. In contrast to graph kernels, however, the proposed framework results in an explicit embedding of graphs from some graph domain $\mathcal{G}$ in a real vector space $\mathbb{R}^n$. Formally, the main contribution of the present book is a general procedure for defining functions $\varphi : \mathcal{G} \to \mathbb{R}^n$ mapping graphs from arbitrary graph domains to a vector space. Based on the resulting graph maps, the considered pattern recognition task is eventually carried out. Hence, the whole arsenal of algorithmic tools readily available for vectorial data can be applied to graphs (more exactly to graph maps $\varphi(g) \in \mathbb{R}^n$). Moreover, as seen in the previous chapter, an embedding specified by $\varphi : \mathcal{G} \to \mathbb{R}^n$ provides us with the possibility to indirectly apply any vector kernel κ to graphs g from $\mathcal{G}$ (Lemma 5.1).

The remainder of this chapter is organized as follows. Next, work related to our graph embedding framework is discussed. This is done in two parts. First, other graph embedding techniques are reviewed. Second, the recently emerged idea underlying our graph embedding framework, the dissimilarity representation for pattern recognition, is summarized. Then, in Section 6.2

the general graph embedding procedure including some basic properties is introduced. Additionally, the close relationship of the proposed embedding procedure to kernel methods as well as to Lipschitz embeddings is clarified. The remaining sections of this chapter are devoted to the crucial task of prototype selection and prototype reduction, feature selection, and dimensionality reduction. In fact, this builds an essential step in our embedding framework. Therefore, various strategies resolving this critical issue are proposed.

6.1 Related Work

6.1.1 *Graph Embedding Techniques*

In recent years various efforts to embed graphs in vector spaces have been made. From another perspective, graph embeddings can be viewed as an extraction of descriptive numerical features from graphs. *Topological descriptors*, for instance, aim at a vectorial summary of the graph's topology. The *Wiener index* [264], defined as the sum over all shortest paths in a graph, is a prominent example of such a descriptor. A large amount of other descriptors are used in chemoinformatics in order to encode molecular compounds (see [265] for an exhaustive survey on topological descriptors). The problem with topological descriptors is that none of them is general enough to work properly on different kinds of graphs [39]. Hence, the choice of the set of numerical features to be actually extracted for a particular graph embedding is somewhat handcrafted and not general at all.

Various graph embedding procedures based on spectral methods [266] have been proposed in the literature [51, 156–162, 177, 266–268]. Spectral graph theory is concerned with understanding how the structural properties of graphs can be characterized using eigenvectors of the adjacency or Laplacian matrix [161][1]. In the seminal contribution of Umeyama [156] the idea of spectral methods is used for the first time for the purpose of exact graph matching (but not yet for graph embedding). The basic idea of Umeyama's algorithm is to perform a singular value decomposition on the adjacency matrices of the graphs to be matched. By means of the sum of the outer products of the sets of corresponding singular vectors, the correspondence between the nodes, i.e. the permutation matrix, is found. A severe shortcoming of this approach is that graphs to be processed have to

---

[1]Hence, spectral methods can also be seen as topological descriptors.

be of the same size. This particular problem is overcome by the work presented in [177]. The authors show how the problem of graph matching can be posed as maximum-likelihood estimation using the apparatus of the EM algorithm. The correspondence between the graph nodes is established in a matrix framework which allows one to efficiently recover matches between nodes using the singular value decomposition. Note that this method is purely structural, meaning that no node or edge labels are taken into account. Moreover, similarly to Umeyama's algorithm this procedure aims at a direct graph matching, i.e. no explicit vector space embedding of graphs is established.

In the follow-up work [51, 159], however, a vector space embedding of graphs based on the spectral approach is proposed. The authors make use of the leading eigenvectors of the graph adjacency matrix to define eigenmodes of the adjacency matrix. For each eigenmode, a number of spectral properties are computed. The resulting property vectors are eventually embedded in a feature space using principal component analysis [247] and multidimensional scaling [224]. In [158] a retrieval task based on a graph spectral characterization is accomplished with a nearest-neighbor search. Another approach for graph embedding has been proposed in [162]. The authors use the relationship between the Laplace-Beltrami operator and the graph Laplacian to embed a graph onto a Riemannian manifold.

A further idea deals with string edit distance applied to the eigensystem of graphs [267]. This procedure results in distances between graphs which are used to embed the graphs into a vector space by means of multidimensional scaling. In [161] the authors turn to the spectral decomposition of the Laplacian matrix. They show how the elements of the spectral matrix for the Laplacian can be used to construct symmetric polynomials. In order to encode graphs as vectors, the coefficients of these polynomials are used as graph features.

In [160, 157] a projection of the graph's nodes onto the eigensubspace spanned by the leading eigenvectors is explored. By means of a clustering approach, the node-to-node correspondence in the established vector space is obtained. Finally, in [268] a strategy similar to Isomap [269] is applied to trees[2]. In this work the geodesic distances between the tree's nodes are computed resulting in a distance matrix for each individual tree. Via multidimensional scaling the nodes are embedded in a Euclidean space where spectral methods are eventually applied.

---

[2]Isomap is a non-linear transformation of input patterns that can be applied to arbitrary domains where a dissimilarity measure is available.

Although graph spectralization exhibits interesting properties which can be used for both direct graph matching and vector space embedding of graphs, this approach remains somewhat limited. For instance, spectral methods are not fully able to cope with larger amounts of noise. This stems from the fact that the eigendecomposition is very sensitive towards structural errors, such as missing or spurious nodes [28]. Moreover, spectral methods are applicable to unlabeled graphs or labeled graphs with severely constrained label alphabets only, making this approach for graph embedding only to a limited extent applicable to graphs extracted from real-world data.

In the present book a novel approach for graph embedding is established. The main ideas for this framework are based on the work on dissimilarity representation for pattern recognition done by Pekalska and Duin [4], which is described next.

6.1.2 *Dissimilarities as a Representation Formalism*

During the past ten years the crucial importance of dissimilarities in the field of pattern recognition and machine learning has been regularly pointed out by various researchers [70, 71, 270–272][3]. However, the idea of using dissimilarities as pattern representation emerged only recently [4] and is picked up in the present book for graph based pattern recognition.

Typically, objects from a certain class are similar with respect to some basic characteristics. Hence, it is the similarity of objects that groups them together to meaningful classes, or in other words the dissimilarity that separates the individual classes from each other. Based on this observation, the authors of [4] infer that a notion of dissimilarity, i.e. proximity, is more fundamental than that of a feature or a class and therefore argue to use the dissimilarities (instead of features) as a primary concept for pattern representation.

The basic idea of dissimilarity representation is to represent a particular object with a number of dissimilarities to a set of prototypical objects. Therefore, rather than a vector of features, a vector of dissimilarities is used in order to represent the patterns and carry out pattern recognition task. More formally, in the traditional approach of statistical pattern recognition,

---

[3]There is also a recent international collaborative CORDIS project about similarity based pattern analysis and recognition (SIMBAD) clearly emphasizing the growing interest in (dis)similarity based pattern recognition (http://cordis.europa.eu, project reference 212250).

a set of features is defined first and the underlying patterns are represented as points in the respective feature vector space. In the dissimilarity approach a dissimilarity measure is imposed and the underlying patterns are represented by their dissimilarities to other objects. In view of this, the feature vector approach can be seen as an absolute representation while the dissimilarity representation can be interpreted as a relative representation of the underlying patterns.

Given that the underlying dissimilarity measure is powerful enough to capture the important differences between patterns, related objects (e.g. objects from the same class sharing some fundamental characteristics) most probably exhibit similar dissimilarities to some reference objects. Consequently, the more similar two objects are, the more similar their corresponding dissimilarity representation will be. In view of this, using dissimilarities as features for a numerical description of the patterns definitely makes sense.

Based on the dissimilarity representation three lines of further processing are pursued in [4]. The first approach directly feeds the dissimilarities into a distance based classifier (e.g. a k-nearest-neighbor classifier). The second idea finds a spatial representation defined according to the underlying dissimilarities. More formally, a vector space $\mathcal{H}$ is found where the patterns are mapped to points such that their distances in $\mathcal{H}$ best reflect the actual dissimilarities originally computed. This mapping can be carried out, for instance, by means of multidimensional scaling [224]. Finally, in a third approach, the dissimilarities are interpreted as a novel vectorial description of the patterns. Based on these dissimilarity vectors, the pattern recognition task is carried out by means of any algorithm working with vectorial data. Hence, from a higher level perspective, the third method allows the embedding of sets of patterns in dissimilarity spaces.

Note that dissimilarities can be computed on structural data as well as on vectorial data (similar to kernels). Consequently, the dissimilarity representation can also be viewed as natural bridge between statistical and structural pattern recognition. In the context of graph based pattern recognition, the first line of research proposed in [4] is already covered by our first reference system, namely the k-nearest-neighbor classifier which directly operates on graph edit distances. Our second reference system which infers a kernel value from dissimilarities can be interpreted as spatial embedding in some implicit existing feature space $\mathcal{F}$. Consequently, the second approach of using dissimilarities proposed in [4] is also covered by one of the reference systems discussed so far. The third approach, however, highly attracts interest for graph based pattern recognition. In the case of graphs the extraction of numerical features, which preserve the rich topological information represented by a graph, is difficult in general (see discussion about graph embedding techniques above). Yet, proximity can directly be derived from graphs using an adequate dissimilarity model. In fact, various existing graph matching paradigms provide us with different dissimilarity models for graphs (see Chapter 2 and particularly [40] for a review of various graph matching techniques).

Clearly, the dissimilarity representation extended to the domain of graphs leads to a universal framework for mapping graphs to real vector spaces. Actually, this third line of research will be employed in the present book for graph based pattern recognition.

6.2 Graph Embedding Using Dissimilarities

6.2.1 *General Embedding Procedure and Properties*

The idea of our graph embedding framework stems from the seminal work done by Duin and Pekalska [4] where dissimilarities for pattern representation are used for the first time. Later this method was extended so as to map string representations into vector spaces [273]. In the current book we go one step further and generalize and substantially extend the methods described in [4, 273] to the domain of graphs. The key idea of this approach is to use the distances of an input graph to a number of training graphs, termed *prototype graphs*, as a vectorial description of the graph. That is, we use the dissimilarity representation for pattern recognition rather than the original graph based representation.

Assume we have a set of sample graphs, $\mathcal{T} = \{g_1, \ldots, g_N\}$ from some graph domain $\mathcal{G}$ and an arbitrary graph dissimilarity measure $d : \mathcal{G} \times \mathcal{G} \to \mathbb{R}$. Note that $\mathcal{T}$ can be any kind of graph set, i.e. the samples in $\mathcal{T}$ can even be synthesized graphs. However, for the sake of convenience we define $\mathcal{T}$ as a training set of existing graphs. After selecting a set of prototypical graphs $\mathcal{P} \subseteq \mathcal{T}$, we compute the dissimilarity of a given input graph g to each prototype graph $p_i \in \mathcal{P}$. Note that g can be an element of $\mathcal{T}$ or any other graph set $\mathcal{S}$. Given n prototypes, i.e. $\mathcal{P} = \{p_1, \ldots, p_n\}$, this procedure leads to n dissimilarities, $d_1 = d(g, p_1), \ldots, d_n = d(g, p_n)$, which can be arranged in an n-dimensional vector $(d_1, \ldots, d_n)$.

Definition 6.1 (Graph Embedding). *Let us assume a graph domain $\mathcal{G}$ is given. If $\mathcal{T} = \{g_1, \ldots, g_N\} \subseteq \mathcal{G}$ is a training set with N graphs and $\mathcal{P} = \{p_1, \ldots, p_n\} \subseteq \mathcal{T}$ is a prototype set with $n \leq N$ graphs, the mapping*

$$\varphi_n^{\mathcal{P}} : \mathcal{G} \to \mathbb{R}^n$$

is defined as the function

$$\varphi_n^{\mathcal{P}}(g) = (d(g, p_1), \ldots, d(g, p_n)),$$

where $d(g, p_i)$ is any graph dissimilarity measure between graph g and the i-th prototype graph.

Obviously, by means of this definition we obtain a vector space where each axis is associated with a prototype graph $p_i \in \mathcal{P}$ and the coordinate values of an embedded graph g are the distances of g to the elements in $\mathcal{P}$. In this way we can transform any graph g from the training set $\mathcal{T}$ as well as any other graph set $\mathcal{S}$ (for instance a validation or a test set of a classification problem), into a vector of real numbers. In other words, the graph set to be embedded can be arbitrarily extended. Training graphs which have been selected as prototypes before have a zero entry in their corresponding graph map. The embedding procedure is illustrated in Fig. 6.1.

The embedding procedure proposed in this book makes use of graph edit distance. Note, however, that any other graph dissimilarity measure can be used as well. Yet, using graph edit distance allows us to deal with a large class of graphs (directed, undirected, unlabeled, node and/or edge labels from any finite or infinite domain). Furthermore, due to the flexibility of graph edit distance, a high degree of robustness against various graph distortions can be expected.

Since the computation of graph edit distance is exponential in the number of nodes for general graphs, the complexity of this graph embedding is exponential as well. However, as mentioned in Chapter 3, there exist efficient approximation algorithms for graph edit distance computation with cubic time complexity [125, 126]. Consequently, given n predefined prototypes the embedding of one particular graph is established by means of n distance computations with polynomial time.

After two graphs, g and g', have been mapped to the vector space, we

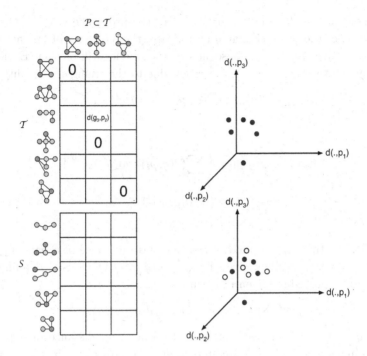

Fig. 6.1 Based on a prototype set $\mathcal{P} \subseteq \mathcal{T}$ the graphs from the training set $\mathcal{T}$ as well as graphs from some additional data set $\mathcal{S}$ are transformed into a vector of dissimilarities. Formally, by means of the proposed embedding for each graph $g \in \mathcal{T} \cup \mathcal{S}$ a vector $\varphi_n^{\mathcal{P}}(g) = (d(g, p_1), \ldots, d(g, p_n))$ is established, where $d(g, p_i)$ represents the distance of the embedded graph g to the i-th prototype from $\mathcal{P}$. Black dots represent embedded graphs from $\mathcal{T}$, while white dots are embedded graphs from $\mathcal{S}$. Note that training graphs, which have been selected as prototypes before, have a zero entry in their corresponding vector.

observe the following relationship[4]:

$$\|\varphi(g) - \varphi(g')\| = (\langle \varphi(g), \varphi(g) \rangle + \langle \varphi(g'), \varphi(g') \rangle - 2\langle \varphi(g), \varphi(g') \rangle)^{\frac{1}{2}}$$

$$= \left(\sum_{i=1}^{n} d(g, p_i)^2 + \sum_{i=1}^{n} d(g', p_i)^2 - 2 \sum_{i=1}^{n} d(g, p_i) d(g', p_i) \right)^{\frac{1}{2}}$$

$$= \left(\sum_{i=1}^{n} (d(g, p_i) - d(g', p_i))^2 \right)^{\frac{1}{2}} \tag{6.1}$$

Hence, the Euclidean distance of a pair of graphs g and g' in the embedded vector space is equal to the square root of the sum of squared differences

---

[4]For the purpose of simplicity we write $\varphi(g)$ for $\varphi_n^{\mathcal{P}}(g)$.

between the edit distances of g and g' to the prototype graphs. Given d is a metric, the more similar g and g' are, the smaller will be the terms $(d(g, p_i) - d(g', p_i))^2$ and, consequently, the smaller will be their Euclidean distance in the vector space. Moreover, due to the triangle inequality

$$|d(g, p_i) - d(g', p_i)| \leq d(g, g') \quad,$$

we have

$$\|\varphi(g) - \varphi(g')\| = \left(\sum_{i=1}^{n} (d(g, p_i) - d(g', p_i))^2\right)^{\frac{1}{2}}$$
$$\leq \left(n \cdot d(g, g')^2\right)^{\frac{1}{2}}$$
$$= \sqrt{n} \cdot d(g, g') \tag{6.2}$$

That is, the upper bound of the Euclidean distance of a pair of graph maps $\varphi(g)$ and $\varphi(g')$ is given by $\sqrt{n} \cdot d(g, g')$. Obviously, defining the embedding procedure given in Definition 6.1 as

$$\varphi_n^{\mathcal{P}}(g) = (d(g, p_1)/q, \ldots, d(g, p_n)/q) \quad,$$

with $q = \sqrt{n}$, the upper bound of the Euclidean distance of a pair of graph maps $\varphi(g)$ and $\varphi(g')$ amounts to $d(g, g')$. Obviously, by means of the normalization by q, the influence of the number of prototypes is reduced. Hence, regardless of the number of prototypes n, it is guaranteed that distances in the resulting embedding space are bounded by the original graph edit distance $d(g, g')$.

6.2.2 Relation to Kernel Methods

Dissimilarity embeddings strongly remind one of kernel methods. Remember that in the kernel approach the patterns are described by means of pairwise kernel functions representing similarity, while in the dissimilarity approach patterns are described by pairwise dissimilarities. However, there is another fundamental difference between kernel functions and dissimilarity embeddings. In the former method, the kernel values are interpreted as dot products in some feature space in an implicit fashion. By means of kernel machines, the pattern recognition task is eventually carried out in this kernel feature space. In the latter approach, the set of dissimilarities is interpreted as novel vectorial description of the pattern under consideration. Hence, no implicit feature space is assumed by our approach, but an explicit dissimilarity space is obtained.

Although conceptually different, the embedding paradigm established by $\varphi_n^{\mathcal{P}} : \mathcal{G} \to \mathbb{R}^n$ constitutes a foundation for a novel class of graph kernels. Due to the closure properties defined in Chapter 5 one can define a valid graph kernel κ based on the graph embedding $\varphi_n^{\mathcal{P}} : \mathcal{G} \to \mathbb{R}^n$ by computing the standard dot product of two graph maps in the resulting vector space

$$\kappa_{\langle\rangle}(g, g') = \langle \varphi_n^{\mathcal{P}}(g), \varphi_n^{\mathcal{P}}(g') \rangle \quad.$$

Of course, not only the standard dot product can be used but any valid kernel function defined for vectors (see Chapter 5). For instance an RBF kernel function

$$\kappa_{RBF}(g, g') = \exp\left(-\gamma \|\varphi_n^{\mathcal{P}}(g) - \varphi_n^{\mathcal{P}}(g')\|^2\right)$$

with $\gamma > 0$ can thus be applied to graph maps. We refer to this procedure as *graph embedding kernel* using some specific vector kernel function.

The graph embedding kernel is very similar to the so called *empirical kernel map* proposed in [274]. The rationale of this procedure is to convert arbitrary similarity measures defined on some pattern space $\mathcal{X}$ into a valid kernel in a principled way. Given a similarity measure $s : \mathcal{X} \times \mathcal{X} \to \mathbb{R}$ which does not necessarily satisfy the conditions of symmetry and positive-definiteness (hence s does not constitute to be a valid kernel), a procedure as defined in Definition 6.1 can be carried out transforming any pattern $x \in \mathcal{X}$ into a vector of similarities. The empirical kernel map eventually suggests to compute the dot product between two similarity vectors, leading to a valid kernel on pairs of patterns from $\mathcal{X}$.

Also, the graph embedding kernel is somewhat similar in spirit to the subgraph kernel proposed in [154]. However, rather than using a potentially infinite set of subgraphs, we restrict our considerations to a finite number of prototypes, i.e. dimensions. Furthermore, rather than counting the number of occurrences of a particular subgraph within some host graph, we employ the edit distance in order to capture graph similarity. Obviously, large values of the kernel function occur when both g and g' are similar to the same prototype graphs. Whenever both g and g' are similar to the same prototype graphs we may conclude that g and g' are similar to each other. Using the graph edit distance rather than counting the number of occurrences of certain subgraphs allows us to flexibly deal with various kinds of distortions that may affect the underlying graphs.

In a recent book graph kernels were proposed that directly use graph edit distances [28] (in analogy to our second reference system). This approach turns the existing dissimilarity measure (graph edit distance) into a similarity measure by mapping low distance values to high similarity values and vice versa. To this end monotonically decreasing transformations are used. Note the fundamental difference between such an approach and our graph embedding procedure. While in the recently proposed methodology the existing dissimilarity measure is turned into a similarity measure (i.e. a kernel function) and subsequently directly plugged into a kernel machine, our procedure uses the dissimilarities to n prototypes as features for a new explicit vectorial description of the underlying object. Therefore not only kernel machines, but also other non-kernelizable algorithms can be applied in conjunction with the proposed graph embedding method.

6.2.3 *Relation to Lipschitz Embeddings*

Our dissimilarity embedding procedure has a close relation to Lipschitz embeddings [275–278]. The basic idea of Lipschitz embeddings is that an object o is transformed into a vector such that each of its components corresponds to the distance of o to a predefined reference set.

Originally, Lipschitz embeddings were proposed to embed metric spaces into other ones with low distortion. In [278], for instance, Lipschitz embeddings are used for similarity searching in metric spaces. The intuition behind Lipschitz embedding is that important information of an object is captured by its distances to the reference sets [278]. In the context of the present book the paradigm of Lipschitz embedding is adopted in order to transform a graph domain $\mathcal{G}$ into a vector space $\mathbb{R}^n$. Note that this approach can be seen as a generalization of the dissimilarity embeddings for graphs proposed in Definition 6.1 where only singleton reference sets are defined.

In order to apply Lipschitz embeddings to graphs (further details will be presented later in this section), the graph edit distance function $d(g, g')$ has to be extended.

Definition 6.2 (Extended Graph Edit Distance). *Consider a single graph g and a set of m graphs $\mathcal{P} = \{p_1, \ldots, p_m\}$. We define functions $f_{min}, f_{max}, f_{mean}$ of the m graph edit distances $\{d(g, p_i)\}_{1 \leq i \leq m}$ as*

$$f_{min}(g, \mathcal{P}) = \min_{p \in \mathcal{P}}\{d(g, p)\}$$

$$f_{max}(g, \mathcal{P}) = \max_{p \in \mathcal{P}}\{d(g, p)\}$$

$$f_{mean}(g, \mathcal{P}) = \frac{\sum_{p \in \mathcal{P}} d(g, p)}{m}$$

Obviously, $f_{min}(g, \mathcal{P})$ and $f_{max}(g, \mathcal{P})$ are equal to the distance from g to the nearest and furthest element $p \in \mathcal{P}$, respectively. The function $f_{mean}(g, \mathcal{P})$ is equal to the average distance from g to all elements $p \in \mathcal{P}$.

Let us assume that a set of graphs $\mathcal{T} = \{g_1, \ldots, g_N\}$ from some graph domain $\mathcal{G}$ is given. We first define a set $\mathcal{Q} = \{\mathcal{P}_1, \ldots, \mathcal{P}_n\}$ consisting of n subsets of $\mathcal{T}$. The n subsets $\mathcal{P}_i \subset \mathcal{T}$ are called *reference sets* of the Lipschitz embedding.

Definition 6.3 (Lipschitz Embedding of Graphs).
The Lipschitz embedding with respect to $\mathcal{Q} = \{\mathcal{P}_1, \ldots, \mathcal{P}_n\}$ is a function $\varphi_{\mathcal{Q},f} : \mathcal{G} \to \mathbb{R}^n$ defined as

$$\varphi_{\mathcal{Q},f}(g) = (f(g, \mathcal{P}_1), \ldots, f(g, \mathcal{P}_n)) \quad ,$$

where $f \in \{f_{min}, f_{max}, f_{mean}\}$.

Obviously, the range of function $\varphi_{\mathcal{Q},f}$ is a vector space where each dimension is associated with a subset $\mathcal{P}_i \subset \mathcal{T}$ and the i-th coordinate value of the embedded graph g is the distance from g to $\mathcal{P}_i$ computed by f_{min}, f_{max}, or f_{mean}.

Similar to the graph embedding based on dissimilarities presented above, the Lipschitz embedding, and in particular the reference sets $\mathcal{Q} = \{\mathcal{P}_1, \ldots, \mathcal{P}_n\}$, can be established on a training set of graphs $\mathcal{T}$. The embedding $\varphi_{\mathcal{Q},f}$, however, can then be applied to any other graph set as well (e.g. a validation or a test set in a classification scenario).

The triangle inequality $(|d(g_1, p) - d(g_2, p)| \leq d(g_1, g_2))$ can be easily extended to the case of subsets $\mathcal{P}$ (see [279] for proofs). That is, regardless whether f_{min}, f_{max}, or f_{mean} is employed, $|f(g_1, \mathcal{P}) - f(g_2, \mathcal{P})|$ is a lower bound on $d(g_1, g_2)$:

$$|f(g_1, \mathcal{P}) - f(g_2, \mathcal{P})| \leq d(g_1, g_2) \quad .$$

Defining the Lipschitz embedding as

$$\varphi_{\mathcal{S},f}(g) = (f(g, \mathcal{P}_1)/q, \ldots, f(g, \mathcal{P}_n)/q) \quad ,$$

where $q = \sqrt{n}$, an upper bound of the Euclidean distance of a pair of graph maps in the embedding space is given by the graph edit distance between the corresponding graphs (similar to Eq. 6.2). In other words, the mapping $\varphi_{\mathcal{S},f} : \mathcal{G} \to \mathbb{R}^n$ is Lipschitz continuous as

$$\|\varphi_{\mathcal{S},f}(g_1) - \varphi_{\mathcal{S},f}(g_2)\| \leq K \cdot d(g_1, g_2)$$

with a constant $K \geq 0$ (the term *Lipschitz embedding* is derived from this basic property). The smallest K is called Lipschitz constant. In our case $K = 1$ or $K = \sqrt{n}$ depending on whether or not the normalization is applied to the graph maps.

If the computational cost of the embedding in a certain application is too high, the Lipschitz embedding can be endowed with heuristics. *SparseMap* [280], for instance, builds up on the idea of Lipschitz embeddings and makes use of two heuristics that aim at reducing the cost of producing the embedding [278]. First, rather than computing the exact distance value $f(g, \mathcal{P})$, an upper bound $\hat{f}(g, \mathcal{P})$ is used. Second, instead of using the whole set $\mathcal{T}$ to define the subsets $\mathcal{P}_i$, a greedy selection based on the *stress* criterion [223] is applied. In our work, however, the original Lipschitz Embedding as defined in Definition 6.3 is employed. Hence, we refer to [278, 280] for further details on SparseMap and its properties.

6.2.4   *The Problem of Prototype Selection*

In our embedding framework, the selection of the n prototypes $\mathcal{P} = \{p_1, \ldots, p_n\}$ is a critical issue since not only the prototypes p_i themselves but also their number n affect the resulting graph mapping $\varphi_n^{\mathcal{P}}(\cdot)$, and thus the performance of the corresponding pattern recognition algorithm. Clearly, a good selection of n prototypes seems to be crucial to succeed with the classification or clustering algorithm in the embedding vector space. A first and very simple idea might be to use all available training graphs from $\mathcal{T}$ as prototypes. Yet, two severe shortcomings arise with such a plain approach. First, the dimensionality of the resulting vector space is equal to the size N of the training set $\mathcal{T}$. Consequently, if the training set is large, the mapping results in (possibly too) high dimensional vectors definitely disabling an efficient computation of basic mathematical operations. Second, the presence of similar prototypes as well as outlier graphs in the training set $\mathcal{T}$ is most likely. Therefore, redundant and noisy or irrelevant information will be captured in the graph maps. More formally, the more similar two prototypes p_i and p_j from some prototype set $\mathcal{P}$ are, the more similar, thus redundant, will be their corresponding entries d_i and d_j in an arbitrary graph map $\varphi_n^{\mathcal{P}}(g)$. Furthermore, assume that $p_i \in \mathcal{P}$ is an outlier, i.e. $d(g, p_i)$ is large for any $g \in \mathcal{T}$. Then, for two arbitrary graphs g and g', the corresponding entries $d(g, p_i)$ and $d(g', p_i)$ will be very large and their relative difference negligibly small. In other words, the respective entry d_i is somewhat irrelevant and lacks discrimination power. It is well known that the inclusion of both irrelevant and redundant information may harm the performance of pattern recognition algorithms [281].

In the present book an adequate selection of prototypes $\mathcal{P} = \{p_1, \ldots, p_n\}$ is addressed by various procedures. First, a number of *prototype selection methods* are discussed [66, 273, 282]. These prototype selection strategies use some heuristics based on the underlying dissimilarities in the original graph domain. The basic idea of these approaches is to select prototypes from $\mathcal{T}$ that best possibly reflect the distribution of the training set $\mathcal{T}$ or that cover a predefined region of $\mathcal{T}$. The rationale of this procedure is that capturing distances to significant prototypes from $\mathcal{T}$ leads to meaningful dissimilarity vectors. The algorithms from this category are discussed in detail in Section 6.3.

A severe shortcoming of prototype selection strategies is that the dimensionality of the embedding space has to be determined by the user. In other words, the number of prototypes to be selected by a certain prototype selection algorithm has to be experimentally defined by means of the target algorithm on a validation set. This procedure is known as *wrapper* method [283]. Since this validation procedure, i.e. optimizing the size of $\mathcal{P}$ on a validation set, is time consuming, a prototype selection method that automatically infers the dimensionality of the resulting embedding space is highly desirable. In order to achieve this goal, various *prototype reduction schemes* [284] – well known from the literature for the task of condensing training sets in nearest-neighbor scenarios – are adopted for the task of prototype selection. In contrast with the heuristic prototype selection strategies, with these procedures the number of prototypes n, i.e. the dimensionality of the resulting vector space, is defined by an algorithmic procedure. The algorithms from this category are discussed in detail in Section 6.4.

A third solution to the problem of noisy and redundant vectors with too high dimensionality is offered by the following procedure. Rather than selecting the prototypes beforehand, the embedding is carried out first and then the problem of prototype selection is reduced to a feature subset selection problem. That is, for graph embedding all available elements from the training set are used as prototypes, i.e. we define $\mathcal{P} = \mathcal{T}$. Next, various *feature selection strategies* [285–288] can be applied to the resulting large scale vectors eliminating redundancies and noise, finding good features, and simultaneously reducing the dimensionality. Note that each feature selected by means of this approach exactly corresponds to one prototype graph from the training set. Thus, this procedure can be interpreted as a delayed prototype selection. Conversely, the prototype selection and proto-type reduction algorithms can be seen as feature selection strategies where the selected prototypes correspond to the selected features. The algorithms from this category are discussed in detail in Section 6.5.

Similarly to dissimilarity embeddings, where the selection of the proto-types is a critical issue, for Lipschitz embeddings the reference set creation techniques are crucial. In order to define reference sets for embedding, one of the proposed prototype selection strategies (discussed in Section 6.3) is extended such that prototype sets rather than prototype singletons are se-lected for the embedding task. In Section 6.6 the proposed solutions for defining the reference sets for Lipschitz embeddings are described in detail.

Finally, the problem of prototype selection is addressed by means of *ensemble methods* [2] in Section 6.7. In fact, through the embedding frame-work we establish not only a general framework for mapping graphs to the real vector space $\mathbb{R}^n$, but also a straightforward approach for building ensemble members in a multiple classifier system.

6.3   Prototype Selection Strategies

The prototypes $\mathcal{P} = \{p_1, \ldots, p_n\}$ serve as reference points in the underlying graph domain in order to transform graphs into real vectors. Hence, the objective of prototype selection is to find reference points which lead to meaningful vectors in the embedding space. Intuitively, prototypes should not be redundant and simultaneously, prototypes should include as much information as possible. Therefore, we should avoid selecting similar graphs and the prototypes should be uniformly distributed over the whole set of patterns. In the present section, six prototype selection strategies are dis-cussed, all of them selecting graphs from $\mathcal{T}$ with respect to the underlying dissimilarity information.

Note that for all of the proposed prototype selection algorithms the size of the prototype set $\mathcal{P}$ is a user defined parameter. Therefore, the num-ber of prototypes actually selected has to be either experimentally defined or fixed beforehand to an arbitrary number. Regarding the task of pro-totype selection as feature selection procedure [287, 289] (i.e. prototypes correspond to features), the basic terminology of *filters* and *wrappers* [283] can be introduced. Filters and wrappers are general strategies for evaluat-ing the quality of subsets of features. The former approach evaluates the individual features by giving them a score according to general characteristics of the training set [281]. Commonly, a fixed number of top ranked features, or alternatively, only features whose score exceeds a predefined threshold on the criterion, are selected for further analysis. In the latter approach the performance of the underlying pattern recognition algorithm on an independent validation set is used as a criterion for feature subset evaluation [283].

In view of this, the first step of prototype selection can be seen as a filter since one can define N sets of prototypes

$$\mathcal{P}_1, \mathcal{P}_2, \ldots, \mathcal{P}_{N-1}, \mathcal{P}_N = \mathcal{T} \quad ,$$

where $|\mathcal{P}_i| = i$ and $\mathcal{T}$ denotes the full set of training graphs. Subsequently, by varying a single parameter, viz. the number of prototypes n, the optimal subset $\mathcal{P}_i$ can be established through a wrapper method.

In order to define a prototype set $\mathcal{P}$ of size n and eventually map graphs into the n-dimensional real space, some special graphs, termed *set median graph* [258], *set center graph*, and *set marginal graph*, will be needed. They are introduced below.

Definition 6.4 (Set Median, Center, and Marginal Graph). *Given a set $\mathcal{S}$ of graphs, the set median graph* [258] *$g_{mdn} \in \mathcal{S}$ is defined as*

$$median(\mathcal{S}) = g_{mdn} = \operatorname*{argmin}_{g_1 \in \mathcal{S}} \sum_{g_2 \in \mathcal{S}} d(g_1, g_2) \quad .$$

The set median graph is the graph whose sum of edit distances to all other graphs in $\mathcal{S}$ is minimal. Intuitively, the set median graph is located in the center of a given graph set. A slightly different concept is given by the set center graph $g_c \in \mathcal{S}$ which is defined as

$$center(\mathcal{S}) = g_c = \operatorname*{argmin}_{g_1 \in \mathcal{S}} \max_{g_2 \in \mathcal{S}} d(g_1, g_2) \quad .$$

Obviously, the set center graph is the graph for which the maximum distance to all other graphs in $\mathcal{S}$ is minimum. In contrast to those graphs located in the center of a given set, the set marginal graph $g_{mrg} \in \mathcal{S}$ is located at the border of a given graph set. Formally,

$$marginal(\mathcal{S}) = g_{mrg} = \operatorname*{argmax}_{g_1 \in \mathcal{S}} \sum_{g_2 \in \mathcal{S}} d(g_1, g_2) \quad .$$

The set marginal graph is thus the graph whose sum of distances to all other graphs in $\mathcal{S}$ is maximal.

Assume there are k different classes of graphs $\omega_1, \ldots, \omega_k$ represented in the training set $\mathcal{T}$. We distinguish between classwise and classindependent prototype selection. Classindependent selection means that the selection is executed over the whole training set $\mathcal{T}$ to get n prototypes, while in classwise selection the selection is performed individually for each of the k different classes $\omega_1, \ldots, \omega_k$. In the latter case, n_i prototypes are selected independently for each class ω_i such that $\sum_{i=1}^{k} n_i = n$. Whether the classwise or classindependent method is more convenient depends on a number of factors, including the size of $\mathcal{T}$, the distribution of the graphs in $\mathcal{T}$, whether or not classes are balanced, and the application.

The prototype selection algorithms used in this book are described below (see also [66]). In order to illustrate the behavior of the different prototype selectors, we provide illustrative examples (see also Section 4.3). The data underlying these examples are two-dimensional vectors obtained through multidimensional scaling applied to the original graph edit distances from the Letter low data set (Fig. 6.2), the Fingerprint data set (Fig. 6.3), and the Webpage data set (Fig. 6.4).

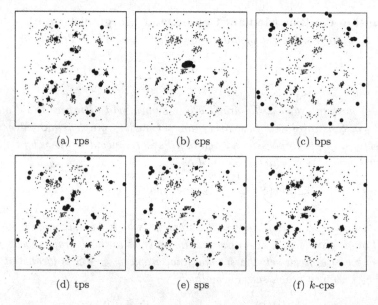

(a) rps	(b) cps	(c) bps
(d) tps	(e) sps	(f) k-cps

Fig. 6.2   Illustration of the different prototype selectors applied to the training set $\mathcal{T}$ of the Letter low data set. The number of prototypes is defined by $n = 30$. The prototypes selected by the respective selection algorithms are shown with heavy dots.

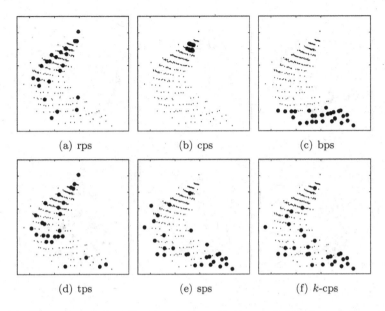

(a) rps	(b) cps	(c) bps
(d) tps	(e) sps	(f) k-cps

Fig. 6.3 Illustration of the different prototype selectors applied to the training set $\mathcal{T}$ of the Fingerprint data set. The number of prototypes is defined by $n = 30$. The prototypes selected by the respective selection algorithms are shown with heavy dots.

Random (rps) A random selection of n unique prototypes from $\mathcal{T}$ is performed. Of course, the Random prototype selector can be applied classindependent or classwise (rps-c). The selection by means of rps-c provides a random selection of n_i prototypes per class ω_i. For a pseudo-code description of this algorithm see Algorithm 6.1.

Algorithm 6.1 Prototype selection by means of rps.

Input: Training set $\mathcal{T} = \{g_1, \ldots, g_N\}$, number of prototypes n
Output: Prototype set $\mathcal{P} = \{p_1, \ldots, p_n\} \subseteq \mathcal{T}$

1: Initialize $\mathcal{P}$ to the empty set $\{\}$
2: **while** $|\mathcal{P}| < n$ **do**
3:    p = random selection from $\mathcal{T}$
4:    $\mathcal{P} = \mathcal{P} \cup \{p\}$
5:    $\mathcal{T} = \mathcal{T} \setminus \{p\}$
6: **end while**

Center (cps) The Center prototype selector selects prototypes situated in, or near, the center of the training set $\mathcal{T}$. The set of prototypes $\mathcal{P} = \{p_1, \ldots, p_n\}$ is iteratively constructed. In each iteration the median of the training set $\mathcal{T}$ is moved to the prototype set $\mathcal{P}$. For a pseudo-code

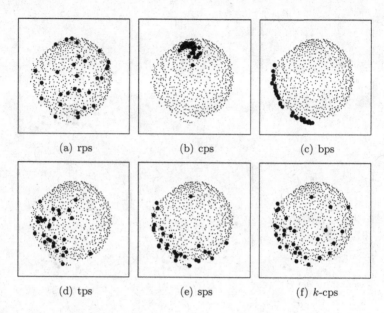

(a) rps	(b) cps	(c) bps
(d) tps	(e) sps	(f) k-cps

Fig. 6.4   Illustration of the different prototype selectors applied to the training set $\mathcal{T}$ of the Webpage data set. The number of prototypes is defined by $n = 30$. The prototypes selected by the respective selection algorithms are shown with heavy dots.

description of this algorithm see Algorithm 6.2.

Algorithm 6.2 Prototype selection by means of cps.

Input: Training set $\mathcal{T} = \{g_1, \ldots, g_N\}$, number of prototypes n
Output: Prototype set $\mathcal{P} = \{p_1, \ldots, p_n\} \subseteq \mathcal{T}$

1: Initialize $\mathcal{P}$ to the empty set $\{\}$
2: **while** $|\mathcal{P}| < n$ **do**
3:     $p = median(\mathcal{T})$
4:     $\mathcal{P} = \mathcal{P} \cup \{p\}$
5:     $\mathcal{T} = \mathcal{T} \setminus \{p\}$
6: **end while**

It seems that the Center prototype selector is not very appropriate for selecting n prototypes. Obviously, both requirements, avoiding redundancy and uniform distribution, are not satisfied. Nevertheless, we mention this prototype selector here for the purpose of completeness. To obtain a better distribution, one can apply the Center prototype selector classwise (cps-c). In this case, supposably, the prototypes mirror the given distribution better than the classindependent version. In Fig. 6.5, 6.6, and 6.7 the difference between classwise (cps-c) and classindependent (cps) prototype selection is

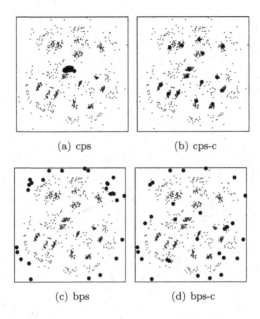

(a) cps   (b) cps-c

(c) bps   (d) bps-c

Fig. 6.5 Classindependent vs. classwise prototype selectors on the Letter low data set. The number of prototypes is defined by $n = 30$. The prototypes selected by the respective selection algorithms are shown with heavy dots.

illustrated on the Letter low data set, the Fingerprint data set, and the Webpage data set, respectively.

Border (bps) The Border prototype selector selects prototypes situated at the border of the training set $\mathcal{T}$. The set of prototypes $\mathcal{P} = \{p_1, \ldots, p_n\}$ is iteratively constructed. In each iteration the marginal graph of the training set $\mathcal{T}$ is moved to the prototype set $\mathcal{P}$. For a pseudo-code description of this algorithm see Algorithm 6.3.

Algorithm 6.3 Prototype selection by means of bps.

Input: Training set $\mathcal{T} = \{g_1, \ldots, g_N\}$, number of prototypes n
Output: Prototype set $\mathcal{P} = \{p_1, \ldots, p_n\} \subseteq \mathcal{T}$

1: Initialize $\mathcal{P}$ to the empty set $\{\}$
2: **while** $|\mathcal{P}| < n$ **do**
3:     $p = marginal(\mathcal{T})$
4:     $\mathcal{P} = \mathcal{P} \cup \{p\}$
5:     $\mathcal{T} = \mathcal{T} \setminus \{p\}$
6: **end while**

In contrast to the Center prototype selector, where many prototypes

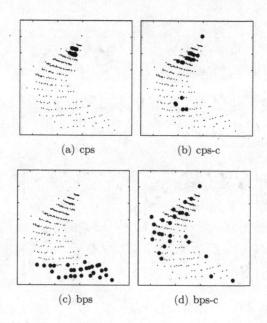

(a) cps   (b) cps-c

(c) bps   (d) bps-c

Fig. 6.6   Classindependent vs. classwise prototype selectors on the Fingerprint data set. The number of prototypes is defined by $n = 30$. The prototypes selected by the respective selection algorithms are shown with heavy dots.

are structurally similar, this kind of selection avoids redundancies much better. However, there are no prototypes selected from the center of the set. Obviously, the requirement of uniform distribution is not satisfied. Furthermore, one has to expect that bps possibly selects outliers. The Border prototype selector can be applied classindependent and classwise (bps-c). In Fig. 6.5, 6.6, and 6.7 the difference between classwise (bps-c) and classindependent (bps) prototype selection is illustrated on the Letter low data set, the Fingerprint data set, and the Webpage data set, respectively.

Targetsphere (tps)   The idea of this prototype selector is to distribute the prototypes from the center to the border as uniformly as possible. The Targetsphere prototype selector first determines the set center graph $g_c = center(\mathcal{T})$. After the center graph has been found, the graph furthest away from g_c, i.e. the graph $g_f \in \mathcal{T}$ maximizing the distance to g_c is located. Both graphs, g_c and g_f, are selected as prototypes. The distance from g_c to g_f is referred to as d_{max}, i.e. $d_{max} = d(g_c, g_f)$. The interval $[0, d_{max}]$ is then divided into $n - 1$ equidistant subintervals of width

$$w = \frac{d_{max}}{n - 1} \; .$$

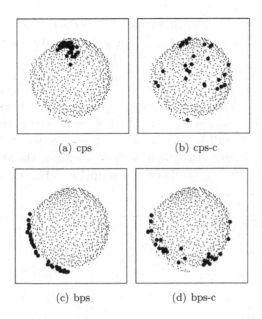

(a) cps   (b) cps-c

(c) bps   (d) bps-c

Fig. 6.7 Classindependent vs. classwise prototype selectors on the Webpage data set. The number of prototypes is defined by $n = 30$. The prototypes selected by the respective selection algorithms are shown with heavy dots.

The $n - 2$ graphs for which the corresponding distances to the center graph g_c are closest to the length of the subintervals in terms of edit distance are selected as prototypes. For a pseudo-code description of this algorithm see Algorithm 6.4.

Algorithm 6.4 Prototype selection by means of tps.

Input: Training set $\mathcal{T} = \{g_1, \ldots, g_N\}$, number of prototypes n
Output: Prototype set $\mathcal{P} = \{p_1, \ldots, p_n\} \subseteq \mathcal{T}$

1: Initialize $\mathcal{P}$ to the empty set $\{\}$
2: $g_c = center(\mathcal{T})$
3: $g_f = \underset{g \in \mathcal{T}}{\mathrm{argmax}}\ d(g, g_c)$
4: $d_{max} = d(g_c, g_f)$, $w = \frac{d_{max}}{n-1}$
5: $\mathcal{P} = \mathcal{P} \cup \{g_c, g_f\}$, $\mathcal{T} = \mathcal{T} \setminus \{g_c, g_f\}$
6: **for** $i = 1, \ldots, n - 2$ **do**
7:      $p = \underset{g \in \mathcal{T}}{\mathrm{argmin}}|d(g, g_c) - iw|$
8:      $\mathcal{P} = \mathcal{P} \cup \{p\}$
9:      $\mathcal{T} = \mathcal{T} \setminus \{p\}$
10: **end for**

The selection of the prototypes using tps considers the distance to the center graph only. That is, the procedure selects n prototypes uniformly distributed in the interval $[0, d_{max}]$. The individual distances between the prototypes selected are not considered. The Targetsphere prototype selector can be applied classindependent as well as classwise (tps-c).

Spanning (sps) The Spanning prototype selector considers all distances to the prototypes selected before. The first prototype is the set median graph $g_{mdn} = median(\mathcal{T})$. Each additional prototype selected by the spanning prototype selector is the graph furthest away from the already selected prototype graphs. For a pseudo-code description of this algorithm see Algorithm 6.5.

Algorithm 6.5 Prototype selection by means of sps.

Input: Training set $\mathcal{T} = \{g_1, \ldots, g_N\}$, number of prototypes n
Output: Prototype set $\mathcal{P} = \{p_1, \ldots, p_n\} \subseteq \mathcal{T}$

1: Initialize $\mathcal{P}$ to the empty set $\{\}$
2: $m = median(\mathcal{T})$
3: $\mathcal{P} = \mathcal{P} \cup \{m\}$, $\mathcal{T} = \mathcal{T} \setminus \{m\}$
4: **while** $|\mathcal{P}| < n$ **do**
5:     $p = \underset{g \in \mathcal{T}}{\operatorname{argmax}} \ \underset{p \in \mathcal{P}}{\min} \ d(g, p)$
6:     $\mathcal{P} = \mathcal{P} \cup \{p\}$
7:     $\mathcal{T} = \mathcal{T} \setminus \{p\}$
8: **end while**

In contrast to tps, where only the distances to the center graph are considered during the selection, sps takes into account all distances to the already selected prototypes and tries to cover the whole training set as uniformly as possible. The Spanning prototype selector can be applied classindependent or classwise (sps-c).

k-Centers (k-cps) The k-Centers prototype selector tries to choose n graphs from T so that they are evenly distributed with respect to the dissimilarity information given by d. The algorithm proceeds according to k-medians clustering [259]. For a pseudo-code description of this algorithm see Algorithm 6.6.

The procedure starts with a prototype set obtained through sps and stops when no more changes in the sets sets $\mathcal{C}_1, \ldots, \mathcal{C}_n$ occur. The prototypes $\mathcal{P} = \{p_1, \ldots, p_n\}$ are then given by the centers of the n disjoint clusters established by k-medians clustering. The k-Centers prototype selector can be applied classindependent as well as classwise (k-cps-c). In contrast to sps, we note that k-cps avoids selecting prototypes from the border by focusing on graphs that are in the center of densely populated

---

Algorithm 6.6 Prototype selection by means of k-cps.

Input: Training set $\mathcal{T} = \{g_1, \ldots, g_N\}$, number of prototypes n
Output: Prototype set $\mathcal{P} = \{p_1, \ldots, p_n\} \subseteq \mathcal{T}$

1: Initialize $\mathcal{P} = \{p_1, \ldots, p_n\}$ by means of sps (see. Algorithm 6.5)
2: **repeat**
3:     Construct n sets $\mathcal{C}_1 = \{p_1\}, \ldots, \mathcal{C}_n = \{p_n\}$
4:     **for all** $g \in \mathcal{T}$ **do**
5:         Find the nearest neighbor $p_i \in \mathcal{P}$ of g
6:         Add g to p_i's corresponding set $\mathcal{C}_i$
7:     **end for**
8:     **for all** sets $\mathcal{C}_1, \ldots, \mathcal{C}_n$ **do**
9:         $c_i = center(\mathcal{C}_i)$
10:        **if** $c_i \neq p_i$ **then**
11:            $p_i = c_i$
12:        **end if**
13:    **end for**
14: **until** no more centers c_i are changed

---

areas (see for instance Fig. 6.2 (e) and (f) for a comparison between sps and k-cps).

6.4   Prototype Reduction Schemes

Different prototype reduction schemes have been proposed in the literature in conjunction with k-nearest-neighbor classifiers [290–292]. These prototype reduction schemes aim at overcoming the three major drawbacks of k-nearest-neighbor classifiers, viz. large storage requirements, large computational effort for distance evaluations, and sensitivity to outliers. In [284] a survey of such prototype reduction methods is provided. The proposed reduction schemes determine a subset $\mathcal{P} \subseteq \mathcal{T}$ such that the elements from the training set $\mathcal{T}$ (or at least a considerable part of them) are still correctly classified using a nearest-neighbor classifier in conjunction with the prototype set $\mathcal{P}$. That is, these reduction schemes reduce redundancy in terms of not selecting similar graphs out of the same class by simultaneously finding significant graphs which help to correctly classify the graphs in $\mathcal{T}$.

In fact, this particular selection paradigm seems to be appropriate in order to find a prototype set $\mathcal{P}$ for dissimilarity embedding. Remember that we use the distances to the prototypes as features for our vectorial description of the considered graphs. Similar objects yield a similar contribution to the vectorial representation of a graph [4]. Therefore, redundant graphs should be omitted. Moreover, it might be advantageous to select representative graphs related to each of the given classes such that the dissimilarity representation becomes most informative. As stated above, the

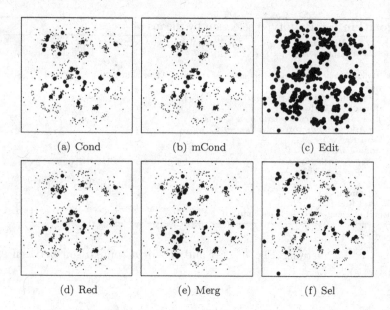

(a) Cond   (b) mCond   (c) Edit

(d) Red   (e) Merg   (f) Sel

Fig. 6.8   Illustration of the different prototype reduction schemes on the Letter low data set. The number of prototypes is defined by the algorithm. The prototypes selected by the respective selection algorithms are shown with heavy dots.

reduction schemes for nearest-neighbor classification account for both of these requirements.

According to the taxonomy of prototype reduction schemes described in [293], we use *selective* prototype selectors where the number of prototypes is *uncontrollable*. These two constraints are motivated through the following considerations. First, the fact that we are dealing with graphs makes the creation of new prototypes quite difficult. For instance, whereas the creation of a weighted mean of two feature vectors is straightforward, the same operation on graphs is highly complex. Second, we want to bypass the time consuming validation of the dimensionality of the resulting embedding space by means of the target algorithm. Hence, we leave the determination of the number of prototypes to the prototype selection algorithm.

In the next subsections the six prototype reduction strategies used in this book are reviewed and adopted to the domain of graphs. All of our reduction schemes make use of a classifier of the nearest-neighbor type (NN) for evaluating the quality of a certain prototype set.

In order to illustrate the behavior of the different prototype reduction schemes, we provide the same illustrative examples as for the prototype

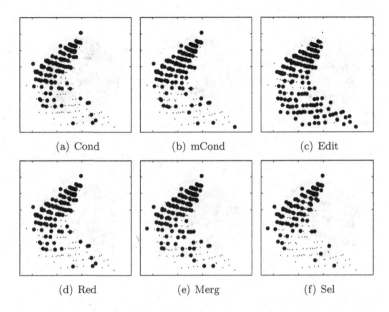

(a) Cond   (b) mCond   (c) Edit

(d) Red   (e) Merg   (f) Sel

Fig. 6.9 Illustration of the different prototype reduction schemes on the Fingerprint data set. The number of prototypes is defined by the algorithm. The prototypes selected by the respective selection algorithms are shown with heavy dots.

selection strategies presented above (Fig. 6.8, 6.9, and 6.10).

Condensing (*Cond*) The idea of condensing a training set $\mathcal{T}$ is to iteratively select graphs $g \in \mathcal{T}$ as prototypes until all graphs from $\mathcal{T}$ are correctly classified using the respective prototypes [290]. As a disadvantage, this procedure depends on the order in which the graphs are processed. For a pseudo-code description of this algorithm see Algorithm 6.7.

Algorithm 6.7 Condensing a training set $\mathcal{T}$ to a prototype set $\mathcal{P}$.

Input: Training set $\mathcal{T} = \{g_1, \ldots, g_N\}$
Output: Prototype set $\mathcal{P} = \{p_1, \ldots, p_n\} \subseteq \mathcal{T}$

1: $\mathcal{P} = \{g_1\}$ and $\mathcal{T} = \mathcal{T} \setminus \{g_1\}$
2: **repeat**
3:      **for all** $g \in \mathcal{T}$ **do**
4:          classify g with a 1-NN classifier using $\mathcal{P}$
5:          **if** g is falsely classified **then**
6:             $\mathcal{P} = \mathcal{P} \cup \{g\}$, $\mathcal{T} = \mathcal{T} \setminus \{g\}$
7:          **end if**
8:      **end for**
9: **until** no misclassification occured

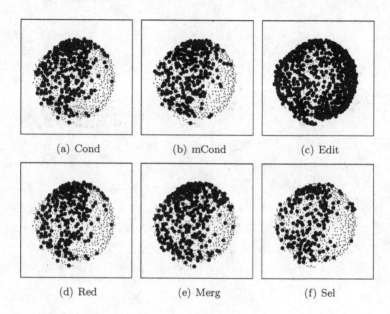

(a) Cond   (b) mCond   (c) Edit

(d) Red   (e) Merg   (f) Sel

Fig. 6.10   Illustration of the different prototype reduction schemes on the Webpage data set. The number of prototypes is defined by the algorithm. The prototypes selected by the respective selection algorithms are shown with heavy dots.

Modified Condensing ($mCond$)   In order to overcome the limitation of order dependency in the condensing method, a modified condensing procedure can be applied [294]. In this scheme the prototypes are selected iteratively from the training set $\mathcal{T}$. We start with a basic set of prototypes containing one graph per class. To this end, for each class, the set center graph is selected as prototype. Then the graphs from $\mathcal{T}$ are classified by means of this initial set of prototypes. Using only the misclassified graphs, the class centers are recomputed and subsequently added to the existing set of prototypes. This procedure is repeated until all graphs from $\mathcal{T}$ are correctly classified.

Both condensing methods (Cond and mCond) possess the property that the number of prototypes selected from a particular class depends on the variation of the graphs in the respective class. That is, if graphs from a certain class differ only little in their structure and labels, only few prototypes are necessary to correctly classify all graphs from this class. Yet, the higher the variety of the graphs in a given class, the more prototypes are selected from this specific class. For a pseudo-code description of this algorithm see Algorithm 6.8.

Algorithm 6.8 Modified condensing a training set $\mathcal{T}$ to a prototype set $\mathcal{P}$.

Input: Training set $\mathcal{T} = \{g_1, \ldots, g_N\}$
Output: Prototype set $\mathcal{P} = \{p_1, \ldots, p_n\} \subseteq \mathcal{T}$

1: Initialize $\mathcal{P}$ and $\mathcal{M}$ to the empty sets $\{\}$
2: **for** all classes ω_j contained in $\mathcal{T}$ **do**
3:     m_j = set center graph of class ω_j using all training graphs $\mathcal{T}$
4:     $\mathcal{P} = \mathcal{P} \cup \{m_j\}$
5: **end for**
6: **repeat**
7:     **for** all $g \in \mathcal{T}$ **do**
8:        classify g with a 1-NN classifier using $\mathcal{P}$
9:        **if** g is falsely classified **then**
10:          $\mathcal{M} = \mathcal{M} \cup \{g\}$
11:        **end if**
12:     **end for**
13:     **for** all classes ω_j contained in $\mathcal{M}$ **do**
14:        m_j = set center graph of class ω_j using the misclassified graphs $\mathcal{M}$ only
15:        $\mathcal{P} = \mathcal{P} \cup \{m_j\}$
16:     **end for**
17: **until** no misclassification occured

Editing (*Edit*) The basic idea of editing a training set $\mathcal{T}$ is to delete outliers from $\mathcal{T}$ [295]. For this purpose, we classify each graph g from $\mathcal{T}$ with a 3-NN classifier. If g is misclassified we assume that this particular graph is an outlier and therefore should not be included in the prototype set. For a pseudo-code description of this algorithm see Algorithm 6.9.

Reducing (*Red*) The idea of reducing is built up on condensing [296]. First, the training set $\mathcal{T}$ is condensed to a prototype set $\mathcal{P}$ according to Algorithm 6.7. Next, each prototype $p \in \mathcal{P}$ is iteratively removed from $\mathcal{P}$. Then, the training graphs are classified using the reduced prototype set $\mathcal{P} \setminus \{p\}$. If all graphs are still classified correctly with this reduced prototype set, the respective prototype is useless and can therefore be omitted. Otherwise, the prototype is necessary and therefore kept in $\mathcal{P}$. For a pseudo-code description of this algorithm see Algorithm 6.10.

Merging (*Merg*) The idea of merging [297] a training set is to define two graph sets $\mathcal{P}$ and $\mathcal{Q}$, where initially $\mathcal{P}$ is empty and $\mathcal{Q}$ contains all training graphs from $\mathcal{T}$. First, an arbitrary graph from $\mathcal{Q}$ is selected as prototype, i.e. moved from $\mathcal{Q}$ to $\mathcal{P}$. Next, we consider the two closest graphs p and q from $\mathcal{P}$ and $\mathcal{Q}$, respectively. If the class of p is not the same as that of q, q is moved from $\mathcal{Q}$ to $\mathcal{P}$. Otherwise, p and q are merged to $p^* \in \mathcal{Q}$, where p^* is the graph from $\mathcal{Q}$ that minimizes the sum of distances to p and q. The accuracy of the NN classifier using $\mathcal{P} \cup \{q\}$ is then compared with the accuracy when $\mathcal{P} \setminus \{p\} \cup \{p^*\}$ is used as prototype set. Whenever the former outperforms the latter, q is moved from $\mathcal{Q}$ to $\mathcal{P}$. Otherwise, p and q are removed from $\mathcal{P}$ and $\mathcal{Q}$, respectively, and p^* is moved from $\mathcal{Q}$ to $\mathcal{P}$. This procedure is repeated until no graphs are left in $\mathcal{Q}$. For a pseudo-code description of this algorithm see Algorithm 6.11[5].

Algorithm 6.9 Editing a training set $\mathcal{T}$ to a prototype set $\mathcal{P}$.

Input: Training set $\mathcal{T} = \{g_1, \ldots, g_N\}$
Output: Prototype set $\mathcal{P} = \{p_1, \ldots, p_n\} \subseteq \mathcal{T}$

1: Initialize $\mathcal{P}$ and $\mathcal{Q}$ to the empty sets $\{\}$
2: **for all** $g \in \mathcal{T}$ **do**
3:     classify g with a 3-NN classifier using $\mathcal{T} \setminus \{g\}$
4:     **if** g is falsely classified **then**
5:         $\mathcal{Q} = \mathcal{Q} \cup \{g\}$
6:     **end if**
7: **end for**
8: $\mathcal{P} = \mathcal{T} \setminus \mathcal{Q}$

Algorithm 6.10 Reducing a training set $\mathcal{T}$ to a prototype set $\mathcal{P}$.

Input: Training set $\mathcal{T} = \{g_1, \ldots, g_N\}$
Output: Prototype set $\mathcal{P} = \{p_1, \ldots, p_n\} \subseteq \mathcal{T}$

1: $\mathcal{P}$ = condensed training set according to Algorithm 6.7
2: **for all** $p \in \mathcal{P}$ **do**
3:     $\mathcal{P} = \mathcal{P} \setminus \{p\}$, *useful* = false
4:     **for all** $g \in \mathcal{T}$ **do**
5:         classify g with a 1-NN classifier using $\mathcal{P}$
6:         **if** g is falsely classified **then**
7:             *useful* = true
8:         **end if**
9:     **end for**
10:    **if** *useful* **then**
11:        $\mathcal{P} = \mathcal{P} \cup \{p\}$
12:    **end if**
13: **end for**

Selecting (*Sel*)   In [298] another algorithm for reducing the training set $\mathcal{T}$ is introduced. This approach is based on the idea of related neighbors. We define $g_j \in \mathcal{T}$ as a related neighbor to $g_i \in \mathcal{T}$ if g_i and g_j are out of the same class, and g_j is nearer to g_i than any other sample $g_k \in \mathcal{T}$ from another class. We use $\mathcal{R}_i$ to denote the set of all related neighbors to g_i. Formally,

$$\mathcal{R}_i = \{g_j \in \mathcal{T} \mid \omega_i = \omega_j \text{ and } d(g_i, g_j) < \min_{g_k \in \mathcal{T}} d(g_i, g_k) , \quad \omega_i \neq \omega_k\} ,$$

---

[5]Note that in this Algorithm NN$(\mathcal{T}, \mathcal{P})$ refers to the classification accuracy of a 1-NN classifier applied to $\mathcal{T}$ using the prototype set $\mathcal{P}$.

Algorithm 6.11 Merging a training set $\mathcal{T}$ to a prototype set $\mathcal{P}$.

Input: Training set $\mathcal{T} = \{g_1, \ldots, g_N\}$
Output: Prototype set $\mathcal{P} = \{p_1, \ldots, p_n\} \subseteq \mathcal{T}$

$\mathcal{P} = \{g_1\}$ and $\mathcal{Q} = \mathcal{T} \setminus \{g_1\}$
while $\mathcal{Q}$ is not empty **do**
   $(p, q) = \text{argmin}_{(p,q) \in \mathcal{P} \times \mathcal{Q}}\, d(p, q)$
   if (class of p) $\neq$ (class of q) **then**
      $\mathcal{P} = \mathcal{P} \cup \{q\}$ and $\mathcal{Q} = \mathcal{Q} \setminus \{q\}$
   else
      $p^* = \text{argmin}_{p_i \in \mathcal{Q}}(d(p, p_i) + d(q, p_i))$
      if $\text{NN}(\mathcal{T}, \mathcal{P} \cup \{q\}) > \text{NN}(\mathcal{T}, \mathcal{P} \setminus \{p\} \cup \{p^*\})$ **then**
         $\mathcal{P} = \mathcal{P} \cup \{q\}$ and $\mathcal{Q} = \mathcal{Q} \setminus \{q\}$
      else
         $\mathcal{P} = \mathcal{P} \setminus \{p\} \cup \{p^*\}$ and $\mathcal{Q} = \mathcal{Q} \setminus \{q\} \setminus \{p^*\}$
      end if
   end if
end while

---

where ω_i denotes the class of the i-th graph from $\mathcal{T}$. The selection of the prototypes is now stated as finding a small number of graphs such that each of these graph has at least one related neighbor. In [298] a procedure is given such that the minimum set is found. In the present book a greedy algorithm using a binary $N \times N$ matrix $\mathbf{A} = (a_{ij})_{N \times N}$ is employed seeking for a small number of prototypes. For a pseudo-code description of this algorithm see Algorithm 6.12.

Algorithm 6.12 Selecting a training set $\mathcal{T}$ to a prototype set $\mathcal{P}$.

Input: Training set $\mathcal{T} = \{g_1, \ldots, g_N\}$
Output: Prototype set $\mathcal{P} = \{p_1, \ldots, p_n\} \subseteq \mathcal{T}$

1: Initialize $\mathcal{P}$ to the empty set $\{\}$, $\mathbf{A} = (a_{ij})_{N \times N}$ where $a_{ij} = 0$ for $i, j = 1, \ldots N$
2: **for** $g_i \in \mathcal{T}$ and $g_j \in \mathcal{T}$ **do**
3:    **if** all $g_j \in \mathcal{R}_i$ **then**
4:       $a_{ij} = 1$ **else** $a_{ij} = 0$
5:    **end if**
6: **end for**
7: **while** not all columns of $\mathbf{A}$ are deleted **do**
8:    $max = \text{argmax}_{1 \le i \le N} \sum_j a_{ij}$
9:    $\mathcal{P} = \mathcal{P} \cup \{g_{max}\}$
10:    delete all columns j of $\mathbf{A}$ where $a_{max,j} = 1$
11: **end while**

6.5   Feature Selection Algorithms

So far, the prototypes are selected from a training set $\mathcal{T}$ before the embedding is carried out. For this prototype selection either some heuristics based on the graph edit distances between the members of $\mathcal{T}$ can be used or well known reducing rules for nearest-neighbor classification are employed. Note that both paradigms in conjunction with our embedding framework can be seen as supervised feature selection methods, i.e. the distances of an input graph g to the retained prototypes $\mathcal{P}$ are the selected features of the vector space embedded graph. Obviously, redundant training graphs as well as outliers are eliminated by means of the proposed prototype selection methods and reduction schemes, while characteristic graphs of the training set $\mathcal{T}$ are retained. Therefore, the resulting features of $\varphi_n^{\mathcal{P}}(g)$, which are equal to the distances of g to characteristic graphs of each class, have a large discrimination power.

In the present section an approach is proposed where primarily all available elements from the training set are used as prototypes, i.e. $\mathcal{P} = \mathcal{T}$. Subsequently, a feature subset selection method is applied to the resulting vectors. In other words, rather than selecting the prototypes beforehand, the embedding is carried out first and then the problem of prototype selection is reduced to a feature subset selection problem. (Remember that each selected feature exactly corresponds to one prototype $p \in \mathcal{T}$.)

Feature subset selection aims at selecting a suitable subset of features such that the performance of a classification or clustering algorithm is improved [283, 286]. By means of *forward selection* search strategies, the search starts with an empty set and iteratively adds useful features to this set. Conversely, *backward elimination* refers to the process of iteratively removing useless features starting with the full set of features. Also *floating search* methods are available, where alternately useful features are added and useless features are removed. For a review on searching strategies for feature subset selection we refer to [286].

Based on the embedding established through $\varphi_N^{\mathcal{T}} : \mathcal{G} \to \mathbb{R}^N$ real vectors with N features are obtained. We denote the full set of features by $\{x_1, \ldots, x_N\}$. In the present section feature selection algorithms with both forward and backward selection strategies are used to define a feature ranking $x_{(1)}, x_{(2)}, \ldots, x_{(N)}$ where $x_{(1)}$ denotes the top ranked feature according to the given feature selection algorithm, $x_{(2)}$ the second-best feature, and so on. Based on this ranking, nested subsets of features

$$\{x_{(1)}\} \subset \{x_{(1)}, x_{(2)}\} \subset \ldots \subset \{x_{(1)}, x_{(2)}, \ldots, x_{(N)}\}$$

can be defined. An optimal subset of features can eventually be found by varying the size of the feature subset. For this second step, a certain pattern recognition algorithm's performance serves us as a quality criterion (thus, similar to prototype selection algorithms a wrapper is applied).

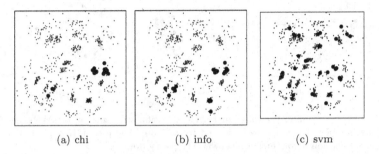

(a) chi   (b) info   (c) svm

Fig. 6.11   Illustration of the different feature selection strategies on the Letter low data set. The number of prototypes is defined by $n = 30$. The prototypes selected by the respective selection algorithms are shown with heavy dots.

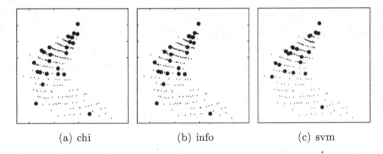

(a) chi   (b) info   (c) svm

Fig. 6.12   Illustration of the different feature selection strategies on the Fingerprint data set. The number of prototypes is defined by $n = 30$. The prototypes selected by the respective selection algorithms are shown with heavy dots.

For feature ranking, six different methods are employed, viz. Chi-square feature ranking, info gain feature ranking, svm recursive feature elimination, PCA, kernel PCA, and MDA. They are discussed in detail below. For the first three methods we provide the same illustrative examples as for the prototype selection strategies and prototype reduction schemes presented above in order to illustrate the behavior of the different feature ranking methods (Fig. 6.11, 6.12, and 6.13).

Chi-square feature ranking (chi)   For this feature ranking criterion to work properly, a discretization of the features is carried out first. This is done by means of *multi-interval discretization* of continuous-valued attributes proposed in [299]. This procedure starts with a binary discretiza-

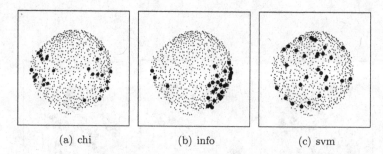

(a) chi   (b) info   (c) svm

Fig. 6.13   Illustration of the different feature selection strategies on the Webpage data set. The number of prototypes is defined by $n = 30$. The prototypes selected by the respective selection algorithms are shown with heavy dots.

tion, i.e. a partitioning of a certain feature's range into two intervals. Formally, assume a set $\mathcal{S}$ of N training samples increasingly sorted according to the considered feature's values is given. Clearly, in order to binarize this feature, $N - 1$ possible cut points $T_1, \ldots, T_{N-1}$, each at the midpoint between successive pairs of examples, exist and have to be evaluated. Let there be k classes $\omega_1, \ldots, \omega_k$ and let $P(\omega_i, \mathcal{S})$ be the proportion of examples in a set $\mathcal{S}$ that have class ω_i. The *class entropy $Ent(\mathcal{S})$* of a particular set $\mathcal{S}$ is then defined as

$$Ent(\mathcal{S}) = -\sum_{i=1}^{k} P(\omega_i, \mathcal{S}) \log(P(\omega_i, \mathcal{S})) \quad .$$

In order to find the "best" cut point for a given feature dividing the feature's range into two intervals $\mathcal{S}_1$ and $\mathcal{S}_2$, the weighted average of their resulting class entropies is computed. That is, the so called *class information entropy $E(T, \mathcal{S})$* of the partition of a set $\mathcal{S}$ into intervals $\mathcal{S}_1$ and $\mathcal{S}_2$ induced by a potential cut point T is computed. Formally, the class information entropy is defined as

$$E(T, \mathcal{S}) = \frac{|\mathcal{S}_1|}{|\mathcal{S}|} Ent(\mathcal{S}_1) + \frac{|\mathcal{S}_2|}{|\mathcal{S}|} Ent(\mathcal{S}_2) \quad .$$

A binary discretization for a certain feature is determined by selecting the cut point T for which $E(T, \mathcal{S})$ is minimal. It can be shown that the best cut point for binarization obtained by means of this procedure is always a boundary point, i.e. a value between two examples of different classes [299].

Given the binary discretization according to the minimization of the class information entropy, the algorithm is applied recursively to the derived subsets of features. A criterion is defined for deciding whether or not a further binary partitioning to a given interval is applied. This criterion is based on information and decision theory and decides for the option (further binarize or not) which minimizes the probability of making a wrong decision. For a more thorough description of this principle we refer to [299]

Given the discretized features, we evaluate the importance of each feature by measuring the χ^2-statistic with respect to the class. Eventually, the features are ranked according their χ^2-statistic by means of a forward selection. We refer to this method as Chi-square feature ranking, or chi for short.

Info Gain feature ranking (info) This feature ranking algorithm is based on mutual information, which is a widely used measure to analyze the dependency of variables. The mutual information $I(X;Y)$ of two random variables X and Y is defined in terms of their joint probability density function $p(x,y)$ and the marginal probability density functions $p(x)$, $p(y)$. Formally,

$$I(X;Y) = \int_Y \int_X p(x,y) \log \left(\frac{p(x,y)}{p(x)p(y)} \right) dx dy \quad .$$

In terms of mutual information, the purpose of feature selection is to find features that have the largest relevance to the target classes in Ω. For discrete feature variables (we use the same discretization algorithm as for Chi-square feature ranking), the integration operation reduces to summation. Moreover, both joint and marginal probability density functions can be estimated by merely counting the observations in the training set. Let $X^{(i)}$ be the infinite set of values the i-th feature x_i can take. The mutual information between a certain feature x_i and the ground truth Ω is defined by

$$I(x_i;\Omega) = \sum_{\omega \in \Omega} \sum_{x_i \in X^{(i)}} p(x_i,\omega) \log \left(\frac{p(x_i,\omega)}{p(x_i)p(\omega)} \right) \quad .$$

The features are ranked according to their mutual dependence to the class information by means of a forward selection. We refer to this method as Info gain feature ranking, or info for short.

SVM recursive feature elimination (svm) In [232] a feature ranking method based on SVM classifiers is introduced . The basic idea of this approach is to use the weights $\mathbf{w}$ of an SVM classifier's hyperplane $f(\mathbf{x}) = \langle \mathbf{w}, \mathbf{x} \rangle + b$, where $\mathbf{w} \in \mathbb{R}^n$ and $b \in \mathbb{R}$, as feature ranking criterion. The rationale is that the inputs that are weighted by the largest value have the most influence on the classification decision. Consequently, if the classifier performs well, those inputs with the largest weights correspond to the most informative features [232]. In the case of SVMs (see Section 5.4.1 for details on SVM training), the term to be optimized is

$$J = \min_{\mathbf{w} \in \mathbb{R}^n} \frac{1}{2} \|\mathbf{w}\|^2 \ .$$

We therefore use $(w_i)^2$ as feature ranking criterion. Particularly, the authors in [232] propose to use a recursive feature elimination procedure (RFE) to define the feature ranking. RFE is an instance of backward feature elimination that iteratively proceeds as follows.

(1) Train the SVM, i.e. optimize the weights w_i with respect to J.
(2) Compute the ranking criterion $(w_i)^2$ for all features.
(3) Remove the feature with smallest ranking criterion.

Obviously, top ranked features correspond to features eliminated last. We refer to this method as SVM recursive feature elimination, or svm for short.

Principal Component Analysis (PCA)   For feature ranking the well known principal component analysis (PCA) [246, 247] can be also applied. Moreover, besides a feature ranking PCA provides us with a linear transformation which basically seeks the projection that best represents the data. That is, PCA finds a new space whose basis vectors (principal components) correspond to the maximum variance directions in the original space. The first principal component points in the direction of the highest variance and, therefore, may include the most information about the data. The second principal component is perpendicular to the first principal component and points in the direction of the second highest variance, and so on.

The ordering of the principal components exactly corresponds to a feature ranking. Consequently, by means of a backward elimination procedure, the principal components with lowest variance can be considered as noise and iteratively removed. Obviously, top ranked features correspond to features eliminated last. For further details on PCA we refer to Section 5.4.2 where the procedure is more thoroughly described.

Kernel Principal Component Analysis (kPCA)   PCA can be kernelized such that also non-linear transformations of the underlying data can be carried out. Similar to PCA, kernel principal component analysis (kPCA) can be used to rank the (transformed) features according to their importance. In contrast with traditional PCA, however, the variance which measures the relevance of a certain feature is computed in an implicitly existing feature space rather than in the original pattern space. For further details on kPCA we refer to Section 5.4.2 where the procedure is more thoroughly described.

Multiple Discriminant Analysis (MDA)   Similarly to PCA, Fisher's Linear Discriminant Analysis (LDA) [288] is also a linear transformation. In contrast with PCA, however, LDA is a supervised transformation method, i.e. LDA takes class label information into account. In its original form, LDA can be applied to two-class problems only. However, one can use a generalization, called Multiple Discriminant Analysis (MDA), which can cope with more than two classes. In MDA, we are seeking a subspace that best separates the classes from each other. For this purpose, we define two measures.

The first measure is called *within-class* scatter matrix $\mathbf{S}_W$ and is defined as

$$\mathbf{S}_W = \sum_{j=1}^{k} \sum_{i=1}^{m_j} (\mathbf{x}_i^j - \mu_j)(\mathbf{x}_i^j - \mu_j)' \quad ,$$

where $\mathbf{x}_i^j$ is the i-th sample vector of class ω_j, μ_j is the sample mean of class ω_j, k is the number of classes, and m_j the number of samples in class ω_j.

The second measure is called *between-class* scatter matrix $\mathbf{S}_B$ and is defined as

$$\mathbf{S}_B = \sum_{j=1}^{k} m_j (\mu_j - \mu)(\mu_j - \mu)' \quad ,$$

where μ denotes the mean of all samples. We seek for a transformation matrix $\mathbf{W}$ which maximizes the between-class measure while minimizing the within-class measure. We make use of the fact that the determinant of a matrix is the product of the eigenvalues, i.e. the product of the data's variances in the directions of the corresponding eigenvectors. Hence, we use the determinant of a matrix as a scalar measure and maximize the following criterion function

$$J(\mathbf{W}) = \frac{\det(\mathbf{W}'\mathbf{S}_B\mathbf{W})}{\det(\mathbf{W}'\mathbf{S}_W\mathbf{W})} \quad .$$

It has been proven that if $\mathbf{S}_W$ is a nonsingular matrix this ratio is maximized when the column vectors of the projection matrix $\mathbf{W}$ are the eigenvectors of $\mathbf{S}_W^{-1}\mathbf{S}_B$ [288]. In order to overcome the problem in case of a singular matrix $\mathbf{S}_W$, we use an intermediate PCA space. That is, the original space is projected onto a space using PCA and then onto the final space using MDA. Note that the matrix $\mathbf{S}_B$ has a maximal rank of $k - 1$, where k is the number of classes. Consequently, we have at most $k - 1$ different and nonzero eigenvalues and therefore, the transformed data points have a maximal dimensionality of $k - 1$.

In contrast with the other five feature selection algorithms no ranking of the features is obtained through MDA. Here we use all $k - 1$ projected features for further processing.

6.6   Defining the Reference Sets for Lipschitz Embeddings

Similar to dissimilarity embeddings, where the task of prototype selection is crucial, in Lipschitz embeddings an adequate definition of the reference sets $\mathcal{Q} = \{\mathcal{P}_1, \dots, \mathcal{P}_n\}$ is also an important issue. In the present book we are interested in a vectorial description of the underlying graphs which enables us to outperform traditional classifiers operating directly on the graph distances. We use three creation methods to define our reference sets, all based on k-Centers prototype selection (k-cps) presented in Section 6.3.

Plain-k-Med   In the first method, the reference sets $\mathcal{P}_i \in \mathcal{Q}$ are equal to the n clusters $\mathcal{C}_i$ found by k-Centers prototype selection. That is, no postprocessing is applied to the partition $\mathcal{C}_1, \dots, \mathcal{C}_n$ and $\mathcal{Q} = \{\mathcal{P}_1 = \mathcal{C}_1, \dots, \mathcal{P}_n = \mathcal{C}_n\}$. In the following, this method with parameter n (number of reference sets) is referred to as Plain-k-Med(n), or P-k-Med(n) for short.

Center-k-Med   In the second method, for each of the n clusters $\mathcal{C}_i$ we iteratively remove the set center graph $c_i \in \mathcal{C}_i$ and add it to $\mathcal{P}_i$ until $\mathcal{P}_i$ consists of m graphs or $\mathcal{C}_i$ is empty. Note that whenever the size of a cluster $\mathcal{C}_i$ is smaller than, or equal to, m ($|\mathcal{C}_i| \leq m$), all graphs from $\mathcal{C}_i$ are moved to $\mathcal{P}_i$ and the cardinality of $\mathcal{P}_i$ is equal to $|\mathcal{C}_i|$. The n sets $\mathcal{P}_i$ developed with this procedure serve us as the reference sets, i.e. $\mathcal{Q} = \{\mathcal{P}_1, \dots, \mathcal{P}_n\}$. We refer to this method with parameters n and m (number of reference sets and maximum size of $\mathcal{P}_i$, respectively) as Center-k-Med(n, m), or C-k-Med(n, m) for short.

Neighbor-k-Med   In the third method, the cluster center c_i of the i-th cluster $\mathcal{C}_i$ is added to the corresponding reference set $\mathcal{P}_i$ (similar to k-cps). Additionally, the $m-1$ graphs that are located the nearest to c_i according to graph edit distance are added to $\mathcal{P}_i$. Formally, if $\{p_{(1)}, \dots, p_{(m-1)}\} \subseteq \mathcal{T}$ are the $m-1$ graphs that have the smallest distance $d(c_i, p_{(j)})$ to center c_i, we define the reference set by $\mathcal{P}_i = \{c_i, p_{(1)}, \ldots, p_{(m-1)}\}$. In contrast with the two other methods (Plain-k-Med(n) and Center-k-Med(n, m)), this method allows multiple occurrences of the same graph g in different reference sets $\mathcal{P}_i$ and $\mathcal{P}_j$ of $\mathcal{Q}$ ($i \neq j$). Moreover, with this method it is guaranteed that the individual reference sets are all of size m. From now on, we refer to this method with parameters n and m (number of reference sets and size of $\mathcal{P}_i$, respectively) as Neighbor-k-Med(n, m), or N-k-Med(n, m) for short.

6.7 Ensemble Methods

Considering our graph embedding framework, the observation that mapping a population of graphs into a vector space is controlled by a set of prototypes is fundamental. One possible procedure to actually get these prototypes is the random selection from the given training set of graphs (see Section 6.3). Obviously, if we repeat the process of random selection a number of times, we can derive different prototype sets which in turn can be used to embed a graph set to different vector spaces. More formally, selecting m times the prototypes randomly, and varying the respective number of prototypes n in a certain interval for each selection, results in m different prototype sets with different cardinality $\mathcal{P}_1 = \{p_{11}, \ldots, p_{1n_1}\}, \ldots, \mathcal{P}_m = \{p_{m1}, \ldots, p_{mn_m}\}$.

In Algorithm 6.13 the applied procedure is described in pseudo-code. Once a graph has been selected as a prototype it becomes temporarily unavailable until all training patterns have been selected as a prototype. This is achieved by a tabu list, which contains all patterns that have been already selected (line 12). The randomized prototype selection is performed on the subset $\mathcal{T} \setminus TABU$ only (line 10). Whenever the tabu list contains all patterns of $\mathcal{T}$, a reset is done such that all training elements become available again (line 7 and 8). The size of each prototype set $\mathcal{P}_i$, i.e. the number of prototypes selected, is determined randomly (line 5). This means that each prototype set $\mathcal{P}_i \in PROTO$ might have a different dimensionality n_i selected out of a predefined interval.

For each prototype set $\mathcal{P}_i$ a mapping $\varphi_{n_i}^{\mathcal{P}_i}$ is defined according to Definition 6.1 which maps a given graph set $\mathcal{T} = \{g_1, \ldots, g_N\}$ to m different vector sets $\mathbf{X}^{(1)} = \{\mathbf{x}_1^{(1)}, \ldots, \mathbf{x}_N^{(1)}\}, \ldots, \mathbf{X}^{(m)} = \{\mathbf{x}_1^{(m)}, \ldots, \mathbf{x}_N^{(m)}\}$. Note that the dimensionality of the vectors in $\mathbf{X}^{(s)}$ depends on the number n_s of selected prototypes. A *classifier ensemble* is a set of classifiers $\{f_1, \ldots, f_m\}$ whose results are combined in some way. The key idea of ensemble meth-

---

Algorithm 6.13 Generating m prototype sets out of one graph set.

Input: Training graphs $\mathcal{T} = \{g_1, \ldots, g_N\}$, number of required prototype sets m,
            and an interval of integers for the dimensionality of the resulting
            feature vectors $[min, max]$

Output: Set $PROTO$ consisting of m different prototype sets of
            size $n_i \in [min, max]$ each

1: initialize $TABU$ to the empty set $\{\}$
2: initialize $PROTO$ to the empty set $\{\}$
3: **for** $i = \{1, \ldots, m\}$ **do**
4:      $\mathcal{P}_i = \{\}$
5:      select n randomly out of $[min, max]$
6:      **for** $j = \{1, \ldots, n\}$ **do**
7:        **if** $|TABU| == N$ **then**
8:          reset $TABU$ to the empty set $\{\}$
9:        **else**
10:        select p randomly out of $\mathcal{T} \setminus TABU$
11:        $\mathcal{P}_i = \mathcal{P}_i \cup \{p\}$
12:        $TABU = TABU \cup \{p\}$
13:      **end if**
14:     **end for**
15:     $PROTO = PROTO \cup \{\mathcal{P}_i\}$
16: **end for**
17: **return** $PROTO$

---

ods is to combine several classifiers such that the resulting combined system achieves a higher classification accuracy than the original classifiers individually [2]. In statistical pattern recognition, a large number of methods for the creation and combination of classifiers have been developed over the past few years. *Bagging*, for instance, creates classifiers by randomly selecting the set of training examples to be used for each classifier [300]. A similar idea is that of *random feature subset selection* [301]. In this method, one randomly selects the features (dimensions) to be used for each feature vector to create a group of classifiers. A third prominent example of classifier creation methods is *boosting*, where classifiers are created sequentially out of a single base classifier by giving successively higher weights to those training samples that have been misclassified [302].

The general methodology of graph embedding in real vector spaces by means of prototype selection can be used in a straightforward manner to build a classifier ensemble. We have shown how one can produce arbitrarily many vector sets out of one graph set. Clearly, for each vector space embedded graph set an individual classifier can be trained and, finally, the results of those classifiers can be combined in an appropriate way (in Appendix C three methods – voting, Borda count, and Bayes' combination – for classifier combination are described in detail). Hence, rather than using elaborated methods for prototype selection, a random method is used to construct a powerful and stable classifier ensemble.

6.8 Summary

In some special cases with some particular graph representations it might be possible to extract numerical features that – more or less accurately – describe the topology of the underlying graphs. However, to this day there exists no universal possibility to embed graphs in vector spaces in a satisfactory way. Spectral methods have to be adopted to a certain problem domain and the definition of other numerical descriptors for graphs is somewhat handcrafted. Moreover, it seems that these methods are not fully able to cope with labeled graphs and structural errors.

The present book eliminates these problems and offers a general graph embedding framework applicable to any kind of graphs in a unified way. Simultaneously, our embedding procedure is able to cope with noisy data. The embedding framework exploits the fact that one of the few mathematical operations which can be carried out in various ways in the domain of graphs is the computation of dissimilarities. Using dissimilarities to a predefined set of prototypical graphs, a vectorial description of input graphs is obtained. Due to the flexibility in its application and high expressiveness in its interpretation, the concept of graph edit distance is used as a basic dissimilarity model. The conceptual simplicity of dissimilarity embeddings, combined with the ability to cope with any kind of graphs as well as with structural errors, makes this graph embedding framework extremely powerful.

For the critical task of prototype selection, six prototype selection strategies, six prototype reduction schemes, and six feature selection algorithms are proposed. In case of Lipschitz embeddings, three reference set creation techniques are introduced. Finally, it is shown how random prototype selection can be used in order to build a classifier ensemble. All of these methods aim at overcoming the problems of too high dimensional graph maps as well as noisy and redundant data.

We observe that our graph embedding procedure is closely related to graph kernels. However, the graph embedding approach is more general than graph kernels for a number of reasons. First, as the map of each graph in the target vector space is explicitly computed, not only kernel machines, but also other non-kernelizable algorithms can be applied to the resulting vector representation. Second, there are almost no restrictions on the type of graphs the proposed method can deal with. It can be applied to directed or undirected graphs, and to graphs without or with labels on their nodes and/or edges. In case there are labels on the nodes and/or edges, these labels can be of any nature, for example, they can be elements from a finite or infinite set of discrete symbols, the set of integer numbers, real numbers, or real vectors. The graphs to be embedded can even be hypergraphs [303]. Third, our method is versatile in the sense that it is possible to integrate domain specific knowledge about object similarity, if available, when defining the cost of the elementary edit operations.

In the next two chapters vector space embedded graphs are used for the tasks of classification (Chapter 7) and clustering (Chapter 8). Thereby the versatility and great power of the proposed embedding procedure will be empirically verified on a number of graph datasets from diverse application fields.

Classification Experiments with Vector Space Embedded Graphs

7

The purpose of computation is insight, not numbers.

Richard Hamming

The purpose of the experimental evaluation described in this chapter is to empirically verify the power and applicability of the proposed graph embedding framework. To this end, several classification tasks are carried out using vector space embedded graphs. The classifier mainly used in the vector space is the support vector machine, or SVM for short [251]. Of course, any other statistical classifier could be used for this purpose as well. However, we feel that the SVM is particularly suitable because of its theoretical advantages and its superior performance that has been empirically confirmed in many practical classification problems[1]. The classification accuracies achieved with SVMs on the embedded graphs are compared against two standard graph classification methods.

In contrast with the high representational power of graphs, we observe a lack of general classification algorithms that can be applied in the graph domain. One of the few classifiers directly applicable to arbitrary graphs is the k-nearest-neighbor classifier (k-NN) in conjunction with some graph dissimilarity measure (here graph edit distance is used). Given a labeled set of training graphs, an unknown graph is assigned to the class that occurs most frequently among the k nearest graphs (in terms of edit distance) from the training set. The decision boundary of a k-NN is a piecewise linear function which makes it very flexible. This classifier in the graph domain

---

[1]Note that in [241] an experimental comparison of various classification algorithms applied to vector space embedded graphs is presented. In this work it has been shown that SVMs generally perform the best among all tested statistical classifiers.

175

will serve us as our first reference system. (See Section 3.4.1 and 4.2 for a more thorough description of the nearest-neighbor classification scheme and the classification accuracies achieved on all graph data sets.)

The second reference system to be employed in the present book is a similarity kernel in conjunction with an SVM (referred to as sim). This approach basically turns the existing dissimilarity measure (graph edit distance) into a similarity measure by mapping low distance values to high similarity values and vice versa. To this end we use a monotonically decreasing transformation. Given the edit distance $d(g, g')$ of two graphs g and g', the similarity kernel is defined by

$$\kappa(g, g') = \exp(-\gamma d(g, g')^2) \quad ,$$

where $\gamma > 0$. Comparing the performance of this similarity kernel with the performance of the embedding procedure might be a first step towards understanding whether the power of our system is primarily due to the embedding process or to the strength of the kernel classifier. (See Section 5.6 for a thorough description of the classification accuracies achieved on all graph data sets using SVMs in conjunction with sim.)

The remainder of this chapter is organized as follows. Next, in Section 7.1 the same classifier (k-NN) as for the first reference system is applied to vector space embedded graphs. This experiment can be understood as a preliminary step to the thorough evaluation of classification scenarios in Section 7.2, where SVMs are used for classification. For the purpose of a clear arrangement, Section 7.2 is divided into five subsections each devoted to one particular embedding system (7.2.1 prototype selection; 7.2.2 prototype reduction; 7.2.3 feature selection and dimensionality reduction; 7.2.4 Lipschitz embedding; 7.2.5 ensemble methods). Finally, in Section 7.3, a summary and overview of the large-scale experiments is given.

7.1   Nearest-Neighbor Classifiers Applied to Vector Space Embedded Graphs

Before the experimental evaluation of SVM classifiers applied to vector space embedded graphs is carried out, a preliminary experiment is of special interest. Traditionally, for classification of graph representations some sort of graph distance is used. In other words, the classification decision in such a scenario only relies on direct dissimilarity information captured through some graph matching process. By means of the proposed graph embedding procedure, in contrast, the dissimilarity information originally used in the graph domain for classification is now used as representation formalism. The task of classification is eventually carried out based on the dissimilarity vectors. Hence, both systems, the original and the embedding approach, use dissimilarities of graphs – albeit in a fundamentally different way. This gives rise to the question whether or not a general loss of information occurs when graphs are transformed into vectors of dissimilarities.

In order to find this out, the first experiment to be conducted is a comparison between nearest-neighbor classifiers applied in both the graph domain and in the vector space established through graph embedding. Applying a classifier of the nearest-neighbor type to the embedded graphs and compare them with nearest-neighbor classifiers in the original graph domain might help in understanding whether or not the representational power of graphs can be maintained in the generated dissimilarity vectors.

For the embedding framework the edit distances optimized for the k-NN classifier are used[2] (see also Section 4.2). For the present experiment the prototype selection strategies are employed only (see Section 6.3). Hence, for the task of graph embedding in real vector spaces two meta parameters have to be validated, namely the prototype selection method and the number of prototypes selected, i.e. the dimensionality of the target feature space. In order to determine suitable values of these two meta parameters, a k-NN classifier using Euclidean distance is applied to each graph set, embedded in a vector space with all of the prototype selectors described in Section 6.3, varying the dimensionality of the embedding vector space over a certain interval.

Thus, for each embedding procedure and each k, the classification accuracy can be regarded as a function of the dimensionality, i.e. the number of selected prototypes. This optimization is illustrated on the Letter low data set in Fig. 7.1, where the classification accuracies on the validation set for each prototype selector (both classindependent and classwise), each dimensionality, and different values for parameter k are shown.

The poor classification accuracy of the center prototype selection (cps) is striking. This prototype selection method, which selects graphs located in the center of the training set only, is definitely not adequate for graph embedding. Too much redundancy and too little information is captured in the resulting vector space embedded graphs. Obviously, the weak selection strategy of cps can be compensated by classwise selection or by selecting a large number of prototypes (in case of Letter low data set more than 300

---

[2]This accounts for all graph embeddings made in the present chapter.

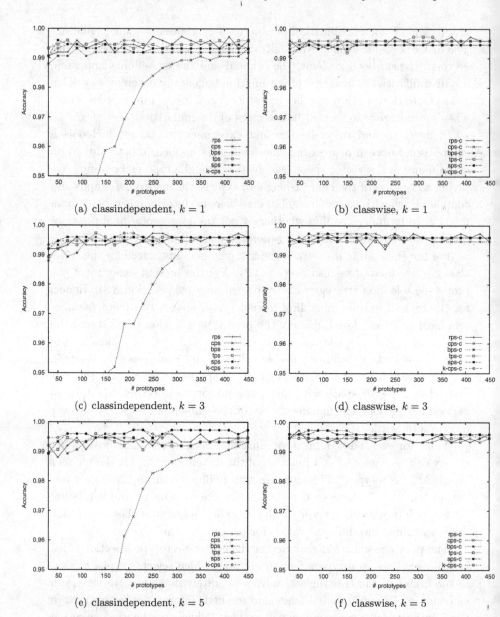

(a) classindependent, $k = 1$

(b) classwise, $k = 1$

(c) classindependent, $k = 3$

(d) classwise, $k = 3$

(e) classindependent, $k = 5$

(f) classwise, $k = 5$

Fig. 7.1 Validation of the prototype selectors on the Letter low data set for a k-NN classifier.

prototypes are necessary to achieve results similar to the other selection strategies).

Whether classindependent or classwise selection is used, the pairwise differences of the classification accuracies among the different selection methods are only marginal (with the exception of cps). Due to the constraint that each class is individually considered in the classwise prototype selection, the different selection algorithms conform to each other even more. That is, the relative difference between the performance achieved by different classwise prototype selectors is smaller than that of different classindependent selections. Similar results can be observed in Appendix D where this validation procedure is illustrated on all remaining data sets.

By means of this procedure, for each prototype selection strategy, the optimal number of prototypes n and the optimal number of neighbors k can be determined for every data set on the validation set. The parameter combination (n, k) that results in the lowest classification error on the validation set is finally applied to the independent test set. The results obtained on the test set by means of this procedure are reported in Table 7.1.

On two data sets, the Fingerprint and Webpage data, the embedding procedure with subsequent k-NN classification completely fails. Regardless of the prototype selection strategy, the classifier in the embedding space always performs statistically significantly worse than the reference system in the graph domain. Due to these poor results, some information loss through graph embedding can be assumed on these two data sets. In addition, some particular deteriorations can be observed on four more data sets (Letter low, Letter medium, Digit, and GREC). Yet, a clear majority of the results achieved in the embedding space do not significantly differ from the results in the graph domain. For instance, on four of the data sets (Letter high, AIDS, Mutagenicity, and Protein) no statistically significant deteriorations can be observed. On Digit and GREC only one prototype selector each, cps and cps-c, respectively, leads to a deterioration of the accuracy with statistical significance. On the other hand, several statistically significant improvements are achieved with the novel embedding framework compared to the reference system. This is the case, for instance, on the AIDS data set for all but one selection strategy (k-cps-c).

Regarding these inconclusive results, no clear answer to the question about the degree of information loss due to graph embedding can be given. Yet, there is empricial evidence that in general k-NN classifiers using graph edit distance and k-NN classifiers relying on graph edit distance based vectors perform similarly. However, the great potential of graph embedding

Table 7.1 Classification accuracy of a k-NN in the graph domain (k-NN) (first reference system see Section 3.4.1 and 4.2) and classification accuracy of a k-NN applied to vector space embedded graphs (using the prototype selectors rps, cps, bps,...). ①/❶ Stat. significant improvement/deterioration compared to the reference system (k-NN) using a Z-test at significance level $\alpha = 0.05$.

Data Set	k-NN	rps	cps	bps	tps	sps	k-cps	rps-c	cps-c	bps-c	tps-c	sps-c	k-cps-c
Letter low	99.3	98.8	98.5❶	98.5❶	98.7❶	99.1	99.1	99.1	99.1	99.3	98.9	99.2	99.1
Letter medium	94.4	93.5	92.1❶	94.4	93.6	93.9	94.0	93.1①	94.1	93.2①	93.6	93.6	93.5
Letter high	89.1	90.0	87.7	90.1	90.7①	89.6	89.2	90.3	90.4	90.0	90.8①	89.9	90.1
Digit	97.4	97.1	95.8❶	98.1①	97.3	97.9	97.9	97.7	97.0	97.4	97.5	97.6	97.7
Fingerprint	79.1	58.9❶	59.8❶	57.9❶	59.1❶	57.6❶	59.3❶	59.8❶	59.3❶	59.4❶	58.7❶	58.5❶	58.0❶
GREC	82.2	82.6	81.6	85.0①	83.0	84.0①	84.0①	83.4	79.9❶	85.3①	82.9	80.8	84.9①
AIDS	94.9	96.1①	96.3①	96.9①	96.9①	96.8①	96.9①	96.2①	96.5①	96.5①	96.3①	96.1①	95.7
Mutagenicity	66.9	66.2	65.9	68.0	65.3	66.1	66.6	65.6	65.2	67.2	65.9	67.5	66.2
Protein	68.5	64.0	64.5	65.0	65.0	65.5	66.0	64.0	64.0	64.0	64.0	64.5	64.5
Webpage	80.6	70.1❶	68.5❶	73.1❶	69.5❶	74.0❶	75.3❶	72.9❶	69.2❶	74.6❶	70.9❶	75.5❶	74.9①

is obvious. Through graph embedding we gain the possibility to access a wide spectrum of classification algorithms beyond nearest-neighbor classifiers. Therefore, there is no need to constrain the embedding classification scheme to this rather simple classification algorithm. The next question to be answered is how more elaborated classifiers, which are not directly applicable to the original graph data, perform on vector space embedded graphs.

7.2 Support Vector Machines Applied to Vector Space Embedded Graphs

Given the graph maps in some vector space, one of the most powerful and flexible classifiers can be applied to them, viz. the SVM (see Section 5.4.1 for a thorough introduction into this kernel classifier). In the present section classification results achieved with this classification procedure are compared to both reference systems (the k-NN and the similarity kernel). For the task of graph embedding, prototype selection, prototype reduction, feature selection and dimensionality reduction, the Lipschitz approach, and ensemble methods are employed.

7.2.1 *Prototype Selection*

7.2.1.1 *Experimental Setup and Validation of the Meta Parameters*

Using prototype selection algorithms for the task of graph embedding in real vector spaces, the number of prototypes n to be selected has to be validated. To this end, each graph set is embedded in a vector space with all of the prototype selectors described in Section 6.3, varying the dimensionality of the embedding vector space over a certain interval. With the resulting vector sets an SVM is eventually trained. We make use of an SVM with RBF kernel[3] which has parameters C and γ. Parameter C corresponds to the misclassification penalty and γ is used in the RBF kernel function $\kappa(x, y) = \exp\left(-\gamma||x - y||^2\right)$. In Fig. 7.2 (a)–(d) such an SVM pa-

---

[3]We make use of the RBF kernel since it is the most widely used kernel and it has been extensively studied in various fields of pattern recognition [5]. In fact, it is unfortunately not always possible to make the right choice of a kernel a priori. Note that in [304] also other kernel functions are applied to the embedded graphs (linear and polynomial kernels). However, it turns out that for the problem of classifying vector space embedded graphs the RBF kernel generally performs best.

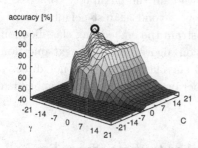

(a) SVM validation, $n = 50$ (the parameter values are on a logarithmic scale to the basis 2)

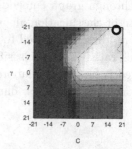

(b) SVM validation, $n = 50$ (the parameter values are on a logarithmic scale to the basis 2)

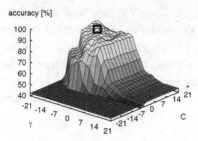

(c) SVM validation, $n = 310$ (the parameter values are on a logarithmic scale to the basis 2)

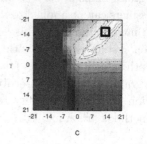

(d) SVM validation, $n = 310$ (the parameter values are on a logarithmic scale to the basis 2)

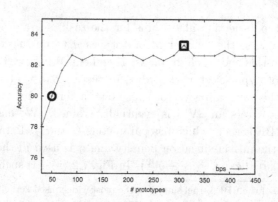

(e) Validation of the number of prototypes

Fig. 7.2   Validation of the meta parameter triple (n, C, γ) on the Fingerprint data set.

rameter validation on the Fingerprint data set is illustrated for two specific numbers of prototypes ($n = 50$ and $n = 310$). In these figures the classification accuracy on the validation set is plotted as a function of C and γ. The best classification result achieved for both numbers of prototypes is marked with a black circle and a black square, respectively. In Fig. 7.3 this specific SVM parameter validation is illustrated on various additional data sets for one fixed value of the dimensionality n and one specific prototype selection method each. It turns out that on all data sets the classification performance is best for large values of parameter C and small values of parameter γ.

The SVM optimization is performed on a validation set for every possible dimension of the target space and every prototype selection method. Thus, for each embedding procedure the classification accuracy can be regarded as a function of the dimensionality and the prototype selector. This complete optimization is illustrated on the Fingerprint data set in Fig. 7.2 (e) where the accuracies for a certain prototype selector (here bps is used) and each tested dimensionality are shown. The best results achieved on the validation set with dimensionality $n = 50$ (red circle) and $n = 310$ (red square) correspond to the optimal result achieved during SVM training and are marked as in Fig. 7.2 (a)–(d).

Finally, for each prototype selection method both the number of prototypes n and the SVM parameters (C, γ) can be determined for every data set on the validation set. In Appendix E this optimization of the parameter triple (n, C, γ) is illustrated for all selection strategies on all data sets. The parameter combination that results in the lowest classification error on the validation set is finally applied to the independent test set.

7.2.1.2 *Results and Discussion*

In Table 7.2 the classification accuracies of an SVM applied to the vector space embedded graphs using prototype selection strategies are given. Additionally, the classification results of an SVM applied to embedded graphs where all available training graphs are used as prototypes is given (referred to as all). For this system no selection of prototypes is carried out but the embedding is given by $\varphi_N^{\mathcal{T}} : \mathcal{G} \to \mathbb{R}^N$. Note that the best result per data set is displayed in bold face. We observe that there is only one data set (Mutagenicity) where the raw embedding without prototype selection outperforms the best performing prototype selector. On all other data sets a selection of prototypes is beneficial. Hence, we conclude that rather than

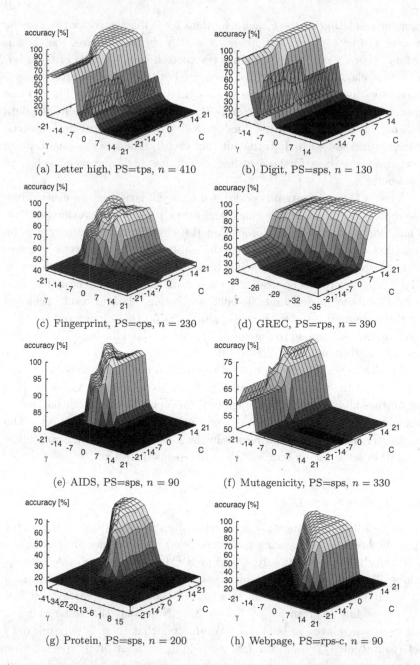

Fig. 7.3   Validation of the meta parameter tuple (C, γ) on various data sets for different prototype selectors (PS) and number of prototypes (n). The parameter values are on a logarithmic scale to the basis 2.

Table 7.2 Classification accuracy of an SVM applied to vector space embedded graphs using all available training graphs (all) and the prototype selectors (rps, cps, bps,...). The best result per data set is displayed in bold face.

Data Set	all	rps	cps	bps	tps	sps	k-cps	rps-c	cps-c	bps-c	tps-c	sps-c	k-cps-c
Letter low	99.2	99.2	98.5	99.2	98.5	99.2	98.8	99.1	99.2	99.2	99.2	**99.3**	**99.3**
Letter medium	94.9	94.8	94.4	94.4	**95.3**	94.3	**95.3**	94.9	94.7	94.7	94.8	94.9	94.4
Letter high	92.5	91.9	90.9	92.5	91.7	92.7	92.5	91.9	91.2	**92.9**	92.4	91.6	92.0
Digit	98.1	98.2	98.0	98.0	98.0	98.5	98.5	98.0	98.0	**98.6**	98.3	**98.6**	98.1
Fingerprint	82.1	81.3	81.5	81.8	82.2	81.8	82.7	82.2	82.4	**83.1**	81.6	82.0	81.7
GREC	91.9	91.7	91.0	90.7	90.7	90.8	90.9	91.8	91.6	91.9	91.7	**92.4**	**92.4**
AIDS	98.0	97.7	97.9	97.5	96.8	98.0	95.2	**98.1**	97.6	98.0	97.9	97.3	97.9
Mutagenicity	**71.9**	70.2	71.1	71.7	71.3	71.1	71.3	70.5	70.2	70.7	71.4	71.5	71.8
Protein	**71.5**	**71.5**	**71.5**	**71.5**	**71.5**	**71.5**	**71.5**	**71.5**	**71.5**	**71.5**	**71.5**	**71.5**	**71.5**
Webpage	**82.4**	**82.4**	82.1	80.8	81.0	80.5	81.9	81.3	80.3	80.1	80.8	82.3	82.3

Table 7.3   Borda count for each prototype selector.

PS	Sum of rank points
sps-c	40
bps-c	42
k-cps-c	44
tps-c	53
k-cps	54
rps-c	55
sps	60
rps	60
bps	64
tps	72
cps-c	73
cps	79

using all available training graphs as prototypes, the selection of a few representative graphs leads to improvements of the classification accuracy in general.

Next we turn to the question which of the prototype selection methods is globally best. To this end a Borda count [2] on the prototype selection methods is applied. For each data set, the prototype selection methods are sorted according to their classification performance in descending order. That is, for a specific data set the best performing selection method is at position one, the second-best method at position two, and so on. The number corresponding to the position in the sorted list is then assigned to each prototype selection method. For instance, on the Letter low data set both sps-c and k-cps-c achieve the best result among all of the proposed methods. Hence, one rank point is assigned to these two methods. Two rank points are assigned to the second best prototype selection method(s), and so on. Finally, for all prototype selection methods the rank points achieved on all ten data sets are accumulated. In Table 7.3 the resulting sum of rank points is given for each prototype selector.

According to Borda count, five out of the the top-six prototype selectors are classwise selection strategies. Hence, classwise selection is clearly superior compared to classindependent selection. As presumed, the center prototype selection method is globally the worst strategy for selecting prototypes for graph embedding (regardless whether classwise or classindependent selection is applied). Considering the top ranked selection methods, we can conclude that there is a tendency that prototype selectors that distribute the graphs more or less uniformly over the whole graph set lead to higher recognition rates. Note that this result reflects the intuitive observation that the prototypes should avoid redundancies and include as much information as possible. The three selection methods sps-c, bps-c, and k-cps-c excel the other methods. Moreover, these three prototype selection methods are not only considered to perform well according to their Borda count. Regarding the results in Table 7.2 we observe that on seven out of ten data sets at least one of these three selection methods achieves the globally best result when compared to all other prototype selectors. (Note that the method all is not considered in this comparison.)

The optimal number n of prototypes selected, i.e. the dimensionality of the embedding vector space, is also of interest. In Fig. 7.4 the average number of selected prototypes relative to all available training graphs is illustrated. Additionally, the standard deviation is also shown for each selection method. The average number of prototypes selected lies somewhere between 40% and 50% in general (except for cps which needs substantially more prototypes in order to achieve good classification results on the validation set). However, the optimal dimensionality of the resulting vector space does not follow a global rule. It crucially depends on the underlying data set as well as the considered prototype selection method. For instance, on the AIDS data set k-cps selects only 4% of all training graphs, while bps-c turns out to be optimal with a selection of 92% of all training graphs on the same data set. With tps-c 11% of all training graphs from the Digit data set are selected, while on the AIDS data set the same selection method performs best with 84% of all available training graphs.

Of course, from the computational complexity point of view, a smaller number of prototypes is preferable, because the smaller the number of prototypes is, the fewer graph edit distance computations have to be performed for transforming graphs into real vectors. As a rule of thumb, especially in cases where no possibility to perform independent validation experiments is given, a classwise selector using about half of the available training graphs as prototypes might be a good choice.

The next evaluations consider the three best prototype selection methods according to the Borda count (sps-c, bps-c, and k-cps-c). In Fig. 7.5 and 7.6 the classification accuracy of an SVM applied to vector space embedded graphs using these three prototype selection strategies are compared against both reference systems (k-NN and sim). Let us first compare the classification accuracies achieved by the embedding framework

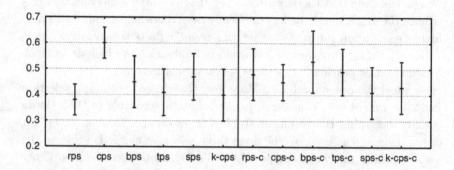

Fig. 7.4 Average and standard deviation of optimized number of selected prototypes (relative to all available training graphs). Shown on the left is classindependent selection, on the right classwise selection.

with the results of the first reference system. In total, the first reference system is outperformed 25 times by our embedding framework while only two deteriorations are observed. Note that none of these deteriorations but 18 of the improvements are statistically significant. Hence, it clearly turns out that the novel procedure of graph embedding and SVM classification is much more powerful than the traditional k-NN in the graph domain.

Next we compare the embedding framework with the similarity kernel sim. It turns out that sim is better than our approach in 11 cases, while the embedding framework outperforms the similarity kernel in 15 cases. Note, however, that ten of the improvements but only two of the deteriorations compared to the second reference system are statistically significant. From these findings we can conclude that the power of our novel approach primarily results from the embedding process itself and not from the strength of the SVM classifier.

One possibility to further improve the classification accuracy achieved on the vector space embedded graphs is to scale the resulting vectorial descriptions of the graphs. Two different procedures are pursued and referred to as *scaling* and *normalizing*. For the first method a linear scaling is applied to each individual feature. Assume max_i and min_i are the maximum and minimum values of the i-th feature x_i in the training vectors. Scaling the features to the interval $[-1, 1]$ means that each feature value x_i is replaced by

$$\hat{x}_i = \frac{2(x_i - min_i)}{max_i - min_i} - 1 \quad .$$

For normalizing, the embedding procedure given in Definition 6.1 in

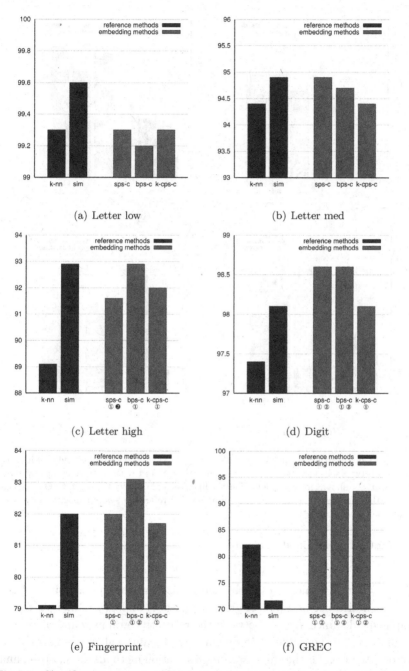

(a) Letter low   (b) Letter med

(c) Letter high   (d) Digit

(e) Fingerprint   (f) GREC

Fig. 7.5 Classification accuracy of SVMs applied to vector space embedded graphs with three prototype selectors (sps-c, bps-c, k-cps-c) compared with both reference systems (①/② Stat. significant improvement over the first/second reference system, ❶/❷ Stat. significant deterioration compared to the first/second reference system using a Z-test at significance level $\alpha = 0.05$).

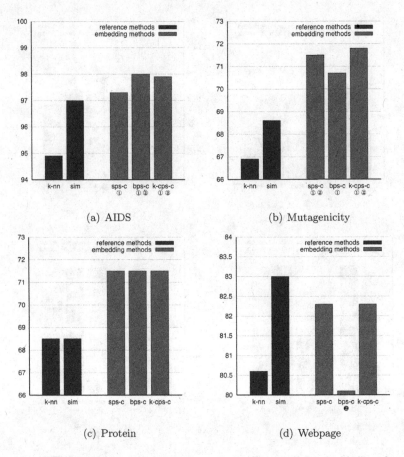

Fig. 7.6   Classification accuracy of SVMs applied to vector space embedded graphs with three prototype selectors (sps-c, bps-c, k-cps-c) compared with both reference systems (①/② Stat. significant improvement over the first/second reference system, ❶/❷ Stat. significant deterioration compared to the first/second reference system using a Z-test at significance level $\alpha = 0.05$).

Section 6.2 is reformulated according to

$$\varphi_n^{\mathcal{P}}(g) = (d(g, p_1)/q, \ldots, d(g, p_n)/q) \quad ,$$

with $q = \sqrt{n}$. By means of such a normalization the upper bound of the Euclidean distance of a pair of graph maps $\varphi(g)$ and $\varphi(g')$ amounts to the graph edit distance $d(g, g')$ between the respective graphs g and g'.

In Table 7.4 the classification accuracies of plain, scaled, and normalized vectors are given for the three prototype selection methods sps-c, bps-c, and k-cps-c. Of course, the whole optimization process of the meta parameters

Table 7.4   Classification accuracies using plain, scaled, and normalized vectors.

Data Set	sps-c			bps-c			k-cps-c		
	plain	scale	norm	plain	scale	norm	plain	scale	norm
Letter low	*99.3*	*99.3*	*99.3*	99.2	99.2	*99.3*	*99.3*	99.2	99.2
Letter medium	*94.9*	94.4	94.7	94.7	94.7	*94.8*	94.4	*94.7*	94.4
Letter high	91.6	92.0	*92.3*	*92.9*	92.8	92.3	*92.0*	*92.0*	*92.0*
Digit	*98.6*	98.5	*98.6*	98.6	*98.7*	*98.7*	98.1	98.5	**98.7**
Fingerprint	*82.0*	81.1	81.9	**83.1**	81.4	81.6	*81.7*	81.1	81.5
GREC	*92.4*	92.0	*92.4*	91.9	92.0	*92.3*	*92.4*	92.1	*92.4*
AIDS	97.3	97.8	**98.1**	*98.0*	97.6	*98.0*	97.9	97.5	**98.1**
Mutagenicity	71.5	*71.6*	71.2	*70.7*	69.8	69.5	**71.8**	71.1	71.0
Protein	71.5	72.5	**73.0**	71.5	62.5	**73.0**	71.5	72.5	**73.0**
Webpage	82.3	**82.7**	82.1	80.1	78.7	*80.4*	*82.3*	79.4	79.6

is independently carried out for both scaled and normalized data. Regarding the results obtained for each of the tested prototype selection strategies individually, the following observations can be made (the best result per prototype selector is displayed in italics). In 15 cases the plain vectors achieve the best result, while in six and 18 cases the scaled and normalized vectors achieve the best result per prototype selector, respectively. Considering the results independently from the prototype selectors, we observe eight cases where the plain vectors achieve the overall best result. In three and 11 cases the scaled and normalized vectors achieve the overall best result on a certain data set, respectively. (These globally best results per data set are displayed in bold face.) Hence, while scaling improves the existing system in a clear minority of the cases, a normalization of the vectors is a clear benefit. Especially on four data sets (Digit, GREC, AIDS, and Protein) the classification system using normalized vectors always achieves better results than with scaled or plain vectors (regardless of the prototype selector actually used).

In Table 7.5 the best possible classification accuracy with plain, scaled (marked by (s)), or normalized (marked by (n)) vectors is compared against the two reference systems[4]. With this improved embedding framework, the first reference system is outperformed by sps-c in nine out of ten data sets.

---

[4]The choice of the best possible system is made on the test set.

Table 7.5 Embedding methods with plain, scaled (s), and normalized (n) vectors vs. reference systems. (①/② Stat. significant improvement over the first/second reference system, ❶/❷ Stat. significant deterioration compared to the first/second reference system using a Z-test at significance level $\alpha = 0.05$).

	ref. systems		embedding methods		
Data Set	k-NN	sim	sps-c	bps-c	k-cps-c
Letter low,	99.3	99.6	99.3	99.3 (n)	99.3
Letter medium	94.4	94.9	94.9	94.8 (n)	94.7 (s)
Letter high	89.1	92.9	92.3 ① (n)	92.9 ①	92.0 ①
Digit	97.4	98.1	98.6 ①②	98.7 ①② (n)	98.7 ①② (n)
Fingerprint	79.1	82.0	82.0 ①	83.1 ①②	81.7 ①
GREC	82.2	71.6	92.4 ①②	92.3 ①② (n)	92.4 ①②
AIDS	94.9	97.0	98.1 ①② (n)	98.0 ①②	98.1 ①② (n)
Mutagenicity	66.9	68.6	71.6 ①② (s)	70.7 ①	71.8 ①②
Protein	68.5	68.5	73.0 (n)	73.0 (n)	73.0 (n)
Webpage	80.6	82.9	82.7 ① (s)	80.4 ❷ (n)	82.3

Seven of these improvements are statistically significant. For bps-c we observe eight improvements whereof six are statistically significant. Finally, for k-cps-c again seven improvements compared to the k-NN can be reported (six with statistical significance). Compared to the second reference system, we observe three deteriorations and five improvements with sps-c, three deteriorations and six improvements with bps-c, and five deteriorations and five improvements with k-cps-c. Note that for each prototype selection method four of the improvements compared to sim are statistically significant. Hence, 12 statistically significant improvements are observed in total, while only one of the deteriorations is statistically significant (bps-c on the Webpage data set).

7.2.2   *Prototype Reduction Schemes*

7.2.2.1   *Experimental Setup and Validation of the Meta Parameters*

In case of prototype reduction schemes the number of prototypes is determined automatically and cannot be influenced by the user. This is a crucial advantage over prototype selection methods where the prototypes and in particular their number are determined by means of the target classifier on a validation set. Hence, with the proposed prototype reduction schemes exactly one embedded graph set is obtained rather than various sets with different dimensionalities. With the resulting vector sets, which are still composed of independent training, validation, and test sets, an SVM is trained. Formally, in the present scenario the SVM parameter pair (C, γ) has to be tuned on the validation set, whereas n, the number of prototypes, is now given by the reduction algorithms. Consequently, these procedures lead to significant speed-ups of the validation process when compared to the previous selection strategies. Assuming that in case of prototype selection the dimensionality n is incrementally validated with an interval size of t, the speed-up factor for the validation procedure is roughly $\frac{N}{t}$, where N is the size of the training set $\mathcal{T}$.

7.2.2.2 Results and Discussion

In Table 7.6 the classification accuracies achieved with all prototype reduction schemes are given. Additionally, results of both reference systems are included in the same table. We observe some statistically significant deteriorations of the embedding framework compared to both reference systems. Especially on the Protein data set various prototype reduction schemes are outperformed by both k-NN and sim. Five additional significant deteriorations can be observed on Letter low, Letter high, and Webpage concerning the second reference system only.

On the other hand, compared to the first reference system, on seven out of ten data sets statistically significant improvements are possible with the embedding system (for instance with cond and mCond). Compared to the second reference system also several improvements can be reported. For instance with mCond, on five data sets improvements compared to sim can be observed. On three data sets (GREC, AIDS, and Mutagenicity) these improvements are statistically significant.

Comparing the prototype reduction schemes against each other, one can conclude that the modified condensing approach (mCond) generally performs best. On five out of ten data sets this reduction scheme leads to the overall best classification result (including the reference methods). We observe that the three reduction schemes cond, mCond, and edit cover the best results per data set in eight out of the ten cases (all but Letter medium and Digit).

In order to compare the prototype reduction schemes with the proto-

Table 7.6 Embedding methods using prototype reduction schemes vs. reference systems. (①/②) Stat. significant improvement over the first/second reference system, ❶/❷ Stat. significant deterioration compared to the first/second reference system using a Z-test at significance level $\alpha = 0.05$).

Data Set	ref. systems		embedding methods					
	k-NN	sim	cond	mCond	edit	red	merg	sel
Letter low	99.3	99.6	99.1	99.2	99.2	99.2	99.1 ❷	98.9 ❷
Letter medium	94.4	94.9	95.1	94.3	95.1	94.3	95.2	95.1
Letter high	89.1	92.9	92.3 ①	92.0 ①	92.5 ①	91.9 ①	91.6 ①❷	92.3 ①
Digit	97.4	98.1	98.4 ①	98.4 ①	98.3 ①	98.4 ①	98.5 ①	98.4 ①
Fingerprint	79.1	82.0	81.4 ①	81.3 ①	82.4 ①	81.4 ①	81.5 ①	81.2 ①
GREC	82.2	71.6	92.0 ①②	91.8 ①②	91.5 ①②	91.3 ①②	90.5 ①②	91.3 ①②
AIDS	94.9	97.0	97.7 ①②	98.0 ①②	97.3 ①	97.3 ①	97.9 ①②	97.1 ①
Mutagenicity	66.9	68.6	70.1 ①	71.6 ①②	70.4 ①	68.5	70.1 ①	69.6 ①
Protein	68.5	68.5	68.5	62.0 ❶❷	62.0 ❶❷	68.0	63.0 ❶❷	67.0
Webpage	80.6	82.9	83.1 ①	83.7 ①	79.2 ❷	82.9 ①	82.4	81.2 ❷

type selection algorithms, the following experiment is carried out. We use the best result of the three reduction schemes cond, mCond, and edit on each data set and compare this classification accuracy with the best result achieved with one of the three prototype selection strategies sps-c, bps-c, and k-cps-c. In Fig. 7.7 this comparison is visualized for all of the ten data sets. Whenever the best classification accuracy of the three classwise prototype selection methods (PS-C) outperforms the best result achieved with one of the three prototype reduction schemes (PRS), the difference between the respective classification accuracies is plotted with a black bar. For all other cases, i.e. for data sets where the best performing prototype reduction scheme outperforms the best performing prototype selector, a gray bar shows the relative difference of the classification accuracies between the two approaches.

We observe that on most of the data sets, i.e. on seven out of ten, the former approach of prototype selection outperforms the novel idea of prototype reduction. Hence, there is a tendency that prototype selection generally performs better than prototype reduction. Yet, using the reduction schemes rather than a heuristic selection might still be beneficial as the cumbersome validation of the embedding space dimensionality can be omitted. Moreover, note that only on one data set the improvement achieved with prototype selection compared to prototype reduction is actually statistically significant (Fingerprint). Summarizing, prototype reduction achieves comparable results to prototype selection. The slight deteriorations observed on some data sets are repaid in terms of substantial reductions of the validation time.

7.2.3   *Feature Selection and Dimensionality Reduction*

7.2.3.1   *Experimental Setup and Validation of the Meta Parameters*

For the feature selection algorithms described in Section 6.5 all available elements from the training set are used as prototypes, i.e. $\mathcal{P} = \mathcal{T}$. Consequently, we obtain real vectors with N features through $\varphi_N^{\mathcal{T}} : \mathcal{G} \to \mathbb{R}^N$. The full set of features is denoted by $\{x_1, \ldots, x_N\}$. Eventually, a feature subset selection method is applied to the resulting vectors in order to define a feature ranking $x_{(1)}, x_{(2)}, \ldots, x_{(N)}$, where $x_{(1)}$ denotes the top ranked feature according to the given feature selection algorithm, $x_{(2)}$ the second-best

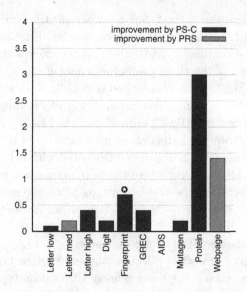

Fig. 7.7 Differences of classification accuracies between classwise prototype selection strategies (PS-C) and prototype reduction schemes (PRS). The symbol ✪ indicates a statistically significant improvement compared to the other system using a Z-test at significance level $\alpha = 0.05$.

feature, and so on[5]. Based on the ranking, nested subsets of features

$$\{x_{(1)}\} \subset \{x_{(1)}, x_{(2)}\} \subset \ldots \subset \{x_{(1)}, x_{(2)}, \ldots, x_{(N)}\}$$

can be defined. An optimal subset of features can eventually be found by varying the size of the feature subset. Hence, each graph set is embedded in a vector space with the feature subset selection methods described in Section 6.5, varying the number of retained features over a certain interval. Next, for each of the resulting vector sets an SVM is trained.

As this SVM optimization is performed on a validation set for every possible dimension of the target space, the classification accuracy can be regarded as a function of the dimensionality, similar to the validation procedure for prototype selection. This final optimization is illustrated on four data sets in Fig. 7.8 where the accuracies for the three feature selection algorithms chi, info, and svm and each dimensionality are shown (the validation on the remaining data sets is illustrated in Appendix G). Regarding these validation results, the conclusion that svm feature selection generally

---

[5]Note that for PCA, kernel PCA, and MDA not only a feature ranking but also a feature transformation is obtained.

performs the best among the three tested feature selection methods can be drawn.

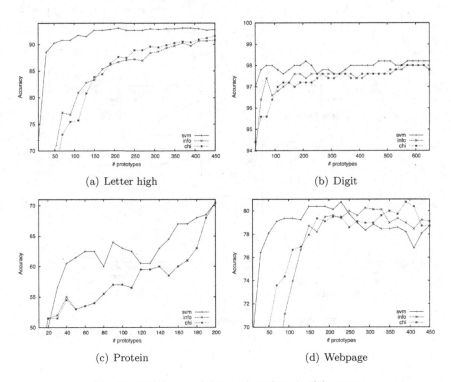

(a) Letter high   (b) Digit

(c) Protein   (d) Webpage

Fig. 7.8   Validation of the number of retained features.

For PCA based feature selection, we use two procedures to determine the optimal dimensionality of the target space. For the first method the validation set is explicitly used to find the number of eigenvectors that have to be retained. Similarly to the procedures described before, for each dimensionality and each possible value of C and γ, an SVM with RBF kernel is trained and its performance is evaluated on the validation set. In Fig. G.3 (solid line) the best classification results achieved on the validation set with the best (C, γ) pair for various dimensionality values are displayed (the validation on the remaining data sets is illustrated in Appendix G). The dimensionality for the final embedding corresponds to the dimensionality achieving the best classification accuracy on the validation set. We refer to

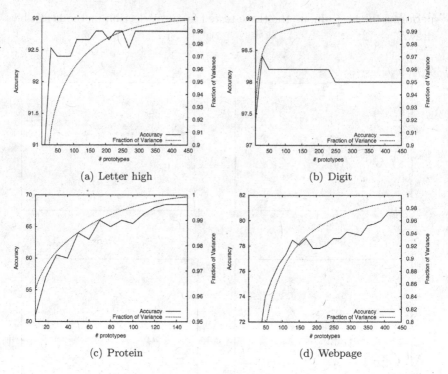

Fig. 7.9   Validation of the PCA space dimensionality.

this first PCA validation procedure as *optimal*.

Together with the accuracy, another curve is shown in Fig. G.3 (dashed line). This curve displays the fraction of the variance kept in the PCA reduced vectors as a function of the dimensionality. As one expects, the fraction of variance monotonically increases with the number of eigenvectors retained. The optimal dimensionality of the target space can now be estimated with a second procedure, where the fraction of variance rather than the classification accuracy on the validation set is used as the decision criterion. We use several cut-off points in the fraction curve, viz. on fractions of 0.95, 0.99, 0.999, and 0.9999 of the captured variance. The number of eigenvectors needed to keep at least these fractions of variance are used for embedding. The great benefit of this second validation procedure is that no classifier has to be trained for determining the dimensionality of the embedding space. We refer to this second PCA optimization procedure as *fraction of variance*. Note that on some data sets, not all cut-off points are reached. For instance, on the Webpage data set with the maximum number of tested dimensions a fraction of variance equal to 0.99202 is obtained. Hence, for this data set only the first two cut-off points are reached.

For the approach with kernel PCA we apply an RBF kernel PCA to the embedding vectors instead of a linear transformation. Hence, in the step of feature transformation the meta-parameter γ of the RBF kernel has to be tuned. Using the kernel PCA reduced data, an SVM with linear kernel $\kappa(x, y) = ||x - y||$ is applied to the non-linearly transformed and reduced data for the purpose of classification. From some higher level of abstraction we observe that both systems (linear PCA in conjunction with an SVM using an RBF kernel, and kernel PCA using an RBF kernel in conjunction with a linear SVM) are quite similar. In Fig. 7.10 both approaches are shown schematically. The first system (solid arrows) transforms the graph domain $\mathcal{G}$ into a vector space $\mathbb{R}^N$. Next, a linear transformation (PCA) for mapping the data into an n-dimensional vector space is used. Finally, a support vector machine with RBF kernel is applied which implicitly maps the graphs into a (possibly infinite) feature space $\mathcal{F}_2$ and labels the objects according to a label space Ω. The second system (dashed arrows), by contrast, uses a non-linear transformation of the data (kPCA via $\mathcal{F}_1$ to $\mathbb{R}^n$) in conjunction with a linear support vector machine. So both systems consist of a linear and non-linear part, and the main difference is the order in which these components are applied.

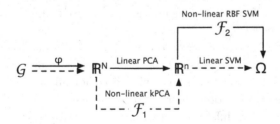

Fig. 7.10   PCA and kernel PCA based classification.

Apparently, one could use a combination of kernel PCA based transformation and non-linear SVM classification. However, with this setting the complexity of the model becomes quite high making an independent validation procedure rather difficult. Hence, we leave this out for future study.

The procedure for the MDA transformed data differs from the validation on PCA data in that no validation set is used. There are two reasons for not using a validation set. First, as the number of dimensions is limited by the number of classes minus one, we always use the maximum possible value. Second, it turns out that for MDA it is more important to provide a large training set for transformation than optimizing the SVM parameter values. Hence, for MDA transformation we merge the validation and training set to one large set. Then the MDA transformation is applied on this new set.

7.2.3.2 *Results and Discussion*

In Table 7.7 the classification accuracies on all data sets achieved with our graph embedding framework in conjunction with the three feature selection algorithms info, chi, and svm are given. For the purpose of comparison, the results of both reference systems are also included in this table. Comparing the feature selection algorithms against each other, one can conclude that, similarly to the validation procedure, the svm approach performs generally best. On nine out of ten data sets svm feature selection leads to the overall best classification result. Furthermore, we observe that info as well as chi are outperformed by both reference systems on several data sets. Yet, with svm feature selection no statistically significant deterioration can be observed. Moreover, by means of svm feature selection the first reference system is outperformed on all but the Letter low data set. Six of these nine improvements are statistically significant. Compared to the second reference system four improvements can be observed whereof three are statistically significant.

We use svm feature selection on each data set and compare the classification accuracy with the result achieved with sps-c prototype selection. In Fig. 7.11 (a) this comparison is visualized for all of the ten data sets. Whenever the classification accuracy of sps-c outperforms the result of svm feature selection, the difference between the respective classification accuracies is plotted with a black bar. For the other cases, i.e. for data sets where the svm selection algorithm outperforms sps-c, a gray bar shows the relative difference of the classification accuracies between the two approaches.

We observe that on six out of ten data sets the approach with sps-c outperforms the feature selection method svm. However, only one of these improvements is statistically significant (Mutagenicity). Out of three

Table 7.7 Embedding methods vs. reference systems. (①/②
Stat. significant improvement over the first/second reference system,
❶/❷ Stat. significant deterioration compared to the first/second reference system using a Z-test at significance level α = 0.05).

Data Set	ref. systems		embedding methods		
	k-NN	sim	info	chi	svm
Letter low	99.3	99.6	98.1 ❶❷	97.7 ❶❷	99.2
Letter medium	94.4	94.9	93.7 ❷	92.7 ❶❷	94.7
Letter high	89.1	92.9	90.9 ①❷	90.5 ❷	92.8 ①
Digit	97.4	98.1	98.2 ①	98.0	98.5 ①②
Fingerprint	79.1	82.0	82.5 ①	80.3 ❷	81.7 ①
GREC	82.2	71.6	91.2 ①②	91.6 ①②	92.2 ①②
AIDS	94.9	97.0	97.5 ①	98.0 ①②	98.1 ①②
Mutagenicity	66.9	68.6	66.6	66.6	68.3
Protein	68.5	68.5	71.5	71.5	71.5
Webpage	80.6	82.9	81.0 ❷	81.9	82.7 ①

improvements achieved by svm feature selection, two are statistically significant (Letter high and AIDS). We conclude that due to this empirical
comparison between svm and sps-c no clear winner can be found. Yet, the
use of all training graphs as prototypes with subsequent feature selection
procedures clearly provides us with a versatile alternative to the heuristic
prototype selectors.

In Table 7.8 the classification accuracies of PCA transformed vector
space embeddings are given. Both optimization procedures are considered,
i.e. the fraction of variance kept in the training set and the optimal classification accuracy on the validation set. Note that the best result per data
set is displayed in bold face. We observe that in eight out of ten cases
the former approach, where the fraction of variance is used as optimization criterion, achieves the best result per data set. Yet, there can be no
specific fraction found as the cut-off point which performs generally the
best. With a fraction of 0.95, 0.99 and 0.9999 three best results per data
set are achieved, respectively. With a fraction of 0.999 two best results
per data set are possible. In view of this, the optimization procedure using the classification accuracy on a validation set as the criterion for the
retained dimensionality (optimal) appears in a better light. On half of the

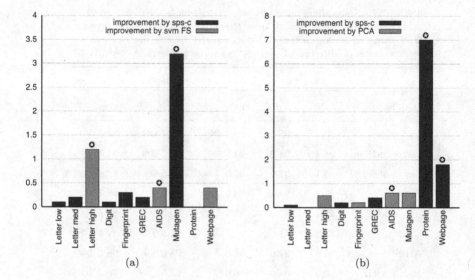

Fig. 7.11   (a) Feature selection strategy (svm) and (b) PCA embedding vs. prototype selection (sps-c). The symbol ✪ indicates a statistically significant improvement compared to the other system using a Z-test at significance level $\alpha = 0.05$.

data sets, this procedure achieves the best possible result. Consequently, a trade-off between the two validation procedures can be observed. While the optimization procedure using the fraction of variance is less time consuming, the optimization procedure using the classification accuracy on the validation set generally performs better.

In Fig. 7.11 (b) a comparison between PCA embedding (we use the optimal criterion) and prototype selection based embedding (we use sps-c as prototype selector) is visualized for all of the ten data sets. Whenever the former outperforms the latter, the difference between the respective classification accuracies is plotted with a gray bar. For the other cases, i.e. for data sets where sps-c outperforms the PCA based embedding, a black bar shows the relative difference of the classification accuracies.

We observe that on half of the data sets the approach with sps-c outperforms the PCA embedding framework. Two of these improvements are statistically significant (Protein and Webpage). Out of four improvements achieved by PCA embedding, only one is statistically significant (AIDS). The poor results achieved by means of PCA embedding on the Protein and Webpage data set motivate some additional investigations. Our experiments are extended in that we use both unscaled and scaled data. Scaled

Table 7.8   Classification accuracies of PCA transformed embeddings where (a) the fraction of variance and (b) the classification accuracy on the validation set is used for defining the PCA space dimensionality.   The best result per data set is displayed in bold face.

Data Set	fraction of variance				optimal
	0.95	0.99	0.999	0.9999	
Letter low	98.8	**99.2**	**99.2**	**99.2**	**99.2**
Letter medium	**95.1**	**95.1**	-	-	94.9
Letter high	92.5	**92.7**	-	-	92.1
Digit	**98.4**	98.3	98.3	-	**98.4**
Fingerprint	67.5	68.7	82.2	**82.5**	82.2
GREC	85.5	91.4	91.8	-	**92.0**
AIDS	93.5	97.5	97.8	**97.9**	**97.9**
Mutagenicity	61.5	65.6	68.9	70.4	**72.1**
Protein	52.5	67.5	**70.5**	-	64.5
Webpage	**82.2**	81.3	-	-	80.5

data is obtained by linearly scaling all individual feature values to the range $[-1, 1]$ (see Section 7.2.1.2 for more details). Of course, the whole optimization process of the meta parameters is independently carried out for both non-scaled and scaled data. On most of the data sets no substantial changes can be observed using scaled rather than plain data. However, on the Fingerprint, the Protein, and the Webpage data set some interesting observations can be made.

In Fig. 7.12 the classification accuracies achieved by both reference methods (k-NN and sim), sps-c with plain and scaled data, and PCA embedding with plain and scaled data are shown. Similarly to prototype selection, in case of PCA embedding the scaling of the data is positively affecting the classification accuracy on both data sets. In contrast to sps-c, in case of PCA embedding the use of a scaling method further improves the classification result significantly. Consequently, the poor result observed with plain data are compensated through scaled data such that no statistically significant deterioriation compared to the prototype selection strategy can be observed any more. Moreover, by means of scaling the classification accuracy achieved by PCA reduced data is increased to 84.0% on Fingerprint data (not illustrated here). In fact, this corresponds to the globally best result among all tested procedures so far. That is, the SVM classifier using PCA embedded data in conjunction with scaling outperforms all other classifiers on the Fingerprint data set with statistical significance.

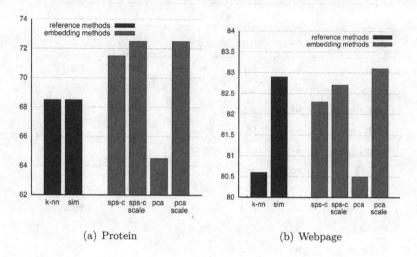

(a) Protein   (b) Webpage

Fig. 7.12   PCA (scale) vs. sps-c (scale) on Protein and Webpage data sets. Through scaling the poor results achieved with PCA embedded graphs can be compensated.

In Fig. 7.13 the results of a comparison between PCA and kernel PCA transformation are shown. As mentioned before, both systems are quite similar in the sense that both approaches have a linear and a non-linear part. Taking into account that both systems are closely related, it is not astounding that they show similar performance on almost all of the ten data sets. Only two statistically significant differences in classification accuracy can be observed, viz. on Letter high, where linear PCA achieves a better result than kernel PCA, and on Webpage, where kernel PCA outperforms the linear PCA.

Regarding the embedding framework applied to MDA reduced data, we observe that the recognition rates are lower than those of the previously reported classification accuracies in general. This can be explained by the fact that when using MDA the maximum possible dimensionality is restricted by the number of classes minus one. For instance, the AIDS data set consists of two classes only and therefore, only one dimensional feature vectors can be extracted through MDA. An SVM trained on these vectors achieves a classification accuracy of 96.8%, which is in fact a remarkable result considering the low dimensional representation. Yet, compared to sps-c, for

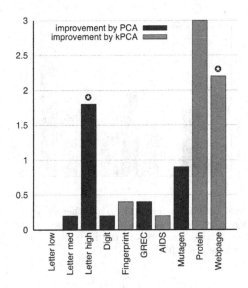

Fig. 7.13 PCA embedding vs. kernel PCA embedding. The symbol ✪ indicates a statistically significant improvement compared to the other system using a Z-test at significance level $\alpha = 0.05$.

instance, this constitutes a statistically significant deterioration. Similar results can be reported on the remaining data sets with the exception of the Webpage data. On this data set, MDA based graph embedding achieves the globally best classification result (see Fig. 7.14). In fact, all other embedding systems are outperformed with statistical significance. Moreover, this procedure is the first subsystem in our embedding framework which is able to significantly outperform the classification accuracy of the second reference system.

7.2.4 *Lipschitz Embeddings*

7.2.4.1 *Experimental Setup and Validation of the Meta Parameters*

For all of our Lipschitz embeddings (Plain-, Center-, and Neighbor-k-Med) the number n of reference sets, and additionally, for Center- and Neighbor-k-Med the (maximum) size m of the reference sets $\mathcal{P}_i$, have to be optimized. In order to determine suitable values of these meta parameters, each graph set is embedded in a vector space with all of the Lipschitz embeddings described in Section 6.6, varying the dimensionality n of the target vector

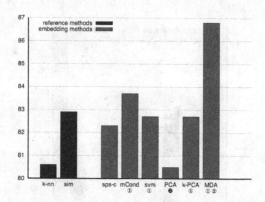

Fig. 7.14   MDA based embedding outperforms all other systems on the Webpage data set. (①/② Stat. significant improvement over the first/second reference system, ❶/❷ Stat. significant deterioration compared to the first/second reference system using a Z-test at significance level $\alpha = 0.05$).

space and the (maximum) size m of the reference sets $\mathcal{P}_i$ over certain intervals[6]. With the resulting embedding vector sets an SVM is eventually trained.

The SVM optimization is performed on a validation set for every possible parameter pair (n, m). Thus, for each embedding procedure the classification accuracy can be regarded as a function of the dimensionality n and the (maximum) size m of the reference sets $\mathcal{P}_i$. This optimization on the validation set is illustrated on the Letter high data set in Fig. F.3 where the accuracies for each dimensionality n, reference set size m, and the distance function f_{min} are shown. Note that for the Lipschitz embeddings based on Plain k-cps, the accuracy of the singleton prototype selector k-cps is additionally shown in Fig. F.3 (a). In Appendix F the validation procedures for Lipschitz embeddings are illustrated on the remaining data sets and all distance functions ($f_{min}, f_{max}, f_{mean}$).

The additional parameter m, which refers to the (maximum) size of the individual reference sets, is optimized to be an integer value out of the set $\{1, 3, 5, 7, 9\}$. Consequently, the validation procedure for both Center-k-cps and Neighbor-k-cps is increased by a factor of five when compared to Plain-k-cps. The best performing parameters for Lipschitz embedding (n, m) and classification (C, γ) are eventually applied to the independent test sets. These results are reported in the next subsection.

---

[6]Note that for P-k-Med the parameter m is not used.

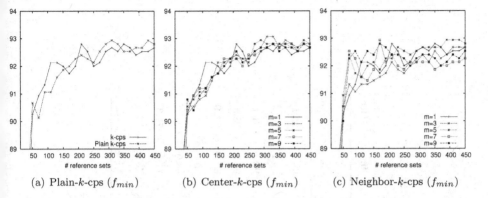

(a) Plain-k-cps (f_{min}) (b) Center-k-cps (f_{min}) (c) Neighbor-k-cps (f_{min})

Fig. 7.15   Validation of the reference set creation techniques for Lipschitz embeddings on the Letter high data set.

7.2.4.2   Results and Discussion

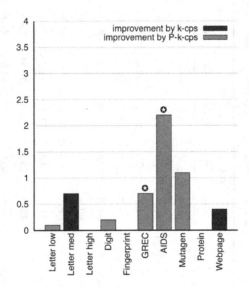

Fig. 7.16   Lipschitz embedding vs. prototype based embedding. The symbol ✪ indicates a statistically significant improvement compared to the other system using a Z-test at significance level $\alpha = 0.05$.

Regarding the classification accuracies given in Table 7.9, the following main findings can be reported. (Note that the best results per data set achieved with the Lipschitz embedded graphs are displayed in bold face.)

Table 7.9 Classification accuracies of Lipschitz embedded graphs. The best result per data set achieved with the Lipschitz embedded graphs is displayed in bold face.

Data Set	P-k-cps(n)			C-k-cps(n, m)			N-k-cps(n, m)		
	f_{min}	f_{max}	f_{mean}	f_{min}	f_{max}	f_{mean}	f_{min}	f_{max}	f_{mean}
Letter low	**99.2**	98.9	99.1	99.1	99.1	99.1	99.1	99.1	99.1
Letter medium	94.5	94.1	94.4	94.7	94.8	94.9	**95.2**	95.1	**95.2**
Letter high	92.3	92.0	**92.5**	92.0	92.0	**92.5**	91.6	**92.5**	91.1
Digit	**98.7**	98.5	**98.7**	98.5	98.5	98.5	98.5	98.5	98.5
Fingerprint	81.9	**81.9**	**81.9**	81.9	**81.9**	**81.9**	**81.9**	**81.9**	**81.9**
GREC	90.8	**91.1**	91.0	90.9	90.4	90.4	90.4	90.4	90.3
AIDS	**98.1**	97.3	97.2	97.4	97.1	97.3	97.6	98.0	97.4
Mutagenicity	71.1	**71.9**	71.2	71.3	71.3	71.3	71.3	71.3	71.3
Protein	**73.0**	**73.0**	**73.0**	**73.0**	**73.0**	**73.0**	**73.0**	**73.0**	**73.0**
Webpage	80.9	80.8	80.9	81.3	81.4	81.0	81.3	**84.2**	81.3

First, among all proposed reference set creation techniques, Plain-k-cps generally performs best. That is, in eight out of ten cases this method leads to the best classification result, and only on the Webpage and Letter medium data sets, one of the other two methods is superior. Therefore, the two methods Center-k-cps and Neighbor-k-cps cannot be recommended in general. The experimental evaluation indicates that they only accidentally perform better than the basic Plain version of k-cps method[7].

Considering Plain-k-cps only, it is remarkable that the extended distance function f_{min} outperforms the other distance functions (f_{max} and f_{mean}) in most of the cases. That is, only on Letter high, GREC, and Mutagenicity the best performing classifier is not relying on f_{min}. Hence, there is a clear tendency that Plain-k-cps in conjunction with f_{min} as extended distance function leads to good Lipschitz embeddings in terms of classification accuracy in the resulting embedding space.

In Fig. 7.16 the Lipschitz embedding classifier based on Plain k-cps in conjunction with f_{min} is compared with the singleton prototype selector k-cps. Note that both systems, Plain-k-cps and k-cps, are based on the same procedure, namely a k-medians clustering applied to the training set of graphs (see also Section 6.3). In the Lipschitz approach the clusters found through k-medians clustering serve as reference sets for the embeddings, while the approach with k-cps uses the set center graph of each cluster as a single prototype for dissimilarity embeddings. Whenever the classification accuracy of the Lipschitz approach outperforms the result achieved with the prototype selector k-cps, the difference between the respective classification accuracies is plotted with a gray bar. Conversely, if k-cps is superior, a black bar shows the difference of the classification accuracies.

We observe that only on Letter medium and Webpage data, the singleton reference sets outperform the extended approach with Lipschitz embeddings. Both improvements are not statistically significant. On the other hand, the Lipschitz approach outperforms the prototype selection method in half of the cases. Two out of these five improvements are statistically significant (GREC and AIDS). That is, allowing general subsets of greater cardinality than one, rather than only singletons, is a clear benefit.

---

[7]However, the results of all reference set creation techniques are reported in the present section for the sake of completeness and should be understood as a report of negative results.

7.2.5   *Ensemble Methods*

7.2.5.1   *Experimental Setup and Validation of the Meta Parameters*

The motivation of classifier ensembles is that errors of an individual classifier can often be compensated by the other ensemble members. In the present book we introduce a general approach to building structural classifier ensembles, i.e. classifiers that make use of graphs as representation formalism (see Section 6.7). The proposed methodology is based on graph embedding in real vector spaces by means of prototype selection. This selection is performed randomized m times such that the procedure leads to m different graph embeddings. Hence, a classifier can be trained for each embedding and the results of the individual classifiers can be combined in an appropriate way. We use voting, Borda count, and Bayes' combination for the task of combination (see Appendix C for further details).

For ensemble methods the question arises how many classifiers should be trained and finally combined to obtain a good classification accuracy. We apply a methodology which is known as *overproduce-and-select* [2]. The idea is to produce a pool of classifiers, followed by a selection procedure that picks the classifiers that are most diverse and accurate. In the present book we make use of the accuracy of the resulting ensembles on the validation set to control the selection of a subset out of the classifier pool. Note, however, that other methods based on the overproduce-and-select paradigm could be used as well [305].

To create a good performing ensemble a sequential floating forward search (SFFS) [286] is applied. The algorithm is given in detail in Algorithm 7.1. First we add the best individual classifier, in terms of the classification accuracy on a validation set, to the ensemble E_1 (line 2). Next, the best fitting classifier f^+, i.e. the classifier that complements the actual ensemble E_k the best, is added incrementally such that an ensemble of size $k + 1$ results (line 5 and 6). Adding a classifier is performed whether or not the accuracy of the resulting ensemble is enhanced. After each forward step, i.e. after the addition of a classifier to the ensemble E_k, a number of backward steps are applied as long as the resulting subsets are getting better than the previously generated ensemble E_{k-1} (line 11–14). In other words, for each classifier in the actual ensemble E_k it is checked whether or not its removal improves the classification accuracy of the parent ensemble E_{k-1}. The classifier that improves the accuracy of the previous ensemble the most is removed. The algorithm does not terminate until m ensembles

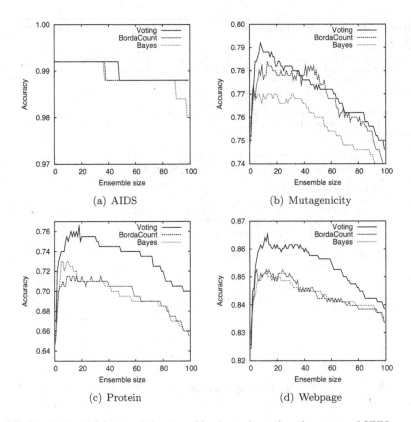

Fig. 7.17   Validation of the ensemble size and members by means of SFFS.

with size $\{1, \ldots, m\}$ are constructed, i.e. the last generated ensemble E_m consists of all available classifiers $\{f_1, \ldots, f_m\}$. Finally, the best performing ensemble E_{max} is returned (line 19).

The size of the initial pool of classifiers is 100 on all data sets. Using the 100 initial classifiers, an SFFS is applied on the validation set for combination via voting, Borda count, and Bayes' combination. In Fig. 7.17 the accuracy of all three combination methods on four data sets is given as a function of the size of the underlying ensemble (the remaining evaluations are given in Appendix H). These curves are plotted in the validation phase in order to find the best performing ensemble members for all combination approaches. In Table 7.10 the optimized ensemble size via SFFS and the corresponding classification accuracies on the validation set are indicated for each data set and combination method.

Algorithm 7.1 Determine the best performing classifier ensemble via SFFS.

Input:　　A set of m classifiers $F = \{f_1, \ldots, f_m\}$ sorted in order of their
　　　　　　individual classification accuracy (f_1 has the highest and f_m
　　　　　　the lowest classification accuracy)
Output:　The best performing classifier ensemble E_{max}

1: Initialize m empty ensembles $E = \{E_1, \ldots, E_m\}$
2: add the best individual classifier to the ensemble: $E_1 = \{f_1\}$
3: intitalize $k := 1$
4: **while** $k < m$ **do**
5:　　$f^+ = argmax_{f_i \in F \setminus E_k} accuracy(E_k \cup \{f_i\})$
6:　　add the classifier f^+ to the ensemble: $E_{k+1} = E_k \cup \{f^+\}$
7:　　$k := k + 1$
8:　　initialize $removed := false$
9:　　**repeat**
10:　　　$removed := false$
11:　　　$f^- = argmax_{f_i \in E_k} accuracy(E_k \setminus \{f_i\})$
12:　　　**if** $accuracy(E_k \setminus \{f_i\}) > accuracy(E_{k-1})$ **then**
13:　　　　$E_{k-1} = E_k \setminus \{f_i\}$
14:　　　　$k := k - 1$
15:　　　　$removed = true$
16:　　　**end if**
17:　　**until** $removed = false$
18: **end while**
19: **return** the ensemble $E_{max} = argmax_{E_i \in E} accuracy(E_i)$ with highest accuracy

---

7.2.5.2　Results and Discussion

In Table 7.11 the classification accuracies on the test set obtained by the optimized ensemble are given for each data set. For the purpose of comparison, the results of both reference systems are also indicated. Comparing the ensemble methods against each other, one can conclude that voting performs generally best (the best result per data set achieved by the ensemble methods is displayed in bold face). On six out of ten data sets this combination method leads to the overall best classification result. Borda count and Bayes' combination, however, achieve only on two and four data sets the best result per data set, respectively.

The ensemble combined by means of voting outperforms the first reference system in nine and the second reference system in eight out of ten cases. Borda count is superior to k-NN and sim in eight and six cases, respectively, while Bayes' combination leads to nine and seven improvements compared to both reference systems. Note that, for all of the three combination methods, seven of the improvements compared to the first reference system are statistically significant. Three of the improvements achieved by Borda count and Bayes' combination compared to the second reference system statistically significant (Fingerprint, GREC, and AIDS). Voting

Table 7.10   Optimized ensemble size and corresponding accuracy on the validation set.

Data Set	voting Ensemble size	voting Accuracy (va)	Borda count Ensemble size	Borda count Accuracy (va)	Bayes Ensemble size	Bayes Accuracy (va)
Letter low	100	99.9	88	99.9	84	99.9
Letter medium	7	96.4	20	96.5	13	96.1
Letter high	6	94.3	37	94.4	21	94.4
Digit	57	98.6	42	98.6	47	98.2
Fingerprint	8	87.0	6	86.0	7	85.0
GREC	20	91.0	21	91.3	17	90.8
AIDS	48	99.2	38	99.2	37	99.2
Mutagenicity	9	79.2	14	78.4	33	77.0
Protein	19	76.5	35	71.5	11	73.0
Webpage	14	86.5	25	85.3	13	85.1

additionally improves the result of sim on the Mutagenicity data set with statistical significance.

In Fig. 7.18 the classifier ensembles combined through voting are compared with the prototype selector sps-c on both the validation set and the test set. Whenever the classification accuracy of the ensemble outperforms the result achieved with the prototype selector, the difference between the respective classification accuracies is plotted with a gray bar. Conversely, if the single embedding classifier is superior to the ensemble method a black bar indicates the respective difference.

We observe that on eight out of ten validation sets the multiple classifier system outperforms the single embedding classifier (note that no significance tests have been carried out on these validation results). Hence, the ensemble method is clearly superior compared to the single classifier during the validation phase. Yet, on the test set, the superiority of the ensemble approach is not as clear as on the validation set. Nevertheless, on six out of ten data sets the multiple classifier system based on random embeddings outperforms the prototype selection based embedding. Two of these improvements are statistically significant (Fingerprint and AIDS). Note that the validation set is used for determining the cost of the edit operations, the SVM optimization, and the ensemble generation trough SFFS. Conse-

Table 7.11 Ensemble methods vs. reference systems. (①/② Stat. significant improvement over the first/second reference system, ❶/❷ Stat. significant deterioration compared to the first/second reference system using a Z-test at significance level $\alpha = 0.05$.)

	ref. systems		ensemble methods		
Data Set	k-NN	sim	voting	Borda count	Bayes
Letter low	99.3	99.6	**99.2**	99.1	99.1
Letter medium	94.4	94.9	95.2	95.2	**95.3**
Letter high	89.1	92.9	92.5 ①	**92.8** ①	**92.8** ①
Digit	97.4	98.1	**98.5** ①	98.4 ①	98.4 ①
Fingerprint	79.1	82.0	83.0 ①②	**83.1** ①②	82.8 ①②
GREC	82.2	71.6	**92.3** ①②	92.1 ①②	**92.3** ①②
AIDS	94.9	97.0	**97.9** ①②	97.8 ①②	97.8 ①②
Mutagenicity	66.9	68.6	**72.4** ①②	71.1 ①	71.2 ①
Protein	68.5	68.5	71.5	68.5	**72.5**
Webpage	80.6	82.9	**83.7** ①	82.6 ①	82.8 ①

quently, the fact that the outstanding results on the validation set cannot be repeated on the test set can be ascribed to an overfitting effect. That is, the overly complex system too strongly adopts to the validation set. Given enough data, independent validation sets could be formed in order to find optimal meta parameters for the individual steps in the embedding and ensemble framework. We leave this out for future work.

7.3   Summary and Discussion

This chapter presents large-scale experiments including classification tasks on ten different graph data sets. The experimental evaluation aims at testing the power and flexibility of the graph embedding framework based on dissimilarity representation.

In a preliminary experiment the vector space embedded graphs have been classified by means of a k-NN scheme. Note that the first reference system used in the present book employs the same classifier in the graph domain. Both systems crucially rely on the same paradigm of graph edit distance. The traditional approach in the graph domain uses the informa-

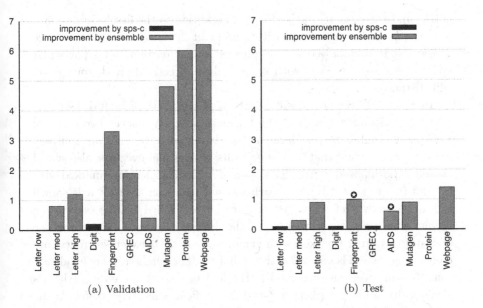

(a) Validation   (b) Test

Fig. 7.18   Accuracy of the ensemble vs. accuracy of sps-c on the validation and test set. The symbol ✪ indicates a statistically significant improvement compared to the other system using a Z-test at significance level $\alpha = 0.05$.

tion of graph edit distance in a direct manner for classification, while the embedding procedure uses the same information in order to define a new representation formalism. Comparing the results of the k-NN in the embedding space with the results of the same classifier in the graph domain leads to the following conclusions. On two out of ten data sets, the k-NN classifier in the embedded vector space is outperformed by the original framework in the graph domain. In general, however, both systems perform quite similarly and in fact also some improvements can be observed achieved with the embedding framework. This is a very interesting result since one could have expected that due to the embedding process some information loss has to be accepted in general.

Given the vector space embedded graphs, the restriction of applying classifiers of the nearest-neighbor type does no longer hold. Hence, in the main classification experiments an SVM as a powerful and flexible statistical classifier is applied to the embedded graphs. We use an SVM with RBF kernel and all of the proposed subsystems for graph embedding, namely prototype selection (PS), prototype reduction schemes (PRS), feature selection (FS) and dimensionality reduction (DIM), Lipschitz embeddings

(LIP), and ensemble methods (ENS). In addition to the first reference system, the k-NN in conjunction with graph edit distance, a second reference system (sim) is employed for the purpose of comparison. This particular system also uses an SVM with kernel values directly derived from graph edit distance.

In Table 7.12 the best result per strategy (PS, PRS, FS, DIM, LIP, and ENS) is indicated for each of the ten data sets. Whenever two or more methods per subsystem achieve the best result on a data set an arbitrary choice is made. Note that for these results besides plain vectors, also scaled as well as normalized vectors have been used for classification (marked with (s) and (n), respectively). For each method and each data set it is shown whether the two reference systems are outperformed by the embedding system (marked with symbol ⇑), or the reference systems outperform the embedding system (marked with symbol ⇓). A tie between reference and embedding system is marked with symbol ⇔. The symbols ① or ② indicate that the improvement compared to the first or second reference method is statistically significant (using a Z-test at significance level $\alpha = 0.05$). At the bottom of Table 7.12 a summary of the improvements achieved compared to both reference methods is given for each subsystem in our embedding framework.

Compared to the first reference system, the different embedding approaches perform very similar. In general, on all but the Letter low data set the traditional classifier k-NN is outperformed by the embedding classifiers. On the Protein data set the result of the k-NN in the graph domain cannot be improved by means of PRS and therefore only eight improvements can be reported for this subsystem in total. For all systems but feature selection, seven improvements with statistical significance can be observed. These significant improvements are achieved on Letter high, Digit, Fingerprint, GREC, AIDS, Mutagenicity, and Webpage. (The approach with feature selection achieves no statistically significant improvement on the Mutagenicity data set.)

Regarding the second reference system, the following observations can be made. Most of the subsystem outperform sim in seven out of ten cases (PS, PRS, DIM, and LIP). The feature selection strategies and the ensemble method achieve improvements on six and eight data sets, respectively. The number of improvements which are statistically significant compared to sim varies from three (FS) up to six (DIM). On two data sets (GREC and AIDS) all subsystems of our embedding framework outperform the second reference system with statistical significance. On Digit and Mutagenicity

Table 7.12   Graph embedding subsystems (prototype selection strategies (PS), prototype reduction schemes (PRS), feature selection algorithms (FS), dimensionality reduction methods (DIM), Lipschitz embedding (LIP), and ensemble methods (ENS)) compared against both reference systems.   ⇑/⇔/⇓ Improvement/equal result/deterioration compared to the first/second reference system. ①/② Statistically significant improvement over the first/second reference system.

Data Set	embedding methods					
	PS	PRS	FS	DIM	LIP	ENS
Letter low	⇔/⇓ sps-c	⇔/⇓ merg (s)	⇓/⇓ svm	⇔/⇓ PCA (s)	⇓/⇓ P-k-cps	⇓/⇓ voting
Letter medium	⇑/⇑ tps	⇑/⇑ sel (s)	⇑/⇑ svm (s)	⇑/⇔ PCA	⇑/⇑ N-k-cps	⇑/⇑ Bayes
Letter high	⇑/⇔ bps-c ①	⇑/⇓ edit ①	⇑/⇑ svm (n) ①	⇑/⇓ PCA (s) ①	⇑/⇓ P-k-cps ①	⇑/⇓ B. count ①
Digit	⇑/⇑ sps (s) ①②	⇑/⇑ cond (s) ①②	⇑/⇑ svm (s) ①②	⇑/⇑ PCA (s) ①②	⇑/⇑ P-k-cps ①②	⇑/⇑ voting ①
Fingerprint	⇑/⇑ bps-c ①②	⇑/⇑ cond (n) ①	⇑/⇑ info (n) ①	⇑/⇑ PCA (s) ①②	⇑/⇓ P-k-cps ①	⇑/⇑ B. count ①②
GREC	⇑/⇑ sps-c ①②	⇑/⇑ cond ①②	⇑/⇑ svm ①②	⇑/⇑ PCA ①②	⇑/⇑ P-k-cps ①②	⇑/⇑ voting ①②
AIDS	⇑/⇑ rps-c ①②	⇑/⇑ mCond (n) ①②	⇑/⇑ chi (n) ①②	⇑/⇑ kPCA ①②	⇑/⇑ P-k-cps ①②	⇑/⇑ voting ①②
Mutagenicity	⇑/⇑ tps-c (n) ①②	⇑/⇑ mCond ①②	⇑/⇑ svm (n)	⇑/⇑ PCA ①②	⇑/⇑ P-k-cps ①②	⇑/⇑ voting ①②
Protein	⇑/⇑ sps-c (n)	⇔/⇔ cond	⇑/⇑ svm (n)	⇑/⇑ PCA (s)	⇑/⇑ P-k-cps	⇑/⇑ Bayes
Webpage	⇑/⇓ sps-c (s) ①	⇑/⇑ mCond ①	⇑/⇓ svm ①	⇑/⇑ MDA ①②	⇑/⇑ N-k-cps ①	⇑/⇑ voting ①
Improvements over k-NN	9× ⇑ 7× ①	8× ⇑ 7× ①	9× ⇑ 6× ①	9× ⇑ 7× ①	9× ⇑ 7× ①	9× ⇑ 7× ①
Improvements over sim	7× ⇑ 5× ②	7× ⇑ 4× ②	6× ⇑ 3× ②	7× ⇑ 6× ②	7× ⇑ 4× ②	8× ⇑ 4× ②

all but one embedding subsystem (ENS and FS, respectively) achieve statistically significantly better results than the second reference system.

In order to compare the results of the different embedding systems, in Table 7.13 the best possible classification accuracy per subsystem is shown for each data set. In a clear majority of all cases, no statistically significant differences between the individual systems can be observed. Yet, some remarkable observations can still be made. For instance, on GREC and Mutagenicity data sets one subsystem (LIP and FS, respectively) is outperformed by all other subsystems with statistical significance. Furthermore, on Letter high, Fingerprint, and Protein we observe that at least one of the methods outperform the worst subsystem with statistical significance. On the Webpage data, the Lipschitz approach even outperforms two subsystems with statistical significance (PS and FS). The most extraordinary results are observed on the two data sets Fingerprint and Webpage where PCA and MDA based embedding achieve statistically significantly better results than all other subsystems.

Since for most data sets only marginal differences exist between the individual systems, no clear advice can be given which of the subsystems should be used for graph embedding in general. In summary, all of the proposed methods can be used for dissimilarity embeddings of graphs. Yet, the dimensionality reduction methods tend to be the methods of choice because of two reasons. First, this particular embedding system achieves the majority of statistically significant improvements compared to the first and second reference systems (seven and six, respectively). Second, dimensionality reduction based graph embedding is the only subsystem able to outperform all other systems with statistical significance, which is achieved on Fingerprint and Webpage data.

Yet, regardless of which subsystem is actually used for embedding, on most of the data sets both reference system are outperformed, and in the majority of the cases these improvements are statistically significant. From this main finding one can conclude that the embedding procedure using dissimilarities with subsequent classification has great potential to outperform classification systems directly working on graph dissimilarity information. Moreover, the second reference system, which actually employs a powerful kernel classifier, is outperformed by our embedding classifiers on most data sets. Therefore, we also conclude that the power of our framework is primarily due to the strength of the novel embedding procedure rather than to sophisticated kernel methods.

Table 7.13 Graph embedding subsystems (prototype selection strategies (PS), prototype reduction schemes (PRS), feature selection algorithms (FS), dimensionality reduction methods (DIM), Lipschitz embedding (LIP), and ensemble methods (ENS)) compared agains each other. (❂ statistically significantly better than the worst system, ❂❂ statistically significantly better than the two worst systems, ❂❂❂ statistically significantly better than all other systems.

Data Set	embedding methods					
	PS	PRS	FS	DIM	LIP	ENS
Letter low	99.3 sps-c	99.3 merg (s)	99.2 svm	99.3 PCA (s)	99.2 P-k-cps	99.2 voting
Letter medium	95.3 tps	95.3 sel (s)	95.1 svm (s)	94.9 PCA	95.2 N-k-cps	95.3 Bayes
Letter high	92.9 bps-c	92.5 edit	93.2 svm (n) ❂	92.1 PCA (s)	92.5 P-k-cps	92.8 B. count
Digit	98.8 sps (s)	98.6 cond (s)	98.7 svm (s)	98.7 PCA (s)	98.7 P-k-cps	98.5 voting
Fingerprint	83.1 bps-c ❂	82.5 cond (n)	82.5 info (n)	84.0 PCA (s) ❂❂❂	81.9 P-k-cps	83.1 B. count ❂
GREC	92.4 sps-c ❂	92.0 cond ❂	92.2 svm ❂	92.1 PCA ❂	91.1 P-k-cps ❂	92.3 voting
AIDS	98.1 rps-c	98.1 mCond (n)	98.2 chi (n)	98.1 kPCA	98.1 P-k-cps	97.9 voting
Mutagenicity	72.3 tps-c (n) ❂	71.6 mCond ❂	69.1 svm (n)	72.1 PCA ❂	71.9 P-k-cps ❂	72.4 voting ❂
Protein	73.0 sps-c (n) ❂	68.5 cond	73.0 svm (n) ❂	72.5 PCA (s)	73.0 P-k-cps ❂	72.5 Bayes
Webpage	82.7 sps-c (s)	83.7 mCond	82.7 svm	86.8 MDA ❂❂❂	84.2 N-k-cps ❂❂	83.7 voting ❂

Clustering Experiments with Vector Space Embedded Graphs

8

> The strategy of cluster analysis is structure seeking although its operation is structure imposing.

Mark Aldenderfer and Roger Blashfield

In the previous chapter, an exhaustive evaluation of the proposed graph embedding framework has been described. In various classification experiments, all of the embedding subsystems are compared against two standard reference methods and against one another. The present chapter goes one step further and addresses the problem of clustering which is part of the unsupervised learning paradigm. For the sake of compactness and due to the fact that all embedding subsystems perform quite similar in the classification experiments, only one of the proposed embedding subsystems is actually employed for the task of clustering. That is, in contrast with the thorough evaluation of vector space embeddings in the supervised learning case, for clustering only three prototype selection strategies are used, viz. sps-c, bps-c, and k-cps-c. The choice of these three prototype selection methods is motivated through their superior performance observed in the classification experiments (see Section 7.2.1.2).

The k-means algorithm [257] is one of the most popular clustering algorithms in pattern recognition and related areas. In the present chapter this particular algorithm is employed for clustering both the original graph data and the vector space embedded graphs. In the graph domain, the original clustering algorithm is modified in the sense that the underlying distance function is given by the graph edit distance and the mean of a certain cluster is defined as the set median graph [258] (see Definition 6.4). We denote k-means applied to graphs as k-medians and use this system as

221

a reference method for the purpose of comparisons. For clustering of the vector space embedded graphs, a kernelized version of the original k-means algorithm is used [260]. We use the same kernel as in the classification experiments, viz. the RBF function. For a more thorough introduction to k-means clustering, as well as its adaptation to the domain of graphs and the application of the kernel trick, see Section 5.4.3.

The intention of the experimental evaluation is to empirically investigate whether kernel k-means based on the proposed graph embedding procedure is able to outperform the standard k-medians clustering algorithm in the original graph domain. To this end, clusterings computed by both methods on all of the ten graph data sets are compared against each other in the present chapter.

8.1 Experimental Setup and Validation of the Meta Parameters

For k-means clustering to work properly, the number of clusters k has to be defined beforehand (the same accounts for k-medians and kernelized k-means, of course). Since we use the same graph data sets for the clustering evaluation as for the classification experiments, class information is available for all of our graph data sets. For the sake of convenience, we define the number of clusters k to be found as the number of classes occurring in the underlying graph set.

The initialization of k-means is commonly done with a random selection of k objects. However, in the present chapter a deterministic procedure is applied. Let us assume a set of N objects $\mathcal{X} = \{x_1, \ldots, x_N\}$ to be clustered is given. In our case the objects $x_i \in \mathcal{X}$ are either represented by graphs from some graph domain $\mathcal{G}$ or by vector space embedded graphs in some vector space $\mathbb{R}^n$. The set of k initial cluster centers $\mathcal{M}_k = \{m_1, \ldots, m_k\} \subseteq \mathcal{X}$ is constructed by iteratively retrieving the set median of $\mathcal{X}$ ($median(\mathcal{X})$) minus the objects already selected. Formally,

$$\mathcal{M}_i = \begin{cases} \varnothing, & \text{if } i = 0 \\ \mathcal{M}_{i-1} \cup median(\mathcal{X} \setminus \mathcal{M}_{i-1}), & \text{if } 0 < i \leqslant k \end{cases}$$

Remember, that the set median of $\mathcal{X}$ is the object $x \in \mathcal{X}$ that minimizes the sum of distances to all other objects in $\mathcal{X}$. Obviously, this procedure initializes k-means (or k-medians) with objects situated in, or near, the center of the respective set.

In order to compare the kernel k-means clustering algorithm applied to vector space embedded graphs with the conventional k-medians algorithm in the graph domain, we use four different clustering validation indices known as Dunn [306], C [307], Rand [308], and Bipartite index [309]. Whereas the two former indices (Dunn and C) do not need any ground truth information, the latter ones (Rand and Bipartite) are defined with respect to the class memberships of the underlying objects. Note that all indices can be applied to both graphs and vectors. In the following we assume that a clustering with k clusters $(C_1, \ldots, C_k)$ of the underlying data $\mathcal{X} = \{x_1, \ldots, x_N\}$ is given.

Dunn Index We define the distance between two clusters C and C' as

$$d(C, C') = min\{d(x_i, x_j) \,|\, x_i \in C, x_j \in C'\} \quad .$$

The diameter of a cluster C is given by

$$\varnothing(C) = max\{d(x_i, x_j) \,|\, x_i, x_j \in C\}$$

and accordingly the maximum diameter of all k clusters is defined by

$$\varnothing_{max} = max\{\varnothing(C_i) \,|\, 1 \leqslant i \leqslant k\} \quad .$$

The Dunn index measures the ratio of the minimum distance of two different clusters and the maximum diameter of a cluster. Formally,

$$\text{Dunn} = min\left\{\frac{d(C_i, C_j)}{\varnothing_{max}} \,|\, 1 \leqslant i < j \leqslant k\right\} \quad .$$

Dunn is considered to be positively-correlated, which means that higher values indicate higher clustering quality.

C Index For computing the C index, one defines

$$c(x_i, x_j) = \begin{cases} 1 & \text{if } x_i \text{ and } x_j \text{ belong to the same cluster} \quad , \\ 0 & \text{else} \quad . \end{cases}$$

Furthermore, Γ is defined by the sum of all distances of objects belonging to the same cluster. Formally,

$$\Gamma = \sum_{i=1}^{n-1} \sum_{j=i+1}^{n} d(x_i, x_j) c(x_i, x_j) \quad .$$

The number of pairs of objects in the same cluster is denoted by a. Formally,

$$a = \sum_{i=1}^{n-1} \sum_{j=i+1}^{n} c(x_i, x_j) \quad .$$

With *min* we denote the sum of the a smallest and with *max* the sum of the a largest distances $d(x_i, x_j)$ where $x_i \neq x_j$. The C index is then defined as

$$C = \frac{\Gamma - min}{max - min} \quad.$$

Obviously, the numerator of the C index measures how many pairs of objects of the a nearest neighboring pairs belong to the same cluster. The denominator is a scale factor ensuring that $0 \leq C \leq 1$. The smaller the C index value is, the more frequently do pairs with a small distance belong to the same cluster, i.e. the higher is the clustering quality (negatively-correlated).

Rand Index   For computing the Rand index we regard all pairs of distinct objects (x_i, x_j) with $x_i \neq x_j$. We denote the number of pairs (x_i, x_j) belonging to the same class and to the same cluster with N_{11}, whereas N_{00} denotes the number of pairs that neither belong to the same class nor to the same cluster. The number of pairs belonging to the same class but not to the same cluster is denoted by N_{10}, and conversely N_{01} represents the number of pairs belonging to different classes but to the same cluster. The Rand index is defined by

$$\text{Rand} = \frac{N_{11} + N_{00}}{N_{11} + N_{00} + N_{01} + N_{10}} \quad.$$

Rand index measures the consistency of a given clustering according to the ground truth, and therefore higher values indicate better clusterings.

Bipartite Index   In order to compute the Bipartite index, we first define the confusion matrix $\mathbf{M} = (m_{ij})_{k \times k}$. Assume a clustering with k clusters $(C_1, \ldots, C_k)$, and a set of k classes $(\Omega_1, \ldots, \Omega_k)$ are given[1]. Note that both clusters and classes form a disjoint cover of all elements, i.e $\cup_{i=1}^{k} C_i = \cup_{i=1}^{k} \Omega_i$. The $k \times k$ confusion matrix is defined by

$$\mathbf{M} = \begin{bmatrix} m_{11} & \cdots & m_{1k} \\ \vdots & \ddots & \vdots \\ m_{k1} & \cdots & m_{kk} \end{bmatrix}$$

where m_{ij} represents the number of elements from class Ω_j occurring in cluster C_i. The problem to be solved with this confusion matrix is to find an optimal unique assignment of the k clusters to the k classes. Such an

---

[1]Remember that in our experiments the number of clusters is equal to the number of classes.

optimal assignment maximizes the sum of the corresponding cluster-class values m_{ij}. Formally, one has to find a permutation p of the integers $1, 2, \ldots, k$ maximizing the sum $\sum_{i=1}^{k} m_{ip_i}$. Let $p = p_1, \ldots, p_k$ be the optimal permutation. The Bipartite index (BP index for short) is defined as

$$\mathrm{BP} = \frac{\sum_{i=1}^{k} m_{ip_i}}{N} \quad .$$

Note that BP gives us the maximum possible classification accuracy of the given clustering. The computation of the BP index can be efficiently accomplished by means of Munkres' algorithm [199] (see Section 3.3.1 for a formal definition of Munkres' algorithm).

Note that other clustering validation indices, such as Davies-Bouldin [310], Calinski-Harabasz [311], Xie-Beni [312], $\mathcal{I}$ index [313], and cluster stability [314], could be also used. However, we feel that a validation based on the four proposed indices covers the different aspects of cluster quality evaluation quite well, and we leave a more exhaustive analysis involving additional indices to future work.

Each of our graph sets is divided into three disjoint subsets referred to as training, validation, and test set. The training set is not used for the clustering experiments. Those meta parameters of the clustering algorithm which cannot be directly inferred from the specific application are optimized on the validation set. For k-medians clustering in the original graph domain as well as for dissimilarity based graph embedding, the same edit distance information as optimized for the classification experiments are used (see Section 4.2). No additional parameter has to be validated for our reference system, the k-medians algorithm. For our novel approach, however, there are three parameters to tune: the prototype selection method, the number of prototypes n (dimensionality of the embedding vector space $\mathbb{R}^n$), and the parameter γ in the RBF kernel. For each of the four validation indices, these three meta parameters are optimized individually on the validation set.

The optimization of the RBF kernel is performed on the validation set for every possible dimension of the embedding space and every prototype selection method. Thus, the four validation indices can be regarded as a function of the dimensionality and the prototype selector. This optimization is illustrated on the Letter low data set in Fig. 8.1 where the scores of all validation indices and each tested dimensionality are shown[2]. The

---

[2]For the sake of convenience, we use $1 - C$ instead of C.

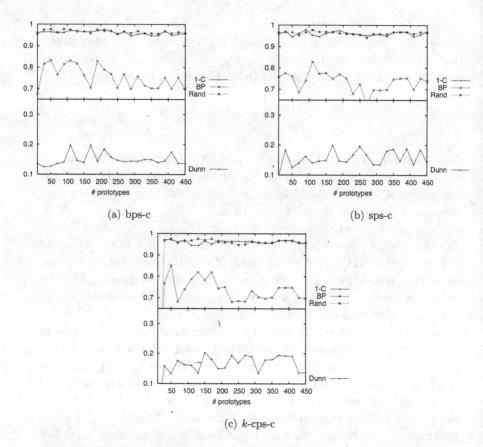

(a) bps-c

(b) sps-c

(c) *k*-cps-c

Fig. 8.1   Validation of clustering indices on the Letter low data set for the three prototype selection strategies bps-c, sps-c, and *k*-cps-c.

illustration of this validation procedure on the remaining data sets is shown
in Appendix I. For each validation index, the best performing prototype
selector with optimal parameter combination is applied to the independent
test set. These results are reported in the next section.

8.2   Results and Discussion

In Fig. 8.2 and 8.3, the clustering validation indices achieved by the best
performing embedding method (kernel *k*-means clustering in the embedding
space) are compared against the validation indices achieved by the reference
method (*k*-medians clustering in the graph domain) on all data sets.

According to Dunn index, the approach of clustering vector space embedded graphs rather than the original graphs is beneficial on nine out of ten data sets (i.e. on all data sets but Mutagenicity where both systems achieve the same Dunn index). Hence, we conclude that the clusters in the embedding space are more compact and better separable than those in the graph domain. Furthermore, on all of the ten data sets, the clusterings in the embedding space outperform the original clusterings according to C index. That is, with the novel procedure in the embedding space, pairs of objects with small distances are more frequently in the same cluster than in the original approach. Note that for both indices Dunn and C the class membership is not taken into account but only the size and shape of the clusters.

In case of BP and Rand index we observe eight cases where the clustering in the embedding space outperforms the clustering in the graph domain and two data sets (Fingerprint and Webpage) where the original graph clustering performs better than our novel approach. In general, the clusterings in the embedding space are more accurate and consistent according to the ground truth than the clusterings in the original graph domain.

In order to get a visual impression of the clusterings, the corresponding confusion matrices $\mathbf{M} = (m_{ij})_{k \times k}$ can be considered. Remember that m_{ij} represents the number of elements from class Ω_j occurring in cluster C_i. For a confusion matrix $\mathbf{M} = (m_{ij})_{k \times k}$ a corresponding $k \times k$ checkerboard plot is generated, where dark squares in the checkerboard represent large values of m_{ij} and bright squares represent small values of m_{ij}. The more elements from class Ω_j occur in cluster C_i, the darker the corresponding square at position (i, j) in the checkerboard plot. For the sake of clarity, the rows of the checkerboard are rearranged such that the squares along the main diagonal are darker than the other squares in the respective row in general. This is achieved by finding a permutation of the rows of the confusion matrix which maximizes the sum of diagonal elements $\sum_{i=1}^{k} m_{ii}$.

Obviously, the grey scale value of the k squares on the i-th line of these figures visualize how the members of a certain class Ω_i are distributed over the different clusters $(C_1, \ldots, C_k)$. Clearly, the better the clustering according to the real class distribution is, the more dark squares can be observed along the main diagonal of these plots by simultaneously showing only few and rather bright squares in the remaining part of the checkerboard[3].

In Fig. 8.4–8.7 confusion matrix plots of four data sets are given for clus-

---

[3]A clustering that perfectly matches the class distribution of the underlying data results in k black squares along the main diagonal while the rest is completely white.

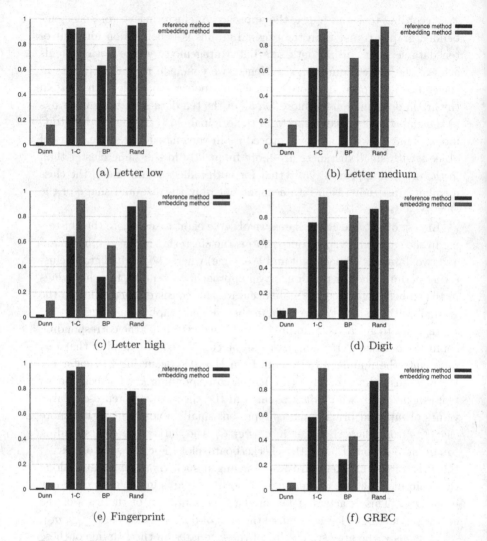

Fig. 8.2   Cluster validation indices in the graph domain (reference method) and the embedding space.

terings in both the graph domain and the embedding vector space (similar illustrations for the remaining data sets are provided in Appendix J). Note that the underlying confusion matrices in the embedding space correspond to clusterings where the BP index is optimal on the validation set.

According to these illustrations, by means of the embedding procedure the quality of the clusterings can be clearly improved when compared to the

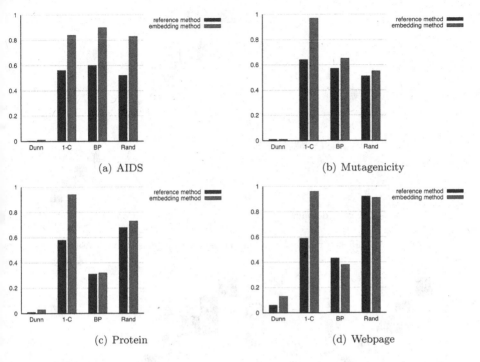

Fig. 8.3 Cluster validation indices in the graph domain (reference method) and the embedding space.

clusterings in the graph domain. Through the embedding process in conjunction with kernel k-means clustering, the number of dark squares along the main diagonal is substantially increased compared to the confusion matrix plots in the graph domain. Simultaneously, the number of grey squares not lying on the main diagonal is decreased. This qualitative comparison well accompanies the quantitative results observed on the same data sets considering BP and Rand indices (which both measure the consistency and accuracy of the clusters found with respect to the underlying classes).

At first glance the meta parameters to be tuned in our novel approach seem to be a drawback compared to the reference system. However, since k-means algorithm is able to find spherical clusters only, these meta parameters establish a powerful possibility to optimize the underlying vector space embedding with respect to a specific validation index.

In case of Dunn's index, for instance, the underlying vector space is optimized such that the resulting clusters are more compact and better separable than the clusters achieved in the original graph domain. In other

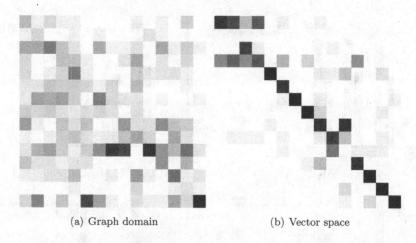

(a) Graph domain   (b) Vector space

Fig. 8.4   Confusion matrix on the Letter medium set (clusters vs. classes).

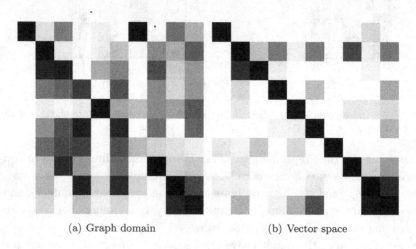

(a) Graph domain   (b) Vector space

Fig. 8.5   Confusion matrix on the Digit data set (clusters vs. classes).

words, the clusters of the data formed through the embedding process can be much better approximated by non-overlapping ellipses than in the original graph domain. In case of BP or Rand index, however, the embedding and clustering are optimized such that spherical clusters are able to separate the data with a high degree of consistency and accuracy according to ground truth. Summarizing, the embedding process lends itself to a methodology for adjusting a given data distribution such that the clustering algorithm is able to achieve good results according to a specific validation criterion.

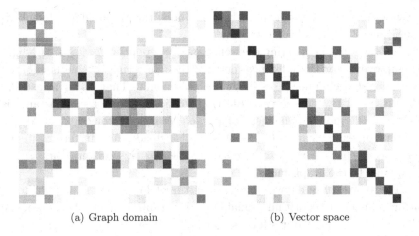

(a) Graph domain   (b) Vector space

Fig. 8.6 Confusion matrix on the GREC data set (clusters vs. classes).

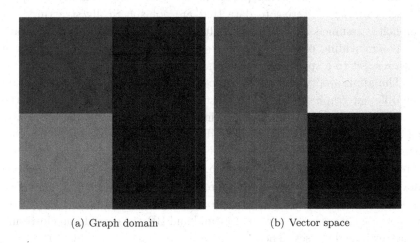

(a) Graph domain   (b) Vector space

Fig. 8.7 Confusion matrix on the AIDS data set (clusters vs. classes).

8.3 Summary and Discussion

In the present chapter a compact experimental evaluation of the graph embedding procedure in a clustering scenario is carried out. In contrast with the experiments conducted for classification, the clustering experiments are non-exhaustive. Only one subsystem of our novel embedding framework is employed for graph embedding, viz. prototype selection strategy. This reduction of empirical investigations accounts for the findings made in the previous chapter, where no clear winner among the proposed graph embedding subsystems has been established.

For the task of clustering the well known and popular k-means paradigm is employed. For the reference method, this clustering scheme is adopted to the special circumstances in the graph domain. That is, for measuring the dissimilarity between two objects the concept of graph edit distance is used. Furthermore, as the mean of a graph set is not defined in general, the concept of set median graph [258] is used instead. For clusterings in the embedding space, a kernelized version of the k-means clustering algorithm is applied to the graph maps.

The power of our novel approach is threefold. First, it makes the k-means clustering algorithm available to the graph domain. Because of the lack of suitable procedures for computing the mean of a graph population, only k-medians algorithm has been traditionally applied to graphs. Second, by means of the embedding procedure we gain the possibility to apply kernel k-means clustering to data that are not spherically structured, as implicitly assumed by the k-means clustering algorithm. Third, by means of the embedding parameters, the resulting vector space can be adjusted with respect to a specific validation index.

The applicability and performance of our novel approach is tested on ten different graph sets with four clustering validation indices. Clearly, the clustering results observed indicate that the proposed methodology of first embedding graphs in vector spaces and then applying a kernelized clustering algorithm has significant potential to outperform clustering algorithms that directly operate in the graph domain. According to the Dunn index, our novel approach outperforms the reference system in nine out of ten cases. Index C indicates that our novel approach outperforms the reference system even on all data sets. According to Rand and BP, the embedding clustering is better in eight cases. These results are summarized in Table 8.1.

There are a number of issues to be investigated in future research. First of all, the experimental evaluation could be extended to all graph embedding subsystems, including prototype reduction or feature selection, for instance. Moreover, cluster ensembles have been introduced recently as a more accurate alternative to individual clustering algorithms [314]. The basic idea of ensemble methods is to combine the partitions of many clustering algorithms applied to a specific data set to one final decision. In [315] a preliminary experimental evaluation using random prototype selection in the embedding framework for clustering ensemble generation is presented (similar to the idea presented in Section 6.7). Finally, other clustering

Table 8.1 Kernel *k*-means clustering
in the embedding space vs. *k*-medians
clustering in the graph domain.

Validation index	wins	ties	losses
Dunn	9	1	0
C	10	0	0
BP	8	0	2
Rand	8	0	2

algorithms applicable to vector space embedded graphs could be investigated (similar to [241] where various classifiers are applied to vector space embeddings of graphs).

Conclusions

9

> We can only see a short
> distance ahead, but we can see
> plenty there that needs to be
> done.
>
> Alan Turing

The present book addresses the issue of graph based pattern recognition. A graph consists of a set of nodes which are possibly connected by edges. In the general case, relevant features of the underlying patterns are stored as labels attached to both nodes and edges. In fact, graphs are a versatile alternative to feature vectors, and are known to be a powerful and flexible representation formalism. The representational power of graphs is due to their ability to represent not only feature values but also binary relationships among different parts of an object. Feature vectors offer no direct possibility to capture such structural characteristics. Consequently, in applications where the patterns at hand are composed of several objects, i.e. in cases where structure plays an important role in the underlying patterns, graphs are definitely more appropriate than vectorial pattern descriptions. The flexibility of graphs stems from the fact that there are no size or labeling restrictions that constrain the representation of a given object. In contrast to feature vectors, where each pattern is represented by a constant number of numerical attributes, graphs allow us to adopt their size and complexity with respect to the size and complexity of the patterns to be modeled.

One of the major drawbacks of graphs is that there is little mathematical structure in the graph domain. That is, most of the basic mathematical operations available for vectors do not exist for graphs or cannot be defined in a standard way, but must be provided depending on the specific applica-

Table 9.1 Pattern recognition in vector spaces $\mathbb{R}^n$ and in graph domains $\mathcal{G}$; advantages $(+)$ and drawbacks $(-)$ compared to the other paradigm.

Properties	$\mathbb{R}^n$	$\mathcal{G}$
representational power	$-$	$+$
available tools	$+$	$-$

tion (often involving a tedious and time-consuming development process). As it turns out, almost none of the common methods for data mining, machine learning, or pattern recognition can be applied to graphs without significant modifications. Second, graphs suffer from their own flexibility. For instance, computing the distances of a pair of objects, which is an important task in many areas, is linear in the number of data items in the case where vectors are employed. The same task for graphs, however, is in general exponential in the number of nodes. Hence, using graphs rather than vectors makes pairwise comparisons inherently more complex. Consequently, while for objects given in terms of feature vectors a rich repository of algorithmic tools for pattern recognition has been developed over the last decades, a lack of algorithmic tools for graph based pattern representation can be observed. In Table 9.1 a summary of the main advantages and drawbacks of graph based and vector based pattern recognition is shown.

Despite adverse mathematical and computational conditions in the graph domain, various procedures for evaluating graph dissimilarity have been proposed in the literature. The process of evaluating the dissimilarity of two graphs is commonly referred to as graph matching. The overall aim of graph matching is to find a correspondence between similar substructures of two graphs to be matched. Based on the matching found, a dissimilarity or similarity score can eventually be computed indicating the proximity of two graphs.

Graph matching has been the topic of numerous studies in computer science over the last decades. Roughly speaking, there are two categories of tasks in graph matching known as exact matching and inexact matching. In the case of exact graph matching, for a matching to be successful, it is required that a strict correspondence is found between the two graphs being matched, or at least among their subparts. Hence, the graph extraction process is assumed to be structurally flawless, i.e. the conversion of the underlying data into graphs must proceed without errors for the matching to be successful.

Due to the intrinsic variability of the patterns under consideration and the noise resulting from the graph extraction process, it cannot be expected that two graphs representing the same class of objects are completely, or at least to a large part, identical in their structure. Moreover, if a node or edge label alphabet is used to describe non-discrete properties of the underlying patterns, it is most probable that the actual graphs differ somewhat from their ideal model. Obviously, such noise crucially hampers the applicability of exact graph matching techniques, and consequently exact graph matching is rarely used in real-world applications. In order to overcome this drawback, it is advisable to endow the graph matching framework with a certain tolerance to errors.

Graph edit distance offers an intuitive way to integrate error-tolerance into the graph matching process and furthermore, there are various applications where this paradigm has proved to be suitable for graph matching. Originally, the concept of edit distance has been developed for string matching, and a considerable amount of variants and extensions to the edit distance have been proposed for strings and graphs. The key idea is to model structural variation by edit operations reflecting modifications in structure and labeling. The main advantages of graph edit distance are its high degree of flexibility, which makes it applicable to virtually all types of graph, and the fact that one can integrate domain specific knowledge about object similiarity by means of specific edit cost functions.

Optimal algorithms for computing the edit distance of two graphs are typically based on combinatorial search procedures that explore the space of all possible mappings of the nodes and edges of the involved graphs. A major drawback of those procedures is their computational complexity, which is exponential in the number of nodes. Consequently, the application of optimal algorithms for edit distance computations is limited to graphs of rather small size in practice.

To render graph edit distance computation less computationally demanding, in the present book a suboptimal approach to graph edit distance computation is proposed. This novel graph edit distance framework is based on Munkres' algorithm originally developed for solving the assignment problem. The assignment problem consists of finding an assignment of the elements of two sets with each other such that a cost function is minimized. In the current book it is shown how the graph edit distance problem can be transformed into the assignment problem. The proposed solution allows for the insertion, deletion, and substitution of both nodes and edges, but considers these edit operations in a rather independent fashion from each other. Therefore, while Munkres' algorithm returns the optimal solution to the assignment problem, the proposed solution yields only an approximate, hence suboptimal, solution to the graph edit distance problem. However, the time complexity is only cubic in the number of nodes of the two underlying graphs.

Using the edit distance, an input graph to be classified can be analyzed by computing its dissimilarity to a number of training graphs. For classification, the resulting distance values may be fed, for instance, into a nearest-neighbor classifier (the first reference system in the present book). Alternatively, the edit distance of graphs can also be interpreted as a pattern similarity measure in the context of kernel machines, which makes a large number of powerful methods applicable to graphs, including support vector machines for classification (the second reference system in the present book).

In several experiments the graph edit distance based on our novel approximation scheme is evaluated. The first finding is that our novel algorithm is much faster than exact computations. Furthermore, the new approach makes graph edit distance feasible for graphs with more than hundred nodes. The second finding is that suboptimal graph edit distance need not necessarily lead to a deterioration of the classification accuracy of a distance based classifier. On two out of three tested data sets, the classification accuracy of a nearest-neighbor classifier remains the same or even improves when the exact edit distances are replaced by the suboptimal ones returned by our novel algorithm. This can be explained by the fact that all distances computed by the approximate method are equal to, or larger than, the true distances. Moreover, an experimental analysis has shown that the larger the true distances are the larger is their overestimation. In other words, smaller distances are computed more accurately than larger ones by our suboptimal algorithm. This means that inter-class distances are more affected than intra-class distances by the novel suboptimal graph edit distance framework. However, for a nearest-neighbor classifier, small distances have more influence on the decision than large distances. Hence no serious deterioration of the classification accuracy occurs when our novel approximate algorithm is used instead of an exact method.

Although it is possible to define graph dissimilarity measures via specific graph matching procedures, this is often not sufficient for standard algorithms in pattern recognition. A promising direction to overcome this severe limitation is graph embedding into vector spaces. Basically, such an embedding of graphs establishes access to the rich repository of algorithmic tools developed for vectorial representations. Revisiting Table 9.1, we observe that through the embedding of graphs in a vector space the lack of algorithmic tools is instantly eliminated and therefore, the minus (–) in the lower right corner of the table (available tools in the graph domain) becomes a plus (+).

The present book's main contribution considers a new class of graph embedding procedures which are based on dissimilarity representation and graph matching. Originally the idea was proposed in order to map feature vectors into dissimilarity spaces. Later it was generalized to string based object representation. In the current book we go one step further and generalize the methods to the domain of graphs. The key idea of this approach is to use the distances of an input graph to a number of training graphs, termed prototype graphs, as a vectorial description of the graph. That is, we use the dissimilarity representation for pattern recognition rather than the original graph based representation. Obviously, by means of this procedure we obtain a vector space where each axis corresponds to a prototype graph and the coordinate values of an embedded graph are its distances to the elements in the prototype set. In this way we can transform any graph into a vector of real numbers.

The problem of prototype selection is an issue in the proposed graph embedding framework. As a matter of fact, the role of the prototypes is crucial as they serve as reference points in the underlying graph domain in order to establish the embedding of graphs. The objective of prototype selection is to find reference points which lead to meaningful vectors in the embedding space. Six possible solutions to the problem of prototype selection are presented in the present book, namely heuristic prototype selection, prototype reduction, feature selection, dimensionality reduction, Lipschitz embeddings, and ensemble methods.

The methods from the first category (prototype selection) select graphs from a given training set of graphs with respect to the underlying dissimilarity information. Six possible algorithms are described in detail. There are selection methods which focus on the center or the border of a given graph population, while other strategies avoid selecting similar graphs and try to uniformly distribute the prototypes over the whole set of patterns. All of the proposed selection strategies can be applied in a classindependent and a classwise way. In the former approach the selection is executed over the whole training set at once, while in the latter case the selection is performed individually for each class. The size of the prototype set is a user defined parameter and has to be experimentally tuned on a validation set.

In order to overcome the time consuming validation of the number of prototypes to be selected, the idea of prototype reduction emerged. This strategy adopts well known prototype reduction schemes originally proposed for nearest-neighbor classification. The six prototype reduction algorithms utilized in the present book have in common that the number of prototypes is determined automatically and cannot be influenced by the user. This is a crucial advantage over the previous method where the number of prototypes is determined by means of the target classifier on a validation set. Hence, these reduction schemes enable us to omit the cumbersome validation of the embedding space dimensionality. The basic idea of these reduction schemes is to determine a subset of prototypes from the original training set such that the elements from this training set (or at least a considerable part of them) are still correctly classified using a nearest-neighbor classifier. That is, these reduction schemes reduce redundancy in terms of selecting similar graphs out of the same class and finding significant graphs which help to correctly classify the graphs in the training set.

A more principled way of embedding graphs in vector spaces is established through feature selection and dimensionality reduction. In contrast to the above mentioned methods of prototype selection and prototype reduction, we use the whole set of training graphs as prototypes. Of course, it can be expected that by using the whole training set as prototypes, we end up with feature vectors of very high dimensionality, which in turn may lead to redundancy and perhaps lower the performance as well as the efficiency of our algorithms in the embedding space. However, these problems may be overcome by feature ranking methods. Based on features ranked according to the six feature selection and dimensionality reduction algorithms employed in the present book, nested subsets of features are defined. By varying their size, an optimal subset of features can eventually be found.

The basic idea of Lipschitz embeddings is very similar to that of dissimilarity embeddings. Yet, rather than using prototypes, sets of prototypes are used for embedding. That is, a graph is transformed into an n-dimensional vector such that each of the components corresponds to the distance of the considered graph to a predefined reference set. Obviously, our dissimilarity embedding framework is a special case of a Lipschitz embedding where singleton reference sets, i.e. reference sets with a sole member, are considered only. In the present book, the proposed embedding framework is also extended towards general Lipschitz embeddings. Three extensions of a prototype selection method are introduced for defining reference sets for Lipschitz embeddings. Note that through the use of a set of subsets rather than singletons, we increase the likelihood that the original distance between two graphs is captured adequately by the distance in the embedding space.

Finally, it turns out that the idea of ensemble methods can also be considered for the difficult task of prototype selection. The great benefit of classifier ensembles is that errors of an individual classifier can often be compensated by the other ensemble members. In this approach, rather than using elaborated methods for defining a single set of prototypes, a randomized selection strategy is applied several times so that the procedure leads to various vector space embeddings of the same graph set. A classifier can be trained for each vector space embedding and the results of the individual classifiers can be combined in an appropriate way. Three different combination strategies are considered in the present book. Furthermore, we take into account that not only the prototypes themselves but also their number has a critical impact on the classification accuracy in the resulting vector space. Consequently, the size of each random prototype set, i.e. the number of prototypes selected, is also determined randomly. This means that each prototype set might have a different dimensionality selected out of a predefined interval.

The embedding procedure proposed in this book makes use of graph edit distance. Note, however, that any other graph dissimilarity measure can be used as well. Yet, using graph edit distance, no restrictions have to be considered on the type of graphs the embedding procedure can deal with. Furthermore, due to the flexibility of graph edit distance, a high degree of robustness against various graph distortions can be expected. Finally, our embedding method is versatile in the sense that it is possible to integrate domain specific knowledge about object similarity, if available, when defining the cost of the elementary edit operations.

Another idea to overcome the lack of algorithmic tools for graph based pattern recognition, which is closely related to graph embedding procedures, is kernel methods. In recent years, kernel methods have become one of the most rapidly emerging sub-fields in intelligent information processing. The vast majority of work on kernel methods is concerned with transforming a given feature space into another one of higher dimensionality without computing the transformation explicitly for each individual feature vector. As a fundamental extension the existence of kernels for symbolic data structures, especially for graphs, has been shown. By means of suitable graph kernel functions, graphs can be implicitly mapped into vector spaces. Consequently, a large class of kernel machines for classification and clustering, most of them originally developed for feature vectors, becomes applicable to graphs. By means of graph kernels one can benefit from both the high representational power of graphs and the large repository of algorithmic tools available for feature vector representations of objects.

The graph embedding procedure proposed in this book can also be seen as a foundation for a novel class of graph kernels. However, in contrast to some other kernel methods, the approach proposed in this book results in an explicit embedding of the considered graphs in a vector space. Hence, not only scalar products, but individual graph maps are available in the target space and thus, not only kernel machines, but also other non-kernelizable algorithms can be applied to the resulting vector space embedded graphs.

The versatility and flexibility of the proposed embedding approach is experimentally verified on ten challenging graph datasets from diverse application fields. The graphs of our benchmark tests represent line drawings from three applications (letters in three distortion levels, digits, and symbols), fingerprint images, HTML webpages, molecular compounds from two screenings (AIDS and mutagenicity), and proteins.

For the classification experiments, two reference systems are used, viz. a k-nearest-neighbor classifier based on graph edit distances and a support vector machine in conjunction with a similarity kernel directly derived from graph edit distance information. The first experiment uses the prototype selection strategies only and compares a k-NN classifier applied to vector space embedded graphs with the first reference method. It turns out that the procedure of first embedding graphs in some vector space with subsequent classification compared to performing the classification directly in the original space of graphs does not necessarily lead to an improvement of the classification accuracy. If the rather poor strategies cps and cps-c are ignored, we observe statistically significant deteriorations compared to the k-NN in the graph domain on three out of ten data sets (Letter low, Fingerprint, and Webpage). On the other hand, on four data sets at least one of the prototype selection strategies outperforms the reference system with statistical significance (Letter high, Digit, GREC, and AIDS). We conclude that no clear winner can be formed comparing the nearest-neighbor paradigm both based on graphs and vector space embedded graphs. Yet, due to the fact that a k-NN applied to vector space embedded graphs achieves similar results as when applied to the original graphs, it appears that no crucial information is systematically lost. Furthermore, one might expect that more sophisticated classifiers applied to embedded graphs have the potential to outperform this traditional graph classification approach.

Therefore, the second classification experiment carried out in this book is a comparison between an SVM classifier applied to vector space embedded graphs (using all embedding subsystems rather than only prototype selection) and both reference systems. The results achieved with our novel framework are convincing. Compared to the first reference method, our embedding systems improve the classification accuracy on nine out of ten data sets (seven of these improvements are statistically significant). Thus, we conclude that SVM classification of vector space embedded graphs, regardless of the subsystem actually employed for embedding, is clearly more powerful than traditional graph classification using a nearest-neighbor classifier in the graph domain.

Regarding the second reference method we observe the following results. The majority of the embedding framework subsystems, viz. the prototype selectors, the prototype reduction schemes, the dimensionality reduction algorithms, and the Lipschitz approach, outperform the SVM in conjunction with the similarity kernel on seven out of ten data sets. The ensemble approach outperforms the second reference system even on eight data sets. At least on three and at most on six out of ten data sets these improvements are statistically significant (achieved with the feature selection and dimensionality reduction embedding system, respectively). The other embedding subsystems outperform the second reference method in four or five cases with statistical significance.(depending on the subsystem actually employed). Given these positive results, the conclusion that the power of our embedding framework classifier is primarily due to the embedding process itself rather than to the kernel classifer is clearly admissible.

Comparing the embedding subsystems with each other, we observe that they perform very similarly in general. An interesting observation is that all of the embedding subsystems are outperformed with statistical significance on at least one data set compared to one of the other subsystems (e.g. the prototype selector is outperformed by the ensemble method on the Webpage data, the prototype reduction schemes are outperformed by the feature selection algorithms on the Protein data, the feature selection algorithms are in turn outperformed on the Mutagenicity data by all other subsystems, and so on). Another interesting point is that the dimensionality reduction algorithm PCA with scaled data outperforms all other systems with statistical significance on the Fingerprint data set. The same applies to the dimensionality reduction method MDA on the Webpage data set. Once again, however, in most of the cases the various embedding subsystems do not differ significantly from one another and it remains difficult to predict which of the subsystems will perform best on unseen data. Or to put it differently, all of the proposed graph embedding subsystems achieve remarkable results and outperform both reference methods on a clear majority of the data sets. Therefore, the novel graph embedding procedure offers a high degree of robustness and flexibility, regardless of the embedding subsystem applied.

The evaluation of the clustering experiments is handled in a more compact manner than the classification experiments. That is, only one subsytem (prototype selection) is used for clustering in the embedding space. As reference system a k-medians clustering is applied to the original graphs. This clustering method works very similarly to k-means clustering, but uses the set median rather than the mean for defining a cluster center (this is necessary as there is no general definition for the mean of a given graph population available). For clustering in the embedding space a kernelized k-means algorithm is used. Compared to standard k-means clustering, this procedure has the advantage that also non-spherical clusters can be found. For the purpose of comparison, four different clustering validation indices are used. Two of these quality measures are defined with respect to the class memberships of the underlying objects while the other two indices do not need any ground truth information. According to the former validation criteria, the clustering of vector space embedded graphs is beneficial on eight out of ten data sets. The clusterings found in the embedding vector space are clearly more accurate and consistent with respect to the ground truth. Regarding the latter criterion, which takes only the size and shape of the clusters into account, we observe that the reference system is outperformed in nine and ten cases. These results indicate that the clusters in the embedding vector space are more compact and better separable than those in the graph domain. Summarizing, we conclude that also in the unsupervised learning experiments the power and applicability of our novel embedding framework is empirically verified.

Overall, the experimental results clearly demonstrate that the dissimilarity embedding framework is advantageous for both graph classification and clustering over traditional approaches using the graph edit distance in a more direct manner. Still there are a number of open issues to be investigated in future research. For example, there seems to be room for developing and investigating additional prototype selectors and feature selection algorithms. Moreover, there might be possibilities for weighting the individual prototypes according to the information given by the prototype selection method (e.g. the cluster size in k-cps). That is, a feature of the embedded graph, i.e. the distance to a prototype, could be weighted according to the importance of this particular prototype. Furthermore, all classification experiments described in this paper are based on SVMs. It would be interesting to conduct exhaustive experiments with other statistical classifiers. A more comprehensive evaluation of the embedding framework in the clustering scenario could also be taken into account in future work. Moreover, the emerging trend of semi-supervised learning is not considered by our novel graph embedding framework so far. The promising results of the ensemble methods on the validation sets ask for a more thorough investigation with multiple validation sets in order to avoid the overfitting effect observed. Finally, in this book we have used only one graph distance measure, viz. the edit distance. Evaluating the proposed embedding method in conjunction with other types of dissimilarity functions could be another rewarding avenue to be explored.

Appendix A

Validation of Cost Parameters

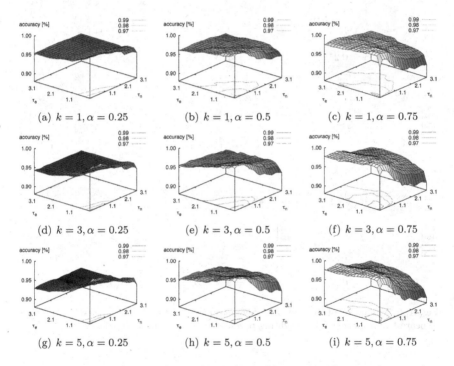

Fig. A.1 Validation of the node and edge insertion/deletion penalty τ_n and τ_e, number of nearest neighbors k, and weighting parameter α on the Letter low data set.

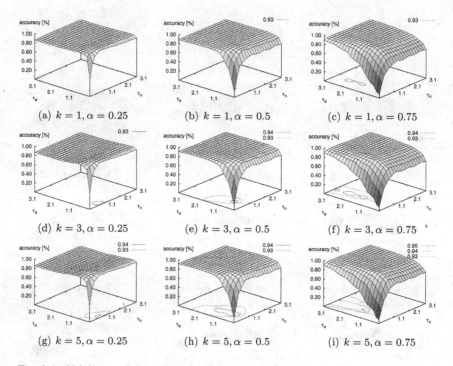

(a) $k = 1, \alpha = 0.25$ (b) $k = 1, \alpha = 0.5$ (c) $k = 1, \alpha = 0.75$

(d) $k = 3, \alpha = 0.25$ (e) $k = 3, \alpha = 0.5$ (f) $k = 3, \alpha = 0.75$

(g) $k = 5, \alpha = 0.25$ (h) $k = 5, \alpha = 0.5$ (i) $k = 5, \alpha = 0.75$

Fig. A.2   Validation of the node and edge insertion/deletion penalty τ_n and τ_e, number of nearest neighbors k, and weighting parameter α on the Letter medium data set.

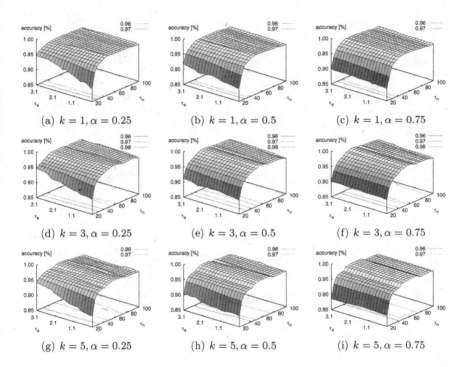

Fig. A.3 Validation of the node and edge insertion/deletion penalty τ_n and τ_e, number of nearest neighbors k, and weighting parameter α on the Digit data set.

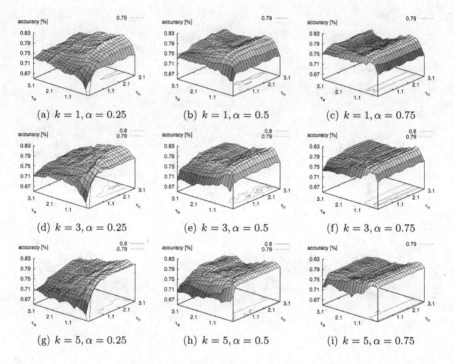

Fig. A.4   Validation of the node and edge insertion/deletion penalty τ_n and τ_e, number of nearest neighbors k, and weighting parameter α on the Fingerprint data set.

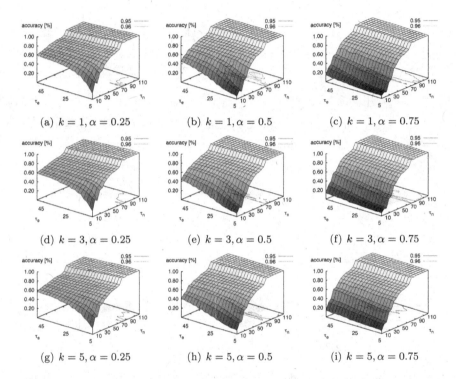

Fig. A.5 Validation of the node and edge insertion/deletion penalty τ_n and τ_e, number of nearest neighbors k, and weighting parameter α on the GREC data set.

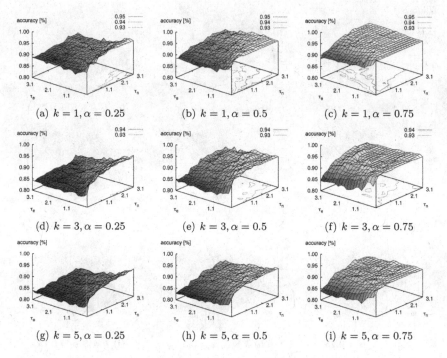

(a) $k = 1, \alpha = 0.25$ (b) $k = 1, \alpha = 0.5$ (c) $k = 1, \alpha = 0.75$

(d) $k = 3, \alpha = 0.25$ (e) $k = 3, \alpha = 0.5$ (f) $k = 3, \alpha = 0.75$

(g) $k = 5, \alpha = 0.25$ (h) $k = 5, \alpha = 0.5$ (i) $k = 5, \alpha = 0.75$

Fig. A.6 Validation of the node and edge insertion/deletion penalty τ_n and τ_e, number of nearest neighbors k, and weighting parameter α on the AIDS data set.

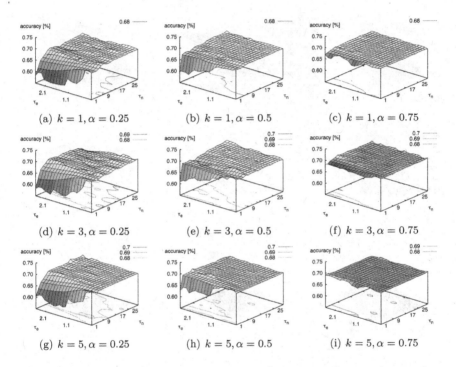

Fig. A.7 Validation of the node and edge insertion/deletion penalty τ_n and τ_e, number of nearest neighbors k, and weighting parameter α on the Mutagenicity data set.

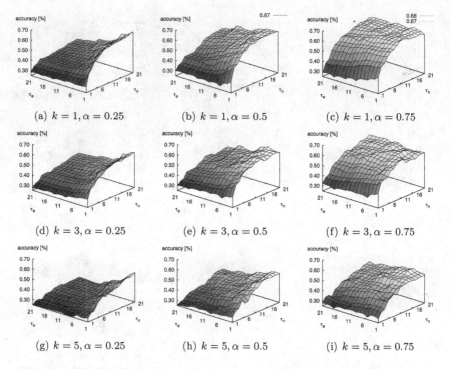

Fig. A.8   Validation of the node and edge insertion/deletion penalty τ_n and τ_e, number of nearest neighbors k, and weighting parameter α on the Protein data set.

Appendix B

Visualization of Graph Data

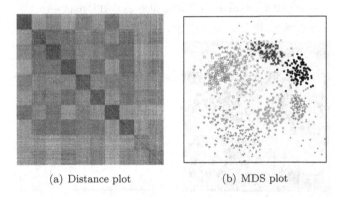

(a) Distance plot   (b) MDS plot

Fig. B.1   Distance and MDS plots of Digit data set.

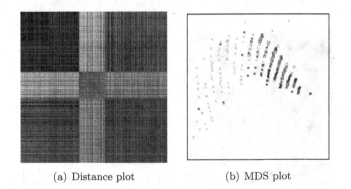

(a) Distance plot   (b) MDS plot

Fig. B.2   Distance and MDS plots of Fingerprint data set.

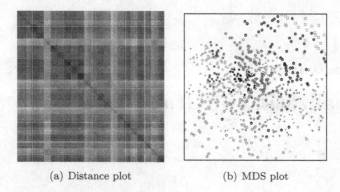

(a) Distance plot   (b) MDS plot

Fig. B.3   Distance and MDS plots of GREC data set.

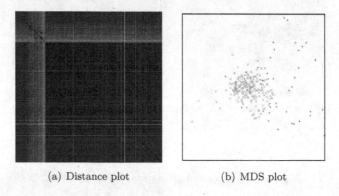

(a) Distance plot   (b) MDS plot

Fig. B.4   Distance and MDS plots of AIDS data set.

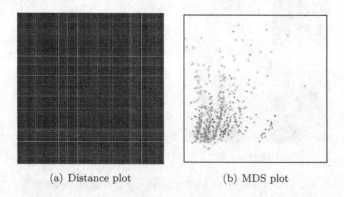

(a) Distance plot   (b) MDS plot

Fig. B.5   Distance and MDS plots of Mutagenicity data set.

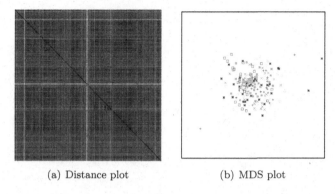

(a) Distance plot   (b) MDS plot

Fig. B.6   Distance and MDS plots of Protein data set.

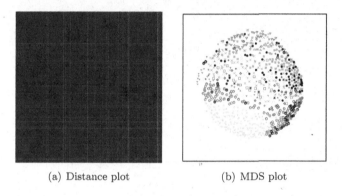

(a) Distance plot   (b) MDS plot

Fig. B.7   Distance and MDS plots of Webpage data set.

Appendix C

Classifier Combination

In the following we assume that we deal with a problem involving k different classes $\Omega = \{\omega_1, \ldots, \omega_k\}$. As any classifier combination method necessarily depends on the type of the m underlying classifiers $f_1, \ldots, f_m$, we distinguish three types of classifiers, viz. *type-1*, *type-2*, and *type-3 classifiers*. Output of type-1 classifiers is exactly one class $\omega_i \in \Omega$. Type-2 classifiers output a ranking list for each classifier f_j, i.e. an ordered list $(\omega_{j1}, \ldots, \omega_{jk})$ including all classes, where ω_{j1} is the class with the highest and ω_{jk} the class with the lowest plausibility according to f_j. Finally, type-3 classifiers output a plausibility value $p(\omega_i)$ for each class ω_i. This plausibility value corresponds to the probability that a test element under consideration belongs to the respective class. Thus, each classifer f_j outputs a vector of size k, $(p_j(\omega_1), \ldots, p_j(\omega_k))$.

Obviously, the combination of the outputs depends on the the type of the underlying classifiers. For type-1 classifers voting methods are typically used [2, 316]. Label ranking methods like Borda count [317] require a sorted label output, i.e. type-2 classifiers. To combine the continuous outputs of type-3 classifiers linear combinations of the individual values have been used [318, 319].

Output of a traditional SVM is one class and thus SVMs are typically type-1 classifiers. Since we want to use not only combiners depending on type-1 but also on type-2 and type-3 classifiers, one has to generalize SVM appropriately. The first generalization, which leads to a type-2 classifier, is simple and straightforward. We make use of the one-against-one scheme for multiclass problems. That is, for every pair of classes an individual binary SVM is trained resulting in $k(k-1)/2$ different SVMs. An unknown test element is assigned to the class that occurs the most frequently among the $k(k-1)/2$ decisions (see Sect. 5.4.1 for more details). Instead of returning only the most frequent class ω_i among the $k(k-1)/2$ SVM decisions, one can extend the j-th SVM of our ensemble to return an ordered list $(\omega_{j1}, \ldots, \omega_{jk})$, where ω_{j1} stands for the most frequent class and ω_{jk} represents the class that has won the fewest SVM decisions. To get a type-3 classifier one can use the so called *probabilistic SVM* [320]. This generalized SVM framework uses the distances in the feature space in order to estimate a probability value $p(\omega_i)$ for each class ω_i. A detailed description of this particular estimation scheme would go beyond the scope of the present thesis and we therefore refer to [320] where the details on probabilistic SVMs are provided.

Based on these three different output formats of the m SVMs, one can use different combination strategies to obtain the final result. In this work we use a *voting* algorithm for type-1 SVMs, a ranking sum method for type-2 SVMs (*Borda count*) and *Bayes' combination* using the plausibility values obtained by type-3 SVMs.

Voting   The class ω_{j1} output by classifier f_j $(1 \leqslant j \leqslant m)$ is regarded as one vote for $\omega_{j1} \in \Omega$. The class that receives the plurality of the votes is choosen by the combiner. This method is often termed *plurality voting* [2]. Of course, one can use more restrictive voting methods with rejection (e.g. *majority voting* where more than 50% of the votes have to be assigned to one class in order to not reject the considered pattern).

Borda Count   Assume that each classifier f_j outputs an ordered list including all classes $\{\omega_i\}_{1 \leqslant i \leqslant k}$. To combine the results of type-2 classifiers one can introduce rank functions $r_j(\omega_{ji})$ for each classifer f_j. Function $r_j(\omega_{ji})$ delivers the position of the class ω_{ji} in the ordered list given by classifier f_j, i.e. $r_j(\omega_{ji}) = i$. Hence, for each class $\{\omega_i\}_{1 \leqslant i \leqslant k}$ the sum of all ranks can be computed, $R(\omega_i) = \sum_{j=1}^{m} r_j(\omega_i)$. Subsequently, the combiner chooses the class $\{\omega_i\}_{1 \leqslant i \leqslant k}$ with the minimum value of $R(\omega_i)$. This combination method is known as *Borda count*.

Bayes' Combination   In this approach the individual plausibility values $\{p_j(\omega_i)\}_{1 \leqslant j \leqslant m}$ are combined to get one plausibility value P_i per class ω_i. Common strategies to combine the plausibility values are given below [321]:

- $P_i = \max(p_1(\omega_i), \ldots, p_m(\omega_i))$
- $P_i = \min(p_1(\omega_i), \ldots, p_m(\omega_i))$
- $P_i = \frac{1}{m} \sum_{j=1}^{m} p_j(\omega_i)$
- $P_i = \prod_{j=1}^{m} p_j(\omega_i)$

Regardless which of these formulas is used, the ensemble eventually chooses the class ω_i with the maximum value of the corresponding P_i. In the present thesis we use the last approach based on the product, which is known as *Bayes' combination.*

Validation of a k-NN classifier in the Embedding Space

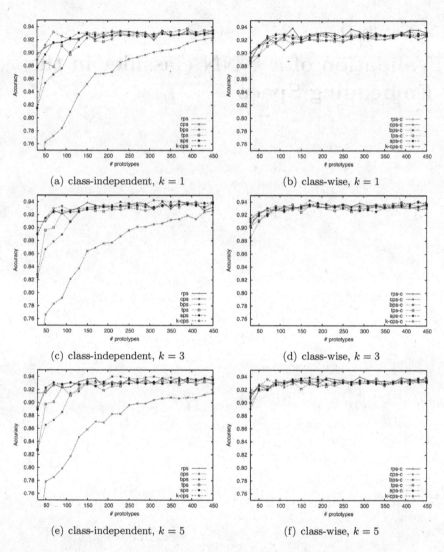

(a) class-independent, $k = 1$ (b) class-wise, $k = 1$

(c) class-independent, $k = 3$ (d) class-wise, $k = 3$

(e) class-independent, $k = 5$ (f) class-wise, $k = 5$

Fig. D.1   Validation of the prototype selectors on the Letter medium data set for a k-NN classifier.

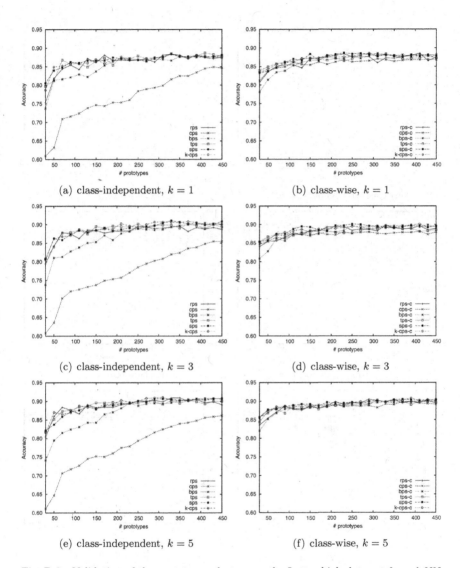

(a) class-independent, $k = 1$ (b) class-wise, $k = 1$

(c) class-independent, $k = 3$ (d) class-wise, $k = 3$

(e) class-independent, $k = 5$ (f) class-wise, $k = 5$

Fig. D.2   Validation of the prototype selectors on the Letter high data set for a k-NN classifier.

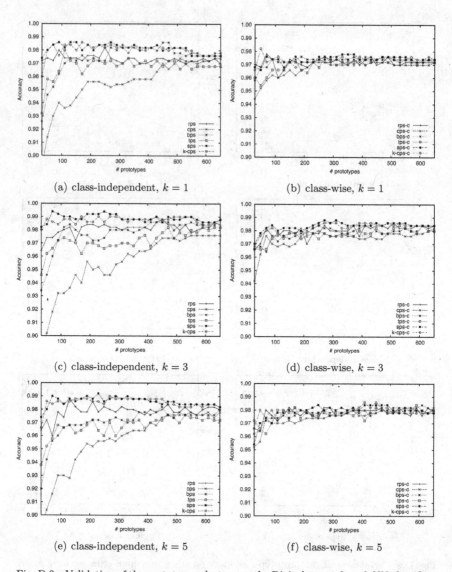

(a) class-independent, $k = 1$

(b) class-wise, $k = 1$

(c) class-independent, $k = 3$

(d) class-wise, $k = 3$

(e) class-independent, $k = 5$

(f) class-wise, $k = 5$

Fig. D.3   Validation of the prototype selectors on the Digit data set for a k-NN classifier.

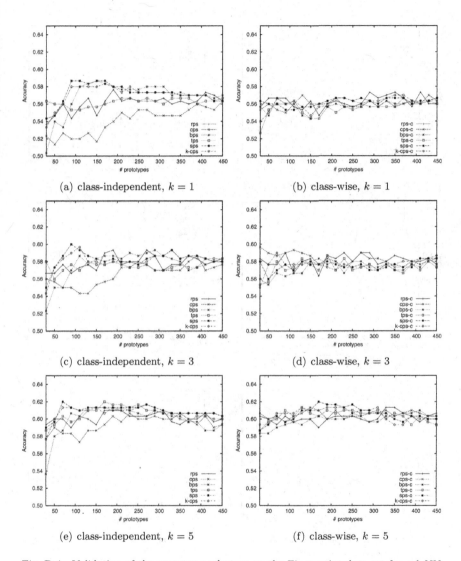

(a) class-independent, $k = 1$

(b) class-wise, $k = 1$

(c) class-independent, $k = 3$

(d) class-wise, $k = 3$

(e) class-independent, $k = 5$

(f) class-wise, $k = 5$

Fig. D.4   Validation of the prototype selectors on the Fingerprint data set for a k-NN classifier.

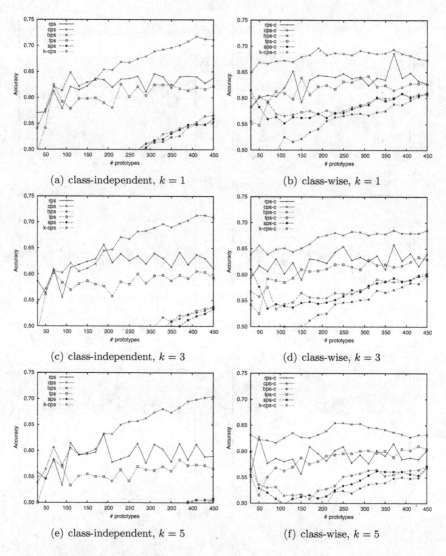

(a) class-independent, $k = 1$

(b) class-wise, $k = 1$

(c) class-independent, $k = 3$

(d) class-wise, $k = 3$

(e) class-independent, $k = 5$

(f) class-wise, $k = 5$

Fig. D.5   Validation of the prototype selectors on the GREC data set for a k-NN classifier.

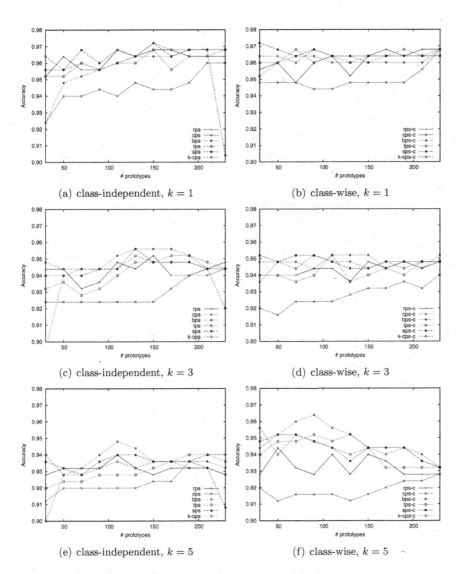

(a) class-independent, $k = 1$

(b) class-wise, $k = 1$

(c) class-independent, $k = 3$

(d) class-wise, $k = 3$

(e) class-independent, $k = 5$

(f) class-wise, $k = 5$

Fig. D.6 Validation of the prototype selectors on the AIDS data set for a k-NN classifier.

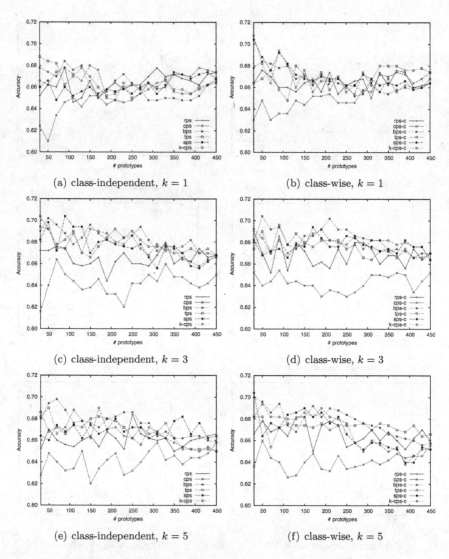

(a) class-independent, $k = 1$

(b) class-wise, $k = 1$

(c) class-independent, $k = 3$

(d) class-wise, $k = 3$

(e) class-independent, $k = 5$

(f) class-wise, $k = 5$

Fig. D.7   Validation of the prototype selectors on the Mutagenicity data set for a k-NN classifier.

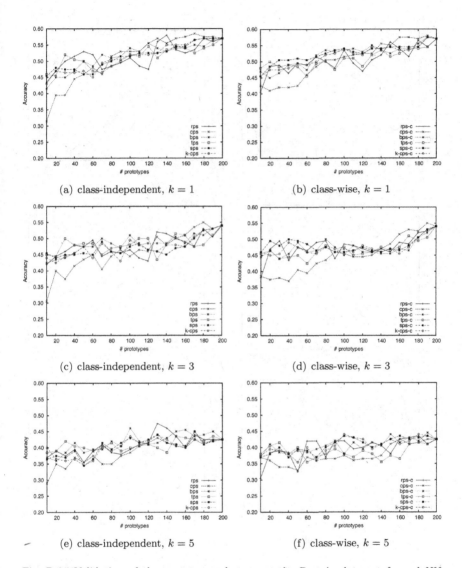

(a) class-independent, $k = 1$

(b) class-wise, $k = 1$

(c) class-independent, $k = 3$

(d) class-wise, $k = 3$

(e) class-independent, $k = 5$

(f) class-wise, $k = 5$

Fig. D.8 Validation of the prototype selectors on the Protein data set for a k-NN classifier.

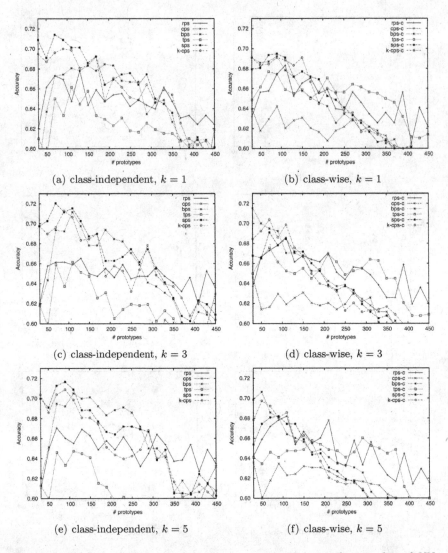

Fig. D.9 Validation of the prototype selectors on the Webpage data set for a k-NN classifier.

Appendix E

Validation of a SVM classifier in the Embedding Space

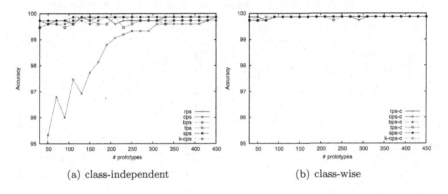

(a) class-independent   (b) class-wise

Fig. E.1   Validation of the prototype selectors on the Letter low data set.

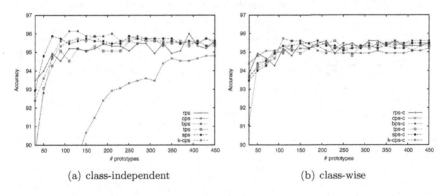

(a) class-independent   (b) class-wise

Fig. E.2   Validation of the prototype selectors on the Letter medium data set.

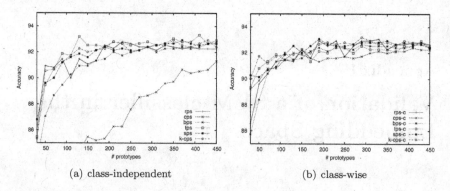

(a) class-independent   (b) class-wise

Fig. E.3   Validation of the prototype selectors on the Letter high data set.

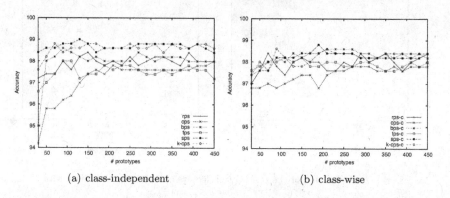

(a) class-independent   (b) class-wise

Fig. E.4   Validation of the prototype selectors on the Digit data set.

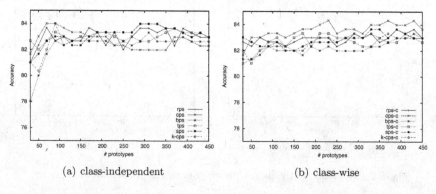

(a) class-independent   (b) class-wise

Fig. E.5   Validation of the prototype selectors on the Fingerprint data set.

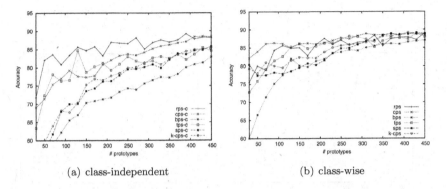

(a) class-independent   (b) class-wise

Fig. E.6   Validation of the prototype selectors on the GREC data set.

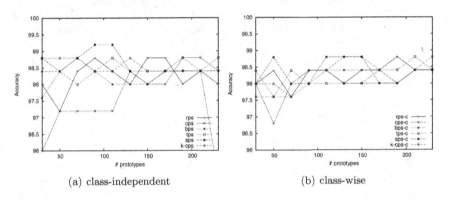

(a) class-independent   (b) class-wise

Fig. E.7   Validation of the prototype selectors on the AIDS data set.

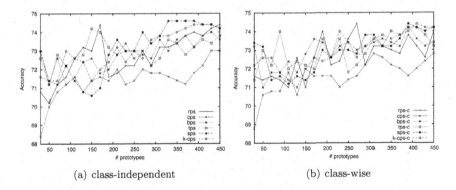

(a) class-independent   (b) class-wise

Fig. E.8   Validation of the prototype selectors on the Mutagenicity data set.

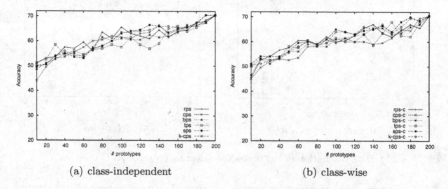

(a) class-independent   (b) class-wise

Fig. E.9   Validation of the prototype selectors on the Protein data set.

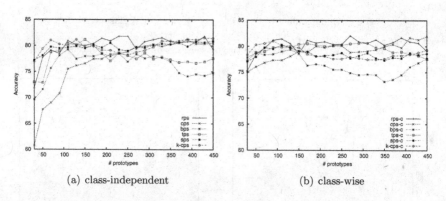

(a) class-independent   (b) class-wise

Fig. E.10   Validation of the prototype selectors on the Webpage data set.

Appendix F
Validation of Lipschitz Embeddings

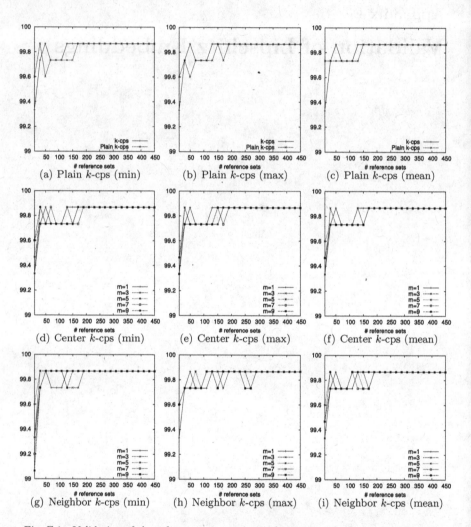

Fig. F.1 Validation of the reference set creation techniques on the Letter low data set.

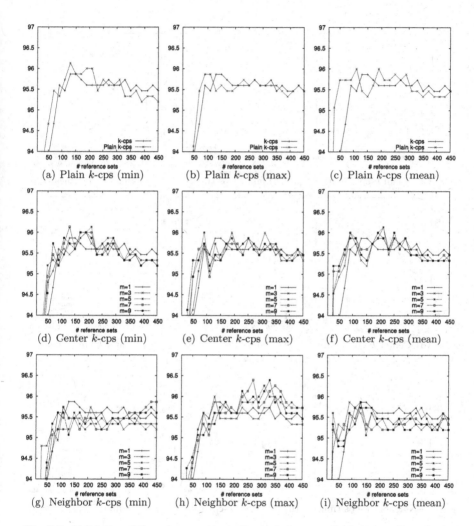

Fig. F.2   Validation of the reference set creation techniques on the Letter medium data set.

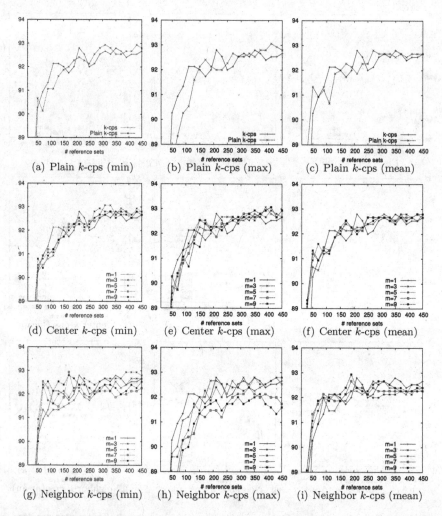

(a) Plain k-cps (min)   (b) Plain k-cps (max)   (c) Plain k-cps (mean)

(d) Center k-cps (min)   (e) Center k-cps (max)   (f) Center k-cps (mean)

(g) Neighbor k-cps (min)   (h) Neighbor k-cps (max)   (i) Neighbor k-cps (mean)

Fig. F.3   Validation of the reference set creation techniques on the Letter high data set.

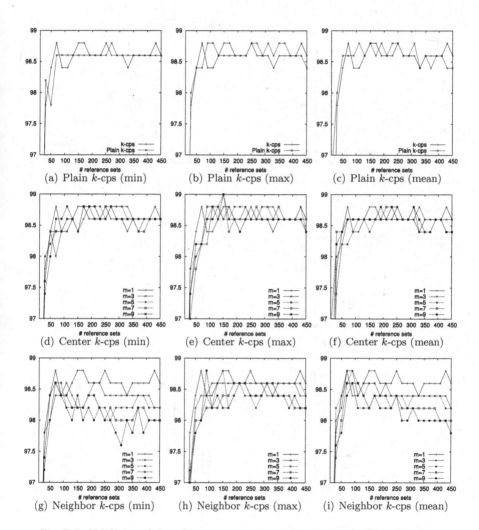

Fig. F.4   Validation of the reference set creation techniques on the Digit data set.

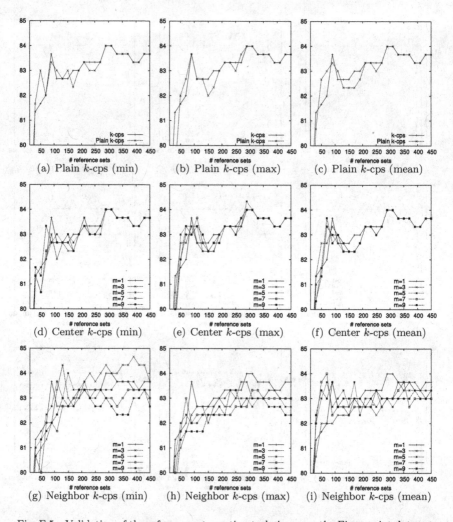

(a) Plain k-cps (min)   (b) Plain k-cps (max)   (c) Plain k-cps (mean)

(d) Center k-cps (min)   (e) Center k-cps (max)   (f) Center k-cps (mean)

(g) Neighbor k-cps (min)   (h) Neighbor k-cps (max)   (i) Neighbor k-cps (mean)

Fig. F.5   Validation of the reference set creation techniques on the Fingerprint data set.

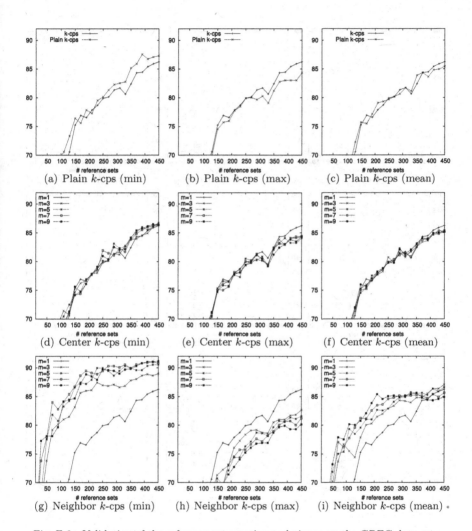

Fig. F.6   Validation of the reference set creation techniques on the GREC data set.

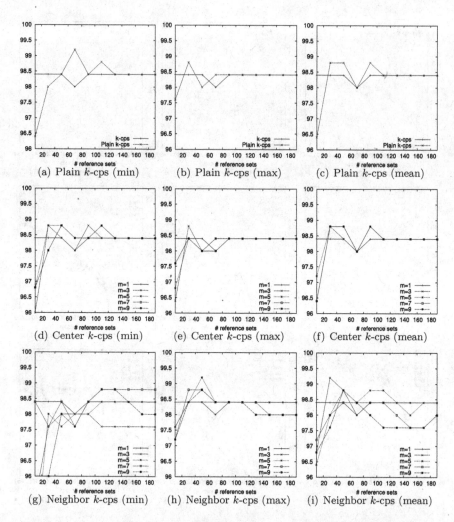

Fig. F.7   Validation of the reference set creation techniques on the AIDS data set.

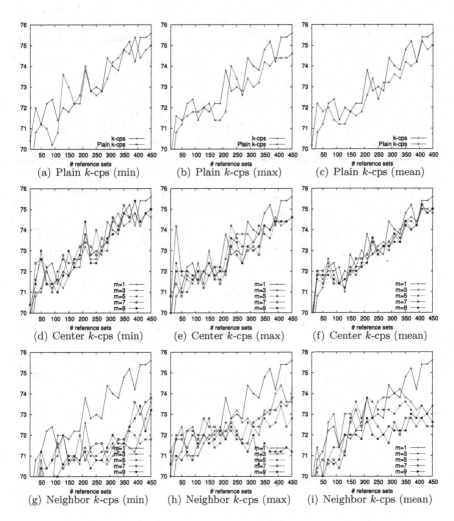

(a) Plain k-cps (min) (b) Plain k-cps (max) (c) Plain k-cps (mean)

(d) Center k-cps (min) (e) Center k-cps (max) (f) Center k-cps (mean)

(g) Neighbor k-cps (min) (h) Neighbor k-cps (max) (i) Neighbor k-cps (mean)

Fig. F.8 Validation of the reference set creation techniques on the Mutagenicity data set.

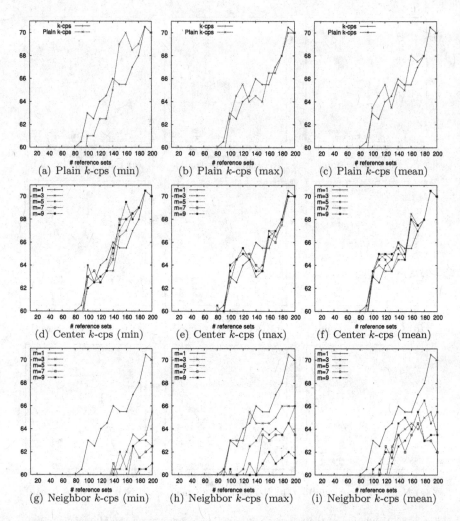

Fig. F.9   Validation of the reference set creation techniques on the Protein data set.

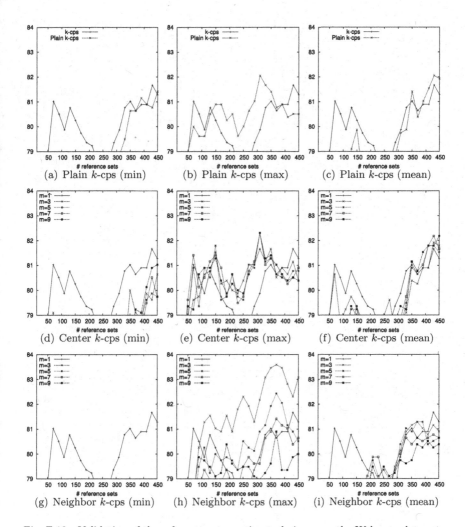

(a) Plain k-cps (min) (b) Plain k-cps (max) (c) Plain k-cps (mean)

(d) Center k-cps (min) (e) Center k-cps (max) (f) Center k-cps (mean)

(g) Neighbor k-cps (min) (h) Neighbor k-cps (max) (i) Neighbor k-cps (mean)

Fig. F.10 Validation of the reference set creation techniques on the Webpage data set.

Appendix G

Validation of Feature Selection Algorithms and PCA Reduction

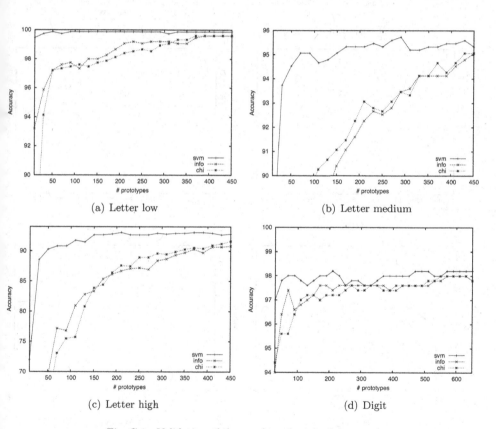

(a) Letter low

(b) Letter medium

(c) Letter high

(d) Digit

Fig. G.1   Validation of the number of retained features.

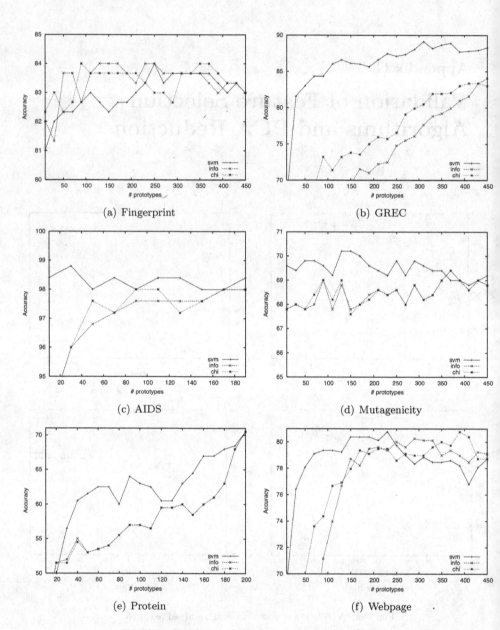

(a) Fingerprint

(b) GREC

(c) AIDS

(d) Mutagenicity

(e) Protein

(f) Webpage

Fig. G.2　Validation of the number of retained features.

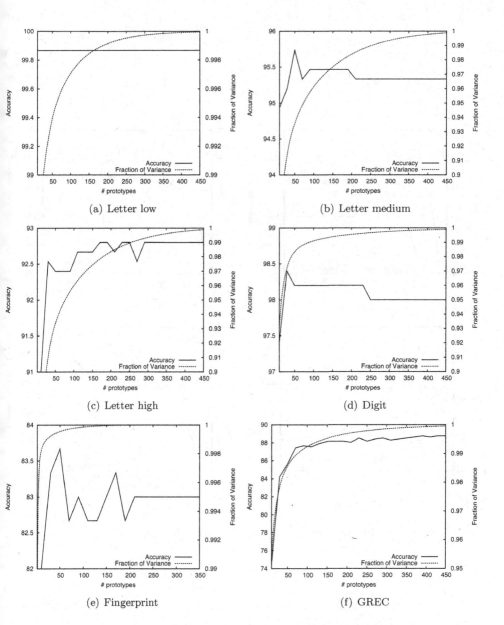

Fig. G.3   Validation of the PCA space dimensionality.

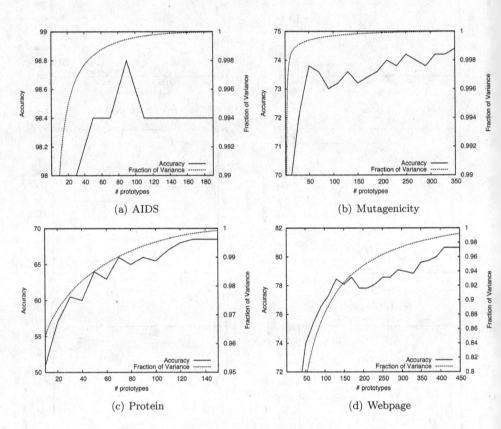

(a) AIDS

(b) Mutagenicity

(c) Protein

(d) Webpage

Fig. G.4   Validation of the PCA space dimensionality.

Appendix H

Validation of Classifier Ensemble

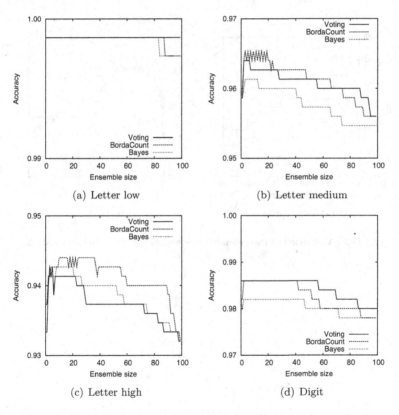

Fig. H.1 Validation of the ensemble size and members by means of SFFS.

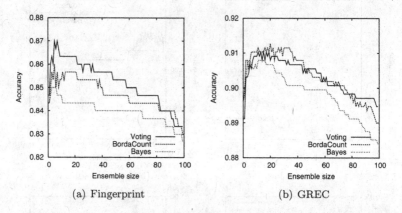

(a) Fingerprint　　　　　　　(b) GREC

Fig. H.2　Validation of the ensemble size and members by means of SFFS.

Appendix I

Validation of Kernel k-Means Clustering

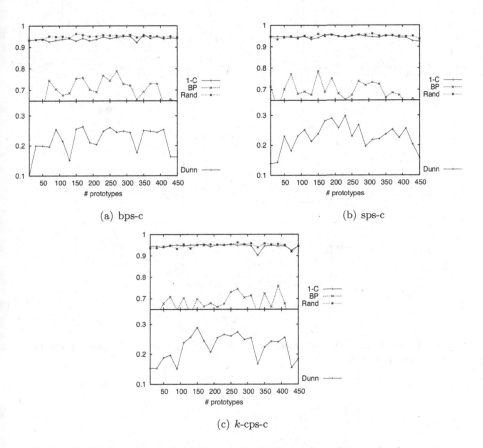

(a) bps-c

(b) sps-c

(c) k-cps-c

Fig. I.1   Validation of clustering indices on the Letter medium data set for three proto-type selection strategies.

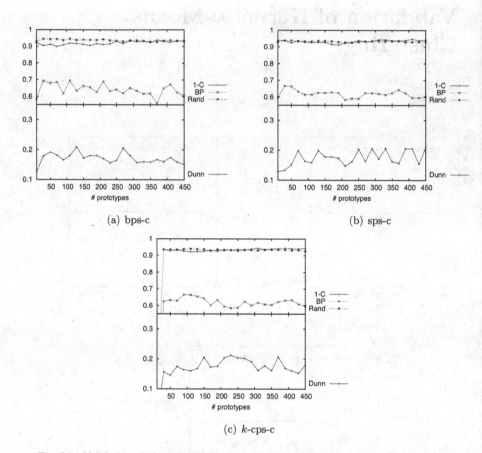

(a) bps-c

(b) sps-c

(c) k-cps-c

Fig. I.2   Validation of clustering indices on the Letter high data set for three prototype selection strategies.

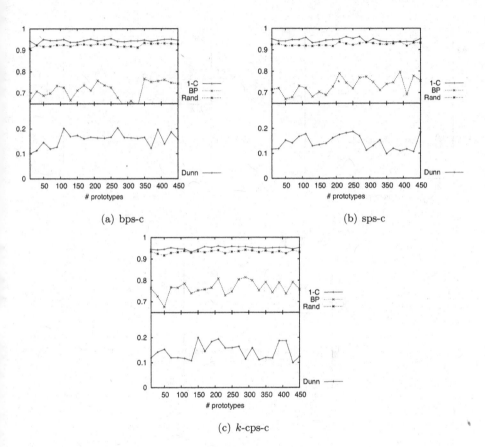

(a) bps-c   (b) sps-c

(c) k-cps-c

Fig. I.3   Validation of clustering indices on the Digit data set for three prototype selection strategies.

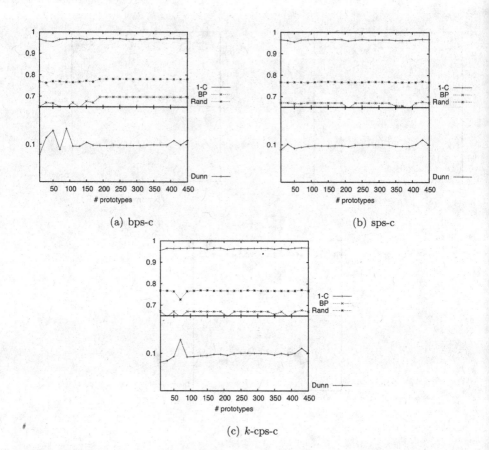

(a) bps-c

(b) sps-c

(c) k-cps-c

Fig. I.4   Validation of clustering indices on the Fingerprint data set for three prototype selection strategies.

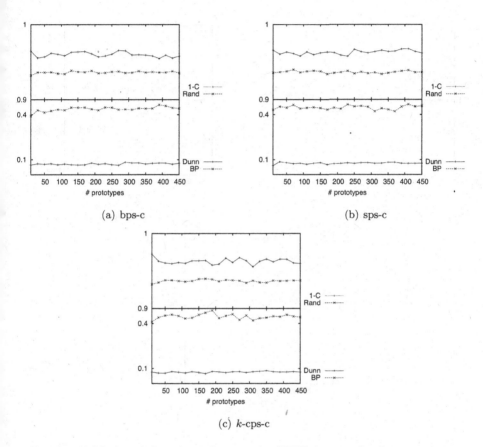

(a) bps-c

(b) sps-c

(c) k-cps-c

Fig. I.5   Validation of clustering indices on the GREC data set for three prototype selection strategies.

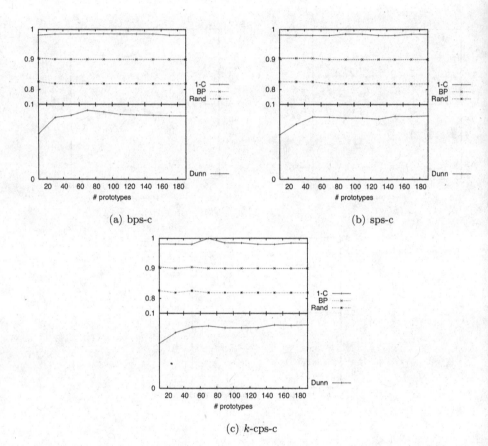

(a) bps-c

(b) sps-c

(c) k-cps-c

Fig. I.6   Validation of clustering indices on the AIDS data set for three prototype selection strategies.

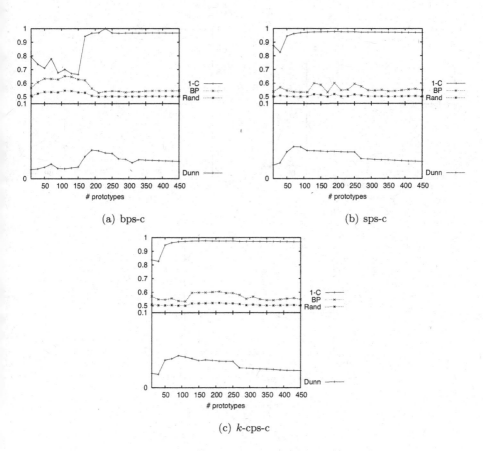

(a) bps-c

(b) sps-c

(c) *k*-cps-c

Fig. I.7   Validation of clustering indices on the Mutagenicity data set for three prototype selection strategies.

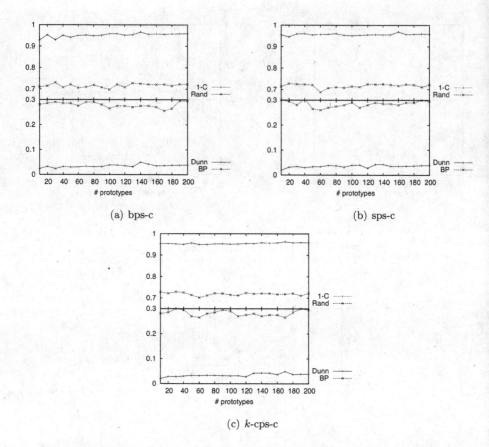

(a) bps-c

(b) sps-c

(c) k-cps-c

Fig. I.8   Validation of clustering indices on the Protein data set for three prototype selection strategies.

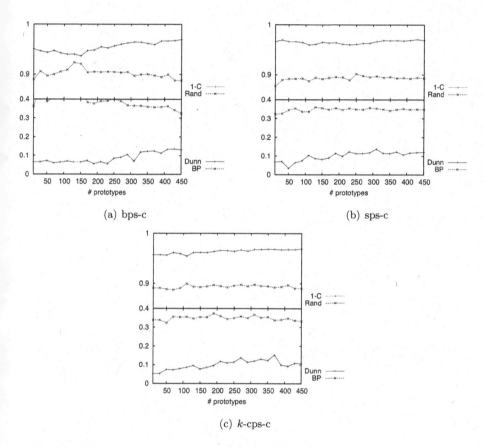

(a) bps-c

(b) sps-c

(c) k-cps-c

Fig. I.9   Validation of clustering indices on the Webpage data set for three prototype selection strategies.

Appendix J
Confusion Matrices

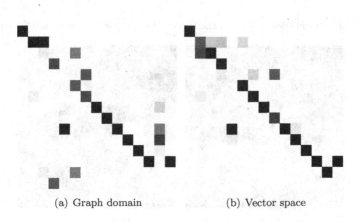

(a) Graph domain   (b) Vector space

Fig. J.1   Confusion matrix on the Letter low data set (clusters vs. classes).

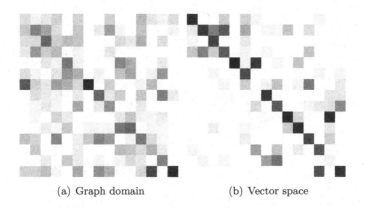

(a) Graph domain   (b) Vector space

Fig. J.2   Confusion matrix on the Letter high data set (clusters vs. classes).

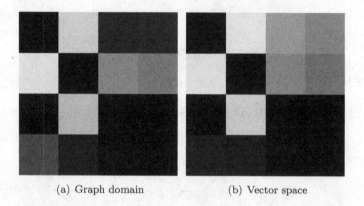

(a) Graph domain   (b) Vector space

Fig. J.3   Confusion matrix on the Fingerprint data set (clusters vs. classes).

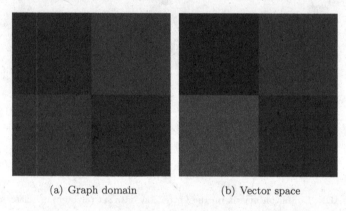

(a) Graph domain   (b) Vector space

Fig. J.4   Confusion matrix on the Mutagenicity data set (clusters vs. classes).

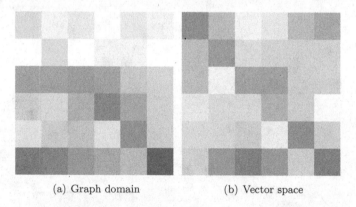

(a) Graph domain   (b) Vector space

Fig. J.5   Confusion matrix on the Protein data set (clusters vs. classes).

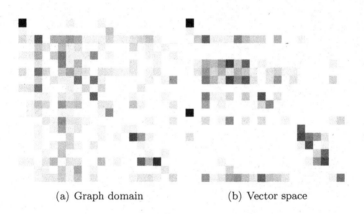

(a) Graph domain   (b) Vector space

Fig. J.6 Confusion matrix on the Webpage data set (clusters vs. classes).

Bibliography

[1] R. Duda, P. Hart, and D. Stork. *Pattern Classification*. Wiley-Interscience, 2nd edition, 2000.

[2] L. Kuncheva. *Combining Pattern Classifiers: Methods and Algorithms*. John Wiley, 2004.

[3] M. Nadler and E.P. Smith. *Pattern Recognition Engineering*. John Wiley & Sons, 1992.

[4] E. Pekalska and R. Duin. *The Dissimilarity Representation for Pattern Recognition: Foundations and Applications*. World Scientific, 2005.

[5] J. Shawe-Taylor and N. Cristianini. *Kernel Methods for Pattern Analysis*. Cambridge University Press, 2004.

[6] J.J. Hull, G. Krishnan, P. Palumbo, and S.N. Srihari. Optical character recognition techniques in mail sorting: A review of algorithms. Technical report, Department of Computer Science University at Buffalo, State University of New York, 1984.

[7] Y. Lu and C.L. Tan. Combination of multiple classifiers using probabilistic dictionary and its application to postcode recognition. *Pattern Recognition*, 35(12):2823–2832, 2000.

[8] L. Zhang, J. Zhu, and T. Yao. An evaluation of statistical spam filtering techniques. *ACM Transactions on Asian Language Information Processing*, 3(4):243–269, 2004.

[9] A. Kolcz and J. Alspector. SVM-based filtering of e-mail spam with content-specific misclassification costs. In *Proc. Workshop on Text Mining TextDM*, 2001.

[10] F. Sebastiani. Machine learning in automated text categorization. *ACM Computing Surveys*, 34(1):1–47, 2002.

[11] A. Vinciarelli. Noisy text categorization. In *Proc. of the 17th Int. Conference on Pattern Recognition*, volume 2, pages 554–557, 2004.

[12] A. Juan and E. Vidal. On the use of Bernoulli mixture models for text classification. *Pattern Recognition*, 35(12):2705–2710, 2002.

[13] R. Bertolami, S. Uchida, M. Zimmermann, and H. Bunke. Non-uniform slant correction for handwritten text line recognition. In *Proc. of the 9th Int. Conference on Document Analysis and Recognition*, volume 1, pages

18–22, 2007.

[14] M. Liwicki and H. Bunke. *Recognition of Whiteboard Notes – Online, Offline and Combination*. World Scientific, 2008.

[15] M. Zimmermann, J.-C. Chappelier, and H. Bunke. Offline grammar-based recognition of handwritten sentences. *IEEE Transactions on Pattern Analysis and Machine Intelligence*, 28(5):818–821, 2006.

[16] R. Kosala and Blockeel. Web mining research: a survey. *SIGKDD Explorations*, 2:1–15, 2000.

[17] N. Zhong, J. Liu, and Y. Yao. In search of the wisdom web. *Computer*, 35(11):27–31, 2002.

[18] A. Schlapbach and H. Bunke. A writer identification and verification system using HMM based recognizers. *Pattern Analysis and Applications*, 10(1):33–43, 2007.

[19] A. Schlapbach and H. Bunke. Off-line writer identification and verification using Gaussian mixture models. In S. Marinai and H. Fujisawa, editors, *Machine Learning in Document Analysis and Recognition*, volume 90. Springer, 2008.

[20] A.K. Jain, S. Prabhakar, and L. Hong. A multichannel approach to fingerprint classification. *IEEE Transactions on Pattern Analysis and Machine Intelligence*, 21(4):348–359, 1999.

[21] M. Neuhaus and H. Bunke. A graph matching based approach to fingerprint classification using directional variance. In T. Kanade, A. Jain, and N.K. Ratha, editors, *Proc. 5th Int. Conference on Audio- and Video-Based Biometric Person Authentication*, LNCS 3546, pages 191–200. Springer, 2005.

[22] A. Serrau, G.L. Marcialis, H. Bunke, and F. Roli. An experimental comparison of fingerprint classification methods using graphs. In *Proc. 5th Int. Workshop on Graph-based Representations in Pattern Recognition*, LNCS 3434, pages 281–290. Springer, 2005.

[23] N. Yager and A. Amin. Fingerprint classification: A review. *Pattern Analysis and Applications*, 7(1):77–93, 2004.

[24] Y. Xu and E.C. Uberbacher. Gene prediction by pattern recognition and homology search. In *Proc. of the Fourth Int. Conference on Intelligent Systems for Molecular Biology*, pages 241–251, 1996.

[25] E. Dougherty. The fundamental role of pattern recognition for gene-expression/microarray data in bioinformatics. *Pattern Recognition*, 38(12):2226–2228, 2005.

[26] R.D. Brown and Y.C. Martin. Use of structure-activity data to compare structure-based clustering methods and descriptors for use in compound selection. *Journal of Chemical Information and Computer Sciences*, 36(3):572–584, 1996.

[27] P. Mahé, N. Ueda, and T. Akutsu. Graph kernels for molecular structures – activity relationship analysis with support vector machines. *Journal of Chemical Information and Modeling*, 45(4):939–951, 2005.

[28] M. Neuhaus and H. Bunke. *Bridging the Gap Between Graph Edit Distance and Kernel Machines*. World Scientific, 2007.

[29] N.A. Fox, R. Gross, J.F. Cohn, and R.B. Reilly. Robust biometric person identification using automatic classifier fusion of speech, mouth, and face expert. *IEEE Transactions on Multimedia*, 9(4):701–714, 2007.

[30] N. Arica and F.T. Yarman-Vural. Optical character recognition for cursive handwriting. *IEEE Transactions on Pattern Analysis and Machine Intelligence*, 24(6):801–813, 2002.

[31] J.G. Wolff. Medical diagnosis as pattern recognition in a framework of information compression by multiple alignment, unification and search. *Decision Support Systems*, 42(2):608–625, 2006.

[32] A.K. Jain, M.N. Murty, and P.J. Flynn. Data clustering: A review. *ACM Computing Surveys*, 31(3):264–323, 1999.

[33] R. Xu and D. Wunsch. Survey of graph clustering algorithms. *IEEE Transactions on Neural Networks*, 16(3):645–678, 2005.

[34] A.K. Jain and R.C. Dubes. *Algorithms For Clustering Data*. Prentice-Hall, Englewood Cliffs, NJ, 1988.

[35] O. Chapelle, B. Schölkopf, and A. Zien, editors. *Semi-Supervised Learning*. MIT Press, 2006.

[36] K.S. Fu. *Syntactic Pattern Recognition and Applications*. Prentice-Hall, 1982.

[37] C. Bishop. *Pattern Recognition and Machine Learning*. Springer, 2008.

[38] H. Bunke. Structural and Syntactic pattern recognition. In C.H. Chen, Pau L.F., and P.S.P. Wang, editors, *Handbook of Pattern Recognition and Computer Vision*, pages 163–210. World Scientific, 1992.

[39] K. Borgwardt. *Graph Kernels*. PhD thesis, Ludwig-Maximilians-University Munich, 2007.

[40] D. Conte, P. Foggia, C. Sansone, and M. Vento. Thirty years of graph matching in pattern recognition. *Int. Journal of Pattern Recognition and Artificial Intelligence*, 18(3):265–298, 2004.

[41] A. Kandel, H. Bunke, and M. Last, editors. *Applied Graph Theory in Computer Vision and Pattern Recognition*, volume 52 of *Studies in Computational Intelligence*. Springer, 2007.

[42] H. Bunke, P.J. Dickinson, M. Kraetzl, and W.D. Wallis. *A Graph-Theoretic Approach to Enterprise Network Dynamics*, volume 24 of *Progress in Computer Science and Applied Logic (PCS)*. Birkhäuser, 2007.

[43] D. Cook and L. Holder, editors. *Mining Graph Data*. Wiley-Interscience, 2007.

[44] K. Borgwardt, C. Ong, S. Schönauer, S. Vishwanathan, A. Smola, and H.-P. Kriegel. Protein function prediction via graph kernels. *Bioinformatics*, 21(1):47–56, 2005.

[45] K. Borgwardt and H.-P. Kriegel. Shortest-path kernels on graphs. In *Proc. 5th Int. Conference on Data Mining*, pages 74–81, 2005.

[46] L. Ralaivola, S.J. Swamidass, H Saigo, and P. Baldi. Graph kernels for chemical informatics. *Neural Networks*, 18(8):1093–1110, 2005.

[47] A. Schenker, H. Bunke, M. Last, and A. Kandel. *Graph-Theoretic Techniques for Web Content Mining*. World Scientific, 2005.

[48] A. Schenker, M. Last, H. Bunke, and A. Kandel. Classification of web

documents using graph matching. *Int. Journal of Pattern Recognition and Artificial Intelligence*, 18(3):475–496, 2004.

[49] B. Le Saux and H. Bunke. Feature selection for graph-based image classifiers. In J. Marques, N. Perez de Blanca, and P. Pina, editors, *Proc. 2nd Iberian Conference on Pattern Recognition and Image Analysis, Part II*, LNCS 3523, pages 147–154. Springer, 2005.

[50] Z. Harchaoui and F. Bach. Image classification with segmentation graph kernels. In *IEEE Conference on Computer Vision and Pattern Recognition*, pages 1–8, 2007.

[51] B. Luo, R. Wilson, and E. Hancock. Spectral embedding of graphs. *Pattern Recognition*, 36(10):2213–2223, 2003.

[52] M. Neuhaus and H. Bunke. An error-tolerant approximate matching algorithm for attributed planar graphs and its application to fingerprint classification. In A. Fred, T. Caelli, R. Duin, A. Campilho, and D. de Ridder, editors, *Proc. 10th Int. Workshop on Structural and Syntactic Pattern Recognition*, LNCS 3138, pages 180–189. Springer, 2004.

[53] R. Ambauen, S. Fischer, and H. Bunke. Graph edit distance with node splitting and merging and its application to diatom identification. In E. Hancock and M. Vento, editors, *Proc. 4th Int. Workshop on Graph Based Representations in Pattern Recognition*, LNCS 2726, pages 95–106. Springer, 2003.

[54] S. Fischer. *Automatic Identification of Diatoms*. PhD thesis, University of Bern, 2002.

[55] D. Maio and D. Maltoni. A structural approach to fingerprint classification. In *Proc. 13th Int. Conference on Pattern Recognition*, pages 578–585, 1996.

[56] J. Lladós and G. Sánchez. Graph matching versus graph parsing in graphics recognition. *Int. Journal of Pattern Recognition and Artificial Intelligence*, 18(3):455–475, 2004.

[57] L.P. Cordella, P. Foggia, C. Sansone, and M. Vento. Fast graph matching for detecting CAD image components. In *Proc. 15th Int. Conference on Pattern Recognition*, volume 2, pages 1038–1041, 2000.

[58] J. Rocha and T. Pavlidis. A shape analysis model with applications to a character recognition system. *IEEE Transactions on Pattern Analysis and Machine Intelligence*, 16(4):393–404, 1994.

[59] P.N. Suganthan and H. Yan. Recognition of handprinted Chinese characters by constrained graph matching. *Image and Vision Computing*, 16(3):191–201, 1998.

[60] P. Dickinson, H. Bunke, A. Dadej, and M. Kraetzl. On graphs with unique node labels. In E. Hancock and M. Vento, editors, *Proc. 4th Int. Workshop on Graph Based Representations in Pattern Recognition*, LNCS 2726, pages 13–23. Springer, 2003.

[61] P.J. Dickinson, H. Bunke, A. Dadej, and M. Kraetzl. Matching graphs with unique node labels. *Pattern Analysis and Applications*, 7(3):243–254, 2004.

[62] P.J. Dickinson, M. Kraetzl, H. Bunke, M. Neuhaus, and A. Dadej. Similarity measures for hierarchical representations of graphs with unique node labels. *Int. Journal of Pattern Recognition and Artificial Intelligence*, 18(3):425–442, 2004.

[63] E. Pekalska and R. Duin. Classifiers for dissimilarity-based pattern recognition. In *15th Int. Conference on Pattern Recognition*, volume 2, pages 12–16, 2000.

[64] E. Pekalska and R. Duin. Automatic pattern recognition by similarity representations. *Electronic Letters*, 37(3):159–160, 2001.

[65] E. Pekalska and R. Duin. Dissimilarity representations allow for building good classifiers. *Pattern Recognition Letters*, 23(8):943–956, 2002.

[66] E. Pekalska, R. Duin, and P. Paclik. Prototype selection for dissimilarity-based classifiers. *Pattern Recognition*, 39(2):189–208, 2006.

[67] R. Duin and E. Pekalska. Possibilities of zero-error recognition by dissimilarity representations. In J.M. Inesta and L. Mico, editors, *Pattern Recognition in Information Systems*, 2002.

[68] R. Duin, E. Pekalska, P. Paclik, and D. Tax. The dissimilarity representation, a basis for domain based pattern recognition? In L. Goldfarb, editor, *Pattern Representation and the Future of Pattern Recognition, ICPR Workshop Proceedings*, pages 43–56, 2004.

[69] S. Edelman and S. Duvdevani-Bar. Similarity, connectionism, and the problem of representation in vision. *Neural Computation*, 9:701–720, 1997.

[70] S. Edelman, S. Cutzu, and S. Duvdevani-Bar. Representation is representation of similarities. *Behavioral and Brain Sciences*, 21:449–498, 1998.

[71] S. Edelman. *Representation and Recognition in Vision*. MIT Press, 1999.

[72] V. Mottl, S. Dvoenko, O. Seredin, C. Kulikowski, and I. Muchnik. Featureless regularized recognition of protein fold classes in a hilbert space of pairwise alignment scores as inner products of amino acid sequences. *Pattern Recognition and Image Analysis, Advances in Mathematical Theory and Applications*, 11(3):597–615, 2001.

[73] A. Guérin-Dugué, P. Teissier, G. Delso Gafaro, and J. Hérault. Curvilinear component analysis for high-dimensional data representation: II. examples of additional mapping constraints in specific applications. In *Proc. Conference on Artificial and Natural Neural Networks*, LNCS 1607, pages 635–644. Springer, 1999.

[74] R. Duin, D. de Ridder, and D. Tax. Featureless pattern classification. *Kybernetika*, 34(4):399–404, 1998.

[75] H. Bunke. Graph-based tools for data mining and machine learning. In P. Perner and A. Rosenfeld, editors, *Proc. 3rd Int. Conference on Machine Learning and Data Mining in Pattern Recognition*, LNAI 2734, pages 7–19. Springer, 2003.

[76] Ch. Irniger. *Graph Matching – Filtering Databases of Graphs Using Machine Learning Techniques*. PhD thesis, University of Bern, 2005.

[77] H. Bunke. Recent developments in graph matching. In *Proc. 15th Int. Conference on Pattern Recognition*, volume 2, pages 117–124, 2000.

[78] E.M. Luks. Isomorphism of graphs of bounded valence can be tested in polynomial time. *Journal of Computer and Systems Sciences*, 25:42–65, 1982.

[79] P. Foggia, C. Sansone, and M. Vento. A database of graphs for isomorphism and subgraph isomorphism benchmarking. In *Proc. 3rd Int. Workshop on*

Graph Based Representations in Pattern Recognition, pages 176–187, 2001.

[80] J.E. Hopcroft and J. Wong. Linear time algorithm for isomorphism of planar graphs. In *Proc. 6th Annual ACM Symposium on Theory of Computing*, pages 172–184, 1974.

[81] K. Zhang, R. Statman, and D. Shasha. On the editing distance between unordered labelled trees. *Information Processing Letters*, 42(3):133–139, 1992.

[82] M. Pelillo, K. Siddiqi, and S. Zucker. Matching hierarchical structures using association graphs. *IEEE Transactions on Pattern Analysis and Machine Intelligence*, 21(11):1105–1120, 1999.

[83] M. Pelillo. Matching free trees, maximal cliques and monotone game dynamics. *IEEE Transactions on Pattern Analysis and Machine Intelligence*, 24(11):1535–1541, 2002.

[84] A. Torsello and E. Hancock. Computing approximate tree edit distance using relaxation labeling. *Pattern Recognition Letters*, 24(8):1089–1097, 2003.

[85] A. Torsello, D. Hidovic-Rowe, and M. Pelillo. Polynomial-time metrics for attributed trees. *IEEE Transactions on Pattern Analysis and Machine Intelligence*, 27(7):1087–1099, 2005.

[86] M.R. Garey and D.S. Johnson. *Computers and Intractability: A Guide to the Theory of NP-Completeness*. Freeman and Co., 1979.

[87] B. Aspvall and R.E. Stone. Khachiyan's linear programming algorithm. *Journal of Algorithms*, 1(1):1–13, 1980.

[88] M Agrawal, N. Kayal, and N. Saxena. PRIMES is in P. *Annals of Mathematics*, 160(2):781–793, 2004.

[89] I. Wegener. *Complexity Theory: Exploring the Limits of Efficient Algorithms*. Springer, 2005.

[90] A.V. Aho, J.E. Hopcroft, and J.D. Ullman. *The Design and Analysis of Computer Algorithms*. Addison Wesley, 1974.

[91] X. Jiang and H. Bunke. Optimal quadratic-time isomorphism of ordered graphs. *Pattern Recognition*, 32(17):1273–1283, 1999.

[92] J.R. Ullmann. An algorithm for subgraph isomorphism. *Journal of the Association for Computing Machinery*, 23(1):31–42, 1976.

[93] L. P. Cordella, P. Foggia, C. Sansone, and M. Vento. An improved algorithm for matching large graphs. In *Proc. 3rd Int. Workshop on Graph Based Representations in Pattern Recognition*, 2001.

[94] L.P. Cordella, P. Foggia, C. Sansone, and M. Vento. A (sub)graph isomorphism algorithm for matching large graphs. *IEEE Transactions on Pattern Analysis and Machine Intelligence*, 26(20):1367–1372, 2004.

[95] J. Larrosa and G. Valiente. Constraint satisfaction algorithms for graph pattern matching. *Mathematical Structures in Computer Science*, 12(4):403–422, 2002.

[96] B.D. McKay. Practical graph isomorphism. *Congressus Numerantium*, 30:45–87, 1981.

[97] H. Bunke and B. Messmer. Recent advances in graph matching. *Int. Journal of Pattern Recognition and Artificial Intelligence*, 11:169–203, 1997.

[98] B. Messmer and H. Bunke. A decision tree approach to graph and subgraph

isomorphism detection. *Pattern Recognition*, 32(12):1979–1998, 1999.

[99] G. Levi. A note on the derivation of maximal common subgraphs of two directed or undirected graphs. *Calcolo*, 9:341–354, 1972.

[100] C. Bron and J. Kerbosch. Algorithm 457: finding all cliques of an undirected graph. *Communications of the ACM*, 16(9):575–577, 1973.

[101] E. Balas and C.S. Yu. Finding a maximum clique in an arbitrary graph. *SIAM Journal on Computing*, 15(4):1054–1068, 1986.

[102] H. Bunke, P. Foggia, C. Guidobaldi, C. Sansone, and M. Vento. A comparison of algorithms for maximum common subgraph on randomly connected graphs. In T. Caelli, A. Amin, R. Duin, M. Kamel, and D. de Ridder, editors, *Proc. of the Int. Workshops on Structural, Syntactic, and Statistical Pattern Recognition*, pages 85–106. Springer, 2002. LNCS 2396.

[103] J.J. McGregor. Backtrack search algorithms and the maximal common subgraph problem. *Software Practice and Experience*, 12:23–34, 1982.

[104] H. Bunke and K. Shearer. A graph distance metric based on the maximal common subgraph. *Pattern Recognition Letters*, 19(3):255–259, 1998.

[105] W.D. Wallis, P. Shoubridge, M. Kraetzl, and D. Ray. Graph distances using graph union. *Pattern Recognition Letters*, 22(6):701–704, 2001.

[106] H. Bunke. On a relation between graph edit distance and maximum common subgraph. *Pattern Recognition Letters*, 18:689–694, 1997.

[107] M.-L. Fernandez and G. Valiente. A graph distance metric combining maximum common subgraph and minimum common supergraph. *Pattern Recognition Letters*, 22(6–7):753–758, 2001.

[108] H. Bunke, X. Jiang, and A. Kandel. On the minimum common supergraph of two graphs. *Computing*, 65(1):13–25, 2000.

[109] W.H. Tsai and K.S. Fu. Error-correcting isomorphism of attributed relational graphs for pattern analysis. *IEEE Transactions on Systems, Man, and Cybernetics (Part B)*, 9(12):757–768, 1979.

[110] W.H. Tsai and K.S. Fu. Subgraph error-correcting isomorphisms for syntactic pattern recognition. *IEEE Transactions on Systems, Man, and Cybernetics (Part B)*, 13:48–61, 1983.

[111] E.K. Wong. Three-dimensional object recognition by attributed graphs. In H. Bunke and A. Sanfeliu, editors, *Syntactic and Structural Pattern Recognition: Theory and Applications*, pages 381–414. World Scientific, 1990.

[112] A. Sanfeliu and K.S. Fu. A distance measure between attributed relational graphs for pattern recognition. *IEEE Transactions on Systems, Man, and Cybernetics (Part B)*, 13(3):353–363, 1983.

[113] H. Bunke and G. Allermann. Inexact graph matching for structural pattern recognition. *Pattern Recognition Letters*, 1:245–253, 1983.

[114] A.C.M. Dumay, R.J. van der Geest, J.J. Gerbrands, E. Jansen, and J.H.C Reiber. Consistent inexact graph matching applied to labelling coronary-segments in arteriograms. In *Proc. 11th Int. Conference on Pattern Recognition*, volume 3, pages 439–442, 1992.

[115] L. Gregory and J. Kittler. Using graph search techniques for contextual colour retrieval. In T. Caelli, A. Amin, R.P.W. Duin, M. Kamel, and D. de Ridder, editors, *Proc. of the Int. Workshops on Structural, Syntactic,*

and Statistical Pattern Recognition, LNCS 2396, pages 186–194, 2002.

[116] S. Berretti, A. Del Bimbo, and E. Vicario. Efficient matching and indexing of graph models in content-based retrieval. *IEEE Transactions on Pattern Analysis and Machine Intelligence*, 23(10):1089–1105, 2001.

[117] K. Riesen, S. Fankhauser, and H. Bunke. Speeding up graph edit distance computation with a bipartite heuristic. In P. Frasconi, K. Kersting, and K. Tsuda, editors, *Proc. 5th. Int. Workshop on Mining and Learning with Graphs*, pages 21–24, 2007.

[118] P.E. Hart, N.J. Nilsson, and B. Raphael. A formal basis for the heuristic determination of minimum cost paths. *IEEE Transactions on Systems, Science, and Cybernetics*, 4(2):100–107, 1968.

[119] M.C. Boeres, C.C. Ribeiro, and I. Bloch. A randomized heuristic for scene recognition by graph matching. In C.C. Ribeiro and S.L. Martins, editors, *Proc. 3rd Workshop on Efficient and Experimental Algorithms*, LNCS 3059, pages 100–113. Springer, 2004.

[120] S. Sorlin and C. Solnon. Reactive tabu search for measuring graph similarity. In L. Brun and M. Vento, editors, *Proc. 5th Int. Workshop on Graph-based Representations in Pattern Recognition*, LNCS 3434, pages 172–182. Springer, 2005.

[121] M. Neuhaus, K. Riesen, and H. Bunke. Fast suboptimal algorithms for the computation of graph edit distance. In Dit-Yan Yeung, J.T. Kwok, A. Fred, F. Roli, and D. de Ridder, editors, *Proc. 11.th int. Workshop on Structural and Syntactic Pattern Recognition*, LNCS 4109, pages 163–172. Springer, 2006.

[122] D. Justice and A. Hero. A binary linear programming formulation of the graph edit distance. *IEEE Transactions on Pattern Analysis and Machine Intelligence*, 28(8):1200–1214, 2006.

[123] M.A. Eshera and K.S. Fu. A graph distance measure for image analysis. *IEEE Transactions on Systems, Man, and Cybernetics (Part B)*, 14(3):398–408, 1984.

[124] M.A. Eshera and K.S. Fu. A similarity measure between attributed relational graphs for image analysis. In *Proc. 7th Int. Conference on Pattern Recognition*, pages 75–77, 1984.

[125] K. Riesen, M. Neuhaus, and H. Bunke. Bipartite graph matching for computing the edit distance of graphs. In F. Escolano and M. Vento, editors, *Proc. 6th Int. Workshop on Graph Based Representations in Pattern Recognition*, LNCS 4538, pages 1–12, 2007.

[126] K. Riesen and H. Bunke. Approximate graph edit distance computation by means of bipartite graph matching. *Image and Vision Computing*, 27(4):950–959, 2009.

[127] A. Cross, R. Wilson, and E. Hancock. Inexact graph matching using genetic search. *Pattern Recognition*, 30(6):953–970, 1997.

[128] I. Wang, K.-C. Fan, and J.-T. Horng. Genetic-based search for error-correcting graph isomorphism. *IEEE Transactions on Systems, Man, and Cybernetics (Part B)*, 27(4):588–597, 1997.

[129] M. Singh, A. Chatterjee, and S. Chaudhury. Matching structural shape de-

scriptions using genetic algorithms. *Pattern Recognition*, 30(9):1451–1462, 1997.

[130] P.N. Suganthan. Structural pattern recognition using genetic algorithms. *Pattern Recognition*, 35(9):1883–1893, 2002.

[131] M.A. Fischler and R.A. Elschlager. The representation and matching of pictorial structures. *IEEE Transactions on Computers*, 22(1):67–92, 1973.

[132] J. Kittler and E. Hancock. Combining evidence in probabilistic relaxation. *Int. Journal of Pattern Recognition and Artificial Intelligence*, 3(1):29–51, 1989.

[133] E. Hancock and J. Kittler. Discrete relaxation. *Pattern Recognition*, 23(7):711–733, 1990.

[134] W.J. Christmas, J. Kittler, and M. Petrou. Structural matching in computer vision using probabilistic relaxation. *IEEE Transactions on Pattern Analysis and Machine Intelligence*, 17(8):749–764, 1995.

[135] R.C. Wilson and E. Hancock. Structural matching by discrete relaxation. *IEEE Transactions on Pattern Analysis and Machine Intelligence*, 19(6):634–648, 1997.

[136] B. Huet and E. Hancock. Shape recognition from large image libraries by inexact graph matching. *Pattern Recognition Letters*, 20(11–13):1259–1269, 1999.

[137] R. Myers, R.C. Wilson, and E. Hancock. Bayesian graph edit distance. *IEEE Transactions on Pattern Analysis and Machine Intelligence*, 22(6):628–635, 2000.

[138] B. Schölkopf and A. Smola. *Learning with Kernels*. MIT Press, 2002.

[139] T. Gärtner. A survey of kernels for structured data. *SIGKDD Explorations*, 5(1):49–58, 2003.

[140] T. Gärtner, P. Flach, and S. Wrobel. On graph kernels: Hardness results and efficient alternatives. In B. Schölkopf and M. Warmuth, editors, *Proc. 16th Annual Conference on Learning Theory*, pages 129–143, 2003.

[141] D. Haussler. Convolution kernels on discrete structures. Technical Report UCSC-CRL-99-10, University of California, Santa Cruz, 1999.

[142] C. Watkins. Dynamic alignment kernels. In A. Smola, P.L. Bartlett, B. Schölkopf, and D. Schuurmans, editors, *Advances in Large Margin Classifiers*, pages 39–50. MIT Press, 2000.

[143] C. Watkins. Kernels from matching operations. Technical Report CSD-TR-98-07, Royal Holloway College, 1999.

[144] K. Borgwardt, T. Petri, H.-P. Kriegel, and S. Vishwanathan. An efficient sampling scheme for comparison of large graphs. In P. Frasconi, K. Kersting, and K. Tsuda, editors, *Proc. 5th. Int. Workshop on Mining and Learning with Graphs*, 2007.

[145] T. Gärtner. Exponential and geometric kernels for graphs. In *NIPS Workshop on Unreal Data: Principles of Modeling Nonvectorial Data*, 2002.

[146] H. Kashima and A. Inokuchi. Kernels for graph classification. In *Proc. ICDM Workshop on Active Mining*, pages 31–36, 2002.

[147] H. Kashima, K. Tsuda, and A. Inokuchi. Marginalized kernels between labeled graphs. In *Proc. 20th Int. Conference on Machine Learning*, pages

321–328, 2003.

[148] R. Kondor and J. Lafferty. Diffusion kernels on graphs and other discrete input spaces. In *Proc. 19th Int. Conference on Machine Learning*, pages 315–322, 2002.

[149] J. Kandola, J. Shawe-Taylor, and N. Cristianini. Learning semantic similarity. *Neural Information Processing Systems*, 15(657–664), 2002.

[150] A. Smola and R. Kondor. Kernels and regularization on graphs. In *Proc. 16th. Int. Conference on Comptuational Learning Theory*, pages 144–158, 2003.

[151] J. Lafferty and G. Lebanon. Information diffusion kernels. In *Advances in Neural Information Processing Systems*, volume 15, pages 375–382. MIT Press, 2003.

[152] J.-P. Vert and M. Kanehisa. Graph-driven features extraction from microarray data using diffusion kernels and kernel CCA. In *Advances in Neural Information Processing Systems*, volume 15, pages 1425–1432. MIT Press, 2003.

[153] J. Lafferty and G. Lebanon. Diffusion kernels on statistical manifolds. *Journal of Machine Learning Research*, 6:129–163, 2005.

[154] J. Ramon and T. Gärtner. Expressivity versus efficiency of graph kernels. In *Proc. First Int. Workshop on Mining Graphs, Trees and Sequences*, pages 65–74, 2003.

[155] T. Horvath, T. Gärtner, and S. Wrobel. Cyclic pattern kernels for predictive graph mining. In *Proc. Int. Conference on Knowledge Discovery and Data Mining*, pages 65–74. ACM Press, 2004.

[156] S. Umeyama. An eigendecomposition approach to weighted graph matching problems. *IEEE Transactions on Pattern Analysis and Machine Intelligence*, 10(5):695–703, 1988.

[157] T. Caelli and S. Kosinov. Inexact graph matching using eigen-subspace projection clustering. *Int. Journal of Pattern Recognition and Artificial Intelligence*, 18(3):329–355, 2004.

[158] A. Shokoufandeh, D. Macrini, S. Dickinson, K. Siddiqi, and S.W. Zucker. Indexing hierarchical structures using graph spectra. *IEEE Transactions on Pattern Analysis and Machine Intelligence*, 27(7):1125–1140, 2005.

[159] B. Luo, R. Wilson, and E. Hancock. Spectral feature vectors for graph clustering. In T. Caelli, A. Amin, R. Duin, M. Kamel, and D. de Ridder, editors, *Proc. of the Int. Workshops on Structural, Syntactic, and Statistical Pattern Recognition*, pages 83–93. Springer, 2002. LNCS 2396.

[160] S. Kosinov and T. Caelli. Inexact multisubgraph matching using graph eigenspace and clustering models. In T. Caelli, A. Amin, R. Duin, M. Kamel, and D. de Ridder, editors, *Proc. of the Int. Workshops on Structural, Syntactic, and Statistical Pattern Recognition*, pages 133–142. Springer, 2002. LNCS 2396.

[161] R.C. Wilson, E. Hancock, and B. Luo. Pattern vectors from algebraic graph theory. *IEEE Transactions on Pattern Analysis and Machine Intelligence*, 27(7):1112–1124, 2005.

[162] A. Robles-Kelly and E. Hancock. A Riemannian approach to graph embed-

ding. *Pattern Recognition*, 40:1024–1056, 2007.

[163] P. Frasconi, M. Gori, and A. Sperduti. A general framework for adaptive processing of data structures. *IEEE Transactions on Neural Networks*, 9(5):768–786, 1998.

[164] A. Sperduti and A. Starita. Supervised neural networks for the classification of structures. *IEEE Transactions on Neural Networks*, 8(3):714–735, 1997.

[165] P.N. Suganthan, E.K. Teoh, and D.P. Mital. Pattern recognition by homomorphic graph matching using Hopfield neural networks. *Image and Vision Computing*, 13(1):45–60, 1995.

[166] P.N. Suganthan, E.K. Teoh, and D.P. Mital. Pattern recognition by graph matching using the potts MFT neural networks. *Pattern Recognition*, 28(7):997–1009, 1995.

[167] P.N. Suganthan, E.K. Teoh, and D.P. Mital. Self-organizing Hopfield network for attributed relational graph matching. *Image and Vision Computing*, 13(1):61–73, 1995.

[168] A. Micheli. Neural network for graphs: A contextual constructive approach. *IEEE Transactions on Neural Networks*, 20(3):498–511, 2009.

[169] F. Scarselli, M. Gori, A.C. Tsoi, M. Hagenbuchner, and G. Monfardini. The graph neural network model. *IEEE Transactions on Neural Networks*, 20(1):61–80, 2009.

[170] Y. Yao, G.L. Marcialis, M. Pontil, P. Frasconi, and F. Roli. Combining flat and structured representations for fingerprint classification with recursive neural networks and support vector machines. *Pattern Recognition*, 36(2):397–406, 2003.

[171] J. Feng, M. Laumy, and M. Dhome. Inexact matching using neural networks. In E.S. Gelsema and L.N. Kanal, editors, *Pattern Recognition in Practice IV: Multiple Paradigms, Comparative Studies, and Hybrid Systems*, pages 177–184. North-Holland, 1994.

[172] L. Xu and E. Oja. Improved simulated annealing: Boltzmann machine, and attributed graph matching. In L. Almeida, editor, *Proc. Int. Workshop on Neural Networks*, LNCS 412, pages 151–161. Springer, 1990.

[173] K. Schädler and F. Wysotzki. Comparing structures using a Hopfield-style neural network. *Applied Intelligence*, 11:15–30, 1999.

[174] B. Jain and F. Wysotzki. Automorphism partitioning with neural networks. *Neural Processing Letters*, 17(2):205–215, 2003.

[175] B. Jain and F. Wysotzki. Solving inexact graph isomorphism problems using neural networks. *Neurocomputing*, 63:45–67, 2005.

[176] A.M. Finch, R.C. Wilson, and E. Hancock. Symbolic graph matching with the EM algorithm. *Pattern Recognition*, 31(11):1777–1790, 1998.

[177] B. Luo and E. Hancock. Structural graph matching using the EM algorithm and singular value decomposition. *IEEE Transactions on Pattern Analysis and Machine Intelligence*, 23(10):1120–1136, 2001.

[178] M. Pelillo. Replicator equations, maximal cliques, and graph isomorphism. *Neural Computation*, 11(8):1933–1955, 1999.

[179] S. Gold and A. Rangarajan. A graduated assignment algorithm for graph matching. *IEEE Transactions on Pattern Analysis and Machine Intelli-*

gence, 18(4):377–388, 1996.

[180] A. Robles-Kelly and E. Hancock. String edit distance, random walks and graph matching. *Int. Journal of Pattern Recognition and Artificial Intelligence*, 18(3):315–327, 2004.

[181] M. Gori, M. Maggini, and L. Sarti. Exact and approximate graph matching using random walks. *IEEE Transactions on Pattern Analysis and Machine Intelligence*, 27(7):1100–1111, 2005.

[182] M.A. van Wyk, T.S. Durrani, and B.J. van Wyk. A RKHS interpolator-based graph matching algorithm. *IEEE Transactions on Pattern Analysis and Machine Intelligence*, 24(7):988–995, 2003.

[183] M.A. van Wyk and J. Clark. An algorithm for approximate least-squares attributed graph matching. *Problems in Applied Mathematics and Computational Intelligence*, pages 67–72, 2001.

[184] A.K.C. Wong and M. You. Entropy and distance of random graphs with application to structural pattern recognition. *IEEE Transactions on Pattern Analysis and Machine Intelligence*, 7(5):599–609, 1985.

[185] A. Sanfeliu, F. Serratosa, and R. Alquézar. Second-order random graphs for modeling sets of attributed graphs and their application to object learning and recognition. *Int. Journal of Pattern Recognition and Artificial Intelligence*, 18(3):375–396, 2004.

[186] V. Levenshtein. Binary codes capable of correcting deletions, insertions and reversals. *Soviet Physics Doklady*, 10(8):707–710, 1966.

[187] R.A. Wagner and M.J. Fischer. The string-to-string correction problem. *Journal of the Association for Computing Machinery*, 21(1):168–173, 1974.

[188] S.M. Selkow. The tree-to-tree editing problem. *Information Processing Letters*, 6(6):184–186, 1977.

[189] A. Robles-Kelly and E. Hancock. Graph edit distance from spectral seriation. *IEEE Transactions on Pattern Analysis and Machine Intelligence*, 27(3):365–378, 2005.

[190] H. du Buf and M. Bayer, editors. *Automatic Diatom Identification*. World Scientific, 2002.

[191] R. Cesar, E. Bengoetxea, and I. Bloch. Inexact graph matching using stochastic optimization techniques for facial feature recognition. In *Proc. 16th Int. Conference on Pattern Recognition*, volume 2, pages 465–468, 2002.

[192] C. Gomila and F. Meyer. Tracking objects by graph matching of image partition sequences. In *Proc. 3rd Int. Workshop on Graph Based Representations in Pattern Recognition*, pages 1–11, 2001.

[193] M. Neuhaus and H. Bunke. A quadratic programming approach to the graph edit distance problem. In F. Escolano and M. Vento, editors, *Proc. 6th Int. Workshop on Graph Based Representations in Pattern Recognition*, LNCS 4538, pages 92–102. Springer, 2007.

[194] M. Neuhaus and H. Bunke. A probabilistic approach to learning costs for graph edit distance. In J. Kittler, M. Petrou, and M. Nixon, editors, *Proc. 17th Int. Conference on Pattern Recognition*, volume 3, pages 389–393, 2004.

[195] M. Neuhaus and H. Bunke. Automatic learning of cost functions for graph edit distance. *Information Sciences*, 177(1):239–247, 2007.

[196] M. Neuhaus and H. Bunke. Self-organizing graph edit distance. In E. Hancock and M. Vento, editors, *Proc. 4th Int. Workshop on Graph Based Representations in Pattern Recognition*, LNCS 2726, pages 83–94. Springer, 2003.

[197] M. Neuhaus and H. Bunke. Self-organizing maps for learning the edit costs in graph matching. *IEEE Transactions on Systems, Man, and Cybernetics (Part B)*, 35(3):503–514, 2005.

[198] H. Bunke. Error correcting graph matching: On the influence of the underlying cost function. *IEEE Transactions on Pattern Analysis and Machine Intelligence*, 21(9):917–911, 1999.

[199] J. Munkres. Algorithms for the assignment and transportation problems. In *Journal of the Society for Industrial and Applied Mathematics*, volume 5, pages 32–38, 1957.

[200] H.W. Kuhn. The Hungarian method for the assignment problem. *Naval Research Logistic Quarterly*, 2:83–97, 1955.

[201] F. Bourgeois and J.C. Lassalle. An extension of the Munkres algorithm for the assignment problem to rectangular matrices. *Communications of the ACM*, 14(12):802–804, 1971.

[202] M. Neuhaus and H. Bunke. A random walk kernel derived from graph edit distance. In D.-Y. Yeung, J.T. Kwok, A. Fred, F. Roli, and D. de Ridder, editors, *Proc. 11th Int. Workshop on Structural and Syntactic Pattern Recognition*, LNCS 4109, pages 191–199. Springer, 2006.

[203] M. Neuhaus and H. Bunke. Edit distance based kernel functions for structural pattern classification. *Pattern Recognition*, 39(10):1852–1863, 2006.

[204] A. Asuncion and D.J. Newman. UCI machine learning repository. University of California, Department of Information and Computer Science. http://www.ics.uci.edu/ mlearn/MLRepository.html.

[205] U. Marti and H. Bunke. The iam-database: an english sentence database for off-line handwriting recognition. *Int. Journal on Document Analysis and Recognition*, 5:39–46, 2002.

[206] H. Bunke and M. Vento. Benchmarking of graph matching algorithms. In *Proc. 2nd Int. Workshop on Graph Based Representations in Pattern Recognition*, pages 109–113, 1999.

[207] K. Xu. Bhoslib: Benchmarks with hidden optimum solutions for graph problems (maximum clique, maximum independent set, minimum vertex cover and vertex coloring). www.nlsde.buaa.edu.cn/ kexu/benchmarks/graph-benchmarks.htm.

[208] H. Bunke and K. Riesen. A family of novel graph kernels for structural pattern recognition. In L. Rueda, D. Mery, and J. Kittler, editors, *Proc. 12th Iberoamerican Congress on Pattern Recognition*, LNCS 4756, pages 20–31, 2007.

[209] E. Alpaydin and F. Alimoglu. *Pen-Based Recognition of Handwritten Digits*. Dept. of Computer Engineering, Bogazici University, 1998.

[210] F. Shafait, D. Keysers, and T. Breuel. GREC 2007 arc segmentation con-

test: Evaluation of four participating algorithms. In L. Wenyin, J. Lladós, and J.M. Ogier, editors, *Graphics Recognition. Recent Advances and New Opportunities*, LNCS 5046, pages 310–320, 2008.

[211] Ph. Dosch and E. Valveny. Report on the second symbol recognition contest. In W. Liu and J. Lladós, editors, *Graphics Recognition. Ten years review and future perspectives. Proc. 6th Int. Workshop on Graphics Recognition)*, LNCS 3926, pages 381–397. Springer, 2005.

[212] R.W. Zhou, C. Quek, and G.S. Ng. A novel single-pass thinning algorithm and an effective set of performance criteria. *Pattern Recognition Letters*, 16(12):1267–1275, 1995.

[213] E. Henry. *Classification and Uses of Finger Prints*. Routledge, London, 1900.

[214] M. Kawagoe and A. Tojo. Fingerprint pattern classification. *Pattern Recognition*, 17:295–303, 1984.

[215] K. Karu and A.K. Jain. Fingerprint classification. *Pattern Recognition*, 29(3):389–404, 1996.

[216] C.I. Watson and C.L. Wilson. *NIST Special Database 4, Fingerprint Database*. National Institute of Standards and Technology, 1992.

[217] Development Therapeutics Program DTP. AIDS antiviral screen, 2004. http://dtp.nci.nih.gov/docs/aids/aids_data.html.

[218] J. Kazius, R. McGuire, and R. Bursi. Derivation and validation of toxicophores for mutagenicity prediction. *Journal of Medicinal Chemistry*, 48(1):312–320, 2005.

[219] Chemical Carcinogenesis Research Information System. http://toxnet.nlm.nih.gov.

[220] H. Berman, J. Westbrook, Z. Feng, G. Gilliland, T. Bhat, H. Weissig, I. Shidyalov, and P. Bourne. The protein data bank. *Nucleic Acids Research*, 28:235–242, 2000.

[221] I. Schomburg, A. Chang, C. Ebeling, M. Gremse, C. Heldt, G. Huhn, and D. Schomburg. Brenda, the enzyme database: updates and major new developments. *Nucleic Acids Research*, 32:Database issue: D431–D433, 2004.

[222] J.B. Kruskal. Multidimensional scaling by optimizing goodness of fit to a nonmetric hypothesis. *Psychometrika*, 29:1–27, 1964.

[223] J.B. Kruskal and M. Wish. Multidimensional scaling. Technical report, Sage University, 1978.

[224] T. Cox and M. Cox. *Multidimensional Scaling*. Chapman and Hall, 1994.

[225] J. Sammon Jr. A nonlinear mapping for data structure analysis. *IEEE Transactions on Computers*, C-18:401–409, 1969.

[226] E. Pekalska, R. Duin, M. Kraaijveld, and D. de Ridder. An overview of multidimensional scaling techniques with applications to shell data. Technical report, Delft University of Technology, The Netherlands, 1998.

[227] O. Chapelle, P. Haffner, and V. Vapnik. SVMs for histogram-based image classification. *IEEE Transactions on Neural Networks*, 10(5):1055–1064, 1999.

[228] C. Leslie, E. Eskin, and W. Noble. The spectrum kernel: A string kernel for SVM protein classification. In *Proc. Pacific Symposium on Biocomputing*,

pages 564–575. World Scientific, 2002.

[229] C. Leslie, E. Eskin, A. Cohen, J. Weston, and W. Noble. Mismatch string kernels for discriminative protein classification. *Bioinformatics*, 20(4):467–476, 2004.

[230] T. Joachims. Text categorization with support vector machines: Learning with many relevant features. In *Proc. European Conference on Machine Learning*, pages 137–142, 1998.

[231] C. Bahlmann, B. Haasdonk, and H. Burkhardt. On-line handwriting recognition with support vector machines. In *Proc. Int. Workshop on Frontiers in Handwriting Recognition*, pages 49–54, 2002.

[232] I. Guyon, J. Weston, S. Barnhill, and V. Vapnik. Gene selection for cancer classification using support vector machines. *Machine Learning*, 46(1–3):389–422, 2002.

[233] G. Baudat and F. Anouar. Generalized discriminant analysis using a kernel approach. *Neural Computations*, 12(10):2385–2404, 2000.

[234] B. Schölkopf, A. Smola, and K.-R. Müller. Kernel principal component analysis. In *Advances in Kernel Methods — Support Vector Learning*, pages 327–352. MIT Press, 1999.

[235] A. Tefas, C. Kotropoulos, and I. Pitas. Using support vector machines to enhance the performance of elastic graph matching for frontal face authentification. *IEEE Transactions on Pattern Analysis and Machine Intelligence*, 23(7):735–746, 2001.

[236] N. Aronszajn. Theory of reproducing kernels. *Transactions of the American Mathematical Society*, 68:337–404, 1950.

[237] M. Aizerman, E. Braverman, and L. Rozonoer. Theoretical foundations of potential function method in pattern recognition learning. *Automation and Remote Control*, 25:821–837, 1964.

[238] R. Duda and P. Hart. *Pattern Classification and Scene Analysis*. John Wiley & Sons, 1973.

[239] B.E. Boser, I. Guyon, and V. Vapnik. A training algorithm for optimal margin classifiers. In *Proc. of the fifth annual workshop on Computational learning theory*, pages 144–152, 1992.

[240] B. Schölkopf, K. Tsuda, and J.-P. Vert, editors. *Kernel Methods in Computational Biology*. MIT Press, 2004.

[241] A. Fischer, K. Riesen, and H. Bunke. An experimental study of graph classification using prototype selection. In *Proc. 19th Int. Conference on Pattern Recognition*, 2008.

[242] K. Müller, S. Mika, G. Rätsch, K. Tsuda, and B. Schölkopf. An introduction to kernel-based learning algorithms. *IEEE Transactions on Neural Networks*, 12(2):181–202, 2001.

[243] H. Byun and S. Lee. A survey on pattern recognition applications of support vector machines. *Int. Journal of Pattern Recognition and Artificial Intelligence*, 17(3):459–486, 2003.

[244] Ch. Berg, J. Christensen, and P. Ressel. *Harmonic Analysis on Semigroups*. Springer, 1984.

[245] H.-T. Lin and C.-J. Li. A study on sigmoid kernels for SVM and the training

of non-PSD kernels by SMO-type methods. Technical report, Department of Computer Science and Information Engineering, National Taiwan University, Taipei, Taiwan, 2003.

[246] H. Hotelling. Analysis of a complex of statistical variables into principal components. *Journal of Educational Psychology*, 24:417–441 and 498–520, 1933.

[247] I. Jolliffe. *Principal Component Analysis*. Springer, 1986.

[248] L. Breiman, J. Friedman, R.A. Olshen, and C.J Stone. *Classification and regression trees*. Wadsworth, 1984.

[249] T.M. Cover. Geometrical and statistical properties of systems of linear inequalities with applications in pattern recognition. *IEEE Transactions on Electronic Computers*, 14:326–334, 1965.

[250] V. Vapnik and A. Chervonenkis. On the uniform convergence of relative frequencies of events to their probabilities. *Theory of Probability and its Applications*, 16(2):264–280, 1971.

[251] V. Vapnik. *Statistical Learning Theory*. John Wiley, 1998.

[252] J.J. More and G. Toraldo. On the solution of quadratic programming problems with bound constraints. *SIAM Journal on Optimization*, 1:93–113, 1991.

[253] C. Burges and V. Vapnik. A new method for constructing artificial neural networks. Technical Report N00014-94-C-0186, AT&T Bell Laboratories, 1995.

[254] E.D. Nering and A.W. Tucker. *Linear Programming and Related Problems*. Academic Press, 1993.

[255] C. Cortes and V. Vapnik. Support vector networks. *Machine Learning*, 20:273–297, 1995.

[256] B. Schölkopf, A. Smola, and K.-R. Müller. Nonlinear component analysis as a kernel eigenvalue problem. *Neural Computation*, 10:1299–1319, 1998.

[257] J. MacQueen. Some methods for classification and analysis of multivariant observations. In *Proc. 5th. Berkeley Symp University of California Press 1*, pages 281–297, 1966.

[258] X. Jiang, A. Münger, and H. Bunke. On median graphs: Properties, algorithms, and applications. *IEEE Transactions on Pattern Analysis and Machine Intelligence*, 23(10):1144–1151, 2001.

[259] L. Kaufman and P. Rousseeuw. *Finding Groups in Data: An Introduction to Cluster Analysis*. John Wiley & Sons, 1990.

[260] I.S. Dhillon, Y. Guan, and B. Kulis. Kernel k-means: spectral clustering and normalized cuts. In *Proc. of the 10th ACM SIGKDD Int. conference on Knowledge discovery and data mining*, pages 551–556, 2004.

[261] B. Haasdonk. Feature space interpretation of SVMs with indefinite kernels. *IEEE Transactions on Pattern Analysis and Machine Intelligence*, 27(4):482–492, 2005.

[262] T. Gärtner. *Kernels for Structured Data*. World Scientific, 2008.

[263] T. Gärtner, J. Lloyd, and P. Flach. Kernels and distances for structured data. *Machine Learning*, 57(3):205–232, 2004.

[264] H. Wiener. Structural determination of paraffin boiling points. *Journal of*

the *American Chemical Society*, 69(1):17–20, 1947.

[265] J. Devillers and A.T. Balaban, editors. *Topological Indices and Related Descriptors in QSAR and QSPAR*. Gordon and Breach Science Publishers, 1999.

[266] F. Chung-Graham. *Spectral Graph Theory*. AMS, 1997.

[267] R. Wilson and E. Hancock. Levenshtein distance for graph spectral features. In J. Kittler, M. Petrou, and M. Nixon, editors, *Proc. 17th Int. Conference on Pattern Recognition*, volume 2, pages 489–492, 2004.

[268] B. Xiao, A. Torsello, and E. Hancock. Isotree: Tree clustering via metric embedding. *Neurocomputing*, 71:2029–2036, 2008.

[269] J.B. Tenenbaum, V. de Silva, and J.C. Langford. A global geometric framework for nonlinear dimensionality reduction. *Science*, 290:2319–2323, 2000.

[270] D. Jacobs, D. Weinshall, and Y. Gdalyahu. Classification with non-metric distances: Image retrieval and class representation. *IEEE Transactions on Pattern Analysis and Machine Intelligence*, 22(6):583–600, 2000.

[271] H. Bunke, S. Günter, and X. Jiang. Towards bridging the gap between statistical and structural pattern recognition: Two new concepts in graph matching. In S. Singh, N.A. Murshed, and W. Kropatsch, editors, *Proc. of the Second Int. Conference on Advances in Pattern Recognition*, LNCS 2013, pages 1–11. Springer, 2001.

[272] L. Goldfarb and D. Gay. What is structural representation. Technical Report TR05-175, Faculty of Computer Science, University of New Bruinswick, 2006.

[273] B. Spillmann, M. Neuhaus, H. Bunke, E. Pekalska, and R. Duin. Transforming strings to vector spaces using prototype selection. In D.-Y. Yeung, J.T. Kwok, A. Fred, F. Roli, and D. de Ridder, editors, *Proc. 11th int. Workshop on Structural and Syntactic Pattern Recognition*, LNCS 4109, pages 287–296. Springer, 2006.

[274] K. Tsuda. Support vector classification with asymmetric kernel function. In M. Verleysen, editor, *Proc. 7th European Symposium on Artifical Neural Netweorks*, pages 183–188, 1999.

[275] N. Linial, E. London, and Y. Rabinovich. The geometry of graphs and some of its algorithmic applications. *Combinatorica*, 15:215–245, 1995.

[276] W. Johnson and J. Lindenstrauss. Extensions of Lipschitz mappings into Hilbert space. *Contemporary Mathematics*, 26:189–206, 1984.

[277] J. Bourgain. On Lipschitz embedding of finite metric spaces in Hilbert spaces. *Israel Journal of Mathematics*, 52(1-2):46–52, 1985.

[278] G. Hjaltason and H. Samet. Properties of embedding methods for similarity searching in metric spaces. *IEEE Transactions on Pattern Analysis and Machine Intelligence*, 25(5):530–549, 2003.

[279] K. Riesen and H. Bunke. Graph classification by means of Lipschitz embedding. Accepted for publication in IEEE Transactions on Systems, Man, and Cybernetics (Part B).

[280] G. Hristescu and M. Farach-Colton. Cluster-preserving embedding of proteins. Technical report, Rutgers University, 1999.

[281] Y. Wang, I.V. Tetko, M.A. Hall, E. Frank, A. Facius, K.F.X. Mayer, and

Mewes H.W. Gene selection from microarray data for cancer classification – a machine learning approach. *Computational Biology and Chemistry*, 29:37–46, 2005.

[282] K. Riesen and H. Bunke. Graph classification based on vector space embedding. *Int. Journal of Pattern Recognition and Artificial Intelligence*, 23(6):1053–1081, 2009.

[283] R. Kohavi and G.H. John. Wrappers for feature subset selection. *Artificial Intelligence*, 97(1-2):273–324, 1997.

[284] J.C. Bezdek and L. Kuncheva. Nearest prototype classifier designs: An experimental study. *Int. Journal of Intelligent Systems*, 16(12):1445–1473, 2001.

[285] K. Kira and L.A. Rendell. A practical approach to feature selection. In *9th Int. Workshop on Machine Learning*, pages 249–256. Morgan Kaufmann, 1992.

[286] P. Pudil, J. Novovicova, and J. Kittler. Floating search methods in feature-selection. *Pattern Recognition Letters*, 15(11):1119–1125, 1994.

[287] A. Jain and D. Zongker. Feature selection: Evaluation, application, and small sample performance. *IEEE Transactions on Pattern Analysis and Machine Intelligence*, 19(2):153–158, 1997.

[288] R.A. Fisher. The statistical utilization of multiple measurements. In *Annals of Eugenics*, volume 8, pages 376–386, 1938.

[289] P. Langley. Selection of relevant features in machine learning. In *AAAI Fall Symposium on Relevance*, pages 140–144, 1994.

[290] P.E. Hart. The condensed nearest neighbor rule. *IEEE Transactions on Information Theory*, 14(3):515–516, 1968.

[291] J.S. Sanchez, F. Pla, and F.J. Ferri. Prototype selection for the nearest neighbour rule through proximity graphs. *Pattern Recognition Letters*, 18(6):507–513, 1997.

[292] D.R. Wilson and T.R. Martinez. Reduction techniques for instance-based learning algorithms. *Machine Learning*, 38(3):257–286, 2000.

[293] S.W. Kim and B.J. Oommen. A brief taxonomy and ranking of creative prototype reduction schemes. *Pattern Analysis and Applications*, 6:232–244, 2003.

[294] V. Susheela Devi and M.N Murty. An incremental prototype set building technique. *Pattern Recognition*, 35(2):505–513, 2002.

[295] P.A. Devijver and J. Kittler. On the edited nearest neighbor rule. In *Proc. 5th Int. Conference on Pattern Recognition*, pages 72–80, 1980.

[296] G. W. Gates. The reduced nearest neighbor rule. *IEEE Transactions on Information Theory*, 18:431–433, 1972.

[297] C.-L. Chang. Finding prototypes for nearest neighbor classifiers. *IEEE Transactions on Computers*, 23(11):1179–1184, 1974.

[298] G. Ritter, H. Woodruff, S. Lowry, and T. Isenhour. An algorithm for a selective nearest neighbor decision rule. *IEEE Transactions on Information Theory*, 21(6):665–669, 1975.

[299] U.M. Fayyad and K.B. Irani. Multi-interval discretization of continuousvalued attributes for classification learning. In *Proc. 13th Int. Joint Conference*

on Artical Intelligence, volume 2, pages 1022–1027. Morgan Kaufmann, 1993.

[300] L. Breiman. Bagging predictors. *Machine Learning*, 24:123–140, 1996.

[301] T.K. Ho. The random subspace method for constructing decision forests. *IEEE Transactions on Pattern Analysis and Machine Intelligence*, 20(8):832–844, 1998.

[302] Y. Freund and R.E. Shapire. A decision theoretic generalization of online learning and application to boosting. *Journal of Computer and Systems Sciences*, 55:119–139, 1997.

[303] H. Bunke, P. Dickinson, and M. Kraetzl. Theoretical and algorithmic framework for hypergraph matching. In F. Roli and S. Vitulano, editors, *Proc. 13th Int. Conference on Image Analysis and Processing*, LNCS 3617, pages 463–470. Springer, 2005.

[304] K. Riesen, M. Neuhaus, and H. Bunke. Graph embedding in vector spaces by means of prototype selection. In F. Escolano and M. Vento, editors, *Proc. 6th Int. Workshop on Graph Based Representations in Pattern Recognition*, LNCS 4538, pages 383–393, 2007.

[305] F. Roli, G. Giacinto, and G. Vernazza. Methods for designing multiple classifier systems. In *Proc. Second Int. Workshop on Multiple Classifier Systems*, LNCS 2096, pages 78–87. Springer, 2001.

[306] J. Dunn. Well-separated clusters and optimal fuzzy partitions. *Journal of Cybernetics*, 4:95–104, 1974.

[307] L. Hubert and J. Schultz. Quadratic assignment as a general data analysis strategy. *British Journal of Mathematical and Statistical Psychology*, 29:190–241, 1976.

[308] W. Rand. Objective criteria for the evaluation of clustering methods. *Journal of the American Statistical Association*, 66(336):846–850, 1971.

[309] K. Riesen and H. Bunke. Kernel k-means clustering applied to vector space embeddings of graphs. In L. Prevost, S. Marinai, and F. Schwenker, editors, *Proc. 3rd IAPR Workshop Artificial Neural Networks in Pattern Recognition*, LNAI 5064, pages 24–35. Springer, 2008.

[310] D.L. Davies and D.W. Bouldin. A cluster separation measure. *IEEE Transactions on Pattern Analysis and Machine Intelligence*, 1(2):224–227, 1979.

[311] T. Calinski and J. Harabasz. A dendrite method for cluster analysis. *Communications in statistics*, 3(1):1–27, 1974.

[312] X.L. Xie and G. Beni. A validity measure for fuzzy clustering. *IEEE Transactions on Pattern Analysis and Machine Intelligence*, 13:841–847, 1991.

[313] U. Malik and S. Bandyopadhyay. Performance evaluation of some clustering algorithms and validity indices. *IEEE Transactions on Pattern Analysis and Machine Intelligence*, 24(12):1650–1654, 2002.

[314] L. Kuncheva and D. Vetrov. Evaluation of stability of k-means cluster ensembles with respect to random initialization. *IEEE Transactions on Pattern Analysis and Machine Intelligence*, 28(11):1798–1808, 2006.

[315] K. Riesen and H. Bunke. Cluster ensembles based on vector space embeddings of graphs. In J.A. Benediktsson, J. Kittler, and F. Roli, editors, *Proc. 8th Int. Workshop on Multiple Classifier Systems*, LNCS 5519, pages

211–221, 2009.

[316] J. Franke and E. Mandler. A comparison of two approaches for combining the votes of cooperating classifiers. In *Proc. 11th Int. Conference on Pattern Recognition*, volume 2, pages 611–614, 1992.

[317] M. van Erp and L. Schomaker. Variants of the Borda count method for combining ranked classifier hypotheses. In *Proc. 7th Int. Workshop on Frontiers in Handwriting Recognition*, pages 443–452, 2000.

[318] S. Hashem and B. Schmeiser. Improving model accuracy using optimal linear combinations of trained neural networks. *IEEE Transactions on Neural Networks*, 6(3):792–794, 1995.

[319] L. Xu, A. Krzyzak, and C.Y. Suen. Methods of combining multiple classifiers and their applications to handwriting recognition. *IEEE Transactions on Systems, Man and Cybernetics*, 22(3):418–435, 1992.

[320] C.F.J. Wu, C.J. Lin, and R.C. Weng. Probability estimates for multi-class classification by pairwise coupling. *Journal of Machine Learning Research*, 5:975–1005, 2004.

[321] J. Kittler, M. Hatef, R. Duin, and J. Matas. On combining classifiers. *IEEE Transactions on Pattern Analysis and Machine Intelligence*, 20(3):226–239, 1998.

Index